D1614098

BRITISH IDENTITIES AND ENGLISH RENAISSANCE LITERATURE

Though British history and identity in the early modern period are intensively researched areas, to date, the role of literature in the construction of 'Britishness' is under-examined. In the past, English history of the sixteenth and seventeenth centuries often overlooked the contribution of Ireland, Scotland, and Wales to the formation of the British state. Historians now describe 'Britain' as a multiple kingdom, with a long history of conflict. In this volume, a team of leading Renaissance literary critics read a broad range of texts from the period, including the plays of Shakespeare, in light of the new British history. Prominent historians respond to the issues raised by the volume. This collection opens up a new kind of literary history and has pressing relevance for discussions of 'Britishness' today. This volume should interest all literary and political historians working on the British identities and Renaissance literature.

DAVID J. BAKER is Professor in the Department of English at the University of Hawai'i at Manoa. He is the author of *Between Nations: Shakespeare, Spenser, Marvell, and the Question of Britain* (1997). His articles have appeared in *Spenser Studies*, *English Renaissance Literature*, and *Critical Inquiry*.

WILLY MALEY is Professor of Renaissance Studies at the University of Glasgow. He is the author of *A Spenser Chronology* (1994), *Salvaging Spenser: Colonialism, Culture and Identity* (1997), and *Nation, State and Empire in the English Renaissance: Colonising Culture* (2002). He has also co-edited an edition of Edmund Spenser's *A View of the Present State of Ireland* (1997).

BRITISH IDENTITIES AND ENGLISH RENAISSANCE LITERATURE

EDITED BY

DAVID J. BAKER

AND

WILLY MALEY

CAMBRIDGE
UNIVERSITY PRESS

PUBLISHED BY THE PRESS SYNDICATE OF THE UNIVERSITY OF CAMBRIDGE
The Pitt Building, Trumpington Street, Cambridge, United Kingdom

CAMBRIDGE UNIVERSITY PRESS
The Edinburgh Building, Cambridge CB2 2RU, UK
40 West 20th Street, New York, NY 10011-4211, USA
477 Williamstown Road, Port Melbourne, VIC 3207 , Australia
Ruiz de Alarcón 13, 28014 Madrid, Spain
Dock House, The Waterfront, Cape Town 8001, South Africa

http://www.cambridge.org

First published 2002

Printed in the United Kingdom at the University Press, Cambridge

Typeface Baskerville Monotype 11 /12.5 pt.   *System* LaTeX 2$_\varepsilon$ [TB]

A catalogue record for this book is available from the British Library

Library of Congress Cataloguing in Publication data
British identities and English Renaissance literature / edited by David J. Baker and Willy Maley.
p.   cm.
Includes bibliographical references and index.
ISBN 0 521 78200 7
1. English literature – Early modern, 1500–1700 – History and criticism.   2. Literature and
history – Great Britain – History – 16th century.   3. Literature and history – Great Britain –
History – 17th century.   4. National characteristics, British, in literature.   5. Identity
(Psychology) in literature.   6. Group identity in literature.   7. Renaissance – Great Britain.
I. Baker, David J., 1957– II. Maley, Willy.

PR 428.H57 B75   2002
820.9′358 – dc21   2001052444

ISBN 0 521 78200 7 hardback

For our parents, John and Marilyn Baker,
and Anne and James Maley

Contents

Illustrations

Contributors

JAYNE ELISABETH ARCHER is a graduate of Exeter and Cambridge Universities. She is John Nichols Research Fellow in the AHRB Centre for the Study of Renaissance Elites and Court Cultures in the Centre for the Study of the Renaissance at the University of Warwick. She recently completed a doctoral thesis entitled 'Women and Alchemy in Early Modern England', in which she used the discourse and practice of alchemy in early modern England both as topics for analysis and as interpretive devices to transform our understanding of the patronage, authorship and agency of early modern women. She is currently converting this thesis into a book, encompassing women's handling of other 'occult' knowledges – astrology, cabbala and natural magic. Further research interests include women's manuscript receipt books and stillroom culture, including the significance of cosmetics, perfumes and cookery in early modern England.

DAVID J. BAKER is Professor of English at the University of Hawai'i. He is the author of *Between Nations: Shakespeare, Spenser, Marvell and the Question of Britain* (Stanford University Press, 1997); his essays on early modern literature and other topics have appeared in such journals as *Spenser Studies*, *ELR*, and *Critical Inquiry*.

PHILIPPA BERRY is a Fellow and Director of Studies in English at King's College, Cambridge. She combines interdisciplinary research in English and European Renaissance culture with work on feminist and postmodern theory. She is the author of *Of Chastity and Power: Elizabethan Literature and the Unmarried Queen* (Routledge, 1989) and of *Shakespeare's Feminine Endings: Figuring Woman in the Tragedies* (Routledge, 1999), and is the co-editor of *Shadow of Spirit: Postmodernism and Religion* (Routledge, 1992). With Margaret Tudeau-Clayton, she is currently editing a volume of essays entitled *The Texture of the Renaissance*, and is working on a study of the discourses of nature in early modern culture.

MARY FLOYD-WILSON is Assistant Professor of English Literature at Yale University. She has published articles on Ben Jonson, Shakespeare, and early modern racial discourse. Her chapter in this volume is part of a larger book project, *Barbarous Theater: Ethnography, Race, and the Emergence of English Identity*, to be published by Cambridge University Press. She is currently co-editing, with Gail Kern Paster and Katherine Rowe, a volume of essays entitled *Reading the Early Modern Passions: A Cultural History of Emotions*.

MATTHEW GREENFIELD is Assistant Professor at the City University of New York, College of Staten Island. He is co-editor of *Edmund Spenser: Essays on Culture and Allegory* (Ashgate, 2000), and has published articles on elegy, Shakespearean nationalisms, the decline of culture theory, and Wittgenstein and the novel in journals including *English Literary Renaissance*, *Shakespeare Quarterly*, *Raritan* and the *Journal of Narrative Technique*. He is completing a book entitled *Satire and Social Memory in Early Modern Britain*.

LINDA GREGERSON is Professor of English at the University of Michigan and author of *The Reformation of the Subject: Spenser, Milton, and the English Protestant Epic* (Cambridge University Press, 1996) and *Negative Capability: Contemporary American Poetry* (University of Michigan Press, 2001), as well as two volumes of poetry, *Fire in the Conservatory* (Dragon Gate, 1982) and *The Woman Who Died in Her Sleep* (Houghton Mifflin, 1996). Her third collection of poetry will be published by Houghton Mifflin in 2002.

ANDREW HADFIELD is Professor of English, University of Wales, Aberystwyth. He is the author of *Literature, Politics and National Identity: Reformation to Renaissance* (Cambridge University Press, 1994), *Spenser's Irish Experience: Wilde Fruit and Salvage Soyl* (Clarendon Press, 1997), and *Literature, Travel and Colonial Writing in the English Renaissance, 1545–1625* (Clarendon Press, 1999). His most recent book is *The English Renaissance, 1500–1620* (Blackwell, 2000). He is currently working on a book on Shakespeare and political culture. Professor Hadfield is a regular reviewer for the *TLS*.

CHRISTOPHER HIGHLEY is Associate Professor of English at The Ohio State University. He is the author of *Shakespeare, Spenser and the Crisis in Ireland* (Cambridge University Press, 1998), and his essays and reviews have appeared in *Spenser Studies*, *Spenser Newsletter*, and *Renaissance*

Drama. He has recently edited, with John N. King, a collection of essays, *John Foxe and His World* (Ashgate, 2001). His current research involves questions of exile and identity among early modern British Catholics.

DEREK HIRST is William Eliot Smith Professor of History and Chair of the History Department at Washington University, St Louis, Missouri, where he has been based since 1975. Previously he was a Fellow of Trinity Hall, Cambridge. He is the author of many works, including *The Representative of the People?* (Cambridge University Press, 1975), and *England in Conflict: England 1603–1660* (Edward Arnold, 1986). He is co-editor of *Writing and Political Engagement in Seventeenth-Century England* (Cambridge University Press, 2000), and his essays have been published in a range of prestigious scholarly journals including *Past and Present*, *History* and the *English Historical Review*.

CHRISTOPHER IVIC is Assistant Professor of English at the State University of New York, College at Potsdam. His articles on cultural identities in early modern Britain and Ireland have appeared in *Ariel*, *Genre*, and the *Journal of Medieval and Early Modern Studies*. He is at present completing a book entitled *The Subject of Britain, 1603–1660*, and he is co-editing a volume of essays on forgetting in early modern culture.

JOHN KERRIGAN is Professor of English 2000 at the University of Cambridge and a Fellow of St John's College. He is the author of numerous essays on early modern, Romantic-period and post-1945 literature; the editor of various works, including *Shakespeare's Sonnets and 'A Lover's Complaint'* (Penguin, 1986); and the author of *Revenge Tragedy: Aeschylus to Armageddon* (Oxford University Press, 1996). He is currently completing *Dislocations: Contemporary British and Irish Poetry* for Oxford University Press, and a study of literature and the British problem, 1603–1707, provisionally entitled *Archipelagic English*.

RICHARD A. MCCABE is a Fellow of Merton College and Reader in English Language and Literature at Oxford University, and a former Fellow of Trinity College Dublin and Pembroke College Cambridge. Author of *Joseph Hall: A Study in Satire and Meditation* (Oxford University Press, 1982); *The Pillars of Eternity: Time and Providence in* The Faerie Queene (Irish Academic Press, 1989); *Incest, Drama and Nature's Law* (Cambridge University Press, 1993); and co-editor, with Howard Erskine-Hill, of *Presenting Poetry: Composition, Publication, Reception* (Cambridge University

Press, 1995). He has recently edited Spenser's *Shorter Poems* (Penguin, 1999) and is currently working on a study of Spenser's response to Gaelic culture.

WILLY MALEY is Professor of Renaissance Studies in the Department of English Literature at the University of Glasgow, and author of *A Spenser Chronology* (Macmillan, 1994) and *Salvaging Spenser: Colonialism, Culture and Identity* (Macmillan, 1997), and co-editor, with Brendan Bradshaw and Andrew Hadfield, of *Representing Ireland: Literature and the Origins of Conflict, 1534–1660* (Cambridge University Press, 1993) and with Bart Moore-Gilbert and Gareth Stanton of *Postcolonial Criticism* (Longman, 1997), and with Andrew Hadfield of *A View of the State of Ireland: From the First Published Edition* (Blackwell, 1997).

ANDREW MURPHY is lecturer in English at the University of St Andrews. He is the author of *'But the Irish Sea Betwixt Us': Ireland, Colonialism and Renaissance Literature* (University Press of Kentucky, 1998) and the editor of *The Renaissance Text: Theory, Editing, Textuality* (Manchester University Press, 2000). He has published articles on Irish and Renaissance themes in a wide range of journals, including *Literature and History*, *Textual Practice*, *Éire-Ireland* and the *Yearbook of English Studies*, and has contributed to such collections as *Shakespeare and National Culture* (Manchester University Press, 1997), *Shakespeare and Ireland* (Macmillan, 1997) and *Shakespeare, Film, Fin de Siècle* (Macmillan, 1999). He is currently working on the history of Shakespeare publishing.

JANE OHLMEYER is Professor of Irish History in the Department of History at the University of Aberdeen. She is a major authority on the new British history, and is author of *Civil War and Restoration in the three Stuart Kingdoms: the Career of Randal MacDonnell, Marquis of Antrim, 1609–1683* (Cambridge University Press, 1993), editor of *Ireland from Independence to Occupation, 1641–1660* (Cambridge University Press, 1995) and *Political Thought in Seventeenth-Century Ireland* (Cambridge University Press, 2000), and co-editor, with John Kenyon, of *The Civil Wars: a Military History of England, Scotland, and Ireland 1638–1660* (Oxford University Press, 1998).

PATRICIA PARKER is Professor of English and Comparative Literature at Stanford University. She is the author of *Inescapable Romance* (Princeton University Press, 1979), *Literary Fat Ladies* (Routledge, 1987), and *Shakespeare from the Margins* (Chicago University Press, 1996). She has co-edited several volumes, including *Shakespeare and the Question of Theory*

(Methuen, 1985), *Literary Theory / Renaissance Texts* (Johns Hopkins University Press, 1986), and *Women, 'Race', and Writing in the Early Modern Period* (Routledge, 1994). An edition of *A Midsummer Night's Dream* is in progress for Arden.

MURRAY PITTOCK holds the Chair in Literature at the University of Strathclyde, and is Convenor of the Scots–Irish Research Network, which engages in research on issues of cultural policy and identity in Scotland and Ireland. He is the author of *Poetry and Jacobite Politics in Eighteenth-Century Britain and Ireland* (Cambridge University Press, 1994), *The Invention of Scotland* (Routledge, 1991), *Inventing and Resisting Britain* (Palgrave), and *Celtic Identity and the British Image* (Manchester University Press, 1999).

PHILIP SCHWYZER recently completed a Ph.D. in English at the University of California, Berkeley, and is Lecturer in Literature at the University of Exeter. His research focuses on antiquity and identity in early modern Britain. His article, 'Purity and Danger on the West Bank of the Severn', recently appeared in *Representations*.

Acknowledgements

The idea for this book came out of conversations with Andrew Hadfield, Christopher Highley and Patricia Parker at the North American Conference on British Studies in Monterey in November 1997. Ray Ryan at Cambridge University Press responded enthusiastically to our initial proposal, and has remained an invaluable adviser, and an infinitely patient guide, as the project has progressed. We are grateful to the anonymous readers who furnished us with much-needed direction at crucial stages in the development of the collection. We were fortunate in securing in Derek Hirst and Jane Ohlmeyer two first-class historians as respondents to a volume that aspired to interdisciplinary status but from a location squarely within literary studies. We were also lucky to have access to some inspiring work by David Armitage, Kate Chedgzoy, and David Scott Kastan, and of course John Pocock, who can be credited with opening the field. Andrew Hadfield suggested a wonderful cover for the book, Mary Lucasse provided technical support on the Pacific side, and Geraldine Gallagher gave some constructive criticism on the Celtic fringe of the Atlantic Archipelago.

Introduction. An uncertain union

David J. Baker and Willy Maley

In recent years, early modern historians who followed up on J. G. A. Pocock's plea for a new subject – 'British history' – have revolutionized the ways in which key events, such as the 'English Civil War', are being investigated (Pocock 'British History'; Russell 'The British Problem'). Under the vexed heading of the 'British Problem', or in the more neutral terms of 'Atlantic Archipelago' or 'Three Kingdoms', these historians have been rethinking from the ground up the supposed 'unity' of what has been called 'Great Britain'. This has included re-evaluations of the relations between crown and parliament, state and empire, centre and peripheries. No recent manifesto exists for the new British history, but its aims might be stated broadly. Starting from the crucible of the 1640s, a historical moment of equal importance to English historians and to those working on Scotland and Ireland, and working backwards and forwards through the various acts of union and empire, the new historiography seeks to comprehend early modern and modern history as a dialectic or dialogue between centres and margins. The purpose is not to rewrite the past, but to reorient our understanding of the interaction between core and periphery in non-Anglocentric ways while recognizing the historical legacy and continuing political reality of Anglocentrism. In principle, at least, the British history does not merely privilege hitherto neglected peripheries – Wales, Ireland, Scotland. Instead, it tries to show how the putative centre – England – and these so-called peripheries mutually implied and responded to one another. At the same time, however, the obvious fact of England's long-term hegemony is in no way denied. Here, Pocock's early influence was crucial. In 1975, the existing early modern history of Britain was usually distributed between studies of two kinds: those that concentrated on England and paid little attention to its status as a 'national' culture within a connected but conflicted British state, and those that saw neighbouring 'national' cultures in merely oppositional terms. Pocock was the first to attempt to bridge the gap. Somewhere between an unexamined Anglocentrism and an equally uninterrogated Anglophobia, he implied, lay as yet unconsidered historical complexities, contradictions, and crossovers. This, therefore, was to be a history that was 'pluralist and multicultural' (Pocock 'British History' 616). Moreover, it would be stringently 'antinationalist', since nationalism, as Pocock stressed, 'entail[s] a high degree of commitment to a single and unitary point of view', and the British history, properly understood, militated against such a perspective (621, 616). It also problematized any standpoint confined to the 'British Isles'. Pocock explicitly called for the 'projection' of British historiography onto the 'global' as well as the 'archipelagic and Atlantic stages'. Such investigations, he said, would involve placing the 'non-European societies in the Caribbean, Africa, Southern Asia, and Oceania' in a 'context of inherent diversity, replacing the image of a monolithic "parent society" with that of an expanding zone of cultural conflict and creation' (619).

Today, the British history is flourishing. As Pocock could say in 1995, the collective efforts of historians had defined a 'field of study well enough established to have both its paradigms and its critics' (Pocock 'Contingency, Identity, Sovereignty' 292). Since then, a succession of conferences and anthologies has confirmed the intellectual vitality of this paradigm and its organizing debates. Both of us have drawn on this historiography in our previous work, and here we have invited literary critics of the English Renaissance to take up, work with, and work upon the paradigm of the British history. They both address that paradigm itself and apply it (with modifications) to a range of texts (literary and otherwise). We should make our commitment clear from the start: we believe that both Renaissance literary studies and the British history of the early modern period could benefit from the disciplinary cross-pollination to which various of the chapters in this volume aspire. The British history is organized around a flexible, trans-island paradigm that is capable of highly nuanced elaboration, and the contributions assembled here show how productively it can be applied outside of its original disciplinary matrix. What these interventions also demonstrate, we would argue, is the value of mutual commentary and critique between those who are at work on the British problem as a historiographical issue and those whose concerns are perhaps more literary, but who are equally concerned with what John Kerrigan calls the 'interactive perplexities' of Britishness. (Indeed, in many of these chapters – Kerrigan's own, for instance – easy distinctions between 'historical' and 'literary' investigation hardly apply.) Not only does the British history put pressure on the lingering

Anglocentrism of much of Renaissance studies, but Renaissance studies can usefully extend, complicate, and resist the British history. For both historians and literary critics, a British approach affords an unrivalled access to matters of identity – political, cultural, linguistic, religious – that were paramount for the English, Welsh, Scots, and Irish of this period.

So far, it is fair to say, literary critics of the Renaissance have not made much of the British history. We often hear that literary critics and historians do not respect each other enough, and that they don't read each other enough, but neither claim is *entirely* true. There has been some interdisciplinary dialogue already, and even a measure of critical cross-dressing. Historians have been engaged in literary criticism, while literary critics have been embroiled in history. Thus we get the strange spectacle of historians writing on *The Faerie Queene* and *Paradise Lost* (Nicholas Canny and Christopher Hill) while literary critics pore over *A View of the Present State of Ireland* and *Observations upon the Articles of Peace made with the Irish Rebels* (Andrew Hadfield and Willy Maley). Two major new monographs from a historian who engages energetically with literature and a literary critic who grapples heroically with history carry on this great tradition of scholarly transvestism (Armitage *Ideological Origins of the British Empire*; McLeod *The Geography of Empire*). Nonetheless, it would be wrong to say that the British history has been substantially taken on board, except by a small number of Renaissance critics (who are often younger or newer to the profession).

The most prominent – and supposedly 'historical' – critical movements have done little to engage the 'matter of Britain'. Indeed, we would argue that both 'Cultural Materialism' and 'New Historicism' have militated *against* British perspectives, relying instead on an older historiography and then using it only to question earlier literary critical practices. (Social history has sometimes been called upon, but this field remains mostly insulated from the British history.) Work on Ireland has sometimes provided the exception to this blindness, but, even then, the problem is compounded. Ireland is treated as exemplary at the expense of Scotland and Wales. There is a paradox here: in the very act of uncovering England through examining Ireland, critics run the risk of repeating the original colonial manoeuvre whereby early modern English officials used Ireland as a way of speaking freely about England. In general, unfortunately, those in literary studies have often neglected large sectors of Britain and long stretches of its history. If the British history can be said to have a paradigm, one can often be detected in

English studies too. As this discipline's very name indicates, it remains tacitly – and thus even more powerfully – Anglocentric.

What, then, do we propose? As we have said, in this volume the editors and the assembled contributors attempt to locate a certain shared ground with British historians and to learn what useful work can be done on that ground. There are, of course, 'thematic' continuities between the two disciplines. The British history concerns itself with divisions, limits, and margins, and all of these have greatly preoccupied literary critics in recent years. We think the connections can and should be tighter. As the chapters here show, Renaissance scholars can help to take the British history a stage further, first of all, by entering into a 'conversation' with historians about the British problem. However, in arguing for such a 'conversation', we should also make clear what we are *not* advocating: a wholesale adoption of historians' objects and methods of study by literary critics. This volume emerges in the aftermath of another – mostly failed – attempt at rapprochement, the aforementioned 'New Historicism'. That critical 'movement' (it was something less than a 'school' and something more than a 'fad') concerned itself, as Steven Mullaney reports, with literature as 'but ... one realm among many for the negotiation and production of social meaning, of historical subjects and the systems of power that at once enable and constrain those subjects' (Mullaney 'After the New Historicism' 21). As they pursued such considerations, the New Historicists often referred to or included the work of historians, British or otherwise, with the sense that literary and historical projects were complementary, if not congruent. As David Scott Kastan now says, 'what is dismaying to many literary scholars is that, having elegantly formulated and explored the productive interrelation of literature and history, ... historians consistently ignore it and us, unconvinced that our formulations of cultural value have any import for their historical understandings. We regularly read their work but historians rarely read ours' (Kastan 'Are We Being Interdisciplinary Yet?' 48). He points out – rightly, in our experience – that as early modern critics have moved toward historians in recent years, '[f]rom historians ... there has been at best indifference, at worst, contempt' (45). Despite its flaws, its chronic and uninterrogated Anglocentrism, the New Historicism did represent a real attempt to take history and historians seriously. For Kastan, the lesson is that 'interdisciplinarity' is suspect: 'it isn't clear that our disciplinary gestures toward one another have brought the practices or even the interests of the two disciplines any closer together' (46). For us, though, the lesson is somewhat different. We think that British historians and literary critics are likely to benefit from one another not when their 'practices' and 'interests' are brought 'closer together', but when they are held at a productive distance from one another. The two disciplines should not be mutually subsuming, certainly. They may not even touch at most points. They should nonetheless, we urge, be mutually informing and mutually critical. It is the gap between these separate disciplines, we suggest, and the tensions that proximate distance generates, that are most likely to stimulate a worthwhile 'conversation'. Thus, like Kastan, we are wary of calling for too precipitate a dialogue in the name of 'interdisciplinarity'. The British history and Renaissance studies, we recognize, each has its own integrity (and internal diversity). While there may be possibilities for valuable collaboration between the two, in the end, as Kastan puts it, they each 'want to do something different' (49). Literary critics and historians both deal with textual remains, but they approach documents of culture in distinct ways, which, while they may be complementary at times, are also often contradictory. The chapters in this volume are not exercises in British history, and they are not meant to be.

We should point out, however, that certain British historians have been saying lately that the manner in which their discipline deals with others must change; some have begun to promote renewed ties with literary critics. A recent report of the North American Conference on British Studies (NACBS) observes that 'British history provide[s] a logical background for students studying English literature', and adds that 'English scholars newly interested in history and historical context are often highly receptive to interchange and collaboration with British historians.' It calls for joint endeavours. Admittedly, it is sometimes hard to know how seriously to take such proposals. In many quarters, as Kastan says, the 'commitment to interdisciplinarity has now become . . . reflexive and sentimental', and historians and critics alike have learned to pay their *pro forma* respects to this ideal ('Are We Being Interdisciplinary Yet?' 47). Then, too, the condescension that Kastan complains of is still on display in much of what historians have to say about critics. Those in literary studies, notes the report, 'can be a great resource'; they might even 'occasionally [participate] in British history courses' ('NACBS Report' 18). Nonetheless, from within a discipline that is often far too circumspect about its boundaries there is emerging, though not without ambivalence, a desire for a British history that is a 'truly interdisciplinary enterprise'.

The chapters in this volume begin to open up just such a possibility. Eventually, we believe, exchanges between British history and early modern literary studies are going to be key in re-vamping both. It is because we value the imperatives of *both* of these disciplines, therefore, that we advance this argument: one of the most important contributions literary critics can make to the British history is to remind historians of the enduring centrality of 'Englishness' within Britain and the relevance of 'culture' to the formation of that identity. At times, the British history has been in peril of leaving 'Englishness' unexamined. Having allowed the dominant partner in the state, England, to mask itself beneath 'Britishness', historians and literary critics alike must be mindful of letting it off the hook, thinking that to explore 'Englishness' is necessarily to promote Anglocentrism. Far from it. As Pocock has suggested, it is precisely English dominance that makes of British history a 'British Problem'. 'English historiography', he said in 1975, 'rests upon a sense of identity so secure as to be unreflective and almost unconscious' (Pocock 'British History' 616). The way round this barrier, we propose, is to go through it, which means tackling Anglocentrism, at home and at root, by focusing on England, because it is Anglocentrism that benefits most from shifting the focus elsewhere. That 'Englishness' which has become an embarrassment for historians can also be an embarrassment of riches for literary critics. State formation and canon formation go hand-in-hand, and scholars of literature are well positioned to provide the analysis of English texts that is essential to fulfilling both sides of Pocock's equation. Histories of the non-English nations as they impinged on England and on the larger British state are invaluable, but so too are accounts of English culture that stress its fissures, and the forgings that writers of various eras entered into in order to assert English nationhood. We should remember that A. J. P. Taylor, commenting on Pocock's plea for a new subject, declared: 'British and its variants now dominate most political institutions except the queen. English dominates the culture and most of the past' (Pocock 'British History' 623). This is precisely where the literary critic can offer assistance in explaining the survival of a specific and strong English culture within a developing British context. *To an extent*, then, we would argue, a certain Anglocentrism in this collection is inevitable and even proper. What Pocock said of the historiography of the early modern period can be said of its literary criticism too: 'there are extremely powerful and valid professional and historical reasons pressing us toward the continuation of the Anglo-centric perspective' (613). One of us has gone so far as to argue that a 'thoroughgoing British literary

criticism' is most likely impossible in principle (Baker *Between Nations* 16).
For better or for worse, Renaissance studies coalesce, and, we suspect,
will continue to coalesce, around iconic texts – 'Shakespeare' – that were
and are implicated in a hegemonic 'Englishness'. As Pocock memorably
put it, '[t]he fact of a hegemony does not alter the fact of a plurality'
('British History' 605). The questions are *to what extent* English studies
must rehearse that hegemony and *how far* they can incorporate the 'fact'
of plurality. This volume places 'Englishness' at centre stage, without
apology but with a thorough examination of the implications of its dominance, however unevenly construed and constructed. At the same time
it provides, through the close reading of texts and attention to form and
genre, a timely reminder of the specificity of literary culture as a key
carrier of national identity, one that is necessarily multiple and mediated
through readings and performances. A multi-centred approach to the
Renaissance does not mean a glib decentring of the subject of English
studies. Rather, it means engaging with the centre in order to show the
interdependency of discourses of dominance and subservience.

Individually, our contributors find different ways to re-draw the map
on which English studies has usually been situated, and collectively this
volume can be understood to be militating for a new map altogether,
one that is not just English, nor just British, but archipelagic or even
global in its scope. As Pocock first pointed out, a British approach must
be intrinsically dynamic; it must unfold a 'plural history, tracing the
processes by which a diversity of societies, nationalities, and political
structures came into being and situating the history of each and in their
interactions the processes that have led them to whatever forms of association or unity exist in the present or have existed in the past' (Pocock
'Limits and Divisions' 320). The 'new British history' actually written
has not, on the whole, been like this, as Glenn Burgess observes; it has
not extended itself through all of the dimensions that Pocock opened
up (Burgess 'Introduction: The New British History' 9). Then again, it
is British historians themselves who are now saying that must happen:
'Many of us believe that we must overcome the insularity that has too
often afflicted British history. To remain viable, we need to demonstrate
that the history of Britain is not merely an "island" story, but indeed a
world story.' If such a story is eventually written, it will be because, in large
part, British history (as now practised) becomes instead a 'truly interdisciplinary enterprise', one that promotes 'studies that interrogate traditional conceptions of Britain and Britishness, rethinking the boundaries
that have been drawn around those subjects' ('NACBS Report' 24).

British Identities and English Renaissance Literature can be thought of as advocating and adumbrating such a rethinking. The chapters in this volume, we believe, begin the work of drawing up a new critical cartography. It is one, we hope, that will map out difference and diversity across borders – geographic, generic, disciplinary – while remaining vigilant to the indelible marks – and inscrutable masks – of dominance and discrimination.

I

Opening the field

CHAPTER I

British history and 'The British history':
the same old story?

Philip Schwyzer

This chapter explores the relationship between two discourses which, rather awkwardly, go by the same name: 'British history'. For the sake of clarity, and with no offence intended to either party, I will distinguish these two claimants to the title in terms of their seniority, nominating them the old British history and the new. By the new British history, I mean that impressive body of work which has emerged, mostly in the 1990s, in response to J. G. A. Pocock's now-famous 'Plea For a New Subject' ('British History'). By the old British history I mean that grand and sprawling narrative, derived largely from Geoffrey of Monmouth's *Historia regum Britanniae* (*c*. 1136), which maintained an extraordinary sway over English and Welsh historical thought from the twelfth century to the beginning of the seventeenth, and beyond.[1]

The significant common ground that exists between these two versions of British history has generally gone unrecognized. This is in part because scholars discussing the old British history have tended to highlight only its most notoriously fanciful (or fraudulent) features: the settlement of Britain by the Trojan Brutus, great-grandson of Aeneas; the prophecies of Merlin; the reigns of King Lear and King Arthur; the angelic prophecy to Cadwalader that the Britons would regain the island's throne. If its facts were mostly fictions, the old British history also stood for certain claims which are now, once again, widely accepted: that the history of Britain is not that of the rise of one people but of the interaction of many; that these islands have never consisted of a single core and its periphery but of several shifting and competing centres; that British history began neither in 1066, nor with the Anglo-Saxon or Roman invasions, but a good deal earlier; and that close cultural contacts between Britain and mainland Europe existed long before the arrival of Julius Caesar. On these points, Geoffrey of Monmouth and modern archipelagic historians such as Hugh Kearney and Norman Davies are in satisfying agreement (Kearney *The British Isles*; Norman Davies *The Isles*).

Beyond such broad affinities, however, the two British histories would appear to have precious little in common. It is certainly the case that practitioners of the new British history have not displayed much interest in Geoffrey of Monmouth and his early modern adherents.[2] Much less have they been inclined to recognize any relationship, genealogical or otherwise, between the two discourses. No doubt there are good reasons for such diffidence. After all, what sort of kinship could the old British history possibly claim with the new? At best, it might be recognized as a buffoonish, mendacious, and embarrassing uncle (Geoffrey of Monmouth playing Toby Belch to John Morrill's Olivia). At worst it would be something far more sinister – the paternal ghost whose appearance heralds something rotten in the state and burdens the living with an intolerable charge: 'Remember me.' Faced with such an uncanny and potentially unwholesome apparition, the new British history might reasonably attempt, like young Hamlet, to deny all affinity without some more conclusive proof: 'The spirit that I have seen / May be the devil [who] . . . / Abuses me to damn me. I'll have grounds / More relative than this.'[3]

The aim of this chapter is to provide those grounds, and also to suggest what might be built upon them. The long-delayed encounter between the two British histories has the potential to deepen our understanding of early modern Britain in a number of ways, shedding light on early modern nationalisms and national identities, on Tudor discourses of legitimacy and empire, on Tudor Wales and its positioning within the wider archipelagic context. To reap these benefits, the new British history must pay closer attention both to the matter of the old British history, and to the complex network of textual and social practices by which that matter was made available for the use of the Tudor state. It will then be in a position to reap a further, and perhaps greater benefit: by facing up to its discredited predecessor, the new British history may just discover the secret of not sharing in its fate. My central task, however, is to provide the necessary 'grounds', and in this I am content to follow Hamlet's lead: 'the play's the thing'. The basis of the affinity between the two British histories lies in a shared proclivity for a certain kind of performance – and, in particular, in a fondness for that old theatrical standby, the stage Welshman.

Whatever mild embarrassment or unease we may feel in the face of the old British history is nothing compared with what the young Philip Sidney was forced to undergo. Sidney's humiliating predicament, and the means by which he overcame it, provide the starting point of my investigation. In February of 1574 this cultivated young Englishman, at rest in Padua in the course of his continental tour, received a letter from his mentor, Hubert Languet. Having dispensed the usual stiff dose of moral and scholarly advice, the Huguenot intellectual adopted a more playful tone to report his reading of a certain author who

would think he had received great injury at my hands if I should call him English, because he again and again declares that he is Welsh, not English. His name is Humphrey Lhuyd, and he is, if not really learned, at any rate well read, though he occasionally makes judgments which seem to lack common sense . . . You are fortunate that your ancestors came from France, for he says that the Saxons from whom the English descend were nothing but pirates and robbers. (Osborn *Young Philip Sidney* 140)

The book Languet had been reading was Humphrey Llwyd's recently published *Commentarioli Brittanicae descriptionis fragmentum* (Cologne, 1572; translated into English in 1573 as *The Breviary of Britayne*). The unfinished final work of the esteemed Welsh humanist, geographer, and antiquarian, Llwyd's survey of Britain had been undertaken at the request of the great atlas-maker, Abraham Ortelius. The *Fragmentum* included a robustly patriotic defence of Geoffrey of Monmouth against the scepticism of two foreign historians, the Italian Polydore Vergil and the Scot Hector Boece. It was one aspect of this defence which particularly incensed Languet. As he complains in the letter to Sidney, Llwyd had 'stolen' from the French their ancient Gaulish leader Brennus and turned him into a Welshman. In other words, Llwyd followed Geoffrey in insisting that the Brennus who sacked Rome in the fourth century BC was in fact 'a perfect Britayne' (Llwyd *The Breviary of Britaine* fol. 53r). Languet had not been slow in exacting revenge for this national insult, albeit unconsciously:

While I was drowsily extending my reading of the good Welshman deep into the night, it somehow happened that my candle ignited the book, and since it had not yet been bound, a good part of it was burned before I could extinguish the fire . . . I was on the point of sending you the scorched remains of my poor Welshman so that you might have your Griffin, his countryman, conduct his funeral; you would, however, solemnize it with a laugh. So, I entreat you, commission Griffin to write an epicede for him in Welsh, and send it to me. (Osborn *Young Philip Sidney* 141)

As far as we know, Griffin Madox, Sidney's Welsh serving-man, did not take up the pen on this occasion. Sidney himself, however, in his reply to Languet, embarked upon a playful but determined defence of Humphrey Llwyd:

Greetings. You certainly accord extraordinary treatment to our poor Cambro-Briton, who has brought upon himself the anger of Apollo and Vulcan for the offence which Brennus committed, but you seem somewhat lacking in generosity when you decide that the offence has not been sufficiently expiated by fire, and also deprive him of what he claims for himself, so to speak, his own patrimony. And where he maintains that the Saxons were pirates and robbers, you see, I readily grant him everything, strong in the awareness of my French heritage.

Next, in a complex punning passage, Sidney warns Languet that the notorious Welsh magician Dr John Dee will not take kindly to this mockery of his countryman. Finally he invokes the testimony of his servant:

Griffin has spoken many things in Master Lhuyd's memory and has given a kind of funeral oration which I solemnized with laughter. In order to efface the brand of stupidity with which you stamp the good Lhuyd, he says, among other things, that so far as Brennus is concerned, Lhuyd was wholly correct, and he proves this from Brennus's name; for in their ancient British language, Brennus meant king and was as common among them as Pharaoh or Ptolemy among the Egyptians . . . By this perhaps feeble reasoning he concludes that the celebrated robber was his countryman. Let me prevail upon you to concede this.

'But I have written all this in jest. Joking aside' (Osborn *Young Philip Sidney* 145). With that Sidney turns to more ostensibly serious matters. Languet was astute enough to detect something forced in Sidney's jesting, evidence that he had touched a nerve. He was presumably unaware that Philip's father Sir Henry, Lord President of the Council in the Marches of Wales, took a deep interest in Welsh antiquities in general and Llwyd's work in particular (he later arranged for Llwyd's unfinished translation of *The Historie of Cambria* to be completed and published). Languet also may not have considered that, as Llwyd had died of a burning fever six years earlier (the moving letter he wrote to Ortelius from his deathbed prefaces the *Fragmentum*), jokes about flames and funerals were in dubious taste. He had clearly failed to grasp the seriousness which attached to the claim that a Briton had conquered Rome centuries before Caesar's invasion of Britain. Recognizing that his joke had fallen flat, Languet was quick to concede the nationality of Brennus in his reply, archly offering 'a few other robbers of this sort from French history to adopt into your nation' (Osborn *Young Philip Sidney* 150). The wording of his response suggests that he had divined the stake that Sidney had in the Britishness of Brennus, however much Sidney tried to conceal it beneath a veneer of light banter. For while the Englishman had only asked Languet to concede that Brennus was Madox's countryman – that is, Welsh – Languet instead pointedly agreed to relinquish Brennus to '*your* nation' (my emphasis).

Why would a scholarly young Englishman have been so concerned to vindicate a Welshman's claim that a pre-Christian warlord was a Briton? Although Brennus has not achieved the lasting fame of a King Lear or a King Arthur (or even an Old King Cole), he was in the early modern period among the most frequently cited heroes of the British history. Geoffrey of Monmouth presents (or invents) Brennus as a complex figure: in his youth, a rebel against his brother, King Belinus; later, the puissant conqueror of Rome. (Some versions made him also the iconoclastic desecrator of the Greek temple at Delphi, where he slew himself after his army was destroyed by a divine – or diabolical – earthquake.) The Tudors' fondness for this mythical conqueror dates back at least as far as 1486, when in a pageant the newly crowned Henry VII was welcomed to Bristol by his 'cosyn' Brennus, supposedly the founder of that city. In the same year, the Welsh bards Lewys Glyn Cothi and Dafydd Llwyd of Mathafarn both dedicated praise poems to Henry VII in which they linked the Tudors' Welsh bloodline with Brennus, or Brân (Meagher 'The First Progress of Henry VII' 69; Johnston ed. *Gwaith Lewys Glyn Cothi*; Richards ed. *Gwaith Dafydd Llwyd o Fathafarn* 27). Brennus was a useful relative to have, for by claiming kinship with the ancient rulers of Britain the Tudors could claim to have fulfilled the prophecy in Geoffrey of Monmouth that the British blood would one day regain the throne. When the second Tudor king was preparing to break with Rome, Brennus proved more useful yet. As the Duke of Norfolk informed a bemused imperial ambassador in 1530, Henry VIII 'had a right of Empire in his kingdom and recognized no superior. There had been an Englishman who had conquered Rome, to wit Brennus' (Koebner " 'The Imperial Crown of this Realm' " 40).[4] Throughout the sixteenth century and well into the seventeenth, Brennus could be invoked as a figure for England's/Britain's independence from, rivalry with, and primordial superiority to Rome. Spenser devotes a stanza to his and his brother's conquests in *The Faerie Queene* (II.10.40). In Jasper Fisher's *Fuimus Troes, or The True Trojanes* (1633, though perhaps written twenty years earlier), the ghost of Brennus watches over the British resistance to the Roman invasion and boasts of his earlier and greater conquest:

> Rome, proudest Rome
> We cloath'd in skarlet of patrician blood
> And 'bout your Capitoll prauns'd our vaunting steedes,
> Defended more by Geese, than by your gods.
>
> (Fisher *Fuimus Troes* A3r)

Although Philip Sidney, unlike his father, seems to have had no particular interest or even firm belief in the British history, he undoubtedly recognized a need to defend a figure so central to England's imperial claims and to militant English Protestantism as Brennus. His own position, had he been forced to articulate it, might have been that he did not know whether or not Brennus existed, but he was certainly British. Sidney was *not* forced to articulate his own position – and that is the real point. It is his method of at once evading and answering Languet's challenge, as much as his stubborn attachment to Brennus, that makes Sidney representative of English thought and practice.

Languet's letter required Sidney to cope simultaneously with the two gaping holes in the armour Tudor patriots had forged out of the British history. The first of these was that it stood on extremely shaky historical foundations, with little more than Geoffrey's word to substantiate the larger part of it and a host of classical sources to contradict it. The extent to which this problem weighed on early modern minds has probably been overemphasized by later historians. When Sidney and Languet exchanged their letters, no significant attack on the British history had appeared in print since Polydore Vergil's *Anglica historia*, published some forty years before, while numerous defences had been published in the meantime. What some have termed 'the battle of the books' consisted in fact of a one-sided thumping of Vergil by a host of outraged English and Welsh writers (the fact that Vergil was an Italian priest undoubtedly helped in whipping up the campaign against his history) (Carley 'Polydore Vergil'). Yet while Geoffrey of Monmouth's position in England and Wales may still have seemed relatively secure, he had long since ceased to carry any weight with the learned on the continent.

The second, and in some ways greater, problem facing English defenders of the British history was that it was not about the English. Everything that made the British history valuable for the purposes of sixteenth-century nationalism – in sum, its vision of the nation as ancient, insular, uncorrupt, and imperial – referred very specifically and exclusively to the nation of the Britons, that is the Welsh. Geoffrey's picture of the Anglo-Saxons was entirely unsympathetic: 'pirates and robbers', not to mention oath-breakers and poisoners. Sidney, of course, could evade this difficulty on a personal level by laying claim to French descent. His response to Languet also shows how the very Welshness of the British history could be turned, paradoxically, to English advantage. Sidney plays the two weaknesses of the British history – its dubious historicity and its essential Welshness – against each other. His goal is to manipulate perceptions so that it is not the history *per se* that looks dubious, but Welshness.

Intriguingly, the book Languet burned includes in its commendation of the Welsh the proud assertion that the English nobility prefer Welshmen to Englishmen as personal servants (Llwyd *The Breviary of Britayne* 60r–v). This passage, coming just a few pages after the matter of Brennus, may have been what prompted Languet to think of Madox. While Humphrey Llwyd ascribed this preference to the superior agility and courtliness of the Welsh, Sidney's letter suggests a more complex relationship, one based in part on a kind of symbolic service which the Welsh were peculiarly equipped to perform. Griffin Madox offers Sidney his last and best hope of wriggling out of Languet's trap. It is the Welshman, not his master, who speaks in Llwyd's memory and offers the proof that Brennus was indeed a Briton. Sidney, meanwhile, represents himself as laughing indulgently and accuses his servant of 'feeble reasoning' before abruptly asking Languet to concede the point. The comic Welshman is called upon to draw fire, defending the crucial yet indefensible position of the Matter of Britain and heroically sacrificing his own dignity for the sake of his English master. Yet Sidney ultimately robs Madox of more than his dignity; he also robs him, paradoxically, of Brennus. As we have seen, Languet does not relinquish Brennus to Wales but rather to Sidney's (unspecified) nation.

From one perspective, Griffin Madox can be counted in the ranks of Welsh defenders of the British history, alongside such men as Sir John Prise of Breconshire, Humphrey Llwyd of Denbigh, David Powel of Ruabon, and the two John Davies (of Brecon and of Mallwyd). These scholars in the humanist tradition deserve to be remembered not only for their adherence to Geoffrey of Monmouth but for their contributions to antiquarianism, philology, chorography, and cartography (Ceri Davies *Latin Writers of the Renaissance*; Gruffydd 'The Renaissance and Welsh Literature'). Even where they were in the position of defending the indefensible, their historical methods were often well in advance of opponents like Polydore Vergil. (Llwyd, for instance, argued for the Britishness of Brennus and his army on the basis of striking linguistic evidence; he cannot be blamed for not knowing, as no one did at that time, that Gaulish was also a Celtic language.) Nevertheless, these scholars suffered the brunt of ridicule by foreign sceptics, most memorably George Buchanan in his history of Scotland (1582): 'the Ancients, as well *Greeks* and *Latins*, will have greater Weight with me, than all the Hodge-Podge trash of *Llud*, raked by him out of the Dunghil, Collections good for nothing but to be laughed at, and to disparage the Collector' (Buchanan's *History of Scotland* 6).

While Llwyd and his colleagues were exposed to the withering scorn of their fellow humanists, the fruits of their work were eagerly co-opted for the service of English power. It deserves to be noted in passing that Llwyd has been credited with coining that soon-to-be-notorious phrase, 'British Empire'. Llwyd was also the first to record the tradition of the Welsh prince Madoc and his discovery and settlement of America in the twelfth century. Both the phrase 'British Empire' and the Madoc story were swiftly disseminated and popularized through the efforts of John Dee, who often served as a kind of bridge between Welsh scholarship and the English court (Henry 'John Dee'; Gwyn Williams *Madoc* 39–40, *Welsh Wizard*; Sherman *John Dee*). While Llwyd's memory was subjected to the withering scorn of Buchanan, English writers like George Peckham and Richard Hakluyt were able to lay claim to the New World for her majesty's empire on the basis of Madoc's discovery.

At the same time, Griffin Madox can be seen as belonging to a very different tradition from that of Welsh scholarship. As the textual creation of Philip Sidney, he stands first in a long ensuing line of 'stage Welshmen'. The Elizabethan and Jacobean stage would feature an array of such Welsh characters, at once laughable and valiant in their defence of Britain's honour. Among the most memorable in this regard is Morgan of Anglesey in *The Valiant Welshman* (1615), whose response to the threat of Julius Caesar's invasion seems calculated to elicit just the right mixture of laughter and patriotic applause from the play's English audience:

From Rome! And I pray you, what a pox ayles her, that you cannot keepe her at home? have you any waspes in her tayles? or live Eeeles in her pelly, you cannot keepe her at home? Harke you me: I pray you, how toth M. Cesar? toth he neede era parbour? Looke you now: let him come to Wales, and her Cousin Caradoc shall trim his crownes, I warrant her.[5]

The language, unmistakably, is that of Shakespeare's Fluellen, the fount from which so many subsequent stage Welshmen flow (though the use of 'her' in place of all other pronouns, common to many stage Welshmen, is not one of Fluellen's tics). Fluellen has many features in common with his predecessor Griffin Madox, including a taste for distinctly fishy historical reasoning: 'There is a river in Macedon, and there is also moreover a river at Monmouth . . . 'tis alike as my fingers is to my fingers, and there is salmons in both' (*Henry V* 4.7.21–5).[6] Again like Madox, Fluellen engages in and is ultimately vindicated in a dispute with a foe of the British history, Ancient Pistol. Pistol is unquestionably a Saxon, a 'pirate and robber', yet his contempt for Galfridian tradition – 'not for Cadwalader and all his goats' (5.1.25), 'Base Troyan, thou shalt die' (5.1.28) – marks him out at the same time as a kind of foreigner, the crass ally of Vergil, Buchanan, and Languet. In this familiar triangle, Shakespeare the playwright takes the puppeteering role of Philip Sidney, putting words in the comic Welshman's mouth and holding him up for sustained mockery throughout the play before rounding rather suddenly on the sceptics. As Captain Gower instructs the humiliated Pistol, 'let a Welsh correction teach you a good English condition'. In other words, 'let me prevail upon you to concede this'.

We are of course free to doubt whether Gower is entirely successful in co-opting Fluellen's victory for the service of Englishness, and also whether Shakespeare fully endorses his attempt. As David Baker has argued, Fluellen can be seen as disrupting the very categories of Welshness and Englishness which Gower hastens to reinscribe (Baker *Between Nations* 54–62). This argument is taken further by Patricia Parker in this volume. Perhaps in the character of Fluellen, as so often, Shakespeare is showing us the wires, while still captivating us with the way the puppets speak and dance. If Fluellen is the model for all future stage Welshmen, he also stands as Shakespeare's ambiguous comment on a pre-existing tradition of Welsh puppeteering and ventriloquization, a tradition whose origins stretch back far beyond the day in 1574 when the young Philip Sidney had to answer an embarrassing question.

Part of the difficulty attached to determining the nature and significance of belief in the British history in the Tudor period is that the majority of its most fervent advocates are neither English nor Welsh, but paper Welshmen invented or ventriloquized by Englishmen. This peculiar set of discursive circumstances follows a pattern already well established in the pre-Tudor era. For instance, English chroniclers had for centuries insisted that the Welsh believed King Arthur would return to lead them to victory against the Saxons. The chroniclers mocked this as a delusion, insisting that Arthur was dead – as Robert Manning succinctly puts it, 'y seye they trowe wrong' (cited Dean *Arthur of England* 27; Keeler *Geoffrey of Monmouth*). Subsequent English historians have tended to take the chroniclers' word about the Welsh, repeating the old claim that the return of Arthur was eagerly anticipated in medieval Wales. Yet when we turn to late-medieval Welsh prophetic literature, we find precious little evidence for this; the redeeming hero awaited by the Welsh is usually called Owain or Cadwalader, while of Arthur there is surprisingly little mention. The sixteenth-century Welsh chronicler Elis Gruffydd asserted that the English were more interested than the Welsh in Arthur, and even attributed to the English the belief that he would rise again (Lloyd-Morgan 'The Celtic Tradition' 9; Padel 'Some South-Western Sites' 240). Thus, it seems, no one 'really' believed that Arthur would return – but everyone believed that someone believed it. Arthur's second coming was, almost by definition, the faith of the other. Yet the tradition survived for centuries, ready and waiting for Henry Tudor to remember and exploit it in the naming of his ill-fated first-born son. It is a remarkable instance of the capacity of belief systems to sustain themselves without the aid of active believers.

A similar situation existed in the later Tudor period with regard to the British history as a whole. English writers felt able to play with it and chuckle over it, while attributing whole-hearted belief in it to the gullible Welsh. Welsh writers indeed believed and defended some of it, but for them the British history remained an exclusively Welsh concern. With very few exceptions, Welsh bards and Welsh humanists were far less captivated by British imperial themes, and far less inclined to fetishize the Tudor bloodline, than the English steadfastly insisted (and insist) they were. Although he coined the phrase, Llwyd did not use 'British Empire' to refer to Elizabeth's dominions, but only to ancient British – i.e., Welsh – conquests. Llwyd and Powel's *Historie of Cambria* flatly dismisses the promise to Cadwalader that the Britons would one day regain the throne as 'blind prophesies', thereby undermining a key part of the Tudor myth. Geoffrey of Monmouth remained an effective tool to be used *against* the English, as when Llwyd and Prise complained of the English violating the original border between England and Wales, the Severn. The presence of a putatively Welsh family on the English throne did not for these patriots lessen the insult of English towns on anciently Welsh territory.

Whatever enthusiasm Prise, Llwyd and Powel may have felt and expressed for the Acts of Union (which after all did much good and little immediate ill to members of their class), their sharp awareness of remaining differences and inequalities prevented them from celebrating the union in the words an English writer would choose: that is, would choose to put into a Welshman's mouth – 'So shall the Briton bloud their crowne againe reclaime. / Thenceforth eternall union shall be made / Betweene the nations different afore' – as Spenser did in *The Faerie Queene* (III.3.48–9). If Merlin's prophecy to Britomart, spoken in his cavern below Carmarthen, bears little resemblance to what was being said or written in Wales at the time, it is highly indicative of what English writers needed to believe the Welsh were saying. Something similar can be argued in the case of that other Tudor 'wizard', John Dee. It is perhaps not too unfair to regard Dee as an Englishman who for a short while presented himself to the English as a Welshman in order to propound a vision of Britain which they were eager to hear from a Welsh mouth (Gwyn Williams *Welsh Wizard*; Sherman *John Dee*).

The point of all this is *not* that the British history cannot have been very relevant to Tudor politics and Tudor power because no one actually believed it. Quite the opposite: the point is that it was highly relevant, but its relevance did not require the participation of true believers among either the English or the Welsh. It required only the likes of Griffin Madox and Fluellen, Merlin and Dr Dee, fictional Welshmen authored by Englishmen. Thus a discourse that at first glance appears to have Wales at its very centre turns out upon inspection to require no Welsh participation and to tell us little or nothing about sixteenth-century Wales.

It is here that I feel obliged to point to an unacknowledged affinity between the disreputable old British history and its modern, outwardly respectable successor. The emergence of the new history seems on the face of it to have involved a welcome proliferation of discourse about Wales, often in articles comparing its fortunes in the early modern period to those of Ireland, or Scotland. Yet it is questionable to what extent many of this crop of articles are really 'about' Wales. In a certain kind of 'new' British historical narrative, Wales figures almost exclusively as the rather dull 'good son' of the expansive Tudor state, its sheepish acquiescence in politics and religion serving to contrast with and highlight the more romantic and interesting histories of the rebellious prodigals, Ireland and Scotland.[7] To take a fairly typical example from an essay by Brendan Bradshaw: 'The integration of Wales within the unitary system proved to be unproblematical. Resistance was rare and politically insubstantial:

latter-day attempts to generate a national movement for secession have consistently failed to mobilise a substantial popular constituency. *Not so with Ireland*' (Bradshaw 'Tudor Reformation' 42–3 – my emphasis).

Where the title had promised equal attention to Wales and Ireland, here the writer invokes Wales only to assert what it was not – note the string of negatives – and what Ireland achieved by not failing like Wales. (Is there an implied dialectic here, with Ireland emerging as the negation of the negation?) Expanding his analysis of why the Acts of Union 'failed [!] to elicit the slightest whimper of protest from the Welsh', Bradshaw cites two major historical factors. Half of his argument rests on an incontestable truth: that the Union suited 'the needs, aspirations, and sensibilities of [the] emergent Welsh gentry'. The other half rests on a false perception: that the Welsh had spent the half-century since Henry Tudor came to the throne in a state of 'euphoric expectation', and were thus deceived into seeing the annexation of their nation as 'liberation by the long hoped-for British deliverer' (Bradshaw 'Tudor Reformation' 47, 49–50, 51, 52). The Welsh, by this account, had the wool pulled over their eyes – but at least it was wool of their own weaving. Bradshaw here appears to be more swayed by the ventriloquized voices of Griffin Madox, Fluellen and their ilk than by actual Welsh evidence. His approach is in fact eerily reminiscent of Sidney's in his letter to Languet. Once again, the slightly feeble-minded Welshman with his naïve faith in the British history is trundled out, not to tell us anything about Wales, but as a foil allowing another archipelagic nation to work out a more complex and sophisticated relationship to Britishness. To paraphrase Shakespeare's Captain Gower: 'let a Welsh comparison teach you a good Irish condition'.

This is by no means to deny the historical importance of comparisons between Ireland and Wales. Ciaran Brady and Christopher Highley have shed light on the intermittent pursuit of a 'Welsh Policy' in Elizabethan Ireland. As Highley notes, 'Writers turned to present-day Wales as an ideal submissive colony, an image of their hopes for Ireland, and therefore they also looked to England's past subjugation of Wales as a precedent for the re-conquest of Ireland' (Highley *Shakespeare, Spenser, and the Crisis in Ireland* 7). Highley demonstrates how works like *Historie of Cambria*, as well as English plays dealing with rebellions in Wales, could have been read as relating to Irish affairs. There is much to be learned from studying the habits of the English colonial mind. One of the lessons, surely, must be that when we pursue comparisons between Ireland and Wales in the Tudor period, we are gazing through the age-old optic of English power. There is a strong potential for England to remain the real (albeit unspoken) subject of such inquiries. As for Wales, it seems stuck in the position of being always already subjugated, always already known. For the comparison to serve its purpose in producing new information about Ireland, it must rely on not discovering anything new or unexpected about Wales.

Is it the case, then, that as far as Wales is concerned the two British histories are, after all, *yr un stori* – the same [old] story? Can the new British history fulfill its titular promise better than the old, and thereby avoid its compromised, co-opted fate? In spite of the pessimistic tone of the last few pages, I remain confident that it can and will. It has at least one enormous advantage over its predecessor: the stories it tells stand some chance of being true. If we can avoid the pitfalls – the chief of which would be mistaking the mere proliferation of discourse for progress – the new British history can lead us to important truths about the literatures of both England and Wales. Getting at the truth about Englishness will involve recognizing how it has distinguished and defined itself, paradoxically, through acts of ventriloquism and disguise. As for the truth about Wales, that surely is to be found not in the ventriloquized utterances of paper Welshmen, but in the richly varied literature produced in three languages in Wales in the early modern period.

NOTES

1 Geoffrey of Monmouth *Histories of the Kings of Britain*. On the afterlife of the British history in early modern England, see Kendrick *British Antiquity*, and Levy *Tudor Historical Thought*.
2 The most important exception is Peter Roberts 'Tudor Wales'.
3 Shakespeare *Hamlet* 2.2.575–6, 580–1 in Greenblatt ed. *The Norton Shakespeare*. Drawing a connection between Hamlet and the British Question is not unprecedented; see Kurland '*Hamlet* and the Scottish Succession?'
4 Norfolk's description of Brennus as an Englishman accords with Parliament's declaration in 1633 that 'this realm of England is an empire'; it is also possible that Chapuys, who recorded the interview, simply failed to grasp the distinction between 'English' and 'British'.
5 R. A. *The Valiant Welshman* (1615), repr. in *Tudor Facsimile Texts* (1913), sigs. E1v–E2r.
6 All references to *Henry V* are from Greenblatt ed. *The Norton Shakespeare*.
7 It must be stressed that the situation is far otherwise in medieval history, thanks in very large part to the work of R. R. Davies; see *Domination and Conquest*, and his crucial series of presidential addresses to the Royal Historical Society on 'The Peoples of Britain and Ireland'.

CHAPTER 2

Revising criticism: Ireland and the British model

Andrew Murphy

> I regret
> The awkwardness.
> But British, no, the name's not right.
>
> (Heaney 'An Open Letter' 29)

In composing these lines, Seamus Heaney was registering his objection to the inclusion of some of his work in the *Penguin Book of Contemporary British Poetry*. Heaney indicates here a resistance by one strand of the population of Ireland to the extension to them of the descriptor 'British'. For many in Ireland, to be called 'British' is to be subjected to a form of nomenclative imperialism, to have foisted upon them an identity which they steadfastly reject. In this context, it should come as no surprise that the welcome accorded to the revitalized Pocockian 'British history' has been a touch more muted in Ireland than it generally has been elsewhere. In Ireland these matters have a greater live charge, not least since the question of whether one adheres to a British or an Irish identity has too often quite literally been a matter of life and death.

Among Irish historians, objections to the new British history have been articulated most clearly by Nicholas Canny. There are a number of factors motivating Canny's resistance to the new approach, including the fear that the new Britannic paradigm may simply be old Anglocentrism dressed up in a new guise. Thus Canny asserts that 'much of what appears as "new British history" is nothing but "old English history" in "Three-Kingdoms" clothing, with the concern still being to explain the origin of events that have always been regarded as pivotal in England's historical development' (Canny 'Irish, Scottish and Welsh' 147–8). Anyone familiar with Canny's career might well have predicted this response, though on slightly different grounds. The strength of Canny's work has always been his articulation of Ireland's place within a broader 'Atlantic world' colonial context. Viewed from within this paradigm, we might say that, conceptually (and by contrast with the Britannic approach), transatlantic distance shrinks and the Irish Sea widens, as the English are presented forging alignments between the Irish and the natives of the New World, thereby contradistinguishing themselves from their Celtic neighbours. From the point of view of this interpretative model, pursuing Irish history within a 'British' context makes little sense, since the Irish are seen, precisely, as having been rigorously disjoined from Britain during the course of the early modern colonial enterprise.

The focus of the present volume is, of course, not history *per se*, but the interconnections between history and literary analysis. For this reason I begin this chapter by attending to Canny's objection to the Pocockian paradigm not just because it indicates a disjunction between the new British history and a particular strand of Irish analysis, but also because Canny's interpretation of Irish history has been so very influential in informing literary critical analysis of early modern Ireland. In fact, the filiations between historical and literary analysis in this arena are of long standing. One of the earliest attempts to work out an Atlanticist linking of Ireland and the New World was offered in D. B. Quinn's *The Elizabethans and the Irish*. This book was written at the Folger Shakespeare Library, 'under guidance' from the Library's then Director, Louis B. Wright, and the volume was, as Quinn later noted, 'mainly intended to help literary students to understand Tudor Ireland' (Quinn 'Reflections' 10). Whether the average literary student or scholar in the late 1960s or the 1970s much cared about relations between the Elizabethans and the Irish is hard to say, but the 1980s certainly saw the emergence of new forms of literary criticism – New Historicism and Cultural Materialism – which were very much concerned with the historical locatedness of literature. A central topic for this revitalized literary historicism was the colonial project in the New World and the work of Quinn and Canny provided historicist literary scholars with a neat way of forging a link back from the distant world of the Americas to the immediate world of the domestic British realm.

A nice example of how this linkage was effected can be seen in the work of Stephen Greenblatt. Greenblatt and Quinn shared an interest in the paradigmatic Atlanticist colonizer, Sir Walter Raleigh – owner of plantation estates in both Ireland and the New World – and both wrote books about Raleigh early in their careers (Greenblatt *Sir Walter Raleigh*; Quinn *Raleigh and the British Empire*). In his seminal 1980 study *Renaissance Self-Fashioning*, Greenblatt constructed a New Historicist framework which he brought into play in delineating the mechanisms of colonialist discourse.

He discusses Columbus's conceptualization of the New World natives and English encounters with west Africa and, in his chapter on Spenser's *Faerie Queene* and *View of the Present State of Ireland*, he links back from the greater colonial world to Ireland, to delineate 'the destruction of Hiberno-Norman civilization [with] the exercise of a brutal force that had few if any of the romantic trappings with which Elizabeth contrived to soften it at home' (Greenblatt *Renaissance Self-Fashioning* 186). In writing about early modern Ireland, Greenblatt drew both on Quinn's *The Elizabethans and the Irish* and on Canny's first book, *The Elizabethan Conquest of Ireland*. Greenblatt's manoeuvrings here provide a model for many of his successors. To take just one example, in Jonathan Dollimore and Alan Sinfield's *Political Shakespeare* (seen by many as a foundational text for British Cultural Materialism) Paul Brown offers an analysis of key Renaissance texts – notably *The Tempest* – in a colonial context. Like Greenblatt, Brown begins with the New World, discussing Shakespeare's connections with the Virginia Company and figuring Prospero's island, conventionally, as emblematic of the American colonies. Later in his chapter, again like Greenblatt, Brown overlays his New World colonial analysis with an Irish narrative, so that Prospero's island becomes a kind of analytical Necker cube, hovering between simultaneously figuring both the New World and Ireland. Like Greenblatt, Brown is indebted to Quinn and Canny for his historical background.

From the mid-1980s onward a distinctive sub-area can be said to have established itself within historicist criticism, focusing on Ireland and Renaissance literature. Work in this sub-area concerned itself with a clearly demarcated set of texts, radiating outward from the central core of Spenser's *View of the Present State of Ireland* and *The Faerie Queene* (notably Book v). A number of critics – many of them contributors to this present volume – have, from the late 1990s onward, attempted to offer a more sophisticated reading of this Irish colonial canon, but, in general terms, it is the Atlanticist model of Quinn and Canny that has served as the central paradigm for literary analysts wishing to engage with this material (see, for example, Lim *The Arts of Empire*).

An over-ready reliance on Atlanticist paradigms has meant that literary scholars have not always been willing to take account of forms of historical analysis which suggest alternative readings of Renaissance textualizations of early modern Ireland and the Hiberno-Britannic relationship. Historicist literary scholars have, in general, been slow to realize that 'History' is no more monolithic a discipline than 'English' is. The injunction that literary analysts should 'get back to history' is an altogether more complex imperative than has often been recognized. Different historiographical frameworks produce contrasting historical narratives. Literary scholars concerned with early modern Ireland might well find it fruitful to attune themselves more closely to the varieties of frameworks that have been constructed by historians of early modern Ireland and to register the fact that the work of many recent historians serves both to unsettle and to complement the early conclusions reached by Quinn and Canny. Literary scholars need, in other words, to be more attentive to the greater range of historiography and to engage with complex 'cross-colonial' models, rather than continuing to rely so heavily on the work of a narrow band of historical analysis.

Interrogations of the Quinn–Canny model within the field of early modern Irish historical studies have intersected with the emergence within Irish historiography of a disparate group of historians who have been shepherded together under the broad rubric of 'revisionism'. Revisionism is something of a portmanteau term and its borders are imprecisely drawn. In its most wilfully blinkered incarnation, it has set out as its programmatic aim the disjoining of history from mythography, so that the task of the historian becomes the dispassionate construction of narratives about the past whose high truth value distinguishes them from, for example, the narratives evolved by historians who write from an avowedly nationalist perspective (Fanning 'The Meaning of Revisionism'). The literary critic might be excused a wry smile in response to revisionism's desire to eschew mythography in favour of pure truth, but to dismiss revisionism out of hand on the grounds of theoretical *naïveté* is to fail to register the altogether more interesting project which lies at the heart of the most considered forms of revisionist analysis. If myopic revisionism sees itself as cutting away nationalist mythography to reveal the truth in history, a more nuanced version of revisionism seeks to attend not to the absolute veracity of history, but to history's particularity, refusing to take traditional structures of interpretation simply on faith.

It is precisely on the grounds of particularity that revisionists have come to question the usefulness of the Atlanticist paradigm. The Quinn–Canny model proposes that English colonial discourse in the early modern period functions through the simultaneous elision and evocation of difference: the Irish are conjoined with the natives of the New World under the index of an alien otherness and are thereby disjoined from co-extensive identity with the English themselves. This is an accurate analysis, in so far as it goes, and, certainly, Quinn and Canny have provided much evidence in support of this view. Indeed, one need only remember Fynes Moryson's well-known characterization of Ireland as '[t]his famous Iland in the Virginian Sea' to appreciate the force of this analysis (Moryson *An Itinerary* 156). However, the Atlanticist paradigm is itself sustained precisely by a process of eliding and evoking difference. Alignments of various kinds between the Irish and the English are downplayed, at the same time as differences between the two population groups (in dress, judicial codes, systems of landholding, language, religion, etc.) are foregrounded. The aim of much revisionist interrogation of the Quinn–Canny position has been, precisely, to query their overarching thesis by refocusing attention on the particularities of the Irish situation, in the process reversing the charge of Atlanticist interpretation by highlighting the long-established links between Ireland and Britain and the disjunctions between a neighbouring Ireland and a wholly alien 'New' World.

Steven Ellis has been in the vanguard of those historians who have sought to interrogate the Atlanticist model. Ellis has not dismissed the Quinn–Canny interpretation out of hand – indeed, he has on a number of occasions acknowledged the value of their approach, observing, for instance, that 'some kind of analysis comparing the colonisation of Ireland with that of other colonised territories is entirely appropriate, not to say essential, in order to understand the Irish experience' (Ellis 'Writing Irish History' 7). Ellis has argued, however, that while the colonial and transatlantic framework may be necessary to an understanding of early modern Ireland it is not, in itself, sufficient. He thus ultimately concludes that 'in the final analysis, colonial models of Irish history . . . raise as many problems as they solve' and has argued in relation to the conflation of Ireland with the New World that '[t]he contrasts between the two peoples – which in the case of the Atlantic World theory are never spelled out – were actually much more important than the comparisons' (Ellis 'Historiographical Debate' 294, 'Writing Irish History' 13). One notes here, however, a certain slippage between a willingness to accept the colonial model while wishing to complicate it and an interrogation of the colonial model which, in practice, serves to disavow it. Such faultlines tend not to be adequately addressed in Ellis's work.

A great many revisionist readings of early modern Ireland focus precisely on the particularity of the differences between the Irish and the New World natives and on the common elements which serve to link Ireland with its immediate neighbour, and thereby further distinguish the Irish from the native Americans. There is, of course, as many commentators have pointed out, a danger in revisionist particularism, in that attention to the specificities of history may lead to an overly atomistic inquiry, such that any kind of interpretative analysis becomes an impossibility (Deane 'Introduction'). In the present context, the career of the historian Hiram Morgan provides an interesting case in point. Morgan, as he notes himself, began his publishing career in 1985 with an article 'about the plantation attempt of Sir Thomas Smith in Ulster [following] the perspective developed by Quinn and Canny'. However, just over five years later, Morgan finds himself declaring that 'I am convinced the colonialist approach is no longer tenable' (Hiram Morgan 'Mid-Atlantic Blues' 54). This is not to say that Morgan is ultimately bereft of any interpretive framework. What I want to stress here is rather the extent to which the interrogation of a specific framework can easily shade into the denial of the validity of that framework. Where we might well want to challenge the Quinn–Canny model as the exclusive interpretation of early modern Ireland, the blank disavowal of its validity seems to fly in the face of the evidence convincingly marshalled in support of their position.

Brendan Bradshaw – in an article critiquing the work of Steven Ellis – has drawn attention to what he perceives as another difficulty with the revisionist approach: its tendency to neutralize what he has characterized as the 'traumatic' or 'catastrophic dimension of Irish history' (Bradshaw 'Nationalism and Historical Scholarship' 341). It is certainly the case that the ferocity with which the Irish have been treated by their neighbours is more clearly handled by a framework which characterizes the Anglo-Irish relationship as fundamentally and ineluctably colonial. Bradshaw's extended relationship to these issues, however, is interestingly complex. In some of his earliest publications Bradshaw sounds surprisingly like a revisionist *avant la lettre* – I am thinking here, for instance, of his 1977 review article on Canny's *Elizabethan Conquest*, where he writes of 'taking possession of our past' in order to 'prevent it from taking possession of us in the form of irrational myths, prejudices, and hatreds' – a procedure he characterizes as a 'purificatory process of demythologization' (Bradshaw 'The Elizabethans and the Irish' 38). In this same article, and in 'The Elizabethans and the Irish: A Muddled Model', Bradshaw also offers a certain resistance to the Atlanticist paradigm on the grounds that it neglects the European intellectual context of Tudor policy in Ireland. For Bradshaw, what we find in early modern Ireland is less the rigorous and relentless grinding out of a colonialist project which mirrors the English programme in the New World, than the confused collision of two antithetical policies, each rooted in disjunct European intellectual traditions. Early modern Ireland is thus, for Bradshaw, the site of a

contest between policies motivated by either an ameliorative humanism
or a form of Protestant political ethics which sought radical solutions to
civic problems.

Bradshaw offers a large-scale working through of this analysis in which
he argues for seeing English policy toward Ireland in the middle decades
of the Tudor period as being liberal and broadly conciliatory, as the
English sought to bring the Irish within the ambit of an Anglo-Irish judicial, tenurial, linguistic, and cultural system by employing, for the most
part, persuasive assimilationist means rather than aggressive coercion
(Bradshaw *The Irish Constitutional Revolution*). In Bradshaw's analysis, this
assimilationist policy faltered as the century progressed (and older forms
of humanism lost ground to radical Protestantism in England), but its
legacy always resonated to a greater or lesser degree in English thinking. There are, of course, as a number of scholars have indicated, defi-
nite problems with this interpretation. Discussing the significance of the
change in Henry VIII's title from 'Lord' of Ireland to 'King' of Ireland in
1541 (one of the symbolic centrepieces – together with 'surrender and regrant', the policy whereby Irish overlords were encouraged to renounce
their traditional Gaelic titles in exchange for British aristocratic ones – of
the 'liberal formula' identified by Bradshaw), Ciaran Brady rejects attempts to characterize this assimilation of the Irish to the community of
the king's subjects in a wholly positive light, pointing out that

> implicit in the Kingship Act itself was the assumption that those who denied
> its statutory authority were traitors to the new Irish king and would be treated
> as such. Thus the dispossession and destruction of rebellious subjects was re-
> garded from the outset as a legitimate right of the Irish government, though
> one which was to be employed with discretion. (Brady 'The Decline of the Irish
> Kingdom' 100)

Brady's intervention here serves to remind us of the gap between the
professed aims of Tudor policy and its effects – intended or otherwise –
on the ground. The problems with Bradshaw's thesis notwithstanding,
however, his analysis does point to the possibility of a useful approach to
early modern Ireland which might operate in parallel with – rather than
in opposition to – the Atlanticist model. By emphasizing the intellectual
roots of Tudor policy in Ireland, Bradshaw provides a useful counter-
weight to Atlanticist analysis by restoring Ireland to its place within a
greater European context, thus necessarily complicating any attempt
to effect a strict conflation of Ireland's experience with that of the New
World. Furthermore, Bradshaw also helps us to register the fact that,

while we can certainly debate the extent to which Tudor humanists were motivated by a greater or lesser degree of self-serving political cynicism, the fact remains that one significant strand of English thinking on Ireland in the early modern period conceived of the Anglo-Irish relationship in assimilationist terms which differed – if only conceptually – from the baldly colonial aims of English settlers in the New World.

This latter point indicates a line of filiation between Bradshaw's work, a revisionist interpretation of early modern Ireland which rejects the binary analysis advanced by nationalist-inflected historiography, and the framework advocated by proponents of the Britannic paradigm. Given this set of connections, it is no surprise that Bradshaw and Steven Ellis – despite having publicly located themselves on opposing sides in the debates over revisionism – have nevertheless, broadly speaking, endorsed the new 'British' history, both co-editing volumes on the topic (Bradshaw and Morrill *The British Problem*; Ellis and Barber *Conquest and Union*). Certainly, the Britannic approach – if informed by the contrasting positions adopted by Bradshaw and Ellis and, crucially, held in parallel with the Atlanticist model – has much to recommend it in attempting to engage with the complexities of Ireland's positioning in the early modern period. David Armitage has made this clear, in drawing on Raymond Gillespie's proposal that early modern Ireland can best be seen as 'a mid-Atlantic polity having some of the features of both the Old World and the New' without being fully part of either. As Armitage observes, this suggestion 'aptly captures the ambiguity of Ireland's position without ruling its peculiarities out of consideration or rendering it utterly exceptional and hence strictly incomparable to other patterns of early modern social and political development' (Gillespie 'Explorers, Exploiters and Entrepreneurs' 152; Armitage 'Greater Britain' 433). Of course, terminological problems still remain and Jane Ohlmeyer has usefully commented that 'if Ireland is to be included in future discourses, perhaps the more cumbersome term "British and Irish Histories" is more appropriate, though not entirely satisfactory' (Ohlmeyer 'Seventeenth-century Ireland' 454). However we square the nomenclative circle, it is clear that an approach to early modern Ireland which engages with the archipelagic in parallel with the transatlantic is likely to prove fruitful for both historians and literary critics alike.

One of the advantages of an archipelagic approach to historical investigation is precisely the shift away from the narrow framework that nationalist historiography sometimes promotes. For nationalists – especially postcolonially minded nationalists – the natural trajectory of history is to effect the emergence of the independent nation state. History itself is thus, as it were, an extended illustration of the principle *tiocfaidh ár lá* (an Irish-language phrase meaning 'our day will come', adopted as a slogan by republican separatists in Northern Ireland). Within this perspective, it seems entirely appropriate to deploy, with respect to the early modern period, a framework which imagines Ireland as a coherent distinctive entity set in opposition to an equally coherent and self-contained England. We need, however, to ask to what extent this framework really is appropriate to an analysis of archipelagic relations in a period which predates the coming into being of an independent sovereign (segment of the island of) Ireland by some three or four centuries. There is much dispute over the extent to which the Irish in the early modern period conceived of the possibility of an Ireland that would be wholly independent of English control, but the fact remains that, for good or ill, the island was in this period incorporated within an English-dominated polity and had been for about four centuries (and would, of course, continue to be so until the third decade of the twentieth century; indeed part of the island continues to be so).

To foreground the extent to which the Irish themselves very often conceived of opposition to the British state in explicitly archipelagic terms is not to deny the broader implications of that opposition or the fact that one form of such opposition did indeed ultimately lead to the greater part of the island of Ireland breaking away from Britain to form an independent sovereign state. The larger point at stake here is the fact that the British archipelago has always functioned as a problematic and uneasy conglomerate, in which the various elements exist in a more or less tense conjunction, dominated by the governmental structures of the south-east part of the largest island. While the Atlanticist and colonial models have each been very useful in bringing to light one aspect of Ireland's relationship to the archipelagic conglomerate, deployed as the only frameworks for viewing this history, they have tended to flatten this complex set of interrelationships into a monochromatic polar binary. Layering the archipelagic approach upon the Atlanticist model serves to open up a much wider field of interpretive possibilities.

Discussing the extent to which the disputes over revisionist historiography have entered the general scene of cultural debate in Ireland, Ronan Fanning suspects that 'there lurks inside every Irish intellectual an historian trying to get out' (Fanning 'The Meaning of Revisionism' 16). However true this may be of the Irish intellectual community, it is certainly the case that literary criticism since the 1980s has been dominated by forms of analysis in which, to adapt from Spenser, Clio has been compelled to lend Calliope her quill. On many occasions, the results have been fruitful and the conjunction has often led to the useful coming together of historians and literary scholars. One of the problems with such inter-disciplinary work, however, is that, in the case of early modern Ireland, literary scholars have tended to align themselves too closely with one particular strand of historical analysis, while failing to notice the extent to which historians have themselves begun evolving other paradigms which might interrogate or complement earlier analyses. The reasons for this are easy enough to find. A New Historicist reliance on the work of Foucault, and a Cultural Materialist alignment with British Marxism, have led proponents of historicism to engage primarily with large-scale structures and systems of power within cultural history. Such an analyt-ical framework can be very usefully deployed in relation to European encounters with the New World, where, for instance, the engagements with wholly new forms of society serve to foreground structures of belief and systems of ideology. Such criticism, following back along the line traced by Quinn and Canny, crosses the Atlantic and discovers filiations between Ireland and the New World. The connections are certainly there to be found and usefully pursued, but they only represent part of the story. As Canny himself has pointed out, the patterns one discovers in early modern Ireland depend to some extent on the particular his-toriographical lens one brings to bear on the period. In common with the historicists, Canny himself seeks to map out large-scale structures of power and the oppositional divisions which they create. By contrast, as Canny notes, '[a]dministrative historians, whose minds are focused on the day-to-day routine in government offices, lay emphasis on the similarity of this routine in Ireland to that in similar offices in England' and, as he goes on to register, such historians have 'rejected the notion that Ireland was being perceived or treated as a colony by English offi-cials. They have been able to do so because they have drawn attention to the consistent attempt of governments to administer the country after the fashion of England, and because they can explain revolt in terms of malfunction in the administration' (Canny *Kingdom and Colony* 9, 11). If historicism is to continue to occupy a central position within literary criticism, it will have to become more alert to the varieties of historiogra-phy deployed by historical scholars. It is to be hoped that an extension of the archipelagic paradigm – in parallel with Atlanticist models – might serve to complicate matters productively.

Contested peripheries

CHAPTER 3

'The lost British lamb': English Catholic exiles and the problem of Britain

Christopher Highley

In October 1608, as part of the Counter-Reformation publishing campaign, the press at St Omers College issued a work by John Wilson – an English priest living in exile and 'supervisor' of the press. *English Martyrologe* responded to Protestant martyrologies like John Foxe's *Acts and Monuments*, as well as to fears that English Catholics were losing touch with their religious heritage. 'I have heere gathered togeather, and restored unto yow againe, that which the injury of tymes had violently taken from yow, and sought to abolish all memory therof' (*2r) (Rhodes 'English Books of Martyrs and Saints' 10–11). Although described in the title as an 'English Martyrologie', the calendar's subjects are drawn from all parts of Britain and Ireland. Saints commemorated in the month of January, for example, include: 'S. Meliorus Martyr' of Cornwall, 'S. Croniacke Confessor' of Scotland, 'S. Beno Priest and Confessor' of North Wales, and 'S. Eoglodius Monke and Confessor' of Ireland. Organized by chronology rather than geography and mingling saints of different regions on the same page, Wilson's text offers a vision of an encompassing Catholicism that integrates the multiple kingdoms, nations, and peoples of the Atlantic Archipelago.[1] This idea of a Catholicism that transcended traditional national boundaries is reinforced in many of the individual saints' stories that tell how, out of love for their 'neighbour-Countreyes', the saints have left their homelands (45). As related in a later martyrology by Jerome Porter (1632), the life of Saint Patrick is exemplary of this boundary-crossing impulse.[2] Patrick, 'Borne of the race of auncient Britons, in that part of Wales now called Pembrookshire', first arrives 'among the inhabitants of Ireland, who then were called Scotts', after being captured and taken there as a slave. Patrick's ensuing career is one of constant physical mobility, thus making him a culturally hybrid, boundary-blurring figure, one 'skilfull, and readie in fower-distinct languages, the Welch, the Irish, the French, and the Latin' (Porter *The Flowers* 287). After his early captivity, he escapes back to Wales, gains an education in France, and is ordained in Rome, before commencing his long-term itinerant ministry in Ireland.

If Porter's and Wilson's texts work to break down rigid ideas of nationhood by imagining a free-flowing, trans-national Catholicism, they also betray a nagging uncertainty about how to characterize 'our little Dominions' and the relationships among them (Wilson *English Martyrologe* *8r). Wilson's unstable terminology speaks both in imperial, centralizing terms of 'our *Great-Britany*, and . . . the Ilands belonging thereunto', and in more separatist, atomizing terms of 'our three Kingdomes, *England, Scotland & Ireland*' (*7v–*8r). While both these formulations play down a hierarchical ordering among the three kingdoms, Wilson's epigraphs – from Matthew Paris and the Venerable Bede – speak exclusively of 'England'. Described by Paris as 'An Iland so shining with Martyrs, Confessours, and holy Virgins', the name of 'England' absorbs two kingdoms and a plurality of cultures (*1r). Wilson's shifting labels for his homeland connect his work to what has come to be known as the 'the problem of Britain' – a problem that encompasses an array of questions about the complex historical relations among the multiple territories, cultures, peoples, and nations of the Atlantic Archipelago.

For exiled Catholic Englishmen like Wilson and Porter, the problem of Britain was central to the task of reimagining a collective identity that had been thrown into crisis by the exigencies of geographical and social displacement. What did 'home' mean to these exiles? What were its territorial boundaries and contours? What peoples and cultures did it include and exclude? Was 'Britain' a meaningful term in their lexicon? Recent historical scholarship by Jane Dawson, Roger A. Mason, Arthur H. Williamson, and others, has established the emergence of Britain as a resonant imaginative construct in English and Scottish Reformation ideology. Interest in Britain as a single territorial, political, and cultural entity of course existed long before the Reformation, most notably in the legendary British empire of King Arthur. After Henry VIII's break with Rome, and especially during the reign of Edward VI, however, English and Scottish Protestants alike seized upon the image of Britain as home to a unified Protestant monarchy, a bulwark against the encroachments of a hostile Catholic Europe (Dawson 'Anglo-Scottish Protestant Culture'; Mason 'The Scottish Reformation'; Williamson 'Scotland, Antichrist and the Invention of Great Britain'; 'Patterns of British Identity').

Even as the new historiography of Britain eschews an Anglocentric perspective, acknowledging the rich multicultural fabric of the early modern Atlantic Archipelago, it remains firmly embedded within an almost exclusively Protestant framework. This chapter aims to reorient the current discussion by asking how the 'British problem' was construed from the other side of the confessional divide and from outside Britain among Catholic exiles during the reigns of Elizabeth and James. John Wilson's evocation in his *English Martyrologe* of a time before the Reformation when Britain and Ireland were imagined as sharing a unifying Catholic faith is, of course, the nostalgic fantasy of an exile. What the fantasy suppresses are the pressures exerted by alternative affiliations centred on national and ethnic identities, affiliations that sometimes conflicted with religious loyalties, and that complicated efforts by exiled Catholics from across the Atlantic Archipelago to reconvert their homelands (Loomie *The Spanish Elizabethans* 217). Scattered across Catholic Europe, the exiles were a heterogeneous assortment of clerics, scholars, and political fugitives, constituting more of a religious diaspora than a unified community with shared principles and aspirations. In fact the diaspora was the epitome of disunity. The Jesuit Robert Persons, a prominent English exile, tellingly entitled his memoir of the struggle to restore Catholicism in England *A Storie of Domesticall Difficulties which the English Catholic Cause and Promoters therof, have had in defending the same, not onely against the violence, and persecution of heretikes, but also by sundry other impediments amonge themselves, of faction, emulation, sedition, and division, since the chaunge of Religion in England*.[3] These self-inflicted 'difficulties' included disagreements over discipline – could Catholics legitimately attend Protestant services? – and strategy – should missionary priests concentrate their efforts on the Catholic gentry or on the common people? Like their co-religionists in England, the exiles were embroiled in 'stirs' that pitted secular priests against Jesuits and supporters of a Scottish succession against backers of the King of Spain. William Allen, nominal head of the English exiles in 1582, found their condition mirrored in the plight of the Children of Israel in the Book of Numbers (verse 16):

I know for certain and from experience that it would be easier to guide to salvation a thousand souls in England than a hundred in this exile, which of itself breeds murmurings, complainings, contradictions and discontent. When Moses leads the people through the desert, he suffers much. Even at the very time that God rains down manna and quails and brings water from the rock they are not satisfied, but their soul is with the flesh-pots of Egypt, Core conspires, Dathan rises in revolt, Abiron is unruly, and they collect round them many partners. This is the peculiarity of exiles.[4]

The courts, the religious and publishing centres, university towns, and seminaries across Europe in which uprooted English Catholics took refuge, may have been havens from persecution, but they were also strange and sometimes hostile places, inducing nostalgia for an ancestral 'home'. 'Outsiders' both in England and in exile, the English refugees – like their counterparts from Wales, Scotland, and Ireland – invariably coalesced into nations in exile, intensely conscious of their country of origin and jealous of the claims of these other 'neighbour' nations with whom the English saw themselves in competition for the limited assistance of Popes and Catholic rulers. Bound together by a shared religious heritage and political cause, the expatriate cultures of England, Wales, Scotland, and Ireland might have made common cause, inventing a collective archipelagic identity. Instead, the diverse expatriate communities cohered tenaciously along national and ethnic rather than confessional lines.

At least in the early stages of the northern Counter-Reformation, members of the various nations in exile made attempts at cooperation. In the first scheme aimed at returning Britain and Ireland to the Papal See, Nicholas Sanders – the Louvain-based theologian, polemicist, and early leader of the English *émigrés* – accompanied the Anglo-Irishman, James Fitzmaurice Fitzgerald, to Ireland with a small expeditionary force funded by Pope Gregory XIII in 1579. Fitzmaurice, after four years on the continent seeking support for resistance to the English presence in Ireland, was appointed Captain General of the Pope's Army while Sanders acted as Papal Nuncio.[5] Their first objective was to secure a 'common front' among traditionally fractious Gaelic leaders against the heretical English 'she-tyrant'.[6] Fitzmaurice and Sanders, inspired by Counter-Reformation zeal, claimed to be fighting not against the authority of the English crown *per se* but against its Protestant usurper. They issued a proclamation calculated to draw in sympathizers from across Elizabeth's territories, including 'Wales, Chester, Lancashire, and Cumberland, where the country people, the best fitted to bear arms, were strongly Catholic'.[7] The mission, though launched in Ireland, aimed – as Sanders's letters make clear – to re-establish the Old Faith throughout the Atlantic Archipelago. To secure a wide appeal, Sanders wanted their initial party to include 'English, Irish, and Scottish priests, at least two of each nation . . . For it is almost certain that soon after war is waged in one of [these] islands, it will be begun in the other, especially if the matter be prudently and cleverly handled' (Wainewright 'Some Letters and Papers of Nicholas Sanders' 17).

Fitzmaurice's death doomed the mission that finally crumbled at Smerwick in November 1580. Although Sanders, who died shortly afterwards, was revered as a patriot by many English Catholics, he provided Protestants with what they saw as an irrefutable link between Catholicism and rebellion (Persons 'Memoirs' 161). In bringing together English and Irish figures and interests, the Fitzmaurice–Sanders enterprise was a remarkable if ill-fated attempt by Catholic exiles at coordinating an ecumenical, inclusive, British–Irish reconversion effort. Such cooperation, however, was short-lived and atypical – Sanders's willingness to work alongside his co-religionists from Ireland would not be imitated by other English expatriates.

While various exiles from Ireland or with Irish connections, including the Anglo-Irish adventurer Thomas Stukeley, the Limerick-born Jesuit David Wolfe, Peter Lombard, and Florence Conry, impressed the special urgency of Ireland's reconversion upon Popes and kings, English exiles seem to have been more sceptical about the strategic opportunities presented by Ireland.[8] The Jesuit organization of its missions, vice-provinces, and provinces along narrow 'national' lines encouraged Englishmen like Persons and Edmund Campion to formulate a specifically English mission (there was no British mission), although it was recognized that the effort to recover England might require a strategy focused on an Anglo-Celtic frontier.[9]

Following Sanders's defeat in Ireland, which coincided with the departure of Persons and Campion on the Jesuit mission to England, Catholic leaders developed a new 'Celtic strategy'. Persons identified several regions that 'as time went on would be best able to further our cause'. These included 'Wales, a region of wide and ample spaces, which was not so hostile to the Catholic religion but yet owing to the lack of labourers, had sunk into a state of dense ignorance'. Persons also mentioned Cambridgeshire and the Anglo-Scottish borders, but the crucial region was Scotland, 'on which country depends the conversion not only of England but of all the lands in the North'.[10] Throughout the 1580s, Persons and William Allen focused their attention on Scotland: promoting the claim of Mary Queen of Scots to the English throne; converting her son, James Stuart, to Catholicism; and planning a military expedition that would pass from Spain to England via Scotland.[11] A Scottish enterprise was close to realization in 1582, when a group led by Persons and Allen met in Paris to coordinate plans with the Duke of Guise (leader of the militant French Catholic League). The group drafted a memorial asking the Pope and King of Spain for 'eight thousand infantrymen' and money to support an army for six to eight months, supposedly long enough to pass through Scotland to London and to overthrow a queen who 'has come

to be hated by everybody'.[12] The memorial's appraisal of possible opposition was crude fantasy: Scots and English would overwhelmingly rally
to the Catholic side (the English population was supposedly two-thirds
Catholic), while 'large and wealthy cities on the route, such as Newcastle,
[and] York . . . will surrender to the army without drawing the sword'.
Ironically linking the arrival of Tudor rule to that dynasty's demise, the
petitioners claimed that their scheme would approximate 'the victory
won by Henry, Earl of Richmond . . . who with a very small band of men
got possession of the kingdom through having a little inside information'
(Persons *Letters* 161, 162).

Although centred on Scotland, the confederacy's enterprise had a
broader trans-national dimension. Persons wanted the Archdeacon of
Cambray, Dr Owen Lewis, to accompany the enterprise in order to
encourage 'the Welsh, his countrymen. [Lewis] will be able to give considerable assistance in this affair . . . on account of the great love [the
Welsh] bear to the Catholic faith' (Persons *Letters* 147). Others urged
that rebellion also be stirred in Ireland.[13] Yet possibilities of an encompassing archipelagic Catholic solidarity were again threatened by
endemic national and ethnic rivalries. According to Persons, a major
obstacle facing the mission in late 1582 was 'a natural jealousy between the two nations of Scotland and England'. To offset this distrust
Persons urged 'that whenever orders . . . come from his Holiness the
two nations are treated as being exactly on the same footing; and this
will be the case if the English see that Mr. Allen, or some such other
Englishman . . . is associated as representing England, with the most
Reverend Archbishop of Glasgow as representing Scotland' (147–8).[14]
By 1584, however, Allen altogether rejected the idea of landing a force in
Scotland, fearful that a Catholic army descending upon England from
north of the border would be mistaken by potentially sympathetic English
Catholics as a hostile force bent on 'subjecting the English to the Scottish
rule. And if once this doubt is injected, it is to be feared that the invading
army will not only have the heretics for enemies, but also the catholics
who will suspect everything from an army marching on them from
Scotland.'[15]

While Allen's anxieties about the threat posed to Catholic political solidarity by national prejudices were never tested on the Scottish border,
they had already been fully played out between English and Welsh exiles
at the English College in Rome.[16] What had been a hospice for English
and Welsh pilgrims to the city was converted in 1578 into a college for
training young men from these countries for the priesthood. The English

students who transferred to Rome from the seminary at Rhemes, how-ever, soon found themselves in conflict with their superiors, the Welshmen Dr D. Morrice Clenock (the Rector) and Mr D. Lewes. Clenock and Lewes were accused by the more than thirty English students of pro-viding inadequate leadership and of showing favouritism to the '7 or 8' Welsh students who now rallied behind their superiors in a 'nationall quarrell' that soon drew in other Welsh and English Catholics in Rome and beyond.[17] The English students complained they were not properly taken care of: during the winter while 'all the Welchemen [were] double apareled', 'the best borne Englishe went . . . with naked thighes and full of lice'. The English also charged Clenock and his countrymen with not wanting newly trained priests to go as missionaries into England – the very reason that had led most of the English students to enter the college in the first place.[18] Fears abounded that the English–Welsh conflict might escalate into broader Anglo-Celtic divisions, Persons reporting a rumour that 'the Scottishe nation had given up a Memoriall that they myght be admitted also to the participation of this new College, and the like was doubtfull of the Irishe'. Persons thought that Clenock, as revenge for the allegations against him, was seeking to admit, 'Welch, Irish, and Scottishe schollers in the Colledge and they three joyning togeather against the Englishe (as easily they are wonte) they might the better hould down the other'.[19] The troubles in Rome reached a crisis point when the English students were expelled; on the verge of leaving the city, they secured an audience with the Pope, persuading him to place the gov-ernment of the college under Jesuit control. In retrospect, Persons saw this original quarrel between English and Welsh exiles at Rome as repre-senting 'the very first root . . . of the great differences that have fallen out since that time among Catholics of our nation' – differences that resulted in the formation of two opposed groups: one strongly pro-Spanish – with Persons himself at the head – the other dedicated to the succession to the English throne of the Scot James VI.[20]

Alongside the 'Many Memorialls, letters and other schrowles' record-ing the national and ethnic tensions in Rome there appeared a published account in Antony Munday's book, *The English Roman Life* (1582).[21] In chapter 6, 'The manner of the dissension in the English College between the Englishmen and the Welshmen', the Protestant Munday gleefully publicizes the English–Welsh conflict to a wider audience. Munday tells how 'Doctor Morris's' enmity toward him helped to secure him the friend-ship of English scholars.[22] For Munday, the episode provided an oppor-tunity to satirize the Pope as well as Catholic belief in demonic possession and exorcism. Munday's main propaganda coup, however, came from the way he was able to exploit the always uneasy relation between the exiles' religious and national loyalties. By showing how he had success-fully ingratiated himself with the English students against the Welsh, Munday – 'our best plotter' as Francis Meres called this writer-cum-spy – flaunted the triumph of national over religious commitments.[23]

While Munday makes no attempt to disguise his confessional biases, Persons, in his accounts of the troubles, lays claim to a dispassionate im-partiality. Yet although posturing as 'voyde of all affection of both parties', Persons cannot conceal an admiration for the English students.[24] In fact, Persons uses the English students' response to their adversities in Rome as a way of affirming their fitness for the rigors of missionary work. As Persons points out, observers could only wonder that if the students used such 'liberty of speech' and 'stand thus immovable before such princes in Rome, what will they do in England before the heretiques'.[25] The English scholars, according to Persons, displayed during their expulsion from the college exemplary discipline, resourcefulness, magnanimity, and wit. They 'were not only ready to pardon whatsoever the Welchmen had done against them, or should do, but also were ready to kisse their feet, and to serve them at table'. To further reconcile 'the two nations', the English students were also willing to make sure that the Welsh got the best 'apparell, books, [and] chambers'. Only one 'English gentleman named Mr Pasquall', Persons wryly adds, 'stept up and said that he [agreed with this arrangement] except in his portion of meate, wherein he desired to be equall to any of the [Welsh], for that his appetite or stomacke yielded to none of theirs'.[26]

Converting an apparent disaster for the fledgeling college into a vindication of 'Englishmens natures', Persons reveals an underlying preoccupation with ethnic identities, a 'racialism' that also informs his most notorious publication, *A Conference*, produced in 1595 under the pseudonym 'R. Doleman', on which he collaborated with 'Cardinal Allen, Sir Francis Englefield and other principal men of our nation'.[27] In the 1580s, Persons and his associates had backed first Mary Queen of Scots and later James, who they hoped could be converted to his mother's faith. Once it became clear that James would remain a 'heretic', they looked elsewhere for a Catholic candidate. Contributing to this search, *A Conference* sets out the rights of various candidates to the English throne and considers the criteria for adjudicating their claims. An English civil lawyer, one of the main speakers in the dialogue, argues that lineal succession and propinquity of blood, while relevant, are finally less important than the election of a ruler by the commonwealth. Then in the book's second part a temporal lawyer analyses the strengths and weaknesses of each candidate, but without, he insists, 'stand[ing] upon the justification or impugning of any one title' (Q5). Nevertheless, it is the Infanta Isabella of Spain who is finally endorsed as the 'one foreign prince . . . likest to beare it away' (2:263).[28]

With its dialogical structure, its tone of impartiality and its basis in scholarly genealogical research, *A Conference* is no simple polemic on behalf of the Spanish Habsburgs and against rival claimants. Yet Persons was clearly disingenuous when he claimed in defence of the book that 'With regard to the King of Scotland nothing is said against him except on the score of his being a heretic.' *A Conference* presents the candidacy of James Stuart as undesirable, not on religious grounds and not because he is a foreigner but because of the type of foreigner he is. Indeed, in a chapter on the respective merits of home-born and foreign-born rulers, *A Conference* argues that England might be well served by a foreign-born prince who would assume the monarchy unencumbered by domestic rivalries (2:193–233). A young unmarried candidate like the Infanta, claims Persons, far from imposing foreign manners on the English, would be readily assimilated into English culture (2:224). In Persons's analysis, the problem with James's candidacy arises first from the proximity of his new to his old realm, where he 'hath forces at hand to woorke his wil', and second from ethnic enmity: 'the aversion and natural alienation of [the Scots] from the English, and their ancient inclination to join with the French and Irish against us' (2:118). Should James gain the crown, Persons reasons, he would inevitably fill the realm with Scots, favouring them over the English, 'as we read that William [the] Conqueror did his Normans . . . to the incredible calamity of the English nation' (2:120). *A Conference* predicts that James's accession would bring about a 'violent union of nations, that are by nature so disunited and opposite, as are the English, Scottish, Irish, Danish, French, and other on them depending, which by this means must needs be planted together in England' (2:121). The authors of *A Conference* were not the only English Catholics to infuse their religious convictions with strong anti-Scottish prejudice and an aversion to union. Guy Fawkes and other gunpowder plotters were motivated by a similar anti-Scottish animus: had their plot succeeded they would allegedly 'have blown [all the Scots] back into Scotland' and immediately issued a proclamation against Anglo-Scottish union. Fawkes and his allies planned to replace James with one of his daughters who was still young enough to be raised an Anglicized Catholic.[29]

Once James became King of England, Persons scrambled to rethink his public approach to the Scot. In a dedication added to his *Treatise of Three Conversions* (1603) 'upon the newes of the Queens death; and succession of the King of Scotland', Persons likened James to the Emperor Constantine. In appropriating a favourite figure from Protestant mythology, Persons noted how both James and Constantine were notable for their pious mothers (Helena and Mary) and both exercised dominion over 'the whole *Ilande of Britany*' (1:*2). Moreover, Constantine's conversion to Christianity after becoming Emperor was a precedent for James's conversion to Catholicism. Perhaps, just as Constantine had 'donated' temporal and ecclesiastical control of Britain and Ireland to the Papacy, so James would once again restore those lands to their proper overlord. Yet even as Persons proclaimed his hope that James would show more tolerance to his Catholic subjects than had 'the olde persecutor' Elizabeth, he remained deeply suspicious of a Scottish succession and the prospect of Anglo-Scottish union. In a letter of July 1603, Persons again likened the arrival of the Scots in England to the coming of the Normans. He advised his correspondent to consult 'the storie of the Abbot [Ingulph] of Croyland . . . who was secretarie to Duke William before he was King of England, and saw the suppression of his nation by the Normanes'. It was a story, claimed Persons, that presented 'a pattern of the tyme to come'.[30] When news of Elizabeth's death reached Rome, Persons observed ominously that the Scots in the city, anticipating their countryman's accession, 'do begin already to exasperate too much in speeches everywhere against the English'.[31]

With the union of the kingdoms dominating political discourse during James's early years in England, *A Conference* was denounced by both Protestants and Catholics for attempting to subvert Anglo-Scottish integration.[32] The Scottish Protestant Sir Thomas Craig 'outed' Doleman as Persons and claimed that the Jesuit in 'working to secure for the Pope the recovery of this famous island' had 'spared no pains in his writings to combat the proposed union of the kingdoms'.[33] Craig refuted Persons's charges that a union would damage England because the Scots were impoverished, 'turbulent, uncivilized, and animated by bitter hatred towards Englishmen' (426). For Craig and other English and Scottish unionists, Anglo-Scottish integration promised – even without the formal unification of their national churches – to create a Protestant island bastion. According to the Protestant Englishmen who edited and published a Catholic plea for toleration from the new sovereign: 'It is very improbable that the uniting of these two Kingdomes of

England and *Scotland* under one King could please [the Catholic petition-
ers]. For the stronger this Kingdome is, the lesse hope have Masse-priests
to prevaile . . . [W]ho can imagine, that the Popes vassals can joy hartily
in the strength of his Majesties Empire, that dependeth not on their Lord
the Pope' (Anon. *The supplication of certaine masse-priests* H1 v–H2r).

Whatever Persons's 'Scottophobia' and opposition to union owed to
an underlying 'racialism', it also had a sound basis in politico-religious
realities. English Catholics were fearfully aware that recusancy laws were
harsher in Scotland than in England and that Scotland was home to a
radical anti-episcopal Protestantism that, they predicted, would infiltrate
England in the event of closer ties between the countries (Levack *The
Formation of the British State* 112). *A Conference* noted warily that James
already 'standeth in awe of this exorbitant and populer power of his
ministers' (2:123); even 'moderate' Protestants like Sir Henry Spelman
warned about the danger to England of 'those fiery spirited ministers
that in the fury of the[ir] zeale have not only perverted the stable government of [the Scottish] church but even wounded the very kingdome
itselfe'.[34] It was English Catholics, though, who had the most to fear from
the Scottish Presbyterians intent on promoting their radical religious
agenda through a 'unioun of these kingdoms under one God and Christ,
one king, one faith, one law'.[35]

In 1600, in a letter to the Earl of Angus, Persons had expressed a wish
'to see both our Realms united together under one Catholic government,
and prince of our own blood'.[36] Yet in the past when Persons and other
Catholic exiles might have appealed to the idea of a unified Catholic
Britain they remained narrowly Anglocentric in outlook. For example,
when promoting the claims of Mary Stuart and James in the 1580s,
Persons and his allies might have exploited a rhetoric of Britishness; yet
Catholics apparently did not conceive the claims of these Scottish princes
in terms of a larger vision of Anglo-Scottish or British unity. Likewise, in
A Memorial for the Reformation of England, Persons's blueprint for a future
Catholic realm written in 1596, the emphasis is exclusively on the English
nation.[37] Although Persons states in the preface that 'what is said in this
Treatise for the Kingdom of England, is meant also for Ireland, so far as
it may do good', he pays no attention to England's relations with Ireland
or to the special problems of governing England's most intractable neighbour (*The Jesuit's Memorial* A3r). Likewise Scotland is neither included in
Persons's plans nor seen as having any special connection to England.
Instead, the northern kingdom figures as one among many 'of our Neighbours oppressed or infected with Heresie, as namely, Denmark, divers

parts near to us, of Germany, Poland, Gothland, Sweedland, Scotland, Muscovy, and the Isles of Zeland' (150). Finally, in an extraordinary elision of Celtic Catholicity, Persons ignores the work and sufferings of Irish and Scots recusants, mentioning only the 'Executions of English Catholick priests' sent to Scotland and Ireland – a sign, he believes, that God has chosen England to be a 'Light and a Lantern to other Nations near unto it' (3). John Bossy, discussing these and other works of Persons, sees in them a 'Greater English' theory of Catholic nationhood in which England was destined to become the catalyst of the northern Counter-Reformation.[38]

Persons's resolute Anglocentrism recognizes the fact that by the later sixteenth century the language and imagery of Britain had become irrevocably linked with the Protestant cause in both England and Scotland. As Jane Dawson has argued, the discourse of British imperial union was first effectively appropriated for religious purposes by English and Scottish Protestant supporters of a marriage alliance between Edward VI and the young Mary Stuart. When political initiatives like this failed, ideas of union and British identity were taken up by an unofficial Anglo-Scottish Protestant culture – one based upon a shared vernacular and the circulation of common religious texts including pre-eminently the Geneva Bible. At the imaginative centre of that culture was the island of Britain, itself a political construct. God, so Protestants argued, had purposefully placed the Scots and English together on an island protected from Catholic Europe by a sea wall.[39] It was this myth of Britain as an enclosed world, a sanctuary for beleaguered Protestantism, that ran contrary to everything for which Persons and his supporters worked. Their objective was to reinscribe England – a country not self-contained but 'situated almost out of the world' – on a map whose centre was at Rome.[40] For Persons and many English exiles the only union worth pursuing was the alternative 'union of the general and universal and Catholic Church and faith'.[41]

NOTES

I would like to thank Susan Kneedler, John N. King, Thomas G. Olsen, David Cressy, and the editors for reading and commenting upon various drafts of this chapter.

The phrase in the title, 'The lost British lamb', is taken from one of Cardinal Allen's letters (qtd in McCoog *The Society of Jesus* 124).

1 For a defence of the term 'Atlantic Archipelago', see Pocock 'The Atlantic Archipelago'.

2 *The Flowers of the Lives of the Most Renowned SAINCTS of the Three Kingdoms ENGLAND SCOTLAND, AND IRELAND Written and collected out of the best authors and manuscripts of our nation.*

3 Persons 'The Memoirs of Father Robert Persons' 48.

4 Knox ed. *The First and Second Diaries of the English College, Douay* lxxvii.

5 On Fitzmaurice's crucial contribution to the emergent coupling of Irish rebellion and Catholic confessional discourse, see Bradshaw 'The English Reformation' esp. 64–6.

6 Quoted in Veech *Dr Nicholas Sanders* 282. See also Ronan *The Reformation in Ireland* 613–15.

7 Quoted in Veech *Dr Nicholas Sanders* 263.

8 On pleas and petitions of Catholic exiles from Ireland for help from leaders of European Catholicism, see Moran *Spicilegium Ossoriense* 59–70 (cited in McCoog *The Society of Jesus* 90 n.28); Silke 'The Irish Abroad'.

9 On the formation of the English mission and its anomalous status within the Jesuit organizational structure, see McCoog 'Establishment of the English Province'.

10 Persons *Letters* 108–9.

11 See McCoog *The Society of Jesus* ch. 5, 'On the Conversion of Scotland' 178–223.

12 Persons *Letters* 161; Persons 'Memoirs' 30–2 for an account of the meeting. Also see McCoog *The Society of Jesus* 187.

13 Allen *Letters* xxxvi.

14 Sanders had earlier foreseen such rivalries, and urged that 'The honourable Nuncio should be an Italian, lest Englishmen might be indignant at an Irishman being preferred before them, or *vice versa*, and the same reasoning applies also to the Scots' (*Miscellanea XII* 17).

15 Allen *Letters* lxiv.

16 Ibid. 79–84.

17 Persons 'Memoirs' 86, 135–6. For a modern history of the college, see Michael E. Williams *The Venerable English College Rome* ch. 1.

18 Persons 'Memoirs' 87, 114.

19 Ibid. 128–30.

20 Ibid. 88–9; also see 'Father Persons' Memoirs (concluded)', ed. and trans. in Pollen 'Notes Concerning the English Mission' 65–9. Opposition to the policies of Allen, Persons, and the Jesuits was eventually led by Thomas Morgan and Charles Paget. Persons accused these two of enlisting support from any exiled Catholics 'given to faction and nationality between English, Welsh, Irish, or Scots' ('Memoirs' 35).

21 Persons 'Memoirs' 87.

22 Persons, 'Memoirs', 83ff., 140–60.

23 Munday *English Roman Life* xvi.

24 'Memoirs' 142.

25 Ibid. 147, 159–60.

26 Ibid. 152–3.

27 Ibid. 159. Persons *A Brief Apologie* 187v, quoted in Loomie *The Spanish Elizabethans* 46. For the sake of convenience I shall refer to the work as being by Persons alone.

28 On English Catholic support for the Spanish Infanta, see Wormald 'Gunpowder' 155–6.

29 Ibid. 161–2. Also see Galloway *The Union of England and Scotland* 80; and Loomie *Guy Fawkes in Spain*.

30 'Memoirs' 216.

31 Quoted in Francis Edwards *Robert Persons* 284.

32 Scottish Catholics generally supported James and Anglo-Scottish union. Arthur Williamson points out that there was 'no Scottish Robert Persons; even Catholic-led opposition [to union] soon conceded the principle and concentrated on the best terms for Scotland' ('Scotland, Antichrist, and the Invention of Great Britain' 45).

33 Craig *De unione* 411–12.

34 Spelnar 'Of the Union' in Galloway and Levack eds. *The Jacobean Union* 176–7, lxviii–lxx. Also see Levack *The Formation of the British State* 118–19.

35 Quoted in Arthur Williamson 'From the Invention of Great Britain' 273.

36 Quoted in Carrafiello *Robert Parsons and English Catholicism* 110.

37 I quote from the first printed edition of the work issued by the Protestant Edward Gee with the title, *The Jesuit's Memorial* (1690).

38 Bossy 'Catholicity and Nationality in the Northern Counter-Reformation', in Mews ed. *Religion and National Identity* 293. My argument is indebted throughout to Bossy's fascinating article. Bossy distinguishes between the 'Greater-Englanders' like Persons and Richard Verstegan and 'Little-Englanders' like the Appellant priests whose defensive Englishness was accompanied by suspicion of the world beyond England (295).

39 Dawson 'Anglo-Scottish Protestant Culture' esp. 103–10.

40 Wilson *English Martyrologe* *1v.

41 Quoted in Carrafiello *Robert Parsons and English Catholicism* 110. Also see Persons *A Treatise of Three Conversions* 1:217.

CHAPTER 4

Making history: Holinshed's Irish Chronicles, 1577 and 1587

Richard A. McCabe

> Not that I... pretend to be familiar with Irish history *as* Irish; but, as a conspicuous chapter in the difficult policy of Queen Elizabeth, of Charles I, and of Cromwell, nobody who had read the English history could be a stranger to the O'Neils, the O'Donnells, the Ormonds... and many scores besides.
>
> De Quincey[1]

As the first Englishman to attempt to write a 'history' of Ireland, Edmund Campion acknowledged his complete ignorance of Gaelic sources. In their absence, he tells us, he extracted much of his information from English chronicles 'wherin the state of Ireland is oft implied' (Campion *Histories of Ireland* 5–6). Like De Quincey, he never knew Irish history '*as* Irish'. He wrote, as did the majority of his successors, not so much of Irish history as of England's Irish problem. As incorporated into Holinshed's *Chronicles of England, Scotland, and Ireland* (1577) by Richard Stanyhurst, Campion's work established the template for writing Irish history from the predominantly Anglocentric perspective opposed by the modern school of 'British history'.[2] Holinshed's title is indicative of the attitudes underlying his compilation: there are no separate chronicles for Wales which had been incorporated into England in 1536, and many contemporary commentators espoused a 'Welsh solution' for the Irish problem in the hope that the country might eventually become 'mearely a West England' (Brady 'Comparable Histories'; Quinn '"A Discourse of Ireland"' 166). The telos of Irish history was to become English history. The problem, however, was that two competing factions, those of the 'Old' and 'New' English, vied for control of the country's development, and their conflicting ideologies occasioned a fundamental divergence in political outlook between the 1577 and 1587 editions of the *Chronicles*.

The edition of 1577 is heavily informed by the opinions of Richard Stanyhurst, a powerful spokesman for the Old English, whose

'Description of Ireland' serves as a preface not only to his own highly polemical account of the reign of Henry VIII but equally to all of the intervening chapters. The entire narrative of Irish history is accordingly framed, and discursively contextualized, by Old English attitudes and prejudices. In the edition of 1587, however, despite the retention of most of the original material, the emphasis is largely reversed by the contributions of John Hooker, an uncompromising adherent of the New English party, whose 'Supplie of the Irish Chronicles extended to this present yeare of Our Lord 1586' constitutes not just a continuation, but a critical reappraisal, of the preceding materials. The previous decade had witnessed a profound transformation in Irish affairs. The military suppression of the House of Desmond irreversibly undermined the might of the Old English and shifted the balance of power toward their New English rivals who emerged as the major beneficiaries of the subsequent Plantation of Munster. By the time Hooker's work appeared in print, Richard Stanyhurst had fled to religious exile on the continent and Edmund Campion, his primary source, had been executed for alleged treason. Readers of the second edition would therefore find Campion's historiography praised in the Irish *Chronicle* and his life and character vilified in its English counterpart (*Chronicles* IV. 447–60). The work had come to embody the very cultural, religious, and political dichotomies it was intended to resolve, and English accounts of 'Irish' history were destined to echo such contradictions for generations to come. Not the least task confronting the practitioners of 'British' history is the precise discrimination of the various parties who, like Edmund Spenser, claim privileged knowledge of the past and present 'state of Ireland'.

From the compiler's viewpoint, Holinshed's Irish *Chronicle* was intended to complement his account of English history, and the reader is habitually referred from one to the other for corroboratory detail or argument. Campion facilitated this process by chronicling the events of Irish history, from the time of the 'conquest' onwards, under the reigns of the relevant English kings thereby ensuring that the work's structure dictates its political outlook. Technically speaking, it was not until 1541 that the Irish Parliament acknowledged an English monarch as 'King' of Ireland, but the anachronism is polemically functional (Lennon *Sixteenth-Century Ireland* 154–5; Ellis 'Tudor State Formation' 56–7). According to New English observers such as Spenser, 'nothinge was given to Kinge Henrye [in 1541] which he had not before from his Auncestors, but onelye the bare name of a Kinge. ffor all other absolute power of Principalitye he had in himselfe before derived from manye former Kinges his famous progenitours and worthie Conquerours of that lande'.[3] The very format of Campion's work ensured that De Quincey's O'Neills and O'Donnells would be written into 'Irish' history as 'enemies' and 'rebels', the same terminology employed in the English chronicles. Whereas Old English families such as the Fitzgeralds and the Butlers are carefully traced back to their earliest known antecedents, Gaelic clans are introduced without any of the elaborate genealogical information that establishes both their identity and their status in Irish annals and chronicles (O Corráin 'Irish Origin Legends and Genealogy' 69–72). In Holinshed they have no autonomous 'history'.

Perhaps the single most remarkable feature of Holinshed's Irish *Chronicle*, and the surest indication of its political outlook, is the comparative neglect of everything that occurred before the 'conquest' – a neglect highly characteristic of colonial historiography. In the 1587 edition, for example, the 'history' of Ireland from creation to 1169 is crammed into a mere twelve pages mostly culled from Giraldus Cambrensis. This was the natural outcome of treating the indigenous population much as ancient Roman historians treat the 'barbarians'. To the extent that 'barbarity' is regarded as a regressive, and almost sociopathic, condition, the native Irish possess a 'history' only in so far as they interact with the 'English' (Hodgen *Early Anthropology* 308). Their history is the record of their recalcitrance to 'civility'. Such Gaelic material as does appear is consequently handled in a highly circumspect fashion. Holinshed's account of the country's 'First Inhabitants', for example, is based upon Cambrensis's somewhat garbled redaction of the eleventh-century *Lebor Gabála Érenn* which provided 'a narrative extending from the creation of the world to the coming of Christianity, and beyond – a national myth which sought to put Ireland on the same footing as Israel and Rome' (Carey *The Irish National Origin-Legend* 1). Holinshed's preface notes that his sources have merely 'set downe what they found in the Irish antiquities' and do not vouch for its veracity. What is at stake, he recognizes, is not historical truth but national pride: Gaelic chroniclers have merely acted as 'all other nations and people that seeke to advance the glorie of their countries, in fetching their beginning with the furthest from some one of ancient antiquitie' (71).[4] Therein lay the danger. Holinshed therefore follows Campion in interpreting the myth of Hiberus, the legendary progenitor of the Irish, as proving that 'the kings of this our Britain had an elder right to the realme of Ireland, than by the conquest of

Henrie the second' (77).[5] An Irish myth of origin is transformed into an English myth of sovereignty.

Stanyhurst's 'Description of Ireland' ostensibly serves the same purpose as Harrison's 'Description of Britain' in providing a chorographical preface to the chronicles by closely relating the development of the land to that of the nation. The salient difference, however, is that the land Stanyhurst refers to as 'my native countrie' was regarded by most Elizabethans as an unruly frontier (17). Even Stanyhurst's own attitude is contradictory. He divides his homeland into two quite distinct areas: 'the English Pale, and Irishrie'. The one is 'civil', the other 'savage' (3). Stanyhurst's topography is equally notable for the meticulous detail of his descriptions of the Pale (and other Anglicized urban centres such as Cork or Limerick) and the vagueness of its account of Gaelic territories.[6] He is far less concerned to describe the 'Irishrie' than to deplore its influence upon his 'native' Pale. His Old English ancestors were 'invironed and compassed with evill neighbours. Neighbourhood bred acquaintance, acquaintance waffed in the Irish toong, the Irish hooked with it attire, attire haled rudenesse, rudenesse ingendered ignorance, ignorance brought contempt of lawes, the contempt of lawes bred rebellion' (5). In this manner cultural and linguistic 'degeneracy' are seen to lead inexorably to political apostasy.[7] 'Civil' Irishmen are Anglophone and Anglophile. Once 'the Irish language was free dennized in the English pale' barbarity 'tooke such deepe root, as the bodie that before was whole and sound, was by little and little festered, and in manner wholie putrified' (4). The denizens of the Pale are 'invironed and compassed' with an 'evill' yet insidiously seductive race. The domain of the 'Irishrie' is full of 'strange and wonderfull places' and those who enter it risk enchantment: 'the verie English of birth, conversant with the savage sort of that people become degenerat, and as though they had tasted of Circes poisoned cup, are quite altered' (69). Such imagery relates the 'Description' as closely to colonial discourse as to patriotic chorography. In fact, Stanyhurst's work is an intricate, and ultimately incoherent, blending of the two, reflecting his own ambivalent status as both a 'native' of Ireland (the land of his birth) and the descendant of 'English' colonists 'invironed' by an alien culture. As Stephen Greenblatt has argued, the cultivation of 'wonder' is a standard topos of colonial writing, and it is therefore significant that most of Stanyhurst's 'wonders' and 'miracles' are taken directly from

Giraldus Cambrensis whose *History and Topography of Ireland* serves as a sort of chorographical preface to the *Expugnatio Hibernica* (Greenblatt *Marvellous Possessions* 1–25; Bartlett *Gerald of Wales* 158–77). The recounting of 'marvels' commonly partakes of 'the rhetoric of otherness', and Stanyhurst's retention of such materials betrays the continuance of fundamentally colonial attitudes toward the Gaelic population (Hartog *The Mirror of Herodotus* 231). So too does the repeated insistence upon the unexploited 'commoditie' of Gaelic territories and the alleged indolence of their inhabitants who seem to be labouring under 'some secret inchantment' (41–2). Such lands are ripe for planting. By 1587 Stanyhurst's Old English tract had unwittingly come to serve a New English agenda.

Stanyhurst's anxieties concerning 'degeneracy', a derogation from one's proper 'gens' or race, severely qualify the view that his 'Description' marks the advent of a form of 'pan-insular patriotism'.[8] 'When [Stanyhurst] insists he is an Irishman', argues Brendan Bradshaw, 'not just an Englishman born in Ireland, when he defends the worthiness of the island and all its inhabitants, whether Irish or ancient English ... he is articulating his sense of national identity in the language of ideological patriotism' (Bradshaw 'Beginnings of Modern Ireland' 83). The argument, however, is inconsistent. Elsewhere Bradshaw speaks of Stanyhurst's 'patronising attitude towards the Gaelic community and his arrogant assumption of the superiority of English civility' (Bradshaw *Irish Constitutional Revolution* 288). In view of this dichotomy we must ask what it means for Stanyhurst to describe himself as an 'Irishman' in a treatise which invariably uses the adjective 'Irish' to distinguish between the denizens of the 'English Pale' (referred to as 'we') and the 'Irish enemie' (referred to as 'they'). How can the same term express both identity and otherness, and in what sort of situation, other than a colonial one, might it be found to do so? Is the adoption of the term 'Irishman' to be regarded as a gesture of solidarity with the majority community or as an act of appropriation by the minority community? Stanyhurst was somewhat nearer the mark when he coined the term 'Anglo-Hiberni' to describe 'Irishmen' such as himself. The hybridity of the phrase better captures the ambivalent nature of his position although, ironically, the coinage was intended to refute allegations of ethnic hybridity: 'these Anglo-Irish [hi ... Anglo-Hiberni] of whom I speak have so thoroughly dissociated themselves from those ancient Irish [antiquis istis Hibernicis] that the lowliest colonist [colonorum omnium ultimus] living in the English Pale [Anglica provincia] would not give his daughter in marriage to the noblest Irish prince' (*De rebus in Hibernia gestis* 30). The Gaelic historian

Philip O'Sullivan Beare was quick to draw attention to the implications of the term 'colonus' in the context of a debate on national identities.[9] For him, the very name of 'Anglo-Iberni' was a monstrosity ('bifrons, monstrosumque nomen'). 'From now on', he concludes, 'let the Irish [Iberni] be called Irish [Iberni]'. The Gaelicized Old English were simply the New Irish ['Noviores Iberni'] (*Zoilomastix* 63). Bradshaw has argued that 'the exigencies of reform . . . not racial antagonism, were the source of [Stanyhurst's] opposition to Gaelicisation', but this is surely to miss the force of O'Sullivan Beare's point (Bradshaw *Irish Constitutional Revolution* 284). Stanyhurst was not merely opposed to Gaelicization but was ardent in the promotion of Anglicization and, as Sir Henry Sidney pointed out, the purpose of cultural Anglicization was political Anglicization: 'neither weare it a small helpe to the assurance of the Crowne of Englande when babes from their cradells should be enured under lerned schoolemasters with a pure Englishe tonge, habite, fasshion, discipline, and in time utterlie forgett the affinitie of their unbroken borderers'.[10] Contemporary Irish commentators recognized that Stanyhurst's programme of 'reform' entailed the eradication of their culture.[11] Hence the ferocity of the response.

It is true that Stanyhurst has some positive things to say of his Gaelic neighbours, particularly during his lengthy rebuttal of Nicholas Harpsfield's crude aspersions (Maley 'Shakespeare, Holinshed and Ireland' 37–40). It is important to recognize, however, that his praise of the Pale is usually unqualified while that of the 'Irishrie' is invariably extenuatory:

> they lacke universities, they want instructors, they are destitute of teachers, they are without preachers . . . and notwithstanding all these wants, if anie would be so frowardlie set, as to require them, to use such civilitie, as other regions, that are sufficientlie furnished with the like helps; he might be accounted as unreasonable, as he that would force a creeple that lacketh both his legs to run, or one to pipe or whistle a galiard that wanteth his upper lip. (14)

One must take account not only of what Stanyhurst says, but of the way in which he says it. His imagery is neither flattering nor unusual. Contemporary colonial treatises frequently represent the process of 'reformation' through the imagery of discipline and physic thereby implying that to Anglicize is to nurture or to cure.[12] Because Stanyhurst supported a policy of reformation in preference to the military solutions increasingly popular in the last quarter of the century, he was obliged to insist upon his neighbours' latent potential for development.[13] Accordingly he became the first commentator to present English readers with a review of Irish literature – or rather of literature written in Ireland – from the time of Saint Patrick to his own day (57–66). He takes a humanist's pride in this learned tradition, yet the vast majority of the writers mentioned postdate 1169 and write in English or Latin. Only one or two are noted to have written 'in Irish' and a very considerable number are Palesmen educated, like Stanyhurst himself, at Oxford or Cambridge. His list of 'learned Irishmen' is immediately followed by the concluding chapter detailing 'the disposition and maners of the meere Irish, commonlie called the wild Irish'. It begins with a notable disclaimer: none of the 'barbarous' customs it describes are to be imputed to 'the citizens, townesman, and inhabitants of the English pale' (67). The final impression is one of difference not similarity.

As his 'Description' is preoccupied with the Pale, Stanyhurst's 'Continuation of the Chronicles of Ireland Comprising the Reigne of Henry the Eighth' is equally preoccupied with the Old English. This is not to say that the Gaelic Irish are absent, but rather that they serve as the raw material for great reputations: the eighth Earl of Kildare is 'made knight of the garter', for example, 'having triumphantlie vanquished the Irish'. It is assumed that the term needs no qualification: everyone knows who 'the Irish' are (277). In any case, the preceding 'Description' has made the ethnic identity of the Fitzgeralds abundantly clear: 'The familie is English, and it is well knowne that the Irish rather feare their force, than love their persons' (48). The emphasis is hardly surprising in view of Stanyhurst's dependence, throughout both the chronicle and the 'Description', on Edmund Campion's 'Two Bookes of the Histories of Ireland', a work written during the author's stay in Dublin as a guest of the Stanyhurst family (Lennon *Richard Stanihurst* 28–9). Campion duly acknowledges his debt to the 'familiar societie and daly table talke' of Stanyhurst's father and recommends his text both to his own 'countrymen' and to 'the Englishe of Ireland' who, he imagines, have far more in common with one another than either has with the 'Irish' (Campion *Histories of Ireland* 6). Campion's allegation that Lord Bermingham is 'now degenerate and become meere Irish' is repeated verbatim by Stanyhurst (54).[14] On matters such as these the perspectives of the 'native' and the Englishman coalesce. Stanyhurst's disquiet is expressed in Campion's words.

As we have seen, Campion had no access to 'Iryshe chronicles'. 'All be they reported to be full freight of lewde examples, idle tales, and genealogies', he announces, 'yet concernyng the state of that wilde people, specially before the Conquest, I am perswaded that with choise and judgement I might have sucked thence some better store of matter, and gladly wold have sought them, had I fownd an interpretour, or understode their toungue' (Campion *Histories of Ireland* 5–6). The importance of this statement can hardly be over-emphasized. It is not just that 'Irish' history is being written without access to Gaelic sources, but that such documents are perceived to differ in kind from their English counterparts. The English chronicler has no use for Gaelic 'genealogies' because he has no interest in Irish identity *per se*. Rather, Irish chronicles may best be used, as Spenser agreed, more for anthropological than for historical purposes, providing evidence 'concernyng *the state* of that wilde people [my emphasis]' rather than reliable accounts of specific occurrences.[15] For this reason they are deemed to be primarily useful for the period 'before the Conquest'. What they might say *of the conquest* is clearly of little importance. All they could provide for the later period are 'lewde examples' of 'rebellion'. Campion's assertion of the crown's title to Ireland is characteristically based on the Act for the Attainder of Shane O'Neill, 'the Irissh ennemye of greatest force' in his day (Campion *Histories of Ireland* 137). Similarly, Stanyhurst's chronicle of the 'Irish' reign of Henry VIII ends not with a rapprochement between the Gaelic Irish and the Old English but between the warring houses of Ormond and Kildare, and it supported the Kildares so strongly that it provoked official censorship (Miller and Power eds. *Holinshed's Irish Chronicle* xvi–xvii; Donno 'Some Aspects' 242–3; Patterson *Reading Holinshed's Chronicles* 11–12; Clegg *Press Censorship* 161). It ends, as it began, in a highly politicized celebration of Old English hegemony.

HOOKER AND THE EDITION OF 1587

If Stanyhurst's inclusion in the 1577 edition of Holinshed may be seen as a 'coup' for the Old English, the effect was radically qualified, if not wholly reversed, by John Hooker's New English contributions to the edition of 1587 (Hadfield *Spenser's Irish Experience* 23–4; Ohlmeyer '"Civilizinge of those rude partes"'). Hooker first came to Ireland in 1567 as the legal agent of Sir Peter Carew who, on the basis of ancient family documents, claimed title to extensive estates in Munster and Leinster which had long been held by families such as the Kavanaghs and the Butlers (Brady *The Chief Governors* 278–80). Carew's claims therefore represented a threat to the vested interests of both 'meare Irish' and Old English parties, and his habit of prosecuting such claims by the scrutiny of ancient records hitherto unknown, or unavailable, to his opponents, was seen as characteristic of the sharp practice of the New English.[16] Sir Henry Sidney prided himself upon the discovery and publication of ancient records supportive of the New English administration.[17] As J. G. A. Pocock has observed, 'the court of record is the kernel of English government' – and nowhere more so than in its colonies (Pocock 'British History' 611). From this viewpoint, Hooker's legal endeavours constitute a paradigm of his historiography. There is a direct, and consciously laboured, connection between his translation of Giraldus Cambrensis's *Expugnatio Hibernica* (incorporated into Holinshed as 'The Conquest of Ireland') and his 'Supplie of the Irish Chronicles'.[18] To those involved in what was increasingly regarded as the reconquest of Ireland, the *Expugnatio* had an almost typological relevance. Cambrensis's lament for the inadequacy of the original conquest effectively established the agenda for its Elizabethan counterpart.

Sir Peter Carew traced his territorial claims to Robert FitzStephen, one of the principal heroes of the *Expugnatio*, to whom Henry II had granted title to considerable lands in Munster and Carlow. The first book of the *Expugnatio* praises FitzStephen as 'the onelie patterne of vertue, and the example of true industrie and labours' (156), while the second alleges that 'old and ancient records' prove 'that the English nation entred not into this land by wrong and iniurie . . . but upon a good ground, right, and title' (221).[19] The translator appends a note insisting on the legality of FitzStephen's claims and the integrity of his motives. Hooker is no mere 'antiquarian': he replaces Holinshed's abridged version of the twelfth-century conquest with an explosive translation of the original 'document' held to legitimize both Carew's private agenda and the public policy it reflected. Its incorporation into the *Chronicles* contextualizes the *Expugnatio* within the ongoing debate between the Old and New English. After 400 years of relative neglect, it suddenly became a crucial target for Gaelic and Old English commentators who were quick to recognize in the act of translation an act of *translatio imperii*. For Hooker, the New rather than the Old English are the spiritual descendants of the *Expugnatio*'s heroes, and the translation is accordingly dedicated to Sir Walter Raleigh, one of the major beneficiaries in the Plantation of Munster (101–10). In a highly symbolic act, Sir Henry Sidney restored Strongbow's tomb in Christ Church Cathedral (Campion *Histories of Ireland* 86). The implication is clear: the heroism of the reconquest complements that of the glorious *Expugnatio* and consolidates, or recovers, its material rewards. The first Earl of Essex's abortive plans to colonize various parts of Ulster are praised on the grounds that 'he was . . . of so heroicall a mind, that if his abilitie had answered his good will, he had not bin a second, neither to Lacie, nor to Courcie, nor to anie the first conquerors of Ulster to the crowne of England' (387). This accounts for the broader thematic relevance of Carew's career within the chronicle as a whole. He is presented as no less than the Elizabethan antitype of his famous ancestor, and Hooker confirms the association when he asserts that eulogies of such figures have been inserted into the chronicle 'after the maner of Cambrensis in his historie' (366). Carew therefore emerges as the perfect knight, 'sincere in religion . . . dutifull to his prince, and faithfull to his countrie, upright in iustice, politike in governement, and valiant in armes' (376). Having taken possession of lands ancestrally held by the Kavanaghs he 'dealt in such good order with them . . . that they all voluntarilie yeelded up their lands . . . and counted themselves happie and blessed to be under his government' (376–7). This is 'history' refracted through a colonial lens, or rather through the lens of colonial wish-fulfilment: benevolent care on the one hand, loving gratitude on the other. The reality was quite different. In effect, Carew practised a private form of St Leger's policy of 'surrender and regrant' whereby original land holders regained their property as mere tenants 'under writing by lease' (377).[20] Since ancestral freehold was hereby degraded into colonial tenancy, the practice encountered widespread opposition and precipitated the so-called Butlers' Wars. Carew was widely condemned for destabilizing the whole region and provoking the defection of loyal subjects, the Butlers being commonly regarded as amongst the most Anglicized of the Old English families (Lennon *Sixteenth-Century Ireland* 184).

The Butlers' Wars were grist to Hooker's mill and he exploits them accordingly. The heroes of his narrative are New English administrators such as Sir John Perrot, Sir Humphrey Gilbert, Sir Nicholas Malby, and the Lord Deputy, Sir Henry Sidney, to whom the 'Supplie' is dedicated. These are presented as men of unquestioned loyalty to the crown, whereas the Old English are invariably suspect because of their close social and religious associations with the Irish 'who the more they were affected to them, their truth and service [was] more doubtfull to hir maiestie' (328). From Hooker's viewpoint, the 'English Pale', in which Stanyhurst took such pride, seemed 'overwhelmed with infinite numbers of caterpillers' (328). The Irish Parliament, of which Stanyhurst's father was elected Speaker in 1568, struck Hooker as 'more like a bearebaiting of disordered persons, than a parlement of wise and grave men' (344). His account of its proceedings is calculated to drive a sharp wedge between the interests of the Old and New English. It was government

policy to increase the number of New English representatives in the
Irish Parliament and the session duly began with an objection to the
number of 'Englishmen' present (343; Bradshaw 'Beginnings of Modern
Ireland' 80–1). The leader of the dissent was Stanyhurst's father-in-law,
Sir Christopher Barnewall, praised in the 'Description of Ireland' as a
consummate scholar, lawyer, and statesman (55–6). Within the pages of
the 1587 edition, Elizabethan readers would therefore find the same figure eulogized by a hereditary Palesman and vilified by a New English
revisionist. The Palesmen's objections are represented in such a manner
as to call into question not merely their political allegiance but also,
more subtly, their ethnic identity. It is as though they are objecting to
'Englishness' itself – 'as did appeere in the sequele of that assemblie,
where everie bill furthered by the English gentlemen was stopped and
hindered by them' (343).

Since Hooker attended this Parliament as the member for Athenry,
personal memoir masquerades as objective narration. The unnamed
'English gentlemen' who valiantly undertook to oppose the 'foule mis-
orders' of the House and instruct his fellow members on 'the dutie of
a subiect' was none other than the chronicler himself (344). The unruly reaction to his intervention led, he claims, to calls for institutional
'reforme'. In response, Hooker produced a document intended to convert the Irish Parliament into a replica of its English counterpart and the
treatise is duly reproduced by way of prescription: 'And here you must
note, that what the kings and queenes of England do in their persons
in England, the same is done in Ireland by the lord deputie . . . who in
the like parlement robes and under the like cloth of estate representeth
hir maiestie there in al things' (345). Although Hooker correctly refers
to Ireland as a 'realme', acknowledging the country's legal status, the
tenor of his remarks leaves little doubt that he opposed any suggestion of
autonomy. Quite the contrary: the concept of the 'realme' is primarily
invoked to facilitate that of the royal prerogative. Parliament, whether
Irish or English, is regarded as subordinate to the monarch 'who is all in
all, the beginning and ending, upon whome resteth and dependeth the
effect and substance of the whole parlement. For without him and his
authoritie nothing can be doone, and with it all things take effect' (357).
Bradshaw has argued that following the passing of the Act of Kingly
Title in 1541 many of the Palesmen 'began to regard themselves more
as subjects of the kingdom of Ireland than as subjects of the Crown
of England' (Bradshaw 'Beginnings of Modern Ireland' 77). This was
precisely the attitude that Hooker opposed. He provoked uproar by informing the Irish Parliament that its deliberations were permitted purely

by 'courtesie' of the Queen 'that she might thereby have the better triall and assurance of your dutifulnesse and goodwill towards hir' (344). The 'realme' of Ireland was the property of the crown and the history of the independent 'kingdom' was to be written as that of the dependent colony.

If Stanyhurst favoured a programme of reform, Hooker placed his confidence in a policy of repression and the difference of outlook is evident in their choice of language. Whereas Stanyhurst employs the imagery of metamorphosis to represent the phenomenon of cultural 'degeneracy', Hooker employs the imagery of reversion to represent the failure of cultural reform. The nature of the 'meere Irish', he tells us, 'is not much unlike to Mercurie called quicke silver, which let it by art be never so much altered and transposed, yea and with fire consumed to ashes; yet let it but rest a while untouched nor medled with, it will returne againe to his owne nature, and be the same as it was at the first' (369). 'A meere Irish gentleman', he alleges,

can hardly digest anie Englishman or English government, and whatsoever his outward appearance be, yet his inward affection is corrupt and naught: being not unlike to Iupiters cat, whome though he had transformed into a beautifull ladie, and made hir a noble princesse; yet when she saw the mouse, she could not forbeare to snatch at him; and as the ape, though he be never so richlie attired in purple, yet he will still be an ape. (433)

'Like as Iupiters cat' was Patrick Fitzmaurice, son of the Baron of Lixnaw, who

notwithstanding he was trained up in the court of England . . . and apparelled according to his degree, and dailie nurtured and brought up in all civilitie: he was no sooner come home, but awaie with his English attires, and on with his brogs, his shirt, and other Irish rags, being become as verie a traitor as the veriest knave of them all.

'Wherein', Hooker concludes, 'appeareth the nature of himselfe, and of the brood of that cursed generation, among whome there is neither faith, nor truth. And therefore they maie be verie well resembled to an ape, which (as the common proverbe is) an ape is but an ape, albeit he be clothed in purple and velvet' (417). The difficulty is that the Fitzmaurices are not 'meere Irish' but Old English. By using the biblical phrase 'cursed generation' to encompass both, Hooker confounds ethnic distinction in simian kinship. Not only are the Old English 'degenerate', they can no more be reclaimed from 'degeneracy' than the country's indigenous 'apes'. The Palesmen's behaviour in Parliament demonstrates 'the corrupt and ungrateful nature of the Irishmen' for 'it is a fatall and inevitable destinie incident to that nation, that they cannot brooke anie English governor; for be he never so iust, upright, and carefull for their benefit, they care not for it' (404). Of crucial significance here is the use of the terms 'Irishmen' and 'nation' – and one is instantly reminded of Captain Macmorris's indignant question in Shakespeare's *Henry V*, 'what ish my nation, who talks of my nation?' (3.2.127). Since MacMorris is a Gaelicized form of FitzMaurice, Hooker certainly speaks of his 'nation' and in a most uncomplimentary way (Maley 'Shakespeare, Holinshed and Ireland' 32–4; Baker *Between Nations* 31–44). A mere ten years after Stanyhurst referred to himself as an Irishman, his 'nation' is now adjudged to have become so 'Irish' as to have developed a natural antipathy to all 'English' governors. The clear implication is that the two have become ethnically distinct. If any form of pan-insular 'nationalism' arose in this period, the New English played a key, if ironic, role in its promotion: it was they, not Stanyhurst, who first identified the diverse inhabitants of the island as constituting one 'nation'.[21]

Hooker's entire narrative is carefully structured around the concept of the royal prerogative, and the issue is drawn to a highly dramatic climax in the matter of the 'cess', the levy imposed by Sir Henry Sidney to defray the costs of his administration. The campaign against its imposition was conducted by 'the noblemen and gentlemen in the English pale, of whome least suspicion of anie evill was thought' (389).[22] The remark is richly disingenuous: the New English were increasingly suspicious of just this type of person. Hooker dismisses the leaders of the campaign as 'busie headed lawiers and malecontented gentlemen' who choose to 'dispute the princes prerogative with their Littletons tenures': 'if they had first . . . looked into the booke of God, they should have found it written there, that it was God himselfe who first made kings and established their thrones . . . that all inferiors and subiects should and ought in all humblenesse and dutifulnesse submit themselves unto the obedience of them for the Lords sake' (390). This is not the language of historical narrative but of the Book of Homilies, and the shift in linguistic register eloquently encapsulates the author's political agenda. Once again, however, ancient 'records' come to the support of the New English cause:

the lord deputie caused a through search to be made in hir highnesse court of the excheker in Ireland, of all the records, for and concerning all and all manner of liberties which at anie time had tofore bin granted to anie person or persons whatsoever: and in the end found that (verie few ancient liberties excepted) all were usurped, or by statute repealed. (389)

The pedantically legalistic diction is intended to enforce the legality of the process. It is interesting to compare Hooker's account with that of Sir Henry Sidney: 'I thought good partlie to justifie my doings, but chiefly to mayntayne Her Majesty's prerogative, and purchase her profitt, to sende over the lord chancellor with matter of ancient recorde to replie against the opposition made by the malcontents against her majesty's prerogative.'[23] The identity of emphasis and coincidence of invective is telling: Hooker writes Irish history from the viewpoint of Dublin Castle.

Hooker's account of the Desmond 'rebellion' forms the perfect conclusion to what is not so much a historical chronicle as a political tract. Stanyhurst had concluded by celebrating the restitution of the Geraldine House of Kildare, but the Geraldines of Desmond were perceived as being amongst the most Gaelicized of the Old English families and therefore as the ultimate exemplum of 'degeneracy'. Their fall is presented as a grim warning to the Old English in general: 'thus a noble race and ancient familie, descended from out the loines of princes, is now for treasons and rebellions vtterlie extinguished and overthrowne; onlie one sonne of the said earles is left, and yet prisoner in the Tower of London' (459). Condemnation of the Desmonds is offset by unwavering praise for the Lord Deputy, Lord Arthur Grey. Despite widespread contemporary criticism, in both England and Ireland, Grey is presented as 'a man of great nobilitie . . . one that feareth God in true religion, and dutifull to hir maiestie in all obedience' (460). The famine that ravaged Munster in the wake of his campaign – and which was laid to Grey's charge even by his own subordinates – is represented as an act of God: 'a heavie, but a just iudgement . . . upon such a Pharoicall and stifnecked people, who . . . made choise of . . . that wicked antichrist of Rome to obeie, unto the utter overthrow of themselves and of their posteritie' (450).[24] The pseudo-biblical diction, deployed throughout the 'Supplie' to lend questionable policy the status of providential plan, indicates the degree to which the issue of religious difference has come to affect official attitudes toward the Old English. As co-religionists of the 'meere Irish' they are necessarily tainted with the suspicion of treason. According to Hooker's account, the Spanish and Italian mercenaries who landed at Smerwick to support the Desmond cause – and were controversially butchered having surrendered their arms – informed Grey that 'they were sent some from the holie father, which had given that realme to king Philip; and some from king Philip, who was to receive and recover that land to the holie church of Rome' (437–8). Writing in his official capacity as

Grey's New English secretary, Spenser corroborates Hooker's account (*Prose Works* 161–2). Seen from this perspective Grey was fighting for the Reformation, and the House of Desmond represented a Trojan horse within the Queen's 'realme'. The insistent emphasis upon the religious character of figures such as Carew, Sidney, and Grey is therefore highly functional, rather than purely pious, and ultimately works to the detriment of the whole Old English party. The exceptional status conferred upon the Anglicized House of Ormond merely enforces the point. The religious issue, ever latent in Hooker's narrative, is carefully crafted to reach a crescendo in his account of the Desmond wars so that 'Irish' history may be seen to afford a moral exemplum of the spiritual value of 'Englishness' – and Protestant New Englishness in particular. A spiritually renewed 'English' nation will complete the conquest undertaken by its heroic predecessors. Hooker therefore concludes his pattern of allusions to the *Expugnatio Hibernica* with the hope that the current Lord Deputy, Sir John Perrot, will 'bring that land to a full and perfect government and regiment; which Giraldus Cambrensis would not warrant could be doone before doomesdaie' (456).

Yet the 'records' by which Hooker put such store were themselves problematic. Cambrensis was of mixed antecedents, being related both to the Marcher lords and to the Welsh aristocracy, and his personal sense of ethnic ambivalence pervades and fractures his canon: 'both peoples regard me as a stranger', he complains, 'one nation suspects me, the other hates me' (Bartlett *Gerald of Wales* 17–18). The earliest account of the 'English' conquest of Ireland is consequently beset by ethnic anxiety. The people Cambrensis consistently refers to as 'Angli' are desperately unsure of their own identity: 'as we be odious and hatefull to the Irishmen', says Maurice Fitzgerald, 'even so we now are reputed: for Irishmen are become hatefull to our owne nation and countrie, and so are we odious both to the one and to the other' (152). Later on, Cambrensis warns of the danger to the original settlers from insolent 'new comes' in a manner that proleptically reflects upon the New English enterprise (226). A palimpsest of racial uncertainties surfaces even through the most assertive passages of Hooker's polemicized translation. As a result, the bewilderingly polysemous nature of the 1587 edition of Holinshed's Irish *Chronicle*, in which divergent layers of historical commentary are variously overlaid, conflated, or juxtaposed, serves as an ironic paradigm for the ongoing process of political and cultural appropriation that the text attempts to justify. As Stanyhurst labours to supply a redaction of Campion's redaction of Cambrensis's redaction of the *Lebor Gabála* (itself a redaction of earlier materials), and

Hooker struggles to appropriate all of them to a cause that none of them favoured, narrative and stylistic inconsistencies betray the worsening contradictions of policy. Writing in a reformist mode Stanyhurst employs images of nurture and physic, but writing as a member of an endangered Old English 'colony' he switches to the imagery of degenerative metamorphosis, thereby disclosing his darkest cultural fears. Writing as an adherent of the New English, Hooker undermines reformist policy by applying the imagery of reversion to both 'meere Irish' and Old English. But colonial ideology is inherently unstable. Because barbarity was regarded as a regressive state, because it was 'even the other daye since Englande grewe Civill', the possibility arose that 'degeneration' and 'reversion' were one and the same: that the rhetoric of superiority was an index of self-doubt (Spenser *Prose Works* 118). In a sense quite unintended by their authors, Holinshed's Irish *Chronicles* came to form an integral part of 'English' history, a record not of 'conquest' but of confusion.

NOTES

The writing of this paper was facilitated by the award of a British Academy Research Readership. I am most grateful for such generous support.

1 De Quincey *Autobiography from 1785 to 1803* in Masson ed. *Collected Writings* I: 225.
2 For a succinct account of the current controversy see Baker *Between Nations* 1–10.
3 Spenser *The Works of Edmund Spenser* IX: 52. Hereafter *Prose Works*.
4 Holinshed *Chronicles of England, Scotland, and Ireland*, 6 vols. (London, 1808). All page references supplied in the text hereafter are to vol. VI of this edition unless otherwise stated.
5 Compare with Campion *Histories of Ireland* 34.
6 Dublin for Stanyhurst is 'the Irish or yoong London' (21).
7 For the development of the Old English community see Aidan Clarke *The Old English in Ireland*; Canny 'Edmund Spenser'. See also Ivic 'Incorporating Ireland'.
8 For the concept of 'gens' and its close association with that of 'lingua' see R. R. Davies 'The Peoples of Britain and Ireland' 9–10; Lennon *Richard Stanihurst* 123.
9 Beare *Selections from the Zoilomastix of Philip O'Sullivan Beare* 61. Hereafter *Zoilomastix*. For a recent engagement with O'Sullivan Beare see Carroll 'Irish and Spanish Cultural and Political Relations'.
10 Sidney is quoted in Campion *Histories of Ireland* 144. For the long-term effects of the policy of Anglicization see Morrill 'The Fashioning of Britain' 24–6.
11 For Geoffrey Keating's response see Comyn ed. and trans. *The History of Ireland* I: 38–41.

12 Images of 'physic' and discipline are essential to Spenser's *A View of the Present State of Ireland*. See *Prose Works* 54, 146, 240.

13 For the change in outlook see Brady 'The Road to the View' in Coughlan ed. *Spenser and Ireland*.

14 Compare Campion *Histories of Ireland* 13.

15 For Spenser's views see *Prose Works* 84–7.

16 Hooker asserts that one of the crucial documents 'had been trodden under the foot, and by that means the letters were almost worn out'. Maclean ed. *The Life and Times of Sir Peter Carew* 72.

17 Henry Sidney 'Memoir' 5. 307. For Hooker's appreciation of Sidney's attention to official documents see Holinshed *Chronicles of England, Scotland, and Ireland* VI: 402.

18 For colonial translation generally see Cronin *Translating Ireland* 47–90.

19 See Scott and Martin eds. and trans. *Expugnatio* 87, 231.

20 For surrender and regrant see Lennon *Sixteenth-Century Ireland* 155–9.

21 For the concept of the nation and its fabrication see Anderson *Imagined Communities* rev. edn (1991) 5–12.

22 See Brady *The Chief Governors* 235–41.

23 Henry Sidney 'Memoir' 8. 183. Philip Sidney's 'Discourse on Irish Affaires' was largely written in defence of his father's policy on the cess. See *Complete Works* III: 46–50.

24 For Sir Warham St Leger's criticism of Grey see *Irish State Papers*, 63. 91. 41 (I).

III

British Shakespeare

CHAPTER 5

1 Henry IV: *metatheatrical Britain*

Matthew Greenfield

My reading of the first part of Shakespeare's *Henry IV* is situated in a region on the periphery of literary criticism, near the border of the movement known as the new British history. In a frequently invoked phrase, J. G. A. Pocock outlined the following research agenda for the new British history: 'British history denotes the historiography of no single nation but of a problematic and uncompleted experiment in the creation and interaction of several nations' (Pocock 'Limits and Divisions' 317). The new British history's penetration of literary studies is as yet in an early stage: many critics are still writing books whose titles contain phrases like 'early modern English culture' – phrases which imagine English culture as a homogeneous entity with clear boundaries, uncomplicated by the British question.[1] Many literary critics, including the author of this chapter, are not equipped to delve seriously into the vernacular literary traditions of Wales and Ireland: we have not mastered the requisite languages. The new British history promises to help us all to develop a less parochial understanding of the Atlantic archipelago in the early modern period.

At the same time, though, we need to recognize that the new British history fits the needs of literary criticism with a slightly suspicious ease: it clears room for a new set of arguments about extensively studied texts, and it allows specialists in the early modern period to tap some of the prestige and intellectual energy of postcolonial cultural criticism. The new British history has also narrowed as well as opened the canon: a high percentage of literary history in this area has focused on particular passages in Shakespeare's *Henry V* and Spenser's *View of the Present State of Ireland* and a small number of other texts (this anthology is an honourable exception). One might argue that we will not have fully demonstrated the new British history's value to literary critics until we can bring it to bear on *Twelfth Night* as well as *Henry V*, on the *Four Hymns* as well as the *View*. Until then, we are treating the problem of British identity as a thematic question rather than a structural feature of literary institutions like the professional theatres and the pamphlet market. Second, some literary critics influenced by the new British history have abandoned many of the methods and resources of their own discipline. For example, Christopher Highley has written a thoroughly persuasive analysis of the Irish subtext of *1 Henry IV*, but his analysis largely ignores the questions explored by a previous generation of Shakespeareans. He has little to say about metatheatricality, genre, the double plot, redemption, inheritance, counterfeiting, or the play's meditation on corruptions of language, and the single sentence in which he mentions Falstaff concerns Falstaff's characterization of Glendower (Highley *Shakespeare, Spenser, and the Crisis in Ireland* 95). I am not criticizing Highley, whose book I greatly admire, but I am suggesting some new questions: what might one accomplish by placing the *literary* features of *1 Henry IV* within a British frame? Conversely, how could one claim to elucidate the political thinking of the plays without considering their dramatic structure? Can the question of Britain in *1 Henry IV* be addressed only in verse, or might Falstaff have something to say about it?

Concern with form, metadrama, and the self-reflexive properties of the plays might seem like the antithesis of historicist criticism, but metatheatricality is one of the conceptual instruments the plays use to work through political questions. When one examines the politics of Shakespeare's second tetralogy through the lens of literary form, striking differences among the plays emerge. Patricia Parker's chapter on *Henry V* in this volume traces a pattern of leaks and breaches in the nation and its rhetoric, but the play imagines those leaks as springing from a container of some sort: a nation, a state, a historical master-plot that frames the comic sub-plots. In *Henry V*, the vexed constructs called 'England', 'Scotland', 'Wales', 'Ireland', and 'Britain' have a certain political reality and exert some imaginative claim on at least some of the characters. *1 Henry IV* works through quite a different political hypothesis. The sympathies of the characters are too mobile, too fluid, to bind them into anything like a 'band of brothers'. Shakespeare wrote the second play of the tetralogy, I suggest, at a moment when it was still possible to imagine a history that did not move teleologically toward the development of the modern nation state – or toward his own *Henry V*.

As Benedict Anderson has famously argued, a nation is constituted by acts of imaginative sympathy – by a sort of conceptual glue that binds citizens together. Anderson takes literary form, convention, and genre much more seriously than most political scientists: he suggests that new forms have the power to create new communities. Anderson assigns two print genres, the novel and the newspaper, a central role in the production of the sense of 'homogeneous empty time' that citizens need to imagine their solidarity with a nation of strangers. Both newspapers and novels represent simultaneous actions by members of a community who are unaware of each other. Newspaper readers participate in a sort of secular ritual of communion, joined with countless anonymous others.[2]

1 Henry IV, though, suggests that this very capacity for sympathy might have the opposite effect, fragmenting communities into small, unstable groupings. This failure of communal sentiment finds its correlative in literary form: the play's characters inhabit shifting, fractured generic environments that resist inclusion in an historical master-plot. The play presents simultaneous actions in multiple sites, including the court, the Boar's Head Tavern, Gadshill, the castles of Hotspur and Northumberland in the marches, Glendower's house in Wales, and the camps and the field of battle at Shrewsbury; and it also introduces a Scottish character and a report of a battle in Scotland. The plot moves between the low decorum of the tavern and the high decorum of aristocratic action, until the two levels partially merge at Shrewsbury. The different sites are sutured together by a series of anxious utterances: at separate moments the thoughts of Hotspur (1.3, 4.1) and the king (1.1) turn to Hal and his drinking companions; Falstaff and Hal in the tavern discuss Hotspur, Glendower, Douglas, and the king (2.4); and the rebels imagine the king thinking of them (3.1).[3] The characters speculate incessantly about what is happening in the play's other sites. A stream of messengers also connects the battlefields to the centres of political authority. The play opens with the receipt of multiple ambiguous or contradictory messages. Unlike Benedict Anderson's newspapers, Shakespeare's messengers do not present simultaneous events: departing at different times and travelling at different speeds are crucial to their dramatic function. They nonetheless compress the imaginative distance between the parts of Britain. At the beginning of *1 Henry IV* Sir Walter Blunt arrives 'Stain'd with the variation of each soil / Betwixt that Holmedon and this seat of ours' (1.1.64–5). Sir Walter's hard riding makes him into an emblem of Britain, a sort of map. The muds of Northumberland and London may be coloured differently, but they are both plastered to the same messenger.

In addition to their speculation and their travel, the play's characters also involuntarily and unknowingly imitate each other. The thieves plan a robbery and the marcher lords and their neighbours plan a rebellion; the king rebukes Hal and Northumberland rebukes his son Hotspur; and at various points different speakers describe not only Blunt but also the king, Hal, Hotspur, Worcester, and a pile of corpses as stained or marked or blotted, whether physically or morally. Almost all of the play's characters deliver meditations on the possibility of one individual acquiring the personality traits of another; all engage in the demarcation or the erasure of boundaries; and all, even the king and his loyal vassals, are rebels. William Empson suggested that the double plots of Renaissance drama almost always involve a magical causality (*Some Versions of Pastoral* 31–4). In *1 Henry IV* that occult sympathy blurs the difference between individuals and undermines their ability to choose how to behave: the plot-magic connects the characters as the dream of nationhood might, but it makes them rebels rather than citizens.

The plotting of *1 Henry IV* binds together not just different sites and different social groups, but also different genres. Although neither the low plot nor the high can be identified with a single genre, the opposition between them relies on opposing clusters of literary kinds. The low plot draws on what C. L. Barber called the 'festive' element of comedy, on the morality play and particularly the Vice figure, and on the cony-catching pamphlet, among other literary kinds (*Shakespeare's Festive Comedy*). The aristocratic plot borrows conventions from the high end of the hierarchy of genres: tragedy, epic, and romance. In the low plot characters speak mostly in prose, in the high plot mostly in poetry. Falstaff can parody various forms of high or poetic speech, including Euphuism and the rhetoric of Puritanism, and Hal, that infamous student of language and power, is genuinely bilingual: he speaks with authority in both court and tavern, in both poetry and prose. The play's use of genres, like its use of diverse locations, suggests a kind of inclusiveness, a totalizing system like the imagined community. The genres, however, like the characters who people them, have a distinct centrifugal tendency.

Glendower's house in Wales has a generic environment quite distinct from that of the rest of the aristocratic plot. Glendower presides over a seduction like those of Spenser's Bower of Bliss or Armida's Island in Tasso's *Gerusalemme Liberata*. His daughter's weeping, her music, and her sexuality, all represented as a kind of overflowing or incontinence, work to feminize her husband and rob him of an Englishness that is gendered male. As William Palmer points out, when Glendower's daughter lulls Mortimer to sleep she repeats in a softer key the 'beastly transformation' of English corpses by Welsh women after the battle in which Mortimer was captured (Palmer 'Gender, Violence, and Rebellion').

Although the seduction apparently succeeds – Mortimer never shows up at Shrewsbury – it is worth noting that, if Glendower is to be believed, the threat of contagion runs in both directions: 'My daughter weeps, she'll not part with you, / She'll be a soldier too, she'll to the wars' (3.1.192–3). When Glendower speaks for his daughter, he implicates himself in the characterization of Wales as a dangerously feminized region. Hotspur insinuates that Glendower's verbosity and his interest in 'mincing poetry' mark him as feminine. Earlier, describing the battle between Mortimer and Glendower, Hotspur had inserted both men into an Iliadic vignette in which their fierceness frightens a personified Severn river into hiding his head 'among the trembling reeds' (1.3.105). In this narrative, Hotspur displaces a potentially debilitating femininity onto the river god. One might say that Hotspur tries to preserve a boundary between epic and romance as well as between the English and the foreign.

Glendower himself succeeds much better at preserving the boundaries around his territory and his genre. When Hotspur refuses to accept the conventions – the ideologies – of Glendower's genre, Glendower withdraws from the main plot of the play and does not reappear. Hotspur ridicules Glendower's claims about his magical powers, but the stage direction seconds Glendower's claim that the musicians he summons are demons. Glendower may or may not have the power to change the weather, but he has turned back three invasions by the forces of Henry IV. From the standpoint of an audience living under Elizabeth I, many of the Welsh prophecies which Glendower recites have some genuine authority, since they have been deployed by both the Tudor state and its opponents. Glendower's daughter's song, which is accompanied by those mysterious musicians, may also represent a form of magic. In Glendower's generic space, different rules may apply. In metadramatic terms, his daughter's use of the Welsh language also creates a boundary, excluding the audience. Although some critics describe this as a coercive imposition of otherness on the un-named daughter, one might see it as granting her some degree of autonomy or privacy.[4] Glanmor Williams argues that Elizabethan audiences in London may have understood some Welsh, but the general effect of the daughter's Welsh speech and song is to place her thoughts partially outside the bounds of the play (*Religion, Language, and Nationality in Wales* 194). In *Henry V*, Shakespeare translates much of the conversation of the French into English, making their conversation transparent to an English theatrical audience. Katherine of France and the Welsh, Scottish, and Irish captains speak varieties of English that the play represents as humorous and even defective. The play's translations and its renderings of dialect function as an analogue to the English army's conquest of France, subordinating the French aristocrats and the British captains to an English linguistic regime. Glendower's daughter, on the other hand, resists conscription into the play's framing structures. She is subordinated to her father but not to Englishness.

Falstaff's metatheatricality also constitutes a form of resistance to the master-plot of history and the play. Like the Vice figure to which Hal compares him, Falstaff has a privileged relation to the audience; of all the play's other characters, only Hal also delivers a soliloquy. Falstaff, like the Vice of the morality plays, dominates the part of the stage closest to the audience (Weimann *Shakespeare and the Popular Tradition in the Theater* 189–91). As David Wiles has shown, this metatheatrical freedom reflected the actual institutional position of the clowns within Elizabethan theatre companies: Kemp and Armin held shares in the Lord Chamberlain's Men, but they also performed independently and even sometimes with other companies (Wiles *Shakespeare's Clown* 99, 143). Hamlet complains that the clowns sometimes improvised and stole the audience's attention from the other actors, 'though in the mean time some necessary question of the play be then to be consider'd' (*Hamlet* 3.2.42–3). In an elegant reading of *1 Henry IV*, James Calderwood argues that Falstaff continuously threatens to create a disturbance of precisely this kind: if his demands are not met, he will secede from the play and puncture its mimetic pretensions.

Calderwood's analysis of the battle of Shrewsbury builds on Empson's suggestion that Hal, standing over the dead Hotspur and the seemingly dead Falstaff, simultaneously addresses both men: phrases like 'great heart' and 'so stout a gentleman' have two meanings, one referring to Hotspur's spiritual qualities and the other to Falstaff's physical ones (5.5.87, 93). The address to Hotspur has great dignity, while the subtext concerning Falstaff seems inappropriately humorous and insulting – it is spoken in Falstaff's own language. When Hal addresses Falstaff explicitly, he heaps more contumely on the supposed corpse. This speech sounds quite astonishingly cruel unless one believes, with Calderwood, that Hal understands that Falstaff is feigning, or at least that Falstaff's death belongs to a different genre from Hotspur's (Calderwood *Metadrama* 68–87). In Renaissance drama clowns often remain immune to the afflictions of their betters: where Marlowe's Faustus is damned for his traffic with the devil, Wagner and Robin apparently suffer only humiliation. Even when clowns are sent off to execution, they continue joking, as if their generic difference makes them invulnerable (Levin *The Multiple Plot* 138–9). When Falstaff rises to his feet, he muses over the dead Percy: 'Why may not he rise as well as I? Nothing confutes me but eyes, and nobody sees me' (5.4.126–7). This nearly explicit allusion to the myriad eyes of the theatre audience threatens to contaminate the whole battle of Shrewsbury with a sense of the fictional. Calderwood suggests that Hal yields credit for the killing of Hotspur because he is worried that Falstaff will reveal that Hotspur's death was also merely a theatrical performance. When a fictional figure from comedy or the morality play enters the alien spaces of history and heroic conflict, it is not clear whose rules and conventions will prevail. One need not accept Calderwood's reading to see Falstaff's resurrection as a disruption.

Falstaff resists not only the historical but also, more specifically, the question of Britain. His difficulty in remembering Glendower's name is symptomatic: 'he of Wales that gave Amamon the bastinado and made Lucifer cuckold and swore the devil his true liegeman upon the cross of a Welsh hook – what a plague you call him?' (2.4.336–9). (In *Henry V*, Fluellen, another Welshman, has a reciprocal memory lapse: 'He was full of jests, and gipes, and knaveries, and mocks – I have forgot his name' (4.7.48–50). The English captain Gower has to prompt Fluellen.) Falstaff inhabits the largest metropolis in Britain; he often seems to live in the late sixteenth rather than the early fifteenth century; and he believes in no magic other than wit. It is not surprising that Falstaff and Glendower never meet: they occupy the opposite ends of the play's hierarchy of decorum: Mistress Quickly, Francis the drawer, Falstaff, and the tavern are at the bottom; the king and his court and the rebels, with their Machiavellian realism and their calculated uses of language, are at the next level; Hotspur, with his commitment to an archaic idea of honour or the simulacrum thereof, maintains a still higher level of decorum; and Glendower with his myths and his magic occupies the highest level of all. Each successive rung of the ladder involves a temporal regression, a movement toward legend and prophecy. No one seems to be able to travel more than one level away from his own natural position. Hal can travel down to Falstaff's environment and up to Hotspur's, Hotspur can visit Glendower, and Glendower once studied law at the Inns of Court, but Glendower never encounters the fat knight, perhaps because too great a generic distance separates them.

The opposite ends of the hierarchy have a curious similarity: in his own way Glendower is as much a maker of fictions as Falstaff, and both tenaciously resist the imposition of alien generic codes. Glendower sticks rigorously to his script and refuses to leave his territory. When Hotspur expresses scepticism about Glendower's assertions, Glendower gravely repeats himself. At this moment he may seem like the antithesis of the gloriously improvisational Falstaff, but Falstaff insists on carrying his own generic environment with him and even imposing the rules of comedy on historical matter. Hal and Hotspur, by contrast, both maintain a certain flexibility. Hal usually blends like a chameleon with his generic environment, while Hotspur alters his conduct to distinguish himself from his companions. In the company of his Machiavellian father and uncle, Hotspur raves and brags in the best heroic manner, while at Glendower's house he becomes cynical and playful, posing as the exponent of common sense. At home he will not touch his wife for fear of contamination with the feminine and the domestic, while at Glendower's house he puts his head in his wife's lap in a parodic imitation of Mortimer's uxoriousness. Despite his continuous and militant self-assertion, Hotspur does not have a stable generic identity, as both Glendower and Falstaff do.

Although Falstaff never meets Glendower, he does meet that other extravagantly heroic figure from the north, the Scottish Douglas. When Douglas attacks him, Falstaff 'falls down as if he were dead' (stage directions at 5.4.76). On an actual battlefield, this would be an extremely risky move, since an assailant would have to be persuaded that a harmless thrust had been mortal. Even then, that assailant might stab again to make sure that one were really dead, as a nervous Falstaff stabs the already dead Hotspur. The peculiarity of the transaction between Douglas and Falstaff highlights the collaboration between the two actors playing the roles: for the pratfall to be effective, both actors need to time their actions carefully. Falstaff, speaking the punning language of the morality Vice, describes Douglas as another figure from medieval theatre: ''Sblood, 'twas time to counterfeit, or that hot termagant Scot had paid me scot and lot too' (5.4.13–14). Termagant, the pagan god of the mystery plays, was known not for military valour but for comical ranting. This helps explain the bifurcated ending of the play, in which Worcester and Vernon are sent off to execution but 'the noble Scot' is released in recognition of his valour (5.5.17). This is the second time Douglas has been captured and released; his first captor was Hotspur. Earlier in the play Douglas assured Hotspur that 'There is not such a word / Spoke of in Scotland as this term of fear' (4.1.84–5), but in the end he fled with his men, fell, and 'was so bruis'd / That the pursuers took him' (5.5.21–2). In Holinshed's account, Douglas crushes one of his testicles when he falls.[5] Even in the play's less explicit version, his capture lacks dignity. It is as if his encounter with Falstaff has contaminated him with a touch of the comic.

Paraphrasing Marx, one might say that the capture of Douglas repeats itself, the first time as history and the second time as farce. Worcester and Vernon meet their tragic ends in a sober and dignified manner, while Douglas seems to inhabit a completely different kind of plot. Like Glendower, Douglas recedes into historical inconspicuousness and generic marginality, where Falstaff eventually joins them. In *1 Henry IV*, Falstaff threatens to take over the play and reconfigure its literary mode: his bulky presence tends to occlude the British question and the plot mechanisms of the history play. As he travels toward the conclusion of *2 Henry IV*, though, he begins to succumb to the plots of history.

Like Falstaff, and like Britain and British identities, Shakespeare's histories are assembled out of heterogeneous materials. Even considered as one ingredient in a sequence of generic hybrids, the history play does not constitute a consistent, coherent set of literary codes. To paraphrase Pocock's grand dictum on the new British history, the phrase 'Shakespeare's histories' denotes no single genre but a problematic and uncompleted experiment in the creation and interaction of several genres. Only by carefully examining the intimate details of generic mixture within these plays will we be able to understand their stories about what it means to be British – or Welsh, English, Scottish, French, Anglo-Norman, Irish, Cornish, a member of the Church, one of a band of brothers, a lady, a monk, a knight, or a witch. As Benedict Anderson suggests, the identity-work of literature has as much to do with form as with topic. When one follows Anderson's lead and examines the structure of *1 Henry IV*, one sees a strange and perhaps unsettling argument: whether or not the consolidation of a nation state is desirable, it will always be impossible, because the sympathies that should bind citizens together will instead separate them into warring factions and incompatible narratives. One might argue that criticism has privileged *Henry V* over the rest of the tetralogy because it supports our own sense that it was inevitable that the nation state would become the dominant and ubiquitous form of political organization. We may disapprove of nations, and we may disagree about their boundaries, but we find it difficult to imagine a world without them.[6]

NOTES

1 David J. Baker begins his first book with a manifesto advocating the introduction of the new British history into literary studies; see *Between Nations* 1–16.
2 The phrase 'homogeneous empty time' comes from Walter Benjamin; see Anderson *Imagined Communities* 24. Anderson may not be wholly correct

in describing this apprehension of simultaneity as a distinctively post-Enlightenment phenomenon; he has to hedge his point when he briefly discusses the Reformation (39–42). Most social scientists follow Anderson in seeing the French Revolution as the first significant crystallization of nationalist sentiment. Liah Greenfeld, though, argues that English nationalism develops earlier, in the sixteenth century. In this she supports the intuitions of most literary critics and historians working on early modern Britain; see Greenfeld *Nationalism*. In a further complication, Linda Colley acknowledges English nationalism as a Reformation phenomenon but argues that *British* nationalism becomes widespread only in the eighteenth century; see *Britons*. Most students of the sixteenth and seventeenth centuries, though, detect frequent attempts to develop a British nationalist rhetoric – which may or may not have seized many imaginations. One cannot develop a precise chronology of nationalism because the nation is a shifty, insubstantial entity, a narrative or a structure of feeling rather than an institution. I borrow the phrase 'structure of feeling' from Raymond Williams; see *Politics and Letters* 168.

3 All Shakespeare citations refer to *The Riverside Shakespeare*, 2nd edn (1997).
4 For the idea that Glendower's daughter has been denied a voice and made into an emblem of alterity, see Howard and Rackin *Engendering a Nation*.
5 See the note to lines 21–2.
6 This chapter has been improved by careful readings by the editors and by helpful suggestions from Steven Burt, Chris Ivic, David Quint, Jennifer Lewin, and Patricia Parker.

CHAPTER 6

Uncertain unions: Welsh leeks in Henry V

Patricia Parker

breaches and leakes moe then man's wit hath hands to stop.
Hooker, *Ecclesiastic Polity* (1597)

In Act 4 of Shakespeare's *Henry V*, immediately following the English king's order to kill the French prisoners, Henry's Welsh deputy Fluellen re-enters the stage he last left invoking 'the true and aunchient pre-rogatifes and laws of the wars' (4.1.67–8).[1] In this scene – punctuated with another reminder of Henry's controversial order – Fluellen delivers his praise of this 'gallant' English king, comparing the Henry 'porn at Monmouth' with the Alexander the Great he pronounces as 'Alexander the Pig' (4.7.13). He then goes on, after the victory at Agincourt, to evoke the 'service' done by 'Welshmen' in 'a garden where leeks did grow', as the origin of their 'wearing leeks in their Monmouth caps' upon 'Saint Tavy's day' (4.7.99–103).

The scene is the apparent high-point of the play and of the effort of this English king, whose 'proto-British' army has included not just Welsh Fluellen but Scots Captain Jamy and Irish Captain Macmorris, the figure who disappears enigmatically from the play after he has posed the puzzling question 'What ish my nation?' (3.3.122). This high-point, however, which is soon to be accompanied by the singing of *Non Nobis* and *Te Deum*, features, in Fluellen's lines on 'Alexander the Pig' and the 'garden' of 'leeks', curious reminders at the moment of victory itself of the 'mockery' suggested by the Chorus to this Act: 'Minding true things by what their mock'ries be' (4 Chorus 53). At the triumph of a king pronounced earlier to be a 'master' of 'tongues' (*1 Henry IV* 2.4.18–20; *2 Henry IV* 4.4.68–78), the scene introduces both a 'Welshed' linguistic variance and what Hippolyta in *A Midsummer Night's Dream* characterized as 'sound, but not in government' (*MND* 5.1.124), evoking the problem of the government of sound, speech, and tongues on which sound government (in every sense) depends.

Welshness pervades this scene of *Henry V*, both explicitly and implicitly. The 'palpable device' by which the battle at Agincourt was won (denied by the Henry who insists that it was won 'without stratagem') depended on what was effectively a moving 'pale' of Welsh archers, protecting Henry's outnumbered forces on the field. The Sir Thomas Erpingham who commanded the Welsh in Henry's camp had already appeared on stage on the eve of Agincourt, both at the moment where the English king borrows his cloak and subsequently pronounces himself to be a 'Welshman' and just before Henry's prayer that 'the fault / My father made in compassing the crown' (4.1.293–4) not be remembered. Though omitted from mention in this scene of Welsh leeks and the Welshing of 'Alexander the Pig', it was also Welsh archers who were commanded under pain of death to carry out the king's order to kill the French prisoners, unbound as they were (as yeomen rather than gentlemen) by the code of conduct that would have restricted their superiors. The order given by Henry was in several historical accounts expressly judged to be repugnant to 'the law of arms' (4.7.2), the phrase used repeatedly by Fluellen. The Welsh deputy's 'Kill the poys and the luggage! 'Tis expressly against the law of arms' (4.7.1–2) appears to apply only as a criticism of the French. Coming, however, immediately after the line in which Henry has ordered 'Then every soldier kill his prisoners, / Give the word through' (4.6.37–8), it inevitably attaches to the English king as well.[2]

It is important for this play's series of *sotto voce* commentaries on Henry and the English cause that it is in the context of this order to kill the French prisoners – something that not even the aggressively named 'Pistol' with his threatening 'cuppele le gorge' does to *his* French prisoner – that the ostensibly faithful Welsh borderer Fluellen compares the English king to 'Alexander the Pig' (4.7.13) and then goes on to evoke a 'garden' full of 'leeks' as an emblem of Welsh fidelity to English kings, summoning in this 'garden' not only the play's repeatedly sounded figure of hopeful enclosure but also its multiple iterations of breaches, faults, and leaks. Critics of *Henry V* who have extended to this play the contributions of the 'new British history' have stressed the ways in which its famous 'fault-lines' extend to its representations of a 'British' (or proto-British) unity, particularly in the scene that introduces Welsh, Scots, and Irish 'borderers' immediately after the resonant rhetoric of Henry's 'Once more unto the breach . . . / Or close the wall up with our English dead' (3.1.1–2), a speech whose exclusive emphasis on 'England' and 'St. George' is followed by this scene of multiple borderers, filled with 'cavities', 'faults', and undermining 'counter-mines'.[3] What I propose to concentrate on is the combination of 'Alexander the Pig' with the scenes following from this 'garden' of Welsh 'leeks', in relation to the undermining of the rhetoric of unity, containment, or enclosure both by 'sound' not 'in government' and by the instabilities within 'British' unity suggested by the dense inter-allusive verbal echoings (or mockeries) of the play itself.

The potential aural 'mockery' of such echoing is directly suggested within the play – in the lines on the 'caves and womby vaultages of France' that 'return your mock / In second accent' (2.4.124–6), an echo-effect that mocks both through the 'damnable iteration' already invoked in these Shakespearean histories (*1 Henry IV* 1.2.90) and by the pro-liferation of differently mocking accents. Fluellen's garden of 'leeks' joins both the play's iterated sounding of the 'garden' as *hortus conclusus* – contained, bounded, enclosed – and (through the ungoverned 'sound' of Welsh 'leeks') its multiplication of fissures, breaches, and faults both territorial and bodily, producing (at the level of echoic 'mockery' and un-governable sound) an 'uncertain union' of its own. The choice of image thus links this 'garden' of 'leeks' to the complex evocation of comparable fissures within the play as a whole, from the Bishops' opening descrip-tion of the 'body' of the king who will later be called 'Harry England' (3.5.48) as an Edenic *hortus conclusus* with ambiguously scoured 'faults' (1.1.34) to the multiple 'breaches' and 'faults' that suggest anything but perfect containment or enclosure: the description of 'pilfering borderers' at the 'marches' or borderlands of 'England' (or its 'in-land') pouring like the 'tide' into a 'breach' (1.2.149); the rebels in the suppressed cause of the 'Marches' (from the Earl of March designated by Richard II as his legitimate heir), described as the 'fault' in the 'little body' of England that 'France' has 'found out' (2 Chorus 16–20); the 'nicks' and 'sin' of the Language Lesson (3.4) followed by the description of 'Albion' or England as a 'nook-shotten isle' (3.5); the reminder of the sin of a 'father' and a 'before-breach' for which the king refuses to take responsibility (4.1.170), in the exchange with the dissenting Williams on the eve of Agincourt, just before explicit invocation of the king's father's 'fault' (4.1.170, 293); the ruined French 'garden' of the Wooing Scene and the Epilogue that links England's loss of this 'world's best garden' (Epil. 7) to another kind of incontinence – the losses of Henry's son that 'made his England bleed' (Epil. 12), and the breaching of the closure of the play itself by the reminder that these losses had already 'oft' been 'shown' upon 'our stage' (Epil. 13), in the reversed ordering of the history plays in which the post-Agincourt period had already provided the focus of the plays of Henry VI. In the final Wooing Scene that places such emphasis on the rhetoric of 'union', the image of the 'garden' laid waste by war is evoked by Burgundy, who presides over the French–English union of the Treaty of Troyes depicted in that scene; but the rhetoric of unity itself is ironized by the remembrance that it is this same Burgundy who subsequently breached this union, a breaching already 'oft ... shown' in the earlier plays the Epilogue so pointedly recalls.[4]

'Breaches' in *Henry V* are also inseparable from its dramatization of England's 'borderers' and the problem of a united 'Britain'. The 'breach' sounded in Henry's rousing speech before Harfleur is introduced into the play not in that scene of assault on what will later be called the 'maiden walls' of France (5.2.322) but rather in the earlier discussion of the danger posed by 'pilfering borderers', the threat at the 'Marches' of England of attack from behind (1.2.140–51), in lines that conjure up the territorial equivalent of a sodomitical rape.[5] 'Breaching' is thus not simply part of the martial rhetoric of phallic assault but linked to the invasion anxiety that haunts that earlier scene, and the play as a whole, as the verso to the recto of its rhetoric of straightforward advance. This potential for reversal is also conveyed in the curiously negative phrasing of Exeter's insistence that the claim to France is neither 'sinister' nor 'awkward' (2.4.85), terms that manage simultaneously to invoke the illegitimate inverse.[6] In the scene of Irish, Scots, and Welsh captains that begins with the pilfering English Bardolph's 'To the breach, to the breach' (3.1.1–2) – a line that is itself both an echo of Henry's rhetoric and a potentially iterative mockery of it – 'breach' sounds in the first words spoken by Welsh Fluellen in the play ('Up to the breach, you dogs!'; 3.2.20) and continues to echo in the 'cavities', 'counter-mines', and 'faults' that undermine its putative representation of a united British force. Undermining territorial 'breaches' sound not only throughout *Henry V* but in the description of Ireland as a 'breach that craves a quick expedient stop' (*2 Henry VI* 3.1.288) in the earlier plays the Epilogue invokes, the combination of bodily and territorial incontinence that represented various borderers as England's 'breech' or 'postern gate', just as a river is described as 'gelding' the opposing 'continent' (3.1.109) in *1 Henry IV*.

The figure of the 'breach', fault, or leak thus works counter to the rhetoric of containment (one of the meanings of 'continence' in the period), both in relation to the stability of 'British' union and with regard to the *hortus conclusus* invoked in Gaunt's famous image of England as an Edenic 'isle' in *Richard II* (2.1.40) or the repeated figure of English dominion as bounded by an enclosing 'Pale'. Welsh Fluellen's memorial garden of Welsh 'leeks', which evokes simultaneously the figure of containment and its inverse, undermines the rhetoric of union as well as any sense of monological single-voicedness within *Henry V*. What I propose to do first, then, is to explore the collocation of the ungoverned 'sound' of Welsh 'leeks' with the professed linguistic defect that produces 'Alexander the Pig' from the mouth of the Welsh borderer who has already entered the play invoking a 'breach', proving his ability to pronounce 'b' as 'b' rather than as 'p' and hence rendering even more striking the sounding of 'Big' as 'Pig' at the high point of the Agincourt victory, in a spectacular instance of 'sound' not 'in government', or verbal incontinence.

Fluellen's apparently encomiastic comparison of Henry to Alexander the Great itself conveys much more than it is able to contain within the boundaries of straightforward praise. As Leeds Barroll, Janet Spencer, and others have demonstrated, Alexander was available not only as a source of emulation but as a reminder of the links between empire, conquest, and theft, through the well-known anecdote in which a pirate accused by Alexander compares his own petty pilferings to conquest as theft on a grander scale. One of the many familiar sources of this anecdote was Augustine's description of wars of conquest as 'brigandage', a passage that already provides the ironic subtext for the 'pillage', 'boot', and 'emperor' of the Archbishop's Fable of the Bees, in the earlier scene of the urging of the war itself (1.2.193–6); (Leeds Barroll *Shakespearean Tragedy* 250–1; Spencer 'Princes, Pirates, and Pigs' 160–77). The repeated invocation of 'Alexander' throughout *Henry V* – from the 'gordian knot' of the Bishops' praise of the new king (1.1) to the 'Alexanders' of 'Once more unto the breach' (3.1.19) and Fluellen's comparison of Henry of Monmouth to Alexander of Macedon in the scene of linguistic varying from 'Alexander the Great' to 'Alexander the Pig' – forges yet another link between the pilfering former tavern companions of the king whose 'pillage' is evoked by the 'soldiers' of the 'emperor' in the Fable of the Bees and Henry's French campaign, already presented in *2 Henry IV* (4.5.184–215) as a deflection of attention from the Lancastrian theft of the crown. The long-established link between Alexander, empire, and thievery provides a more complex resonance to Henry's exhortation of his soldiers at the siege of Harfleur, where Henry himself will threaten pillage and rape if it refuses to surrender ('On, on, you noblest English / Whose blood is fet from fathers of war proof! / Fathers that, like so many Alexanders, / Have in these parts from morn to even fought', 3.1.17–20). In this scene of the killing of the French prisoners and the garden of Welsh 'leeks', the

ostensible Welsh slip of the lip that produces 'Alexander the Pig' as part of
Fluellen's apparently complimentary comparison, deflates the heroism
of the comparison itself, producing a lingual 'mockery' by putting the
comparison of 'Harry England' to a conquering 'Pig' into the mouth of
the apparently most faithful 'borderer' of the play. As David Quint has
observed, Alexander was in still other ways an ambivalent comparison,
as the ruler whose killing of Cleitus (specifically invoked by Fluellen
here) was a classical exemplum of unbridled violence, appearing at the
moment of Henry's 'one unmitigatedly blameworthy deed – the killing
of the French prisoners' (Quint 'Alexander the Pig' 52, 60). In this part
of the Alexander story, Cleitus's mocking of Alexander's pretensions to
be the son not of his father but of Jupiter Ammon – the mock for which
Alexander runs him through with a spear – comes mimetically close to
other father–son lineages within the play, where Henry (casting off both
his surrogate father Falstaff and his father the 'conveyor' Bolingbroke)
is placed rhetorically in the more exalted line from 'Edward III' and
the 'Black Prince', eliding the deposition and usurpation which make
his frequently invoked 'pedigree' not 'even' but 'crooked', in all of the
senses this play exploits.

Welsh Fluellen's comparison of Henry to Alexander the 'Pig' brings
so many ironic resonances to bear on the idealized English king at the
height of the Agincourt victory that well-known productions of the play
frequently omit it, as if the shocking comparison of this 'mirror of all
Christian kings' to a 'Pig' were too dissonant to contain within any unified representation, either of Henry or of his loyal Welsh deputy. Yet it
is as much a part of the more ironic Folio text of the play as the opening
scene which exposes the ulterior motives of the bishops in promoting the
war or the Epilogue that calls attention to the breaching of the rhetoric
of 'union' at its end. The historical Henry's attempts to place himself
within the legitimate royal line rather than the illegitimate ('sinister' or
'awkward') one had already been evoked in the king's recounting of his
attempts to remedy the 'faults / My father made in compassing the
crown' (4.1.293–4) on the eve of Agincourt. It is thus even more intriguing that in this scene of Fluellen's apparent Welsh mistake, the English
king born at 'Monmouth' (and made 'Prince of Wales', as sign of another
form of 'conveyance') is placed yet again not in the usurping Lancastrian
line but in that of the patriarch Edward III. Welsh Fluellen's other apparent slip in this scene (4.7.92), citing Edward as Henry's *grandfather* of
famous memory' (rather than his *great*-grandfather'), is usually taken to

be a Shakespearean 'mistake'. It also, however, subtly elides an entire generation, relating Henry directly to the legitimate patriarch associated with conquest in France by replacing his own genealogical grandfather (John of Gaunt, progenitor of the Lancastrian line) and eliding (in the accompanying reference to his 'great-uncle Edward the Plack Prince of Wales', father of Richard II) the intervention of the 'fault' of the conveyor Bolingbroke. ('Plack' itself, like 'porn at Monmouth', may suggest 'placket' or another kind of breach, in the mingling of low and high, kings and clowns, that characterizes this entire Lancastrian series.)[7]

Fluellen's 'Alexander the Pig' – contributing by its 'Welshed' variance an inversion of the play's heroic rhetoric – associates Henry with the darker side of this classical figure, already linked with a constructed pedigree, impulsive violence in the killing of a friend, and the association of conquest and empire with pilfering. What Fluellen insists is only 'a little variations' – 'is not "pig" great? The pig, or the great, or the mighty, or the huge, or the magnanimous, are all one reckonings, save the phrase is a little variations' (15–18) – is a 'variation' or difference that turns his apparently enthusiastic encomium back upon itself, introducing a Welshing alteration that is clearly the playwright's deliberate choice, since, as I have noted, Fluellen manages elsewhere to pronounce 'b' as 'b'. 'All one reckonings' here ('the pig, the great, the mighty, the huge, the magnanimous') insists on unity or 'oneness' – multiple 'variations' adding up to a single 'reckoning' or sum. Even apart from the shocking 'pig', however, the calculation of apparent synonymies remains both a troubling and an uncertain union. 'Reckoning' reverberates with more disturbing echoes, of the 'heavy reckoning' (4.1.134–5) already invoked by the commoner Williams ('if the cause be not good, the King himself hath a heavy reckoning to make', 134–5), a sense of 'reckoning' that includes not just adding up but calling to account, just as Welsh Fluellen's synonymy of 'great' and 'pig' undoes the apparent unity of the encomium it so elaborately constructs. This uncertain union – like the ideological rhetoric of unity in multiplicity in the Fable of the Bees, whose undermining subtext is the comparison of conquest to 'brigandage' – tends no more to the teleology of a unified calculation, 'reckoning,' or sum than the bishops' hopeful image of 'many' working to 'one' end in the Bee simile itself (1.2.208–12), or Bolingbroke's hope that his newly subjected co-conspirators might 'March all one way' (*1 Henry IV* 1.1.15) in *1 Henry IV*, a teleology belied by the breached closure of that same play, which ends with the dispatching of Hal, the Prince of Wales, 'towards

Wales, / To fight with Glendower and the Earl of March' (5.5.39–40), a
pointed reminder of the threat at England's borderlands or marches as
well as to the legitimacy of Lancastrian rule (Highley *Shakespeare, Spenser
and the Crisis in Ireland* 67–85).

The curiously reversed form of Fluellen's tortured comparison – that
'as Alexander kill'd his friend Clytus, being in his ales and his cups; so also
Harry Monmouth being in his right wits and his good judgments, turn'd
away the fat knight with the great belly doublet' (44–8) – famously recalls,
on the eve of the short-lived English victory in France, both the figure
of the banished Falstaff (the other father linked with thievery) and other
'friends' killed by this king: Bardolph executed for his theft of a *pax* whose
substitution for the chronicles' 'pyx' provides a *sotto voce* commentary on
the invading Henry's theft of the 'peace' and the former 'bedfellow'
Scroop among the rebels in the suppressed March cause (2.2.), the other
possible referent (as Gary Taylor notes) for the 'best friend' that Henry
has 'kill'd' (38–40; *Henry V* ed. Taylor 245). The comparison offered by
the ostensibly faithful Welsh borderer thus manages to return attention
not only to the Falstaff (or 'Oldcastle') already associated with Wales
(the figure whose name he claims to have 'forgot', 50) or the 'crooked'
Bolingbroke whose paternity and line his son (like Alexander) has sought
to replace, but also to the suppression of the Cambridge rebellion in Act 2,
where the name of 'March' – and the threat from the Welsh (and other)
marches associated with the Earl of March earlier described as rightful
'owner' of the English crown (*1 Henry IV* 4.3.94) – is also ostensibly 'forgot'.

It may be significant, therefore, in relation to the selective 'forgetting'
that suppresses threats to Henry's rhetoric of both unity and 'right', that
it is precisely at this point in this scene of Fluellen's 'Alexander the Pig'
and 'garden' of 'leeks' that Warwick makes his first appearance in the
play (4.7.55). For this same 'Warwick' (a dramatic character compounded
from two separate historical figures) had already appeared in the earlier
Shakespearean histories the Epilogue recalls – both as a figure at Agincourt who subsequently witnessed the losses of Henry's son that made
his 'England bleed' and as a central player in the rise of the suppressed
'right' of the Marches, heirs of the Cambridge executed by Henry V, an
execution decried in those plays by Cambridge's son the future Duke of
York as an act of 'bloody tyranny' (*1 Henry VI* 2.5.100). The appearance
of 'Warwick' here thus brings on stage a character who had appeared in
plays that had already ironized in advance Henry's ideological rhetoric
of proceeding with a 'rightful hand' (1.2.293), by dramatizing a perspective from which this rhetoric was (to use Exeter's rhetorically inverted

phrasing) both 'awkward' and 'sinister', in the sense of reversed and illegitimate.

Fluellen's comparison of 'Alexander's life' with 'Harry of Monmouth's life' that is 'come *after* it' (32) invokes the linear historical model of humanist *imitatio*, routinely translated into English as 'following'. The reversed order, however, of the Shakespearean history plays them-selves – explicitly highlighted by the Epilogue to *Henry V* – compli-cates the very model of *linear* history, presenting the subsequent losses of the son *before* his father's victories and breaching the apparent te-los or 'perfection' of *Henry V* by pointing *back* in its Epilogue to this dramatic beginning, plays that include the return of the heirs of the executed Cambridge from the borderlands or marches to claim the English crown from its Lancastrian usurpers. Fluellen's comparison of Henry to 'Alexander the Pig' invokes a figure evocative of this breached ouroborus structure: 'It is not well done, mark you now, to take the tales out of my mouth ere it is made and finished' (4.7.43). As a fig-ure of the incomplete, fracted, or unfinished, this 'tale' (or 'tail', in the familiar Shakespearean pun) taken out of the 'mouth' ironically recalls the unctuous encomium of completion with which the play it-self began, the Archbishop's marvelling (regarding the apparently now faultless Edenic-body of the king) at how 'things are perfected' (1.1.69), an idealized image of closure whose strangely ambiguous phrasing ('scouring faults') leaves uncertain whether the 'faults' themselves have disappeared. Fluellen's breached or unfinished 'tale' (or in his charac-teristic pluralizing, 'tales' that fail to add up to a single unified 'reck-oning') provides the counterpart here to the brokenness or breaching the Epilogue evokes immediately following the multiple references to 'broken English' (5.2.246) in the Wooing Scene. The putative 'stage Welsh' of Fluellen's own 'broken English' (including his varying inabil-ity to pronounce 'b' except as 'p') destabilizes the representation both of the play's vaunted proto-'British' unity and the rhetorical idealiza-tion of this 'mirror of English kings'. Like the Epilogue, it renders *Henry V* both 'fracted and corroborate' (to borrow a phrase from the scene of the Falstaff whose name is 'forgot'), breaching both unity and clo-sure through the fiction of a professedly Welsh tongue. It also recalls, at the high point of Agincourt and from the mouth of an apparently *loyal* Welsh borderer, the monstrous ouroborus or 'beastly transforma-tion' of English bodies by Welshwomen who put English tails in mouths, a transformation too scandalizing for 'continent tongues', evoked at the opening of *1 Henry IV* (1.1.44), in lines that have inspired much of the re-examination of Shakespeare's histories in the wake of the 'new British history'.

In the context of the selective forgetting that already dominates this scene, it is important that the 'garden' of Welsh 'leeks' is presented in the rhetoric of the 'memorable', a term iterated in this play more than in any other by Shakespeare. Both 'Alexander the Pig' and this memorial 'garden' appear in the scene in which 'Agincourt' is first revealed as the place of the heroic English victory (*'King Hen.* What is the castle call'd that stands hard by? / *Montjoy.* They call it Agincourt'; 4.7.88–9). The buried sense of 'Again' – of iteration or repetition – sounded in the name is underscored by its immediate association with the 'memorable' and memory, making the effort of containment or enclosure an effort to 'waste the memory of former days' (*2 Henry IV* 4.5.215), as the dying Bolingbroke had advised in the scene where he counselled foreign war as a deflection of attention from a faulty title. The association of the French battlefield with the memorable – in the sense of what is to *be* remembered in time *to come* – is marked first in Henry's response to the name ('Then call we this the field of Agincourt, / Fought on the day of Crispin Crispianus'; 90–1). 'Crispin Crispianus' itself recalls within the play the resonant rhetoric of the St Crispin's Day speech ('Be in their flowing cups freshly remembered'; 4.3.54), including the lines where the curious invocation of the 'Talbot' who never fought at Agincourt, along with the rollcall of other names familiar from the earlier plays of Henry VI ('Bedford and Exeter, / Warwick and Talbot, Salisbury and Gloucester'), simultaneously recalls to memory the plays that the Epilogue will remind the audience had already preceded *Henry V* upon 'our stage', breaching the self-contained 'perfection' of the play by reminders of the already-staged undoing of its final 'union'. The association of the battlefield at Agincourt with the 'memorable' is marked here by Henry's memorializing gesture.

It is into this scene of simultaneous memorializing and strategic forgetting that the play introduces the putative historical origin of the Welsh wearing of leeks on Saint Davy's Day, as a memorial of Welsh service to English kings:

FLU. Your grandfather of famous *memory*, an't please your Majesty, and your great-uncle Edward the Plack Prince of Wales, as I have read in the chronicles, fought a most prave pattle here in France.
KING HEN. They did, Fluellen.
FLU. Your Majesty says very true. If your Majesties is *remerb'red* of it, the Welshmen did good service in a garden where leeks did grow, wearing

leeks in their Monmouth caps, which, your Majesty know, to this hour is
an honorable badge of the service; and I do believe your Majesty takes no
scorn to wear the leek upon Saint Tavy's day.

KING HEN. I wear it for a *memorable* honor; For I am Welsh, you know, my good
countryman.

FLU. All the water in Wye cannot wash your Majesty's Welsh plood out of your
body, I can tell you that. God pless it, and preserve it, as long as it pleases
his Grace, and his Majesty too!

KING HEN. Thanks, good my countryman.

FLU. By Jeshu, I am your Majesty's countryman, I care not who know it. I
will confess it to all the world. I need not to be ashamed of your Majesty,
praised be God, so long as your Majesty is an honest man. (4.7.92–115,
italics mine)

The emphasis here on memorializing and the 'memorable' as a selec-
tively constructed 'remembrance' is compounded by the fact that this
passage is itself a fictive construction of Shakespeare's invention, with
no corroboration from any independent history. Fluellen's recalling of
Welsh service in the 'prave pattle' fought by 'Your grandfather of famous
memory' and 'your great-uncle Edward the Plack Prince of Wales, as
I have read in the chronicles' – continues (including in the sound of
'prave' that suggests 'depraved') the substitution of 'p' for 'b'. 'As I have
read in the chronicles' calls attention to the act of chronicling, forging,
or constructing 'history' itself, as well as the querying elsewhere in the
play (including in these Agincourt scenes) of the reliability of testimony
or accounts. Memory is stressed in 'If your Majesties is *rememb'red* of it,
the Welshmen did good service in a garden where leeks did grow'. Both
the repeated image of the 'garden', however, and the absence of any
authority outside Shakespeare for this 'garden' of Welsh 'leeks' call attention to the wider context of the image within *Henry V*, including its
relation to the unstable containment of the *hortus conclusus* threatened by
iterated breaches – in a play that has already added multiple inventions
to its chronicle sources, including the comparison of the 'mirror of all
Christian kings' to 'Alexander the Pig'.

The apparently loyal Fluellen (whose name pointedly evokes an anglicized Llewellyn, the last genuine 'Prince of Wales', the title whose
appropriation by the English crown stands as a sign of imperial English
control) may be made to speak here out of both sides of his mouth. The
'Monmouth' of the 'Monmouth caps' in which these 'leeks' function as
a remembrance or memorial of a 'garden' of 'leeks' (as well as the birth-
place of this king and former Prince of Wales) was itself an uncertain
borderline, a bilingual or two-tongued boundary between England and

Wales that looked in more than one direction at once. Henry's reply that the wearing of the 'leek' is a *'memorable* honour' (104) which he observes because he too is 'Welsh' (105) links this Henry of Monmouth (from the 'marches' or borders between England and Wales) with the multiple 'marches' connected with Wales in particular.[8] But Henry's 'I am Welsh', as Andrew Gurr points out, also recalls to memory the fact that this English king's 'chief acquaintance with Wales was his long training in siege warfare during the succession of rebellions against his father' (Gurr *Henry V* 181). It thus re-imports a memory (in the midst of this passage devoted to the 'memorable') not only of the extension of English dominion over these particular borderers but of the threat from the Welsh marches that haunted all three Lancastrian reigns – in the visiting of the sins of another 'grandfather' on his children and his children's children (the biblical figure frequently summoned in the chronicles for the effect of Bolingbroke's original 'fault'): the aftermath of the Cambridge rebellion, apparently contained by the execution of the rebels but ultimately (as Hall puts it) rising to destroy the 'walls' of Henry's own 'house'.[9]

The sense that this 'garden' of 'leeks' as a memorial of Welsh fidelity may be working in multiple directions is strengthened by the ambiguous response of the borderer Fluellen in these very lines ('I need not to be ashamed of your Majesty, praised be God, *so long as your Majesty is an honest man*'; 4.7.114–15, italics mine). For it is precisely at this moment of the querying of the king's honesty that the commoner Michael Williams enters (bearing a name that links him with both Wales and Shakespeare's 'Will'), linking this scene of 'Alexander the Pig' and Welsh 'leeks' with the dissident voice of the figure who had questioned, on the eve of Agincourt, whether the king's 'cause' was 'just' or his quarrel 'honorable' (4.1.128–9). As Annabel Patterson has observed, this dissenting Will's questioning is never satisfactorily answered within the play (Patterson 'Back by Popular Demand' 90–1). When he reappears here, in the midst of the exchange between Henry and Welsh Fluellen devoted to the king's honesty as well as 'leeks', a curious set of parallels is set up between Williams the dissenting Englishman with the Welsh-sounding name, wearing a glove in his 'cap' as memorial of his challenge to the honesty of the king, and the Welsh borderer who has cited the wearing of memorial 'leeks' in Welsh caps as an 'honorable badge' of Welsh 'service' (4.7.101), including to a king he 'need not to be ashamed' of 'so long as' he is 'an honest man' (113–15).[10]

Though the king pits them against one another, in a complicated dissimulation that is anything *but* 'honest', Fluellen's apparently faithful borderer's voice comes close in this scene to Williams's subversive class voice when the Welsh deputy responds (to the king's reference to a 'gentleman') that 'Though he be *as good a gentleman as the devil is, as Lucifer and Belzebub himself*, it is necessary, look your Grace, that he keep his vow and his oath' (4.7.137–43, italics mine). The links become even more suggestive when the 'leeks' worn in Welsh or 'Monmouth' caps (4.7.100) and the glove worn in Williams's become associated with the glove of Williams himself, which Henry puts in Fluellen's cap as soon as Williams exits, claiming (to compound the dishonesty still further) that it is the glove he had taken at Agincourt from the helm of French Alençon ('When Alanson and myself were down together'; 154–5) and instructing Fluellen that 'If any man challenge this, he is a friend to Alanson, and an enemy to our person' (156–7). The ruse thus identifies the dissenting English commoner with the French enemy to England, a threat to Henry's 'crown' and the 'person' of the king. It also compounds the series of memorial tokens that started from the Welsh 'leek', with a recall of the threat of the 'law Salique' with which the play and war began, since 'Alanson' or 'Alençon' (as Gurr observes) was the name intimately associated with its historical re-emergence in the debate over Elizabeth's proposed marriage to Alençon, an alliance that threatened to reverse Henry V's conquest of France. Williams thus gets complexly associated with the French enemy Alençon whose name recalls a threat to Henry's 'crown' as well as Elizabethan debates over the 'law Salique', while Welsh Fluellen wears in his cap, in lieu of a Welsh 'leek', the dissenting Williams's glove, sign of his challenge to the justice of the king's cause and the entire war of English expansion. At this point in the scene, as Fluellen goes in search of Williams, Warwick and Gloucester enter, both of them 'memorable' figures who recall the threat to Henry's crown, as well as English dominion, dramatized in the plays of Henry VI that the Epilogue recalls: the 'incontinent' aftermath of Agincourt and the Cambridge rebellion that made 'England bleed', from a combination of challenges from the French, English dissidents, and the marches or borderlands of England.

The entire exchange in which Fluellen apprehends Williams as a 'traitor' ('a most contagious treason come to light'; 4.8.20–1) – on the assumption of his league with Alençon – explicitly recalls the scene of the Cambridge rebellion, of 'traitors' condemned as the 'fault' in England that 'France' has 'found out' (2 Chorus), including in lines delivered to Warwick, the figure whose name is inextricably associated with the suppressed claim from the marches already revealed to be anything but

'treason' in the plays of *Henry VI*. The echoes of the Rebellion Scene
become even more prominent as Williams is given monetary 'crowns'
(57, 60) by the king to wear 'for an honor in thy cap / Till I do challenge
it' (59–60), lines that echo not only the wearing of 'leeks' in caps as a
'memorable honor' (4.7.102) but the punning association of monetary
'crowns' with the threat to Henry's 'crown' in the Rebellion Scene, here
in the context of a future 'challenge' (4.8.60). The entire exchange – with
the Williams who continues to insist that his challenge to the king was
the king's own 'fault' (4.8.54) – suggests something left unfinished, a dissident voice that is anything but contained. Even the sustained attention
called by Welsh Fluellen to the sorry state of this common man's 'shoes'
(4.8.70) provides an ironic remembrance of Henry's rousing invocation
of 'Crispin Crispianus', patron-saint of shoe-makers, in his speech on the
memorable 'day' of Agincourt, subtly challenging the equalizing rhetoric
of its 'band of brothers'. This invented set of interactions between Welsh
Fluellen, the dissident Williams, and the recently victorious English king
is routinely shortened or cut in productions that strive for a more unified
representation of both Agincourt and Henry. It reintroduces, however,
striking recalls of the Cambridge revolt, whose simultaneously historical
and theatrical irony was that the aftermath of its suppression involved the
undermining of the 'walls' of this king's own 'house'. It also introduces
an exchange involving both a name shared by the Shakespearean 'Will'
who created these additions and a borderer linked with 'leeks' and a
Wales that (together with England's other borderlands or marches) had
already played a major role in the 'oft . . . shown' losses of everything that
Agincourt had won.

   The same scene that contains (or fails to contain) the disquieting
'variations' of the Welshing that produces 'Alexander the Pig' thus introduces the 'leek' as a memorial of Welsh service to English imperial
extension, in an invented 'garden' of 'leeks' (4.7.99) that not only echoes
the multiple soundings of breached enclosures elsewhere in the play but
leads to a dizzying series of challenges to Henry's rhetoric of English
as well as 'British' unity, at the moment of the Agincourt victory itself.
The 'leeks' that function, like the memorializing of Agincourt or Saint
Crispin's Day, as a 'memorable honor' (104) introduce into this play
the ungoverned sound of 'leaks' that suggest the opposite of containment. The evocation of a 'leek' in this scene of the Agincourt victory
may even – in yet another ungoverned sounding – recall (as Frankie
Rubinstein has suggested) the iterated 'law Salique' of the speech used

to justify Henry's claim to the 'world's best garden': France (Rubinstein *A Dictionary of Shakespeare's Sexual Puns* 145). This possibility (which may on the surface seem unlikely) may be strengthened by the homophonic sounding of French 'lique' in 'leek', in a period in which the 'leek' was subject to precisely such homophony; and perhaps, as Rubinstein suggests, by the seemingly gratuitous exchange on 'salt' and 'leek' (5.1.9–10) inserted immediately before the Wooing Scene, where the spectre of the 'law Salique', already evoked in the name of 'Alençon', returns in the Treaty of Troyes and marriage of Henry to the French king's daughter, weakening the Agincourt victory by placing the future son of this uncertain French–English union in the position (once again) of holding his claim through the female, a weakness already exposed in the dramatization of the losses that made 'England bleed'. The French 'Kate' whose marriage to Henry constitutes the principal 'article' of this Treaty is the foreign woman with whom he 'compound[s]' the boy who lost this 'world's best garden' (Epilogue 7), another breach, fault, or leak in a 'garden', park, or pale, ominously sounded in the 'broken English', 'English broken' of that scene (5.2.244–6). The highlighting of the importance of such female links, in the possible echo of 'Salique' in the 'leek' that curiously reappears immediately before this Wooing Scene, might even recall, once again, the breach or fault in the argument through the female that would undo Henry's own dominion, revealing it to be not lawful or 'right' but the 'awkward' or 'sinister' inverse.

In the plays of *Henry IV* in which Hal figures as both 'Prince of Wales' and putative master of 'tongues', the danger to English domination or containment (as well as continence) comes not from the women of France but from the women of Wales – not only from the Welshwomen who cram 'tails' into 'mouths' and other orifices, but from the enchantments of the daughter of Owain Glyn Dwr, exercised on the Earl of March, the designated English heir. The final Act of *Henry V* recalls both this Welsh female threat (in the scene of 'salt' and 'leeks' in which a leek is forced into a mouth) and the 'witchcraft' of French women associated with the already-dramatized losses that made 'England bleed', linking 'Gallia' and 'Gaul,' Wales and France, front and back of England. The 'law Salique' related to the threat of dependence on foreign women continues to haunt the final Wooing Scene – where, once again, the image of a 'fault' returns ('the liberty that follows our places stops the mouth of all find-faults'), in the 'kiss' that simultaneously seals this French–English union and ironically recalls, in the 'witchcraft' (5.2.275) of French Katherine's lips, its post-Agincourt reversal. Henry's 'stops the mouth of all find-faults, as I will do yours' (5.2.272–3) evokes (in 'stops') the containing of a 'fault' or 'breach' (as in the description of Ireland as a 'breach that craves a quick expedient *stop*' in *2 Henry VI*). It also, however, calls attention to the stopping of a 'mouth', the bodily orifice evoked in the iterated 'mouths' of the play as a whole, including the 'Monmouth' of the scenes of 'Alexander the Pig' and the find-fault Will.

The emphasis in the play's final scene of Welsh 'leeks' is even more specifically on the 'mouth' as well as on a 'Welsh correction'. English Pistol's being forced to 'eat' a 'leek' (with the threat of an even bigger one held in reserve) joins the play's multiple images of cramming, forcing, or stuffing a mouth – from the Prologue's 'cram / Within this wooden "O"' (Prol. 12–13) to the striking image of the Chorus to Act 2 ('digest / Th'abuse of distance, force a play'; 2 Chorus 31–2), lines that suggest in 'force' both 'rape' and stuffing a mouth (*farcir*) and add to the play's other orifices the oral figure of incorporation or 'digestion' (which might extend to the 'farced title' of kingship itself). Such digestion returns in Henry's denunciation of the 'fault' of the Cambridge rebels ('If little faults, proceeding on distemper, / Shall not be wink'd at, how shall we stretch our eye / When capital crimes, chew'd, swallow'd, and digested, / Appear before us'; 2.2.54–7) and – as something *forcibly* 'digested' – in the French discovery of 'the losses we have borne, the subjects we have lost, the disgrace we have digested' (3.6.126–8). When the English 'Pistol' – whose name evokes the phallic assault of the war itself – is forced more passively to 'eat' Fluellen's 'leek', the lines place a similar emphasis on the problem of incorporation or digestion ('*Flu.* I peseech you heartily, scurvy, lousy knave, at my desires, and my requests, and my petitions, to eat, look you, this leek, because, look you, you do not love it, nor your affections, and your appetites, and your disgestions doo's not agree with it'; 5.1.22–27). Even the 'jesting' or mockery within this 'digesting' (conveyed by the spelling of 'disjestion' in this scene where Fluellen insists 'if you can mock a leek, you can eat a leek'; 5.1.37–8) is linked with 'leeks' through the 'gleeking' (74) or mocking by Pistol of this Welsh 'gentleman' and 'ancient tradition', a mockery for which being forced to eat the leek is a form of 'Welsh correction'. If the play invokes invasion anxieties in the scene of 'pilfering borderers' linked with the threat of a sodomitical breaching by the Scottish 'dog' (1.2.218), this final scene of Welsh leeks – iterating the forceful figure of incorporation or 'digestion' – suggests (in an ostensibly simply comic mode) the difficulty of incorporating even the apparently 'model' borderer Wales, just as 'Alexander the Pig' and the 'garden' of 'leeks' had issued from the mouth of the play's apparently most loyal 'borderer'.

Gurr suggests that Fluellen's forcing of Pistol to eat his 'leek' comes with the sexual suggestiveness of 'cock', a suggestion rendered more plausible by the fact that the phallic-shaped leek was already associated with a bodily 'tail' and by the repeated linking of Welsh leeks with the obscene gesture of the Spanish 'figo' or 'fig' earlier in the play. The brandishing of this leek in performance, in place of a sword or other instrument of war, as well as the suggestion of a second 'leek' (5.1.62) invariably in performance made to be of monstrous size, may provide both a *reductio ad absurdum* and a deflating mimicry of the phallicism of the war. Given Fluellen's repeated invocation of the 'Roman disciplines' of war, this final image of the forcing of a phallic 'leek' into an unwilling mouth (following the multiple images of the forcing or raping of mouths and other bodily orifices within the play as a whole) may also evoke the 'Roman discipline' that was the most forceful of displays of humiliation of an enemy, familiar oral counterpart of Pistol's threatened 'fig'.[11] Being forced to eat a Welsh leek thus provides – like the bodily invasion or breaching suggested by the Spanish 'figo' – yet another variation on Fluellen's image of 'tales' and 'mouth' from the scene of 'Alexander the Pig' and the 'garden' of 'leeks', as well as the threat of the 'beastly transformation' by Welshwomen that haunts these English histories. This scene whose image of a 'leek' in a 'mouth' suggests both bodily ends raises the prospect yet again (at what should be the play's victorious close) of ongoing trouble – as Pistol's 'earnest of revenge' (5.1.63) and 'All hell shall stir for this' (68) echo a famous moment in the 'Roman' imperial wars in which what had seemed to promise peace is breached or broken yet again. This final scene of Welsh 'leeks' – in which a notorious English pilferer is made to 'eat' the 'leek' of the Fluellen whose name recalls the last true 'Prince of Wales' – suggests both a Welsh 'correction' and the cycle of revenge (in both directions) which in these histories works against any final teleological closure or 'perfection', breaching the concluding language of 'peace' and union in these final scenes of *Henry V*, the putative telos or 'end' of the entire dramatic series.

The celebration of the English victory at Agincourt in Act 4 and the Chorus celebrating Henry's triumph at the opening of Act 5 are thus surrounded by exchanges preoccupied with Welsh 'leeks', first in the scene of 'Alexander the Pig' and the 'garden' of Welsh 'leeks' cited as the origin of the wearing of 'leeks' in 'Monmouth' caps, and then in the scene of this 'Welsh correction'. The multiple associations of these

Welsh 'leeks' – with the breaching of the 'garden' that figures so prominently as an ideological figure of containment and national unity, with the Welshing of 'Alexander the Pig', the combined threats from the marches, French 'Alençon', and the common 'Will', and the repeated problem of 'digestion' – suggest (even as the 'leek' is made to stand as a sign of loyalty to English dominion) the much more subtle anxieties of incorporation and invasion linked with the ongoing instability of England's 'borderers'. Linked with the problem of continence and containment in both senses – of ungoverned sound and of incorporating troublesome borderers into the 'body' of England – these 'leeks' may also underscore the irony that this very play was cited in influential New Historicist writing as substantiation of the teleological argument that subversion is always ultimately contained.[12] (Lest it be objected that such *subversion*, if it exists at all, is 'merely' verbal, the frequent cutting of so many of this play's multiple iterations of breaches and leeks, or of the 'pig' of the scene of Fluellen's 'Alexander the Pig', may provide its own telling witness to what is literally 'unfitting' about such passages.) In this echo-chamber of a play – where the iterated sounding of '*breaches*' and '*faults*' is part of what undermines its official rhetoric of 'British' as well as English unity – the multiple soundings of Welsh '*leeks*' are part of 'sound' not only not 'in *government*' but not traceable to any individual character's intent. *Henry V* invites such an emphasis on the aural in its opening Chorus, which reminds the audience how much will depend on the ear, in a play where there is so much more than meets the eye (1 Chorus 23–34). The play associated with ultimate closure and containment in the debate over 'subversion and containment' in these Lancastrian histories is thus the very play breached not only by repeated reminders of the incontinence of the 'little body' of England but by the ungoverned sounds, apparent slips of the lip and reminders of what is strategically banished from memory, which have as one of their effects the drawing of attention to the attempt at *containment* itself.

Containment is also in this play finally inseparable from its relationship to the concerns of the broader 'British' history, past and present. The alternative, non-Anglocentric British history – famously part of Pocock's original plea for 'the plural history of a group of cultures situated along an Anglo-Celtic frontier and marked by an increasing English political and cultural domination' – opens at least the possibility of a more decentred vision of 'Britain', even as it acknowledges the history of 'English political and cultural domination' that made this more plural and varied history increasingly monological or single-voiced (Pocock 'British History' 605).

What I would like to suggest with regard to *Henry V* – the play so frequently conscripted (with the aid of strategic cutting) to the heroic voicing of English dominion over faithful borderers and of 'Englishness' itself – is that it provides, in its own multiple (and ultimately unstoppable) contrary voices, a decentring critique of the rhetoric of a dominated unity or oneness, suggesting, in the very play that the current Prince of Wales once praised for teaching him how to be a king, leaks that perhaps still have not been contained.

NOTES

1 All Shakespeare citations, unless otherwise noted, are from *The Riverside Shakespeare*; the epigraph is from Hooker, *Ecclesiastic Polity* (1597) v.ix.par. 2 ('There . . . will be alwaies evils, which no arte of man can cure, breaches and leakes moe then man's wit hath hands to stop').

2 See the Introduction to Gurr *Henry V*; and *inter alia*, in relation to Henry's claim to have won Agincourt 'without strategem' (*Henry V* 4.8.108), the discussion of *Henry V* in Kastan *Shakespeare and the Shapes of Time*.

3 See, among other examples of this ongoing work, Baker ' "Wilde-hirissheman" '; Highley ' "If the Cause be not good": *Henry V* and Essex's Irish Campaign' in *Shakespeare, Spenser and the Crisis in Ireland* 134–63; Holderness ' "What ish my nation?" '; Neill 'Broken English and Broken Irish'. Examination of 'faultlines' in *Henry V* owes a debt to Dollimore and Sinfield's 'History and Ideology', although subsequent readings have tended to differ from the argument concerning the containment (or unity) of England's borderers presented in that essay and in Philip Edwards *Threshold of a Nation*.

4 On the figure of 'breaches' and 'faults', the 'preposterous' reversal of chronological order in the two tetralogies of Shakespearean history plays, and the relation between the 'marches' or borderlands and the Marches (including the Earl of March who was Richard II's designated heir), see Parker *Shakespeare from the Margins* chs. 1 and 5.

5 See Parker *Shakespeare from the Margins* 42–3.

6 'Sinister', in this period, means 'illegitimate' as well as 'left' (in contrast to Henry's rhetoric of proceeding with a 'rightful hand'); 'awkward' means literally 'reversed' (or 'awk') and is a synonym for 'preposterous' in the period, as the historical entries for these terms in the *OED* make clear.

7 On 'conveyance' and its exploitation in these Shakespearean histories, see Parker *Shakespeare from the Margins* ch. 5. I owe the suggestion concerning 'plack' (or 'placket') and 'porn' to David Baker.

8 Essex was known to wear the leek on Saint David's Day as well as Elizabeth, and to identify himself strongly with the Welsh. The Marches (or Earls of March) – including the descendants of the executed Cambridge (through his marriage to Mortimer's sister) – had extensive holdings in Wales as well as Ireland.

9 'Wales' in Hall, as well as in the variant spellings of other contemporary texts, was also frequently spelled 'Walles' (see Hall *Chronicle* 62).

10 David Baker has reminded me that 'so long as your Majesty is an honest man' (4.7.114–115) is preceded by the earlier 'as long as it pleases his Grace, and his Majesty too!' (4.7.108–9) – on which see *Henry V* ed. Taylor 249.

11 On the likely monstrous size of the threatened second leek, see (*inter alia*) *Henry V* ed. Taylor 263.

12 See, for example, the critique of the 'containment' argument of Greenblatt's 'Invisible Bullets' in Baker *Between Nations* 22–5.

CHAPTER 7

Delving to the root: Cymbeline, Scotland, and the English race

Mary Floyd-Wilson

As a romance of ancient Britain, Shakespeare's *Cymbeline* plays fast and loose with its primary historical source, Holinshed's *Chronicles of England, Scotland, and Ireland*. Recognizing that the historical Cymbeline paid peaceful tribute to the Romans, critics have noted that Shakespeare seems to have superimposed the rebellions of Guiderius and Arviragus onto their father's reign (Jones 'Stuart *Cymbeline*' 88). In the face of these chronological confusions, as well as the play's more notorious anachronisms, some scholars have dismissed the romance's historical strands as 'merely ornamentation'.[1] Yet *Cymbeline*'s disruption of Holinshed's narrative actually points to broader historiographical concerns. The play's inverted chronology unsettles the authority of Britain's chronicle history and taps into the uncertainties already present in Holinshed – the discrepancies between the English and Scottish histories of ancient Britain. This chapter will reconsider *Cymbeline*'s debt to Holinshed within the related contexts of the Anglo-Scottish union and the period's revisionary historiography.

Cymbeline criticism has traditionally seen a connection between the play's references to Britain's fabled Trojan history and the Jacobean union project, yet much of this scholarship presumes a harmonious vision of Britain's past and future.[2] More recently, critical attention has been paid to the drama's historiographical tensions (its implicit scepticism toward the Brutish myths and its anxious acknowledgement of native barbarism), but these readings have neglected the Anglo-Scottish politics that helped generate these tensions.[3] Moreover, literary scholars concede that Shakespeare drew on the Scottish chronicles for a single episode in the play, but no one has seriously considered the possibility that *Cymbeline*'s central plot may be an amalgamation of Scottish and English histories – despite the fact that the English chronicle of Arviragus's and Guiderius's reigns presents itself as a rejoinder to the Scottish version of events.[4] We need to reassess *Cymbeline* with the understanding that most early Jacobean history writing sought to adjudicate in some way 'the conflicting and hostile accounts of English and Scottish historians'.[5]

Generated by the ethnological tensions of the early seventeenth century, *Cymbeline* spins out an English historical fantasy in which the Scots submit to Anglo-British rule and the English emerge as a race unaffected by Britain's early history of mingled genealogies and military defeats. *Cymbeline*'s allusions to the competing claims in English and Scottish histories might be aligned with the current efforts in British historiography to represent Britain in non-Anglocentric terms. However, I will argue that the play also responds to a strain of contemporary pressures within early modern historiography that gave rise to modern Anglocentricism: the antiquarians' embrace of England's Anglo-Saxon ancestry. In other words, the traditionally Anglocentric bent of British history was shaped in part by early modern England's investment in ethnic distinctions. While union advocates may have relied on the assimilative effect of depicting Britain's future as a revival of its past, those historians attesting to English-Saxon roots aimed to extricate the English people from a history of Briton savagery, Roman domination, and Scottish kinship. I contend that Shakespeare's *Cymbeline* romanticizes the nascent historiographical impulses toward English exceptionalism that the new British history now aims to redress.

SHAKESPEARE'S HISTORIES

Comparing the Scottish and English versions of the events in Holinshed that informed Shakespeare's play not only reveals significant historical discrepancies, but it also helps to clarify how remarkably anxious the English historians were to repudiate the Scots. According to the English *Chronicles*, the Scottish historians have distorted the past by ascribing to the Scots and Picts 'what notable feat soever was atchived by the old Britains against the Romans'.[6] While both the Scots and the English acknowledge that Cymbeline's son Guiderius led the Britons in a rebellion against Rome, they disagree on whether or not the Scots played a role in this conflict. They are aware of 'diverse opinions and variable reports of writers touching the partile conquest of this Iland by the Romans, [and] the death of Guiderius' (*E* 35), but the English chroniclers will only concede that Guiderius was 'a man of stout courage' who died in battle (33). In the Scottish version, however, the southern Britons prove helpless without the Scots' support: the Roman army immediately 'vanquished Guiderius in battell, so that . . . he was constreined to send to Caratake king of Scots for aid against the common enimies of both nations' (*S* 45).

Reports of Arviragus's reign create an even greater schism. The English *Chronicles* establish rather tentatively that Arviragus's marriage to Genissa, daughter to the Roman emperor Claudius, reinstated Britain's tributary relationship with Rome (*E* 36). Arviragus later rebels on account of 'pride', but his Roman wife's 'good mediation' restores peaceful relations (36) and re-establishes Britain's prudent submission to Rome. Yet Holinshed also indicates that the subject of Arviragus's reign remains a historiographical problem: historians cannot agree on when Arviragus ruled Britain, or whether 'this supposed marriage betwixt Arviragus and the daughter of Claudius is but a feined tale' (36). More pointedly, Holinshed asserts that the Scottish chroniclers have mistakenly merged the legend of Voadicea or Boadicea with Arviragus's story (42).

When we turn to the Scottish *Chronicles*, the rebellion against Roman rule is described not as insubordination on Arviragus's part, but as a populist movement against him for having spurned his Scottish queen Voada. In the Scottish version, Arviragus is already married to Voada, King Caratake's sister, when he chooses to marry Genissa. The second marriage was an 'act manie of the Britans disallowed; the more in deed, because he had faire issue alreadie by Voada' (*S* 46). It is in defence of their abandoned Scottish queen that the betrayed Britons join forces with the Scots and Picts against Arviragus and the Romans. Eventually Arviragus is persuaded to renounce Genissa, but the Romans prevail by 'fortune' (47). From the Scottish perspective then, British defiance against Rome is not simply an exercise in bravado, it is an action that unifies the disparate peoples of Britain in the face of a faithless king and a foreign invader. The Britons, Scots, and Picts rally behind their Scottish queen and seek to preserve future ethnic unity in Arviragus and Voada's 'faire issue'.

Voada becomes a ghostly presence in the English *Chronicles*. Holinshed insists that the Scots' historian Boece has confused Arviragus with Prasutugus, who emerges much later in the historical narrative as the husband of Boadicea, southern Britain's warrior queen (*E* 42).[7] This is as close as the English historians come to giving a name to Arviragus's Scottish wife. It is Voada's erasure from the English *Chronicles* that attests to her importance. Voada represents a history of mingled ethnic identities: the rebellious Britons have not only intermarried with the Scots, but they repeatedly appealed to their northern neighbours for aid when battling the Romans. For the English, Boece's Arviragus violates decorum less for marrying two women than for having a Scottish wife who generated the shared sympathy of Britons, Picts, and Scots. The Britons' loyalty to their Scottish queen over and above their 'British' ruler and his Roman wife underscores a messy ethnological history that the English chroniclers choose to ignore. Rather than affirming a history that binds the Britons to a female Scot and her Pictish rebels, the English historians place their emphasis on the peaceful civility of Roman rule.

In terms of historiographical patterns, the implicit debate in Holinshed regarding Arviragus and Guiderius reiterates the conflict between Scottish and English historians over the legend of Caesar's conquest of Britain. It is Geoffrey of Monmouth's fabulous account of Caesar's invasion which set the terms of this debate. Despite Britain's downfall, Geoffrey insisted that the Britons demonstrated their valiant nature by twice driving Caesar away, and 'even in defeat . . . [they] withstood him whom no nation of the earth had been able to withstand' (*Histories of the Kings of Britain* 65). The Scottish historians later intervene in this narrative with their own claims to valour; in their account, the Britons only succeeded in defeating Caesar 'at first because the Scots and the Picts were helping them', and once they forfeited the aid of their northern allies, the Britons were easily subdued (Nearing, Jr 'The Legend' 921). Holinshed refutes those 'Scotish writers [who] report, that the Britains, after the Romans were the first time repelled . . . refused to receive aid of the Scotish men the second time, and so were vanquished' (*E* 31).

After King James's accession, Scottish union advocates cite Caesar's conquest as the consequence of ancient disunity. As one Scottish author contends, it was 'by the perpetuall discords of the Brittons, Scotish, and Pights, [that] the Romans maid there conquest in the iland'.[8] In less diplomatic terms, Scottish union commissioner Sir Thomas Craig not only claimed that the 'dissensions of the island paved the way for Caesar's invasion', but he also identified degeneracy as the cause of southern Britain's subsequent losses of liberty: 'by abandoning themselves to luxury, [they] relapsed into cowardice, and so opened the island first to the Saxons and then to the Danes, who encountered little resistance from the effeminate and luxury-loving natives' (Craig *De Unione* 211, 414–15). For the Scottish historians, Britain's encounters with Caesar become another rallying point for Scotland's claims to an inherent independence, which the Scots traditionally characterized as 'unlike that of England – [since it] was unsullied by either conquest or feudal submission' (Mason 'Scotching the Brut' 64; Craig *De Unione* 463–4).

With the publication of Camden's *Britannia* (1586), the significance of Caesar's conquest of the Britons was transformed utterly. Although diplomatic in his treatment of Geoffrey's mythography, Camden indicated that the official beginning of Britain's recorded history was Caesar's *Commentaries*. Caesar had described the Britons as a savage race of people, lacking husbandry and practising barbarous customs: 'Groups of ten or twelve men have wives together in common, and particularly brothers along with brothers, and fathers with sons; but the children born of the unions are reckoned to belong to the particular house to which the maiden was first conducted.'[9] Without Geoffrey's fiction that Caesar had recognized the Britons as kin, the ancient description became a harsh portrait of a primitive culture. Where Geoffrey saw evidence of his people's noble ancestry, Camden saw mere barbarians. In *Britannia*, the Roman conquest was conceived to be the turning point in British history – a salutary period that brought civilization to the savage Britons. Once interpreted as cultural advancement, ancient Britain's submission to Rome became a model in the logic of 'progress', which dictated, in turn, that the Anglo-Britons would transmit this civility by eradicating the residual barbarism of Scotland and Ireland (Canny 'The Ideology of English Colonialization' 588–9).

Yet the loss of a Trojan ancestry also meant that the genealogy of Caesar's primitive Britons had become indistinguishable from the savage races that early modern Britain sought to subdue. In Edmund Bolton's words, once Geoffrey's history is 'abolished there is a vast Blanck upon the Times of our Country, from the Creation of the World till the coming of Julius Caesar',[10] and this blank period lends credence to the argument that ethnological distinctions made between and among Britain's early inhabitants collapse in the absence of genealogical myths. As Scottish historian John Major argued in *A History of Greater Britain* (1521),

all men born in Britain are Britons, seeing that on any other reasoning Britons could not be distinguished from other races; since it is possible to pass from England to Wales, and from Scotland by way of England to Wales, dryshod, there would otherwise be no distinction of races . . . I reckon both Scots and Picts to be alike Britons . . . [11]

It is deeply ironic that a central justification for England's colonial enterprises – the model of Britain's submission to Rome – depended on the obliteration of the Britons' exclusivity. Without clear ancestral ties to the Roman empire, the ancient Britons did not simply resemble the barbarous Picts and Scythians, they joined their mingled ranks.

Yet the revisionary historiography of Richard Verstegan's *A Restitution of Decayed Intelligence* (1605) implies that England's prejudice against the Scots reframed the historical significance of Caesar's invasion yet again. While he acknowledges quite plainly that the episode is an embarrassment in British history, Verstegan also dismisses the encounter as irrelevant to the question of *English* origins. In one of the earliest tracts to insist upon England's Saxon ancestry, Verstegan diffused the most threatening aspect of Caesar's portrait of the Britons: they were a polyandrous, therefore savagely effeminate, society. According to Verstegan various historians:

> wryteth that *Ceasar* in his comentaries saith, that the Englishmen of his tyme had but one woman to serve for ten or twelve men, whereas in deed *Ceasar* never said so, or could so say, for that hee never knew or hard [heard] of the name of Englishmen, seeing their coming into *Britaine* was almost 500. yeares after [Caesar's] death. (Verstegan *Restitution* v)

As descendants of the Saxons, the English had not yet arrived in Britain when Caesar made his conquest. Although Verstegan claims that James is descended from English-Saxon kings, he is much more ambiguous about the racial status of the Scots themselves.[12] This uncertainty proves even more significant when we consider Verstegan's contention that the English-Saxon race had maintained its integrity despite Danish and Norman invasions. As he explains it, the Danes and Normans who came to England were of Germanic extraction.

What ultimately differentiated the myth of Anglo-Saxonism from other genealogies was its racial element (MacDougall *Racial Myth* 129). By reworking Tacitus, who located heroic virtue in the Germanic races' barbaric customs, Verstegan is able to suggest that the Saxons have gained civility not at the expense of their vigour and ruggedness but by virtue of these inherent traits. As opposed to the other mingled populations of Britain, the English-Saxons had supposedly preserved an undiluted genealogy through their adherence to chastity and liberty: not only had they never been conquered, but unlike the polyandrous Britons they were also chaste in marriage (Verstegan *Restitution* 42–50). Verstegan's assertions indicate how Jacobean politics might have reshaped England's historical narrative. As one historian has observed:

> [a]fter 1603, Geoffrey of Monmouth and the old British History rapidly lost credibility and British terminology was consequently freed of its Brut-ish connotations . . . the parallel rise of Anglo-Saxonism and the search for an ancient Gothic constitution merely reinforced the irrelevance of the Scottish past and the Englishness of Britain. (Mason 'The Scottish Reformation' 186)

Once the Saxons displaced the Britons as the progenitors of English history, all of Britain's early martial activity – the valiant acts, the barbarous rebellions, the female savagery, and the ignoble losses – could be ascribed to the clamouring Scots.

CYMBELINE'S HISTORIOGRAPHY

A primary critical crux of *Cymbeline* is that the play's most reprehensible character, the anonymous queen, also voices the most exalted account of Britain's past.[13] Rather than pay tribute to the Romans the queen instigates Britain's rebellion by invoking the legend of Caesar:

> Remember, sir, my liege,
> The kings your ancestors, together with
> The natural bravery of your isle, which stands
> As Neptune's park, ribb'd and pal'd in
> With rocks unscaleable and roaring waters,
> With sands that will not bear your enemies' boats
> But suck them up to th'topmast. A kind of conquest
> Caesar made here, but made not here his brag
> Of 'Came, and saw, and overcame:' with shame
> (The first that ever touch'd him) he was carried
> From off our coast, twice beaten: and his shipping
> (Poor ignorant baubles!) on our terrible seas,
> Like egg-shells mov'd upon their surges, crack'd
> As easily 'gainst our rocks. For joy whereof
> The famed Cassibelan, who was once at point
> (O giglet fortune!) to master Caesar's sword,
> Made Lud's town with rejoicing-fires bright
> And Britons strut with courage.
>
> (3.1.17–34)

Like Voada in the Scottish *Chronicles*, Cymbeline's nameless queen puts Britain in a position of divided yet (from an English perspective) equally degrading allegiances to an effeminate Scottish/British savagery on one side and to Roman rule on the other. As a second wife and 'step-dame', the queen is marked as an outsider who has infiltrated a formerly exclusive domain, and her historical perspective simultaneously represents Caesar's Britons, Geoffrey's Britons, the meddling Scottish historians, and the ancient rebellious Scots. Once we identify the queen as a Scoto-Briton, the insularity of her nationalism becomes a mocking indictment of the British Isle's mingled stock. Given that these Scoto-Britons already yielded to the Romans when Caesar conquered their island,

Cloten's assertion that they 'will nothing pay for wearing [their] own noses' (3.1.13–14) not only invites our ridicule but further highlights the play's ethnological interests. As Camden jests in *Britannia,* the Britons and Romans became so intermingled during the Roman occupation that any historian seeking Trojan origins for the British may as well look to the Romans.[14]

Linking Cloten and the queen to the rebellious Scots recasts their British patriotism as Scottish bravado and justifies the play's celebration of Britain's willing submission to Rome. Having been 'dissuaded by [his] wicked queen' (5.5.464), Cymbeline's rebellion is condemned not only as an effeminately barbarous act, but as an ethnically loaded one as well. Recalling both the matriarchal household of the Britons in Caesar's description and the Britons' devotion to Voada in Boece's history, the British king's defiance is a symptom of uxoriousness. However, Cymbeline's compliance in Act 5 signifies ancient Britain's advancement toward civility and provides a historical model of submission for Scotland to emulate in its union with England. Yielding Britain's early history to the Scots allows the play to censure the Britons' rebellion and undermine the Scottish claim that their people have remained undefiled by conquest.

While the nameless queen may represent the menacing link between female rule and British barbarism, Cloten and his mother are not simply primitive savages. They are barbarians who have become more monstrous in their adoption of cosmopolitan manners and customs. As G. Wilson Knight observed, Cloten's 'worst qualities' are 'habitually associated by Shakespeare with foreign travel or foreign birth' (*The Crown of Life* 136–7). He spends most of his time duelling, bowling, serenading his 'mistress', and his zealous devotion to courtly fashions marks him as ridiculous. His mother assumes a more Machiavellian posture, and her interest in herbs and poisons connects her scheming to its continental origins.[15] By portraying these characters as superficially refined, Shakespeare further underscores their affiliation with Scots, whose close ties with France made them more cosmopolitan than the English in certain ways (Pocock 'Two Kingdoms and Three Histories?' 305). Hence, the play's censure of Cloten and the queen not only denotes the rejection of Britain's originary savagery, but it also renounces the horizontal appropriation of behaviour as a civilizing process.

Bound up in *Cymbeline*'s dissection of Britain's early history are more expansive questions about the generative roots of civility and barbarism: is barbarism purged by the passing of time, conquest, or the appropriation of customs? These questions are explored more extensively in the characterization and actions of Posthumus. Posthumus is Cloten's modern counterpart, and, as such, he embodies both the civilized progression of the British people and their potential for further growth.[16] Estranged from Britain and his wife Imogen, Posthumus represents a Scotland that is poised but not yet prepared to receive England's embrace in union.[17] It is not coincidental that the play introduces Posthumus as a man with mysterious origins: the court gentlemen observe that they cannot 'delve him to the root' (1.1.28). His obscure ancestry recalls the Scots' status in Camden's *Britannia*, which finds only Britons and Anglo-Saxons in Britain's early history and insists that the Scots could not be readily identified. *Cymbeline*'s first scene establishes that the unveiling of Posthumus's genealogy is the play's implicit narrative, made plain on a visual level when he doffs his Italian weeds and assumes the apparel of a Briton peasant.

While the parallels between Cloten and Posthumus point to an ethnological link, the characters' differences suggest that Posthumus is the more refined Scot. Hand in hand with the revelation of Posthumus's genealogy goes the play's exploration of how, and to what degree, the early modern Scoto-Britons have gained civility. Like the queen and Cloten, Posthumus sees himself in Caesar's portrait of the early Britons, but, unlike them, he stresses the Britons' advancement over time:

> Our countrymen
> Are men more order'd than when Julius Caesar
> Smil'd at their lack of skill, but found their courage
> Worthy his frowning at. Their discipline,
> (Now mingled with their courages) will make known
> To their approvers they are people such
> That mend upon the world.
>
> (2.4.20–6)[18]

Posthumus does not merely celebrate the 'natural bravery' of the isle but praises his countrymen's civilized gains in discipline and order. His own virtues have been nurtured by the British court, for the king '[b]reeds him and makes him of his bed-chamber, [and] / Puts to him all the learnings' of the time (1.1.42–3). Yet Posthumus's storyline also implies that he has underestimated how much further his 'people' may need to 'mend'. His vulnerability to foreign influence, his lack of faith in 'Fidele', and his violent temper are the residual vestiges of Scottish barbarism. To eradicate these boorish traits, Posthumus must 'be embrac'd by a piece of tender air' and take a submissive role in his reunion with 'Britain' (5.5.437–8).

As his prophecy states, once Posthumus is 'embraced', Britain will flourish:

When as a lion's whelp shall, to himself unknown, without seeking find, and be embrac'd by a piece of tender air: and when from a stately cedar shall be lopp'd branches, which, being dead many years, shall after revive, be jointed to the old stock, and freshly grow, then shall Posthumus end his miseries, Britain be fortunate, and flourish in peace and plenty. (436–43)

For those Shakespeareans who have connected *Cymbeline* to the Anglo-Scottish union, Posthumus's prophecy looks forward to a united Britain as the fulfillment of Merlin's prediction in Geoffrey of Monmouth that 'the *British Empire* after the *Saxons* and *Normans*, shall return againe to her auncient *Stocke* and *Name*'.[19]

Yet critics tend to gloss over the prophecy's two-pronged struc-ture, often conflating Posthumus's 'embrace' with the recovery of the 'lopp'd branches', identified by the soothsayer as Arviragus and Guiderius (Marcus *Puzzling Shakespeare* 135). The text deliberately sep-arates Posthumus's murky and mingled roots from the genealogical branches of Imogen's brothers, whose own identities had been obscured by a 'search so slow / That could not trace them' (1.1.63–4). While some readers have suggested that the 'lopp'd branches' represent Wales and the exiled Britons of Tudor mythography, this interpretation is challenged by the princes' aliases, Polydore and Cadwal, which subtly allude to the fictional status of Geoffrey's tales (Wickham 'Riddle and Emblem' 110; Marcus *Puzzling Shakespeare* 134). 'Polydore' recalls the historian Polydore Vergil, best known for his challenges to the *Histories of the Kings of Britain*. 'Cadwal' may hint at the noted problem that Geoffrey's Cadwallader appeared to be a distorted version of Bede's Cadwalla.[20] While their false names suggest that the Trojan mythography has overshadowed the English peoples' genuine origins, their actual names prove just as counterfeit. The 'Arviragus' and 'Guiderius' of Holinshed have no real correspondence to Shakespeare's idealized brothers. Guiderius sums up their mysterious status: 'I and my brother are not known.'[21]

Although disguised as Cambro-Britons, Guiderius and Arviragus re-side in a world removed from British historiography.[22] The play's other narrative threads raise the problems of tracing a people's history – the un-certainties that mingling, conquest, and transmigration produce – but the princes' timeless, pastoral scenes concern an atemporal interplay between Britain's natural environment and the brothers' extraordinary temperaments. Cymbeline's lost sons function as foils to the precariously civilized Posthumus and the monstrously 'incivil' Cloten, for unlike these representative Scots, Arviragus and Guiderius have an inherent civility that belies their savage surroundings and excels courtly breeding. Belarius repeatedly marvels at their innate virtues:

> O thou goddess,
> Thou divine Nature; thou thyself thou blazon'st
> In these two princely boys: they are as gentle
> As zephyrs blowing below the violet,
> Not wagging his sweet head; and yet, as rough,
> (Their royal blood enchaf'd) as the rud'st wind
> That by the top doth take the mountain pine
> And make them stoop to th' vale. 'Tis wonder
> That an invisible instinct should frame them
> To royalty unlearn'd, honour untaught,
> Civility not seen from other, valour
> That wildly grows in them, but yields a crop
> As if it had been sow'd.
>
> (4.2.169–81)

The boys share more than an analogous relationship with the rude and gentle winds: this correspondence also denotes the mutuality between their nature and the nature of the place. Unlike continental courtly manners, which signify artifice or portend degeneracy, the princes possess an innately wild civility that is 'untaught', 'unlearned', and resistant to decay. They are paradoxically hardy and gentle, civil and barbaric. Moreover, these mixed qualities are fashioned from within and without: both internal valour and Britain's harsh climate 'enchaf[es]' their blood; an invisible 'instinct', simultaneously savage and royal, 'frame[s]' them. The entangled imagery of wild growth, husbandry, intrinsic heat, and external conditions points to a harmonious convergence between the princes' natures and the natural elements that belies the passage of time.

Although the brothers appear to exist outside the temporal world, their status as warriors is celebrated by a peculiar allusion to a specific event in Holinshed's Scottish chronicles that occurs almost 1,000 years after Cymbeline's reign. When Posthumus recounts the glorious deeds of Arviragus and Guiderius, an attendant lord responds, 'This was strange chance: / A narrow lane, an old man, and two boys' (5.3.51–2). The phrase refers to a farmer and his two sons in the Holinshed's *Historie of Scotland* who were working in a field adjacent to a battle between the Scots and the Danes. When they see the Scots fleeing in fear, they place 'themselves overthwart the lane, beat them backe whome they met fleeing' (*S* 155). In striking contrast to the Scottish accounts of Arviragus and Guiderius, this passage describes the Scots in a moment of cowardice, retreating from the battlefield. The history does not explicitly identify the farmer and his sons as Scots, but praises them instead for taking up the Scottish cause and turning the battle around. By re-enacting the circumstances of this battle *Cymbeline* challenges Scotland's claims of invincibility. More significantly, though, the allusion frames Arviragus and Guiderius as anachronistic figures in Roman Britain. With one swift reference, the play shifts its history forward to the period of Anglo-Saxon rule.

In the same scene that links the brothers to Anglo-Saxon Britain, a British captain enters for no apparent purpose other than to announce ''Tis thought the old man, and his sons, were angels' (85). It may strike us as a throwaway line, until we consider how a commonplace glorification of English-Saxon roots rests on the similarity between 'Angles' and 'Angels'. In his *Remains Concerning Britain* (1605) Camden exalts England's Saxon ancestry by recounting the Venerable Bede's story of how Bishop Gregory recognized the 'Angleshmen', 'for they have Angelike faces, and seeme meete to be made coheires with the Angells in heaven'.[23] On its own, the 'angel' reference hardly seems persuasive; however, the play takes an antiquarian turn in Act 5 that sends us back to Camden's *Remains* and his enthusiastic embrace of England's Saxon heritage. The soothsayer Philharmonus provides the court with what has struck many scholars as a tediously belaboured interpretation of Posthumus's prophecy:

> The piece of tender air, [Cymbeline's] virtuous daughter,
> Which we call *mollis aer*; and *mollis aer*
> We term it *mulier*: which *mulier* I divine
> Is this most constant wife, who even now
> . . .
> Unknown to you [Posthumus], unsought, were clipp'd about
> With this most tender air . . .
> The lofty cedar, royal Cymbeline,
> Personates thee: and thy lopp'd branches point
> Thy two sons forth; who, by Belarius stol'n
> For many years thought dead, are now reviv'd,
> To the majestic cedar join'd; whose issue
> Promises Britain peace and plenty.
>
> (5.5.447–59)

Philharmonus's construction of '*mollis aer*' and '*mulier*' may remind us of the etymological derivations that comprise antiquarian Anglo-Saxon studies.[24] What has not been considered, however, is the striking similarity between the soothsayer's etymology and the phrasing of Camden's statement that the English people are predominantly Saxon in origin. In his description of the Saxons, Camden writes:

This warlike, victorious, stiffe, stowt, and rigorous Nation, after it had as it were taken roote heere about one hundred and sixtie yeares, and spread his branches farre and wide, being mellowed and mollified by the mildenes of the soyle and sweete aire, was prepared in fulnes of time for the first spirituall blessing of God . . . (Camden *Remains* 16)

The parallels between this account of the Saxon race and Shakespeare's text are intriguing: the soothsayer's interpretation resonates with the historian's natural imagery in its references to a tree, its branches, and the effects of the 'sweete aire'. The most compelling link, however, is Camden's use of the word 'mollified' and Philharmonus's etymological discussion of '*mollis aer*'. In the *Remains*, Camden indicates that the mollifying effects of Britain's isle, its sweet air and mild soil, civilized the rude Germanic stock, and that this somatic metamorphosis transformed them into the English race. Shakespeare's '*mollis aer*' also refers to the English climate, or its tender air, before gathering its analogical meaning as Posthumus's 'constant wife'. While Shakespeare's prophecy echoes Camden in its recognition of England's Saxon roots, it also revises its source by characterizing the Scots as the nation to be mollified. Although Posthumus's genealogy remains murky, he is clearly differentiated from the stock and branches of the majestic cedar and just as clearly identified as the object of Britain's civilizing embrace. When we read *Cymbeline* alongside Camden, the prophecy implies that Arviragus and Guiderius, as the Saxon branches, are innately civil.

Just as Arviragus and Guiderius enter the play's course of events by way of the battlefield, the Anglo-Saxons entered English history as conquerors. In celebrating England's Germanic heritage, however, Camden recast the Saxon invasion as a transplantation of 'Angles, Englishmen or Saxons by Gods wonderfull providence' (16). Anticipating the exceptional traits of *Cymbeline*'s 'angels', the historian celebrates the perfect match between the Saxons' hardy barbarism and Britain's 'soyle and sweete aire'. In this originary myth, providence, environment, and genealogy have come together to produce a race of people who will resist the cycle of degeneration implicit in the translation of empires. In staging this historiographical rediscovery of England's Saxon origins, Shakespeare's *Cymbeline* helps establish the exclusivity of English history. By locating

Britain's future growth in the English people's untainted ancestry and native soil, *Cymbeline* anticipates some of the ethnographic myths that will give shape to succeeding chapters in Anglocentric historiography.

NOTES

1 I refer to Joan Warchol Rossi's characterization of the play's criticism a generation ago in '*Cymbeline*'s Debt to Holinshed' 104.

2 On the Anglo-Scottish union and Tudor mythography, see Jones 'Stuart *Cymbeline*' 84–99 and Wickham 'Riddle and Emblem'; on the play's pro-union sentiments, see Marcus *Puzzling Shakespeare* 106–48 and Jordan *Shakespeare's Monarchies* 69–106.

3 John E. Curran, Jr, argues that the play discredits Geoffrey of Monmouth's history in favour of the new historiography ushered in by Camden's *Britannia* (1586); 'Royalty Unlearned, Honor Untaught' 277. Jodi Mikalachki also reads the play as deeply engaged in historiographical issues and contends that it stages the 'exclusion of originary female savagery' from English history; 'The Masculine Romance of Roman Britain' 303.

4 It is customarily presumed that the play's singular debt to Holinshed's *Historie of Scotland* is the refrain in Act 5 'Two boys, and old man twice a boy, a lane' (5.3.57), which I discuss in the second half of this chapter. (All Shakespeare quotations follow the Arden edition of *Cymbeline*, edited by J. M. Nosworthy, and are cited parenthetically in the text.) Rossi appears to be alone in her acknowledgement that other portions of the play may also be derived from the Scottish chronicles ('*Cymbeline*'s Debt to Holinshed' 111).

5 D. R. Woolf identifies this as the explicit goal of Edward Ayscu's *A Historie Contayning the Warres, Treaties, Marriages, and Other Occurrents betweene England and Scotland* (1607) in *The Idea of History in Early Stuart England* 59. Woolf observes that 'little attention has thus far been paid to [the union project's] importance in early Jacobean historical writing' (55).

6 Holinshed *Chronicles* (1587) – *The description and Historie of England* 41. John Bellenden's translation of Hector Boece's *Scotorum Historia* is presumed to be the primary source of Holinshed's *Historie of Scotland*; on the Scottish history's sources and authorship, see Mapstone 'Shakespeare and Scottish Kingship' 160–1. References to the English (*E*) and Scottish (*S*) chronicles are cited parenthetically in the text.

7 Mikalachki identifies Cymbeline's queen with the Boadicea of Holinshed's *The description and Historie of England* but overlooks the Scottish *Chronicles* in her discussion. She does note, however, that John Fletcher's *Bonduca* drew on the Scottish 'account of Voada, a northern queen'; see 'The Masculine Romance of Roman Britain' 311 n. 32.

8 'A Treatise About the Union of England and Scotland' in Galloway and Levack eds. *The Jacobean Union* 49.

9 Julius Caesar *The Gallic War* V:253. Craig cites the Britons' polyandry as evidence of their barbarous past (*De Unione* 389).

10 Bolton in *Hypercritica* (1618) quoted in MacDougall *Racial Myth* 23.

11 [Mair] Major *A History of Greater Britain* (1521) 1.4.18.

12 My understanding of Verstegan's implied opposition to the Scots is derived from Christopher Highley's paper 'Saxons, Britons, and the Jacobean Union', delivered in the 'English and Scots' seminar at the 1997 meeting of the Shakespeare Association of America.

13 On this scene as a critical 'stumbling block', see Mikalachki 'The Masculine Romance of Roman Britain' 303–5.

14 Camden *Britain*, trans. Philemon Holland (1610) 88.

15 In ' "Drug-Damn'd Italy" ' Olsen identifies the queen as the Italianate 'Machiavel-poisoner' and her son as an 'English Ape' (288–9).

16 On Cloten as a parody of Posthumus, see Hartwig 'Cloten, Autolycus, and Caliban' 91–103.

17 Marcus contends that Posthumus represents the 'Post Nati' – James's Scottish subjects born after his accession to England's throne, who in the 1608 legal case were 'declared citizens, entitled to recourse at English law' (Marcus *Puzzling Shakespeare* 124).

18 I have followed the Globe text in adopting the second Folio's reading of 'mingled', rather than Nosworthy's use of the Folio's 'wing-led'.

19 Quoted in Jones 'Stuart *Cymbeline*' 90.

20 Curran 'Royalty Unlearned, Honor Untaught' 286.

21 For these points, see Curran 'Royalty Unlearned, Honor Untaught' 286–7. For a contrary view, see Boling 'Anglo-Welsh Relations in *Cymbeline*'. In Boling's reading, the brothers are representative of Wales and its historical subjection to an anglicizing and civilizing process.

22 On the brothers' 'exclusion from history', see Mikalachki 'The Masculine Romance of Roman Britain' 314.

23 Camden *Remains* 16.

24 Mikalachki notes that the 'display of pseudo-etymology recalls the involved and equally fanciful antiquarian derivations of the name *Britain*' ('The Masculine Romance of Roman Britain' 320).

IV

Union questions

CHAPTER 8

Reinventing the matter of Britain: undermining the state in Jacobean masques

Philippa Berry and Jayne Elisabeth Archer

This chapter traces a literary discourse of and around Union – one that affords an important parallel, but also a suggestive contrast, to the political debate on this question which was staged in early Jacobean society. That debate, despite its occasional use of poetic imagery, concentrates on the forms which Union could or should take; in the Jacobean masque, however, a literary version of the same debate remaps the new Britain via subtle explorations of the inherent mutability of states, as these texts oscillate between contrasting images: on the one hand, of binding or fixing the new state, and, on the other, of radically excavating or undermining that English kingdom which 'Britain' was expected imminently to replace. In the process, the masques uncover a distinctive 'matter' of Britain, in the form of a cultural but also a geo-physical residue that is shaped not only by a re-membered and reimagined archaic past (derived from ancient and antiquarian sources) but also by alchemical and scientific interest in the hidden resources of the land. As the masques position themselves at the intersection of these processes of reminding and re-mining, they perform a quasi-archaeological function, whereby they 'indent' and dissolve an existing national identity in order to discover or excavate its archaic precursors. In this process, Elizabethan tropes of the English body politic as a grassy mound, green bower, or adamantine rock are figuratively 'undermined', while what is repeatedly revealed is an emblematic lacuna, hole, or gap at the centre of the new state. This masque-like 'discovery' of a new Britain that, borrowing a device from mannerist garden design, (re-)founds itself upon a grotto-like recess or cavity poses important questions about the paradoxical situation of England within a United Britain.

One of many riddling prophecies invoked in connection with the accession of James VI of Scotland to the English throne was 'When hemp is spunne, England's done', and a recurring theme in these semi-dramatic events is a reassimilation or dissolution of 'England' into an archaic (implicitly Celtic) past.[1] Although troped in James's entry to London as the privileged (and privy) 'Chamber' of his new kingdom, direct references to 'England' are notably absent from the Jacobean masque, as the former potency of the Elizabethan state is figuratively elided beneath the diverse façades of Britannia. A recurring image of the English realm under its unmarried queen was as a hollow, quasi-feminine receptacle. Yet in these Jacobean representations, England is emblematically buried, to be replaced by very different conceptions of a hollow British state, whose recessive or subterranean spaces suggest both the archaic origins of the new kingdom and its potential resources for the future.

A HOLLOW REED: THE ENGLISH STATE UNDER ELIZABETH

Critical assumptions about the firmly bounded nature of the Elizabethan state, especially as represented in relation to the body of an unmarried female monarch, run very deep. Only consider Peter Stallybrass's much-cited essay, 'Patriarchal Territories', where, in a critical tour-de-force that is nonetheless based on a reading (common to many critics) of her 'virgin' body as completely sealed, Stallybrass argues that the motif of physical enclosure was central to representations of Elizabeth and/as the Elizabethan state:

> The [Elizabethan] state, like the virgin, was a *hortus conclusus*, an enclosed garden walled off from enemies. In the Ditchley portrait, Elizabeth I is portrayed standing upon a map of England. As she ushers in the golden age, she is the imperial virgin, symbolizing, at the same time as she is symbolized by, the *hortus conclusus* of the state . . .
> But not only was Elizabeth the maker of that 'paradeice' or 'gardein'; her enclosed body was that paradise (a word derived from the Persian *pairidaeza*, meaning a royal enclosure) projected onto a religious plane, her body was the garden of the Song of Songs, which was interpreted both as the body of the Virgin and as the body of a Church that John King portrayed as 'a several, peculiar, enclosed piece of ground', a *hortus conclusus* that 'lithe within a hedge or fense', separated off from '*the grape of Sodome* or *cluster of Gomorrhe*'. (Stallybrass 'Patriarchal Territories' 130–1)

Stallybrass is right in his assertion that the enclosed garden is a recurring emblem of the English state under Elizabeth. Yet his invocation of this essentially medieval *topos* requires some modification. For example, literary allusions to Elizabethan England as a bounded (and implicitly island) state often invested these bounds with a quasi-sexual permeability, as in the cartographic self-description of Shakespeare's lustful Venus, who tells Adonis: 'since I have hemm'd thee here / Within the circuit of this ivory pale, / I'll be a park, and thou shalt be my deer'.² At the same time, they could also imply a more ambiguous lack of distinctive boundaries *within* the state. Many such references occur, of course, in plays which explore the results of poor government or civil war, such as *Richard II*, where 'This fortress built by Nature for herself' (2.1.43) is 'now leas'd out . . . / Like to a tenement or pelting farm' (2.1.59–60), and where 'our sea-wallèd garden' has 'her hedges ruined' by civil strife (3.4.44–6).³

A number of critics have pointed out that the complex web of allusions to England within *Richard II* has a striking contemporaneity with the restive England of Elizabeth in the final decade of her reign; yet not only does its figurative opposition of substance to hollowness articulate a recurring theme in Elizabethan representations of the state; it also anticipates the Jacobean relocation of England in relation to a British polity. For it is not only civil unrest, but also imperialist ambition, that requires the royal birth-passage imagined by Gaunt repeatedly to be vacated, in a manner both like and unlike the empty tomb in Jerusalem toward which its offspring are figuratively oriented:

> This nurse, this teeming womb of royal kings,
> Feared by their breed and famous by their birth,
> Renowned for their deeds as far from home
> For Christian service and true chivalry
> As is the sepulchre, in stubborn Jewry,
> Of the world's ransom, blessèd Mary's son.
>
> (2.1.51–6)

In its opposition of fullness and plenitude with mystical vacancy, the movement of this passage, from 'nurse' and 'teeming womb' to the empty 'sepulchre' of Christ, suggestively relocates English royal identity through its metonymic proximity to a foreign and uniquely holy 'tomb': one whose potency depends, paradoxically, upon its emptiness. Hence the centre of this paradisal realm is already (*before* the 'fall' attributed to Richard) defined by loss and absence rather than by presence. On Richard's deposition, this paradox assumes material form in the 'bank of rue' (a floral monument defined by the loss and regret which rue represents) that the Gardener proposes to plant in memory of Richard's 'weeping queen'; this trope derives from a long-established emblematic representation of the state as the mound, bank, or hill, upon which a monarch stood or sat.

A notable allusion to the state-as-mound occurs in Edmund Spenser's 'April Eclogue' for *The Shepheardes Calender*, where we are told of Eliza/ Elizabeth:

> See, where she sits upon the grassie greene,
> (O seemely sight!)
> Yclad in Scarlot like a mayden Queene,
> And Ermines white.[4]

Although a poetic frame or boundary is constructed around this much-cited image (by Hobbinoll's recitation of Colin's song), it is striking that the Elizabethan state is imaged here as an unbounded tract of land, since 'greene' denotes 'A piece of public or common grassy land situated in or near a town or village, from which it often takes its name, a "village green".'[5] One implication in this image of the 'greene' is that the English monarch's power is based upon the open 'commons' or common land, rather than on a private or *enclosed* aristocratic estate; however, the indistinct boundaries of Eliza's 'grassie greene' also reinforce the eclogue's covert expression of Protestant anxiety about the queen's possible marriage to a Catholic prince: Spenser's semi-bridal figuration of Eliza/beth (in a putatively ironic anticipation of her proposed marriage to the French Duc d'Alençon) accounts for the implicit openness of her realm, as his eclogue's subsequent emphasis upon her toilette invests Eliza's grassy environment – her state – with the attributes of a bridal bower which may soon be vacated (as a result of marriage to a foreign prince). The implication of the 'April Eclogue', that the Tudor polity is a secretive yet vulnerable space within which the monarch is paradoxically both present and absent, anticipates Colin's subsequent allusions to Dido's 'herse' and Pan's 'green cabinet' in the November and December 'Eclogues'. (It also invests John of Gaunt's later evocation of Richard II as a type of absentee landlord with a plausible topicality amidst the political unease of the mid-1590s.) Thus Spenser's 1579 poem allusively articulates the curious motif of a (necessary?) political hollowness within the English state. The ambivalently erotic dimension of this hollowness is stressed in its reference to Eliza as 'Pan and Syrinx's daughter without spotte', who is engendered through the *hollow reed* which Pan played on after Syrinx's metamorphosis.

Hence a distinctive strand of Elizabethan political imagery configures the English state under Elizabeth not so much as an enclosed garden but rather as a hollow receptacle that is repeatedly on the point either of being vacated (in quasi-imperialist movements beyond its boundaries), or of attracting a violating/inseminating intrusion from outside. In two dramatic events staged near the end of Elizabeth's reign there were highly suggestive anticipations of the Jacobean re-deployment of this imagery. On Shrove Tuesday 1595, when the future accession of James VI of Scotland was already regarded by many at court as a political necessity, the lawyers of Gray's Inn performed 'The Masque of Proteus and the Adamantine Rock' at their Christmas revels, in a daring allusion to the political tensions attendant on this realization.[6] In its representation of the antimasque forces of disorder, presided over by Proteus, the god of ceaseless transformation, this masque dramatizes a threat to the pivotal centrality of England within the region of the British isles, as Proteus's magnetic or 'adamantine' rock is substituted for the familiar mound or rock of state so often used in Tudor pageantry, and is appropriated by Scotland. We are told that Proteus is able, through his power, to 'remove and plant' this rock in a new location:

> whereas he should appoint: assuring him,
> That the wide Empire of the Ocean
> (If his foretelling spirit faild him not,)
> Should follow that, wheare ere it should be sett.
>
> (ll. 152–5)

Like the polar star, we are told, this rock 'draws the needle to the North': it relocates the political centre of gravity, or 'the wide Empire of the Ocean', in relation to Scotland. Against the allurements of this rock, the Christmas Prince posits Elizabeth herself, the masque's royal spectator, as the 'trew *adam*ant of hartes' (our emphasis), who effortlessly draws her loyal subjects back to a state of *adam*ic grace. Ultimately, Proteus's rock splits apart to reveal the Prince and his knights, before Proteus and his water gods are re-enclosed therein. Since Elizabeth is herself the 'blessed rock' of 'Britton land', it is concluded, Proteus's hollow rock is a superfluous gift. Yet emphasis upon the negative magnetism and historical mutability of the Elizabethan court is the central motif of Ben Jonson's *The Fountaine of Selfe-Love: or Cynthia's revells* (staged in 1600), which subjected this court to a final satire (albeit one thinly masked under the guise of courtly compliment).[7] For the 'christall *mound*, a note of monarchie, and symbol of perfection', is here a *gift*, presented to Cynthia by her loyal courtiers at the play's close. Moreover, the state-as-gift is ironically embedded in a play that is uniquely concerned with the ephemeral commodities or accessories of ever-changing courtly fashion. By implication, the English state is now perceived as an especially luxurious commodity:

an object, in other words, that is no longer stable but in circulation, and is threatened with a mirror-like shadow of 'declining night' through its infection by the consumerist 'maladies' of a decadent court. The veiled Cynthia, queen and moon goddess, who at her full moon is poised on the verge both of eclipse and of a final decision about the succession, declares enigmatically 'Our empire is but of the darker halfe', although she concludes that 'A vertuous *Court* a world to vertue drawes'. It seems plausible that Jonson's allusion in *The Fountaine of Selfe-Love* to the English court's negative as well as positive magnetism gestures toward an anticipated invasion from the North; certainly the evidence of these two texts suggests that by the late 1590s the magnetic properties attributed to the English state were in crisis. On James's accession, however, this mysterious imagery of magnetism would become explicitly allied with the project of Union. At the same time, a quasi-magnetic memorial affiliation is explored, between the archaic past and an imagined British future, as diverse representations of barbarous disorder – 'native forms' or 'native manners' – are invoked as a kind of moral and memorial touchstone. Indeed, an important figurative strand within Union-inspired literature expands on classical allusions to the British as 'the nations on whom the Pole Star looks down', whose island 'lies under the Great Bear', the constellation 'that circleth ever in her place' (never disappearing beneath the horizon).[8] Following the acceptance of Copernicus's hypothesis of the earth's planetary status, both the new Britain and its ruler are equated with the polar stars as the 'loadstone' or fixed point within the newly mobile globe in *The Masque of Beautie* (1608), where James as another Phoebus is revealed to be a source of stellar rather than solar light, since 'his attractive beames, that lights these skies /... (though with th'*Ocean* compass'd) never wets / His hayre therein, nor wears a beames that sets' (ll. 389–91).[9] The paradoxically 'fixed' movement of the new Britain or Albion is here compared (with the help of Inigo Jones's machinery) to the movement of the heavens around the 'hinge' of the polar stars: 'Still turne, and imitate the heaven / In motion swift and even ... But let your state, the while, / be fixed as the Isle' (ll. 399–400, 404–5).

UNION AND THE SECRET CHAMBERS OF THE PAST

In his 1611 *Theatre of the Empire of Great Britain* John Speed would describe chronology as 'the onely touch-stone [or magnet] to the truth of histories'. A few years earlier, when Sir Francis Bacon compliments James in his *Advancement of Learning* (1605) on the centrality accorded to memory in his kingly intelligence, correct historical 'remembrance' is associated with a final, providential fixing of both national identity and royal genealogy:

Plato's opinion sometimes comes into my mind, which maintains, *That knowledge is nothing else but remembrance; and that the mind of man by nature knows all things, once redimed and restored to her own native light, which the cloudy vault or glorious tabernacle of the body had orespread with darkness.* For certainly the best and clearest instance for this Assertion shines in your Majesty . . .
[T]his happy and glorious event; . . . that this island divided from all the world, should be united in it self; by which that ancient oracle given to *Aeneas,* which presaged rest unto him; *Antiquam exquirite Matrem;* should be fulfill'd upon the most noble nations of England and Scotland, now united in that name of *Britannia, their ancient Mother,* as a Pledge and Token of the Period and Conclusion, now found of all Wandrings and Peregrination. *So that as massive bodies* once shaken, feel certain trepidations before they fix and settle; so it seems probable, that by the Providence of God, it hath come to pass, *That this Monarchy, before it should settle and be establish'd in your Majesty and your Royal Progeny* . . . it should undergoe so many changes, and vicissitudes, as prelusions of future stability.[10]

Bacon's Latin tag from Book III of the *Aeneid* associates James's project of Union with Aeneas's oracular advice from Apollo, to 'seek out your ancient mother'. The additional association of *exquiro* with an investigation or 'searching into', however, was rather more applicable to the memorial aspects of Union, since in several Jacobean masques the mound, hill, or cliff of state is literally cleft open to reveal its inner secrets. These numerous acts of discovery imply not so much the insemination of the formerly virgin English soil as the revelation of archaic, pre-English forms of materiality. In this staging of a distinctive form of national anamnesis, the early Jonsonian masques of *Blacknesse* and *Beauty* ally what subsequent masques would term 'native forms' and 'native manners' with a dark racial difference, as the roles of Ethiopian nymphs played by Queen Anna and her ladies imply a highly emblematic revision of the gross, feminized materiality that had persistently shadowed courtly compliment to Elizabeth I, now invested with a prodigious fertility and magnetic potency.[11] As later masques similarly configure a formerly abjected 'British' past as the gateway to a new future, their quasi-archaeological or geological preoccupations uncover a mobile fluidity or hollowness at the centre of the new political entity. By excavating and redefining 'native forms' and 'native manners', the Jacobean masque attempts to realize and harness chaos, in the form of the subterranean potency of the state, along with its archaic past, in order to create a space (both figurative and material) in which new political forms – and manners – can be inaugurated.

The Britain reimagined in the masques is unequivocally the scene of a new fruitfulness, in which opposing principles, including England and Scotland, female and male, nature and science, are repeatedly united in order to forge 'some strange, and curious peece' – or peace.[12] It is also the site of implicit anxiety, however, both about the putative 'barbarism' of the past, and about the ambiguous character of the secreted centre to this national identity. This anxiety is equally apparent, yet quite differently staged, in Jonson's *An Entertainment . . . at Theobalds* and Thomas Campion's *Lord Hay's Masque*, both performed early in 1607, at the height of the Union debate. In each event, James's new kingdom is situated in relation to a secret and concealed space, whose combination of especial sanctity with an inherent duality of meaning (plausibly denoting both the new state's elided English centre and its pre-English origins) is suggestively figured by double veils. In *An Entertainment*, performed when the great house of Theobalds in Hertfordshire was given to James I by Robert Cecil, recently appointed Earl of Salisbury, the Roman conception of the household gods is used to treat themes that, although apparently specific to the event, resonate suggestively with the Union debate. The company:

being entered into a gallery after dinner; there was seene nothing but a traverse of white, acrosse the roome: which sodainely drawne, was discovered a gloomie obscure place, hung all with black silkes, and in it only one light, which the GENIUS of the house held, sadly attir'd; his Cornucopia ready to fall out of his hand. (ll. 2–8)

The Genius is sad because he must 'in the twylight of sere age, / Begin to seeke a habitation new; / And . . . . himself engage / Unto a seat, his fathers never knew' (ll. 16–19). Yet:

the black vanishing, was discovered a glorious place, figuring the Lararium, or seat of the household gods, where both the Lares, *and* Penates, *were painted, in copper colours; erected with Columnes and Architrabe, Freeze, and Coronice, in which were placed divers Diaphanall glasses, fill'd with transparent waters, that shew'd like so many stones, of orient and transparent hiewes.* (ll. 26–32)

In this inner sanctum, where a new, more elaborate, order of household gods has seemingly been installed, the dispensation of fate is revealed by Mercury and the three Parcae; the Genius will remain, but will now serve Queen Anna, and through her, King James: 'Then, GENIUS, is thy period come, / To change thy Lord: thus, Fates doe doome' (ll. 71–2). In Roman antiquity, the Penates were often understood as the guardian deities of

the state as well as of the individual household (since the state was understood as the union of households); through this modest spectacle,
therefore, what seems obliquely alluded to is the historical redefinition
of the English genius, both through its change of lord and in its intended
assimilation into a new geographic order, in imagery that implies memorial recession (into the Lararium or inner shrine of the house, and into
the depths of ancient culture) as well as the end of a historical 'period'.

Lord Hay's Masque celebrates the marriage of James's Scottish-born
former favourite, James, Lord Hay, with an English heiress, Honora
Denny. Its complex scenery again depicts Britain's inner sanctum as a
'shrouded' place of concealment: of darkness, shadows, and obscurity.[13]
The higher stage, 'enclosed with a double veil', is only gradually un-
veiled, to reveal a grove with enchanted trees of gold, and, at the centre,
Diana's tree. Diana/Cynthia does not herself appear in the masque,
but Night is her spokeswoman in the attempt to defend her 'holy forest' (by implication, the Elizabethan idea of England) against the assault on its nymphs by Phoebus's knights (James's Scottish lords), who
have been metamorphosed into trees in punishment for this transgres-
sion. At the climax of the masque, however, the darkly veiling powers of
Night and Diana suddenly yield, as the trees move to reveal the 'native
forms' of the male masquers, and the earth effectively admits the 'native'
(British or Celtic) priority and authority of the Scottish knights:

> Night and Diana charge,
> And th'Earth obeys,
> Opening large
> Her secret ways,
> While Apollo's charmèd men
> Their forms receive again.
>
> (ll. 416–21)

Although this masque ends with a celebration of marriage, it also
seems explicitly concerned to safeguard the secret and enclosed 'chastity'
of England, represented by Diana's 'holy' tree, around which the freed
knights are required to make a final solemn procession. Yet its secret
grove is evocative of antiquarian accounts of Druidic rites in ancient oak
groves, while its emphasis upon the relationship of the opening Earth to
'native forms' implies that alongside the sanctity of place (Diana's grove,
England) an originary claim of residence, relegitimated by the trope of
marriage or union, can also be made by the race which the knights
represent. In both these events, the constitution of Britain is dramatized

firstly through processes of veiling/revelation, and secondly through an interrogation of the 'secret' spaces, the hidden energies, that are being reclaimed for a new matter of Britain.

In Renaissance texts of natural philosophy as well as alchemy the examination of the forms and processes of matter was often figured as an opening followed by a descent into the bowels of the earth, represented as a watery cave or grotto, followed by the philosopher's triumphant re-emergence with greater wisdom and spiritual insight. Hinting at both the prophetic and the political potential of such an investigation, this commonplace was expounded in François Rabelais's *Cinquiesme Livre*:

[W]hen you're back in your world, bear witness to the fact that the great treasures and wonderful things are underground... Your philosophers who complain that everything has been written by the ancients, nothing new has been left for them to invent, are only too evidently wrong. What appears to you of heaven and what you call phenomena, what the earth offers to your sight, what the sea and other waters contain, is not to be compared with what is hidden inside the earth.[14]

Behind this philosophical motif lay scientific as well as political imperatives. Following Tycho Brahe, who devised 'Crypteria' and garden 'caves' in which to pursue his alchemical and astronomical experiments, Sir Francis Bacon was to choose 'large and deep caves' for the natural philosophical work pursued in his *New Atlantis*.[15] Bacon designed an island-grotto for the artificial lake he excavated at Gorhambury House, while Thomas Bushell, his former laboratory assistant, designed the Enstone Marvels in Oxfordshire, a grotto enclosed within a house that served for a kind of philosophical hermitage (Strong *The Renaissance Garden* 127, 130). Dark, wet, and warm, such spaces, it was believed, provided the womb-like conditions necessary for the generation of metals. Like Elizabeth, James appeared eager from the start of his reign to exploit the potential material benefits of this philosophical tradition, continuing her patronage of the engineers and chymists who promised to transmute the old matter of England and Scotland into the gold of a prosperous, imperial Britain.[16]

Yet in the Jonsonian masques of Union the opening of the earth is troped as an inherently dangerous process, since it is associated with both antimasque as well as masque elements, and with the dissolution, as well as the constitution, of political forms. In *Hymenaei* (1606), Jonson's most explicit masque of Union, it is male representatives of the disorderly humours and affections that need to be directed appropriately, both within Union and in marriage, who emerge first from a mine or grotto within the masque machine:

the first part of which was a μικρόκοσμος, or *Globe*, fill'd with *Countryes*, and those gilded; where the *Sea* was exprest, heightened with silver waves. This stood, or rather hung (for no *Axell* was seene to support it) and turning softly, discovered the first *Masque* . . . which was of the *men*, sitting in faire *composition*, within a *mine* of several metalls: to which, the lights were so placed, as no one was seene; but seemed, as if onely REASON, with the splendor of her crowne, illumin'd the whole Grot. (ll. 633–42)

Through their distinctive setting in a mine or 'Grot', the moral disorder which the men represent is allied with the hidden richness of the earth, and by implication with the mineral wealth of James's new kingdom. Indeed, Jonson's specific allusion may be to English mineral wealth and related industries, since his patron, William Herbert, third Earl of Pembroke, was a major shareholder, along with Robert Cecil, in the two English mining companies of the day, whose Elizabethan royal charters were renewed by James in 1604 and 1605.[17]

In *The Haddington Masque* of 1608 (a marriage masque for which the Earl of Pembroke was himself one of the male masquers), a parted red cliff, emblematic of the defloration of the bride (from the English family of Radcliffes), reveals the hidden resources of Britain/England in the form of Vulcan's subterranean forge, situated within '*an illustrious* Concave' in the rock. The grotesque as well as grotto-esque character of this secret domain is personified by the monstrous Cyclops, whose potential disorder has been harnessed in service to Vulcan/James as divine 'artificer', in order to fashion 'some strange, and curious peece': a material copy of the celestial sphere. The complimentary reference, to James's projected creation of heaven on or within earth in the new Britain, once again allies Britain with a paradoxical fixity in movement equivalent to that of the celestial (and magnetic) poles. It also hints, though, that a quasi-colonial exploitation of English economic resources, as well as skills, will be central to this process; certainly English smiths and iron-works were claimed by William Camden, as early as 1586, to enjoy an international reputation.[18] The abundant potential energy latent in Britain as a new kind of 'artificer' is figured by the Cyclops, whose use of their hammers to 'strike a time' for the final dance suggests the necessary intersection of industry with harmony in the new Britain. A similar theme, of a curiously inward-looking empire, determined to exploit its own resources more fully, would be treated more explicitly in *Tethys Festivall*.

Jonson's first explicitly identified 'antimasque', in *The Masque of Queenes* (1609), develops these subterranean motifs, although once again it encodes them with an overtly negative valency. His hags or witches emerge from an 'ougly *Hell*', declaring themselves 'faythfull Opposites / To *Fame* and *Glory*', and threaten to 'Mixe Hell, with heaven; and make Nature fight / Within her Selfe; loose the whole henge of Things / And cause the Endes runne back into their Springs' (ll. 147–9). Yet in spite of their opposition to the 'henge' or hinge upon which Union figuratively depends, the witches repeat a central motif of Union through their very attraction to division: this is their desire to 'cleave the ground, as low as lies / Old shrunke-up Chaos; and let rise / Once more his darke, and reeking head' (l. 311–13). Moreover, the *Queenes* antimasque dramatizes the necessary relationship between political 'Endes' and their chaotic, watery 'Springs', between Union and the 'antique' origins of the state – or what the witches refer to as 'native manners' (l. 142) – as an *anteriority* or pre-history that is also 'Anti-' or *antic*. The structural affinity of the masque's representations of virtue and vice, as 'faythfull Opposites', is of course implicit in the turning stage machinery of Inigo Jones, which replaces the 'ougly *Hell*' with the House of Fame. Moreover, the witches are not dispelled forever on the appearance of the masque of Fame, led by the queen as Bel-Anna, queen of the Ocean; instead, like the Cylops in *The Haddington Masque*, their archaic monstrosity is implied to be a necessary attribute of the new Britain, once properly directed, for they are 'led, as Captives, bound' (l. 472) before the queens' three chariots in the final triumph. The message is seemingly that the new political golden age, in asserting its 'antique birth', must address the full complexity of an archaic historical legacy, reopening the question of 'native manners' in order successfully to bind or contain the turbulent energies of place, or of 'Dame Earth'. Yet whereas the elemental mechanism of Union in *The Haddington Masque* was the fire of Vulcan's forge (as it had been air in the preceding masque of *Hymenaei*), the Elizabethan role accorded here to Anna, as a Cynthia-like queen of the Ocean, implies that the watery boundary of the sea is what most obviously binds or unites the new Britain.

THE OBSCURE SPRINGS OF THE NEW BRITAIN:
WATERY ENDS AND BEGINNINGS

Thus the Jacobean masque accords different elements subtly different tasks in shaping the new matter of Britain. Yet the emblematic function of water in these masques is arguably that of greatest importance, not only as a receptacle nor simply as a vehicle for constituting Britain, but also as a more 'subtle' aspect of national origin: its rediscovered 'Spring' or source. In the alchemist's work of *solve et coagula*, the *solutio*, the dissolution of the old matter in the alembic, was the first step which catalysed a reduction into the *nigredo*, or blackening, as the primary ingredients were broken down into a formless, watery state (the *prima materia*), prior to their reconstitution in a superior form – the first stage of which was the whitening of the substance, termed the *albedo*. In the first two Jonsonian masques the alchemical imagery of *solutio* enjoys a figurative prominence which appears to allude both to the dissolution of a redundant image of England and also to the necessary relationship between James as Albion (a name of Britain which signified whiteness) and the kingdom's original black-print, in the form of a watery primal source that is ultimately implied to be both African and English.

Several antiquarian studies had credited Ethiopia and Egypt as the originary fonts not simply of the arts and sciences, but of Scottish (and thus British) identities.[19] In *The Masque of Blacknesse* the Ethiopian nymphs are the daughters of a river (Niger) which several ancient authorities equated with the Nile, as Jonson notes, and granddaughters of the ancient Oceanus, described by Homer as 'backward-flowing', and as the source from which all the gods are sprung. In keeping with this emblematic origin, the Nymphs' quest is paradoxically for a *beginning* which can complete an end – specifically, for the syllable 'Brit' which precedes '-tania'. Magnetically drawn to the future Britain by their quest for a more refined or white beauty (personified by James as Albion), the daughters of Niger are advised by Aethiopia, the moon goddess, to wash in 'that purer brine / And wholesome dew, call'd *Ros-marine*' (339–40): this was a synonym for the alchemical solvent (and coagulant) of mercury, whose homonymic affinity with the herb rosemary also evokes the idea of memory of a former state. (Mercury was also a central constituent in the 'fucus', a cosmetic preparation that was black when applied but whose effect was to whiten the face.) Yet while this focus upon whitening clearly alludes to the alchemical stage of the *albedo*, *The Masque of Blacknesse* leaves this transformation unaccomplished. Moreover, in their final dance, the 'indenting' of white Albion's earth by the dark yet watery footprints of these 'Daughters of the subtle flood' implies a dissolution and reclamation of national identity that parallels yet chiastically inverts their own anticipated metamorphosis.[20]

In early modern Britain the materiality of 'blackness' was specifically associated with the wisdom of ancient Egypt and Ethiopia (with which

Egypt was often conflated), but this blackness is explicitly allied with Celtic antiquity in Camden's description of the ancient Britons' use of woad:

There groweth an herbe in Gaule like unto Plantaine, named Glastum, that is Woad, with the juice whereof, the women of Britaine, as well maried wives as their young daughters anoint and die their bodies all over; resembling by that tincture *the colour of Æthiopians*, in which maner they use at some solemne feasts and sacrifices to goe all naked. (Camden *Britannia* 31)

The masque's closing motif of 'indenting' implies that ultimately the Ethiopian nymphs themselves serve as the remembered agents of the process of national transmutation, providing, as it were, the genetic *prima materia* from which the new 'British' king derives, Solomon-like, his wisdom and power. In their black antiquity, however, they have an obvious affinity not only with the apocryphal figure of Sheba, but also with the Egyptian moon goddess Isis, whom Aethiopia appears to represent. Richard Linche, for example, observes that 'the Aegyptians... worshipped the Moone under the name of Isis and her they depicted covered with a blacke and sable vesture in token that of her selfe shee giveth no light' – veils which remind us of those which shroud the occluded inner chamber of a new national identity at the beginning of *An Entertainment... at Theobalds* and *Lord Hay's Masque*.[21]

In the succeeding *Masque of Beauty*, performed two years later, a second *solutio* or dissolution is accomplished, as the nymphs are finally 'received' into the river Thames, or 'Thamesis', whose name reminds us that one of its sources is the English river named the Isis:

> Rise, aged *Thames*, and by the hand
> Receive these *Nymphes*, within the land:
> And, in those curious *Squares*, and *Rounds*,
> Wherewith thou flow'st betwixt the grounds
> Of fruitfull *Kent*, and *Essex* faire,
> That lent thee gyrlands for thy haire:
> Instruct their silver feet to tread,
> Whilst we, again to sea, are fled.
>
> (ll. 300–7)

The Ethiopian nymphs' final 'reverence to the place' is identified once again with a dance-like mobility, but also with the 'curious' (a word which currently had the implication of strange, even occult) serpentine movement of a specifically English river, now reconfigured as an emblem of the assimilation of dark African origins. John Thornborough evoked a not dissimilar process when he described Union in terms of a 'transfusion', used by 1601 of pouring liquid from one vessel to another: 'So now it concerneth all, and every one Subject, both of England, and Scotland, to participate in the common obedience, transfused into all, under the government of one' (Thornborough *A Discourse* 107–8).

In its staging of a mechanical and grotto-esque version of that 'green cabinet' which Spenser had used to figure the Elizabethan state, the Jacobean masque allies a new Britishness with the obligatory reinvestigation of the material components and 'springs' of British identity. Through their incorporation and development of motifs borrowed from diverse discourses – from the new science, engineering, garden design, and alchemy, as well as from classical literature and myth – these events produce a stylized version of James's new kingdom in which alternative narratives of origin are assimilated or 'transfused' with the familiar Elizabethan motifs of sovereignty, with the result that England's former territorial substantiality is effectively dissolved or undermined. What replaces this, however, is a distinctly mobile or hollow version of the site, in which a pre-English origin, whether watery or subterranean or both, is troped as the concealed spring, centre, or hinge of the new matter of Britain. While this obscure and grail-like origin often has grotesque attributes to signify its perceived barbarism, it is also depicted as a site of enormous fertility and abundance, whose formerly concealed resources are implied to be newly available for detailed investigation – and hence for exploitation.

NOTES

1 Cited by Sir Francis Bacon in his essay, 'Of Prophecies': 'whereby it was generally conceived that after the princes had reigned which had the principial letters of that words hempe (which were Henry, Edward, Mary, Philip, and Elizabeth), England should come to utter confusion, which, thanks be to God, is verified only in the change of name, for that the King's style is now no more of England but of Britain'. See Dobin *Merlin's Disciples* 112.

2 Shakespeare *Venus and Adonis* ll. 229–31. Citations are taken from the Arden edition.

3 Citations from Shakespeare *Richard II* are taken from the Arden edition.

4 Spenser *The Shepheardes Calender* (1579), Aprill, ll. 55–8.

5 *OED* 'green', definition 12 a. The earliest citation is 1477.

6 This masque was discussed in a very perceptive account by Marie Axton *The Queen's Two Bodies* ch. 7.

7 The first, quarto, title of the play is *The Fountaine of Selfe-Love*. See Herford and Simpson *Ben Jonson* IV – *Cynthia's Revels* V.vii.15–23, V.xi.3–4, 174. The

play is exactly contemporary with William Gilbert's *De Magnete*, published in London in 1600. For Jonson's subsequent exploration of magnetism in *The Magnetic Lady* (1632), see McFarland 'Jonson's *Magnetic Lady*'.

8 Lucan *Pharsalia* 1 458–60; *Diodorus Siculus* III.v.21; Homer *The Iliad* I.xviii. 487–9.

9 All quotations from Jonsonian masques are from Herford and Simpson *Ben Jonson* VII.

10 Bacon *Advancement of Learning* I: 2, II: 61.

11 For an account of this less complimentary 'shadow' to Elizabeth's courtly cult, see Berry *Of Chastity and Power*, especially ch. 6.

12 Jonson *The Haddington Masque* (l. 252).

13 In his *Thomas Campion*, David Lindley gives a very detailed and interesting discussion of this masque and its relationship to the Union debate (176–90).

14 François Rabelais *Works* ch. 47 715–16.

15 Bacon *New Atlantis* (1627) in *A Critical Edition* 480–1.

16 On Elizabeth's patronage of engineers and chymists, see Webster 'Alchemical and Paracelsian Medicine'. In using the term 'chymists' we follow the precedent set by Principe *The Aspiring Adept* 8–9.

17 See Donald *Elizabethan Copper* 242, where the names of shareholders in 1605 are listed, and Hamilton *The English Brass and Copper Industries* 82, where shareholders of the Mineral and Battery Works are listed.

18 In Camden's *Britannia* (1610), Birmingham is described as 'echoing with the noise of the Anvils, for here are great numbers of Smiths, and other Artificers in Iron and Steel, whose performances in that way are greatly admired both at home and abroad' (I: 609).

19 According to Pausanias, one of the cultic titles of Aphrodite was Malaenis, meaning 'Black', while Zeus, the king of the gods, was worshipped as Scotitas (the dark Zeus) in a region of Laconia. (*Pausanias: Description of Greece* 4 vols. trans. W. H. S. Jones (London: Heinemann, 1918–35) VIII. vi. 5, III. x. 6.) There were several Latin translations of Pausanias' Greek text printed in Europe during the sixteenth and seventeenth centuries.

20 For a fuller account of Jonson's use of alchemical imagery in these masques see Archer '[A] Black Art' in 'Women and Alchemy'.

21 Cartari *The Fountaine of Ancient Fiction* sig. H2r.

CHAPTER 9

Mapping British identities: Speed's Theatre of the Empire of Great Britaine

Christopher Ivic

When King James VI of Scotland was proclaimed king of England in March of 1603, he not only united the crowns of England and Scotland but also became the first composite monarch of two islands, three kingdoms, and four nations. Throughout his reign, the early years especially, James, the self-proclaimed British king, sought to incite discourse on Britain and Britishness, to foster a British national consciousness. According to Francis Bacon, James desired to 'imprint and inculcate into the hearts and heads of the people, that they are one people and one nation'.[1] Many of James's subjects, then, found themselves rethinking their place within an emergent multi-national British polity. The impact James's composite kingship had on English imaginings of the dynastically united kingdoms and their heterogeneous subjects is particularly evident in John Speed's *Theatre* (1611), the earliest comprehensive atlas of England, Wales, Scotland, and Ireland. As an enactment of space, place, and people, the *Theatre* bears ample witness to the ways in which cartography and chorography contributed to the classification of the inhabitants of the three kingdoms in the wake of King James VI/I's accession.[2]

The title of Speed's atlas suggests that James's British project was not entirely unsuccessful. Speed borrows the word 'Theatre' from Ortelius's *Theatrum orbis terrarum*;[3] the reference to 'Great Britain', however, echoes James's preferred nomenclature for the island. In a proclamation of 20 October 1604, James declared 'Wee have thought good to discontinue the divided names of England and Scotland out of our Regall Stile, and doe intend and resolve to take and assume unto Us in maner and forme hereafter expressed, The Name and Stile of KING OF GREAT BRITTAINE, FRANCE, AND IRELAND' (Hughes and Larkin eds. *Stuart Royal Proclamations* 1:96). If Speed was influenced by James's British project, the king in turn was indebted to cartographers. James highlights the role cartography played in fashioning his royal title when he notes that his new 'Name and Stile' is taken from 'the true and ancient Name, which God and Time have imposed upon this Isle, extant, and received in Histories, in all Mappes and Cartes, wherein the Isle is described' (*Stuart Royal Proclamations* 1:97). Although James's remark hints at the potential ideological uses of cartography for delineating and disseminating images of a united Britain, by no means is Speed's *Theatre* merely a vehicle for royal propaganda. The ideological and cultural work that Speed's cartographic images and chorographic descriptions of Britain and Ireland perform is much more complex than critics have hitherto acknowledged.[4] Speed's maps of Ireland and Ulster, though, come closest to the official view from Whitehall in that they work to promote the plantation and the cultivation of British subjects on the other side of the Irish Sea.

Dedicated to the 'MOST HIGH AND POTENT MONARCH, IAMES, OF GREAT BRITAINE, FRANCE AND IRELAND KING ... INLARGER AND VNITER OF THE BRITISH EMPIRE, RESTORER OF THE BRITISH NAME, ESTABLISHER OF PERPETVALL PEACE', Speed's *Theatre* announces itself as a text ideologically invested in the invention of Britain, an invention that was pervasive in the early years of James's reign.[5] One map in the *Theatre* that appears most committed to James's vision of 'one people, brethren and members of one body' is the map that opens the atlas, 'The Kingdome of Great Britaine and Ireland' (fig. 1) – the only map that in a single image displays James's Atlantic kingdoms (*Stuart Royal Proclamations*, 1:19). In his *Historie*, Speed, like many of his contemporaries, praises James for 'restoring to the *Iland* her ancient Name, *Brittania*'.[6] A similar strategy of praise is inscribed on Speed's map of Britain and Ireland. Of the two coins on the map, one depicts the female figure 'Britannia', who was often invoked as a symbol of unity and a common British identity during the first decade of James's reign, while the other portrays the ancient British king and restorer of peace 'Cvnobilin'. The representation of Cunobelinus (Cymbeline) functions as a compliment to James, who credited his reign as one that brought peace to Britain and Ireland and whose motto was *Beati Pacifici*. James's introduction of new coins such as the 'Unite' as well as the 'Thistle Crown' – a coin which on its obverse side depicts the English rose and on the reverse the Scottish thistle, thereby literally serving to circulate union propaganda – probably inspired the inclusion of these coins and the images inscribed on them (Grueber *Handbook of the Coins of Great Britain*).

That the map of Great Britain and Ireland celebrates the union of the crowns is also evident in the inclusion of the panoramas of London on the map's left-hand side and Edinburgh to the right of Scotland. These panoramas ostensibly honour the residences of Great Britain's two Parliaments. But can they not also be read as a poignant allusion to James's failed attempt at parliamentary union? Dynastic union, Bacon warned James in 1604, would not simply obliterate centuries of Anglo-Scottish hostilities: 'it is true that there are no natural boundaries of mountains, or seas, or navigable rivers; but yet there are badges and memorials of borders' (III:223). Indeed, the unwillingness to forget the past plagued Anglo-Scottish relations: '[o]ne of the main sources of animosity between Englishmen and Scots was the memory of previous armed conflict between them' (Levack *The Formation of the British State* 193). If Speed's map of Britain and Ireland works to obscure those former hostilities, it paradoxically draws upon and therefore re-awakens memories of them. The map's representation of Edinburgh is adapted from an earlier manuscript (BL Cotton MS Augustus I.ii.56) depicting the 1544 assault by English forces on the city (Skelton *County Atlases* 37). Speed has remodelled the original: the earlier manuscript map's image of an encroaching English army bearing the cross of Saint George has been erased and in place of the soldiers stand trees. Beneath the harmonious surface of Speed's map of Great Britain and Ireland, however, lies an unsettling reminder of previous Anglo-Scottish conflict.

While I support traditional readings of the *Theatre* as a monument to regal union and the brief period of peace that ensued, I want to argue that Speed's atlas is less certain, even anxious, about cultural union. Consider, for example, the general maps of England and Scotland. Inscribed in the margins of these maps are representatives of each nation. Gracing the map of England is a hierarchically ordered society of nobles, gentry, and city and country folk. Thus, the cartographic image presents not just the land but also socially diverse representatives of Englishness. What makes England 'England' is both the land and its inhabitants: England, as it were, is mapped onto itself. Adorning the map of Scotland are James and Anne, king and queen of Great Britain, France, and Ireland, along with the two princes, Henry and Charles.[7] James, as his title makes clear, is a composite monarch. Just as the text presents James in his preferred name and style, however, it also figures him as a supranational monarch of distinctly Scottish origins. Speed, to be sure, insists on the cultural and genealogical proximity of Lowland, non-Gaelic Scots and the English. The 'southern people' of Scotland, he writes, 'are from the same Original with vs the *English*, being both alike the *Saxon* branches' (*Theatre* 130). Just as Speed posits Anglo-(Lowland)Scottish cultural proximity, however,

Fig. 1 'The Kingdom of Great Britaine and Ireland', John Speed, *Theatre of the Empire of Great Britaine* (London 1611). Reproduced by permission of the Huntington Library, San Marino, California.

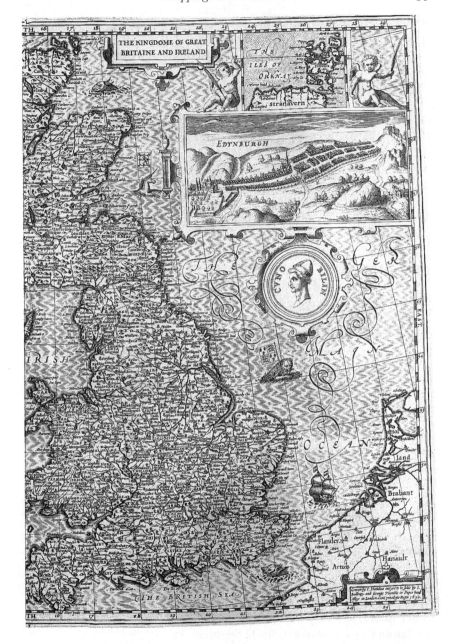

his reference to 'the English' as 'us' reinscribes difference. When Speed, speaking of Ptolemy, says 'he calleth this our Iland GREAT BRITAIN, & IRELAND, BRITAIN THE LESSE' (2), to whom does 'our' refer? Is this possessive pronoun used inclusively, referring to all the island's inhabitants – a British community – or does it refer exclusively to the English?

To what extent, then, is the *Theatre* committed to James's vision of 'one people, brethren and members of one body'? Speed's atlas of the British Isles is dedicated to the king, its title reflects James's British project, but where are the signs of, to quote Bacon, a 'commixture of bodies' (III:92)? The bodies on the margins of the maps of England and Scotland figure as sites of distinct national representation. The map of Great Britain and Ireland, on the other hand, contains no figures in the margins.[8] The *Theatre* inscribes physical embodiments of Englishness and Scottishness. Britishness, however, never inhabits a body.

Well, almost never. The *Theatre*'s frontispiece, of course, portrays a 'BRITAINE' (fig. 2). This tattooed Briton, though, is less a representative of contemporary Britishness than an archaic relic of a primitive past. Moreover, by including images of 'A DANE', 'A ROMANE', A BRITAINE', 'A SAXON', and 'A NORMAN', Speed's frontispiece draws attention to Britain's heterogeneous genealogical roots. The *Theatre*, therefore, shows little interest in retrieving a homogeneous British subject from the dim horizon of antiquity. Indeed, in his *Historie* Speed writes '[a]s touching the first *Inhabitants* and original *Names* of the *Iland*, things so far cast into the misty darkness of obscurity and obliuion . . . there is no hope left vs so lately borne to discover them' (5). Perhaps this explains why the text accompanying Speed's map of Great Britain and Ireland is given over to antiquarian discourse about a Roman province: the opening chapter is entitled 'The British Ilands proposed in one view in the ensuing map. With a generall description of *Great Britaine* vnder the romans.'[9] Only after the general map of Great Britain and Ireland has been displayed, only after '*Great Britaine* vnder the romans' has been described, does Speed turn to the 'three kingdomes that are (in present) the chiefe Bodies of GREAT BRITAINES MONARCHIE' (2). Of signal importance here is Speed's use of the plural: that is, the three separate kingdoms, and, I would add, peoples, of England, Scotland, and Ireland.

Sir Henry Spelman's anti-union tract of 1604, *Of the Union*, affords a better understanding of English resistance to James's British project. 'If the honorable name of England', Spelman writes,

be buried in the resurrection of Albion or Britannia, we shall change the goulden beames of the sonne for a cloudy day, and drownde the glory of a nation

Fig. 2. Frontispiece, John Speed, *Theatre of the Empire of Great Britaine* (London 1611).
Reproduced by permission of the Huntington Library, San Marino, California.

triumphant through all the worlde to restore the memory of an obscure and barberouse people, of whome no mention almoste is made in any notable history author but is either to their owne disgrace or at least to grace the trophyes and victoryes of their conquerors the Romans, Pictes and Saxons.[10]

Little attention has been paid to the *Theatre*'s prefatory material, which includes a commendatory inscription by Spelman. Given the nasty things Spelman says about Britain in his anti-union tract, what was there in the *Theatre* for Spelman to commend? Perhaps the *Theatre*'s identification of Britons as not only artefacts of the past but also artefacts to be left in the past. The text on the reverse of the map of the British Isles informs the reader that 'wee will (by example of best Anatomists) propose to the view the *whole Body*, and *Monarchie* intire . . . and after will dissect and lay open the particular Members, Veines, and Ioints (I meane the Shires, Riuers, Cities, and Townes) with such things as shal occurre most worthy our regard, and most behouefull for our vse' (1). Although the *Theatre* opens with a cartographic representation of the entire body of James's realm – Great Britain and Ireland – this geographic body is ultimately subject to dissection. As the *Theatre* turns its attention to amplifying English and politically assimilated Welsh counties, to exhibiting a general map of Scotland as well as a general map of Ireland and four of its provinces, any sense of Britishness as a cultural identity is displaced in favour of distinct identities: a point reinforced by the atlas's separate books and, moreover, the individual title pages devoted to England, Wales, Scotland, and Ireland. Not surprisingly, when the octavo miniature atlas of the *Theatre* appeared in 1627, *Great Britain* was dropped from the title and replaced with *England Wales Scotland and Ireland Described*.

Speed's enterprise, however, does not altogether abandon James's British project. If the *Theatre*'s handling of the British origin-myth is strained, it expresses less uncertainty about the cultivation of British subjects on the other side of the Irish Sea, where the contingencies of state and the fluidity of nations collided. The Fourth Book of the *Theatre*, consisting of Speed's general map and description of Ireland along with maps and descriptions of four Irish provinces (Connaught, Leinster, Munster, and Ulster), is, I want to suggest, informed by the Jacobean plantation of Ulster. Plantations were nothing new to Ireland. Previous efforts in Laois and Offaly (1556) and the plantation of Munster (1585) were carried out with some success; less successful were Sir Thomas Smith's (1570) and Walter Devereux's (1572–3) failed attempts at establishing colonies in Ulster. Distinguishing the 1609 Ulster plantation from preceding ones in

Ireland is the official introduction of British, that is, 'English, or Inland Scottish', planters.[11] What cannot be underestimated is the pervasiveness of the words 'Britain', 'British', and 'Britons' in Ulster plantation literature. For example, Sir Arthur Chichester, the Lord Deputy of Ireland, writing in 1611, speaks of 'every undertaker and servitor of the British nation'; throughout his *Book of the Plantation of Ulster* (1619), the surveyor Nicholas Pynnar refers to 'British undertakers', 'British tenants', 'British families', and to those 'of British birth and descent'; and Sir Thomas Phillips, writing in the early years of King Charles I's reign, remarks of 'six Thousand *Brittish* Bodies'.[12] Letters to and from Ireland and tracts on the plantation map a collective identity onto the British planters, who are identified as not only coming from the same island but also sharing a common lineage – 'of British birth and descent'. Addressing James in 1608–9, Bacon described 'unions and plantations' as 'the very nativities or birth-days of kingdoms'. For Bacon, Ireland was to serve as the site of an emergent Britishness, or, to pursue Bacon's metaphor, a pregnant Ireland was due to give birth to 'another Britain' (*Letters and Life* IV:116).

Before turning to Speed's Irish maps, I want to acknowledge Linda Colley's influential work on the invention of a British identity, which, she argues, emerged only after 1700. In an article that reflects intelligently on the new British history, Colley highlights two crucial components in British identity formation: first, that 'Britishness was never just imposed from the center, nor can it be understood solely or even mainly as the result of an English cultural or economic colonization of the so-called Celtic Fringe'; secondly, that 'what most enabled Great Britain to emerge as an artificial nation, and to be superimposed onto older alignments and loyalties was a series of massive wars between 1689 and 1815 that allowed its diverse inhabitants to focus on what they had in common rather than what divided them'.[13] But what about the plantation of British subjects in Ulster? Writing to the Earl of Salisbury on 10 May 1610, John Davies informs the Lord High Treasurer:

we published by proclamation in each county, what lands were granted to British undertakers, and what to servitors, and what to natives: to the end that the natives should remove from the precincts allotted to the Britons, whereupon a clear plantation is to be made of English and Scottish, without Irish, and to settle upon the lands assigned to natives and servitors, where there shall be a mixed plantation of English and Irish together.[14]

This passage defines Britons (English and Scottish planters) in opposition to the native Irish. Britishness, therefore, was to come about with the displacement and erasure of the native Irish. Speed's maps of Ireland, I will argue, participated in this attempted imposition from the centre of British subjects in Jacobean Ulster. Furthermore, what many, though not all, incoming British planters had in common was a Catholic Irish other.[15] Colley, though with a later period in mind, herself notes that 'Ireland was in many respects the laboratory of the British Empire' ('Britishness and Otherness' 327). Ulster plantation literature bears witness to the many voices that joined James and Bacon in viewing the English and Scots as British, in naming them Britons.

Early modern English maps of Ireland were an essential resource for those involved in the conquest, colonization, and administration of the kingdom. 'As of 1550 the English had little knowledge of Ireland beyond the Dublin Pale'; but by 1610 (the date of the publisher's imprint on Speed's Irish maps), 'ministers were familiar with the physical and political geography of the kingdom . . . with Robert Lythe's surveys of Munster and Leinster (1568–71), the two John Brownes' survey of Connaught (1580s), Richard Bartlett's survey of Ulster (1597–1603), and Francis Jobson's work throughout the island providing a geographic basis for its government and administration' (Peter Barber 'England II' 61). In the wake of the 1603 conquest, if not earlier, a specific cartographic genre dominated Irish map-making: namely, government plantation surveys.[16] Irish plantation surveys came about as huge amounts of land were transferred from rebellious Gaelic Irish and Old English subjects to English and Scottish colonists. Many of these plantation surveys are still extant in manuscripts, including 'A plott of the six escheated Counties of Vlster' (BL Cotton MS Augustus I.ii.44), believed to be the work of the English surveyor Francis Jobson. I draw attention to this specific map because included among those named as recipients of confiscated land is John Davies, who, according to this map, was awarded 1,000 acres in Clonaghmore and Gravetagh. Solicitor-general (1603–6) and then attorney-general (1606–19) in Ireland, author of *A Discovery of the True Causes why Ireland was never Entirely Subdued* (1612), Davies played a leading role in orchestrating the carve-up and plantation of the six escheated Ulster counties, counties that 'had been surveyed and mapped by 1609 and for which grants on paper had been assigned the following year' (Canny *From Reformation to Restoration* 166). It is precisely Davies, as we shall see, who identifies Speed's cartographic images of and chorographic discourse on Ireland with the plantation project.[17]

Rather than maintaining a strict separation between politically motivated, officially commissioned manuscript maps of Ireland and distinctly

aesthetic, antiquarian, commercial interests that underpinned the production of printed atlases, it is crucial to consider the interplay between
aesthetics and ideology, the aesthetic ideology of Speed's printed atlas –
an atlas that doubtless reached a greater audience than the majority of
manuscript maps. Unlike an official, detailed plantation survey, Speed's
general map of Ireland, as well as his charts of the Irish provinces,
would not have provided much practical help to the newly arrived British
planter. Yet, as Davies's contribution to the *Theatre* attests, his maps did
perform another function. At the conclusion of his general description
of Ireland, Speed proposes to show his readers Ireland 'as now it is,
first in generall, and then in parts' (139). By no means did Speed's spatial
anatomization of Ireland elude Davies's eye. In his commendatory poem
prefacing the *Theatre*, he writes:

> The faire *Hibernia* that Westerne Isle likewise,
> In every *Member, Artire, Nerue,* and *Veine*
> Thou by thine *Arte* dost so Anatomize,
> That all may see each parcell without paine.
> (sig. ¶ 2)

By drawing an analogy between the cartographer and the anatomist,
Davies brings into the open the ideological import of Speed's Irish maps.
In relation to early modern maps of Ireland, Davies's analogy is not
inappropriate. Both anatomical and cartographic discourse are given
over to the organization of space: the former spatializes the interior of
the human body, whereas the latter maps out the body politic. Just as the
anatomist flays and dissects the corpse, so too the cartographer displays
and dismantles the conquered colonial landscape. Likewise, just as early
modern anatomists surveyed the interior of dead bodies and inscribed
(their) names upon the body's internal organs, the colonial cartographer
performed a spatial and territorial reformation of the anatomized body
politic (Sawday *The Body Emblazoned* 24, 25). The corpse upon which
the cartographer mapped English economic, legal, political, and social
forms was an anatomized Gaelic political culture. Thus, the cartographic
image works to erase the memory of fragmented and highly unstable
Irish and Old English lordships with a coherent image of a reformed
landscape.

The candid emphasis in Davies's poem on exposing Ireland, then,
implies no neutral, disinterested antiquarian gaze. The emergence of
surveying and mapping, although far from systematic, enabled the
conquest and colonization of Ireland. Cartographic representations of

post-conquest Ireland continued to open it up, but for purposes other than the merely military. As Davies's commendatory poem makes clear, by fixing Ireland as the object of the colonizers' gaze – 'That all may see each parcell without paine' – early modern readers of Speed's appropriately named *Theatre* are placed in the position of voyeur: readers are invited to gaze upon a domesticated landscape. As the word 'parcel', which could mean a part of the country or a piece of property, suggests, Davies – who in his *A Discovery of the True Causes why Ireland was never Entirely Subdued* refers to James's 'British undertaker' and speaks of a 'mixed plantation of British and Irish' – associates Speed's aesthetically pleasing cartographic depictions of 'faire *Hibernia*' with contemporary plantation literature, such as Thomas Blenerhasset's *A Direction for the Plantation in Vlster* (1610), and, although a less obvious text, the 1607 augmented edition of Camden's *Britannia*, which sought to advertise and promote Ireland to prospective British planters by exposing the lush Irish land to their view (Davies *Discovery* 221, 222).

Camden's *Britannia* began as an antiquarian study of Roman Britain; however, the 1607 edition, dedicated to King James, shows much interest in Jacobean Ireland. Not only does Camden insert a general map of contemporary Ireland; he also 'improves the description of Ulster and northern Connaught, regions of which cartographers had just begun to give a recognizable picture' (Gottfried 'The Early Development' 125). Furthermore, the revisions to the Irish section of the 1607 edition were inspired by proposals for the plantation project in Ulster.[18] In the section on Ulster, Camden describes a land 'so full of forrage, and so fertile, that it easily gratifies the Industrious husbandman'.[19]

Camden's *Britannia* is the source for much of the chorographical description in the *Theatre*, and the Irish section is no exception. Consider, for example, Speed's description of Ulster's soil:

This equall temperature causeth the ground to bring forth great store of seuerall Trees, both fit for building, and bearing of fruit; plentifull of grasse for the breeding of Cattle, and is abundantly furnished with Horses, Sheepe and Oxen; the Riuers likewise pay double tribute, deepe enough to carry Vessels either for pleasure or profit, and fish great store . . . though in some places it be somewhat barren, troubled with *Loughes, Lakes*, and thicke Woods, yet is it euery where fresh, and full of Cattle and forrage, ready at all times to answer the husbandmans call. (144)

This last line explicitly echoes the 1607 edition of *Britannia*. If this topographical description serves to encourage plantation in Ulster, so too does Speed's map of the province, which 'rank[s] as the most care-fully considered and internally harmonious synthetic map of any part of Ireland to be published since 1564' (Andrews *Shapes of Ireland* 113). Camden notes that to 'keep [the Irish] in subjection and order . . . this hither part was formerly divided into three Counties, *Louth*, *Down*, and *Antrimme*; and now the rest is divided into these seven Counties, *Cavon*, *Fermanagh*, *Monaghan*, *Armagh*, *Colran*, *TirOen*, and *Donegall* or *Tirconell*' (1007). With its delineation of Ulster's counties, Speed's map serves to disseminate an image of topographical stability: a sense of stability re-inforced by the map's inset displaying the fort at Enniskillen and the numerous fortifications in Armagh, Monaghan, and Tyrone, commu-nicating an image of the formerly rebellious province as a secure and stable land. Camden's account of Ulster also emphasizes past rebellions. 'But as the soil for want of culture, is rough and barren', he writes, 'so the Inhabitants, for want of education and discipline, are very wild and barbarous' (1007). Camden's reference to the 'wild and barbarous' Irish is, however, qualified by the following gloss: 'This is to be under-stood of the Irish Inhabitants, who are now so routed out and destroyed by their many Rebellions, and by the accession of Scots (who for the most part inhabit this Province) that there are not supposed to be left 10000 Irish, able and fit to bear arms in *Ulster*' (1007). Both Camden and Speed present an image of a depopulated yet fortified Ulster awaiting plantation.

The subject of plantation also motivates Speed's general map of Ireland (fig. 3). In his pioneering work on cartography, J. B. Harley called for a historicized 'cartographic semantics' alert to a map's 'total image': that is, the geographic image and the accompanying marginal emblems, descriptive notes, and decorations (Harley 'Meaning and Ambiguity in Tudor Cartography' 22, 36). 'If the emblems that qualify and frame the maps are part of an ideological dialogue', argued Harley, 'then it is more probable that the geography itself is discursively embed-ded within broader contexts of social action and power' (Harley and Zandvliet 'Art, Science, and Power' 14). The essay in which Harley in-vited cultural historians to pay particular attention to a map's 'total image' cites Speed's map of Ireland as a prime example. Reprinted in the left margin of the map of Ireland are illustrations of 'gentle', 'civil', and 'wild' Irish men and women. More than mere decoration, this vertical ordering of colonial subjects – 'gentle' on top, 'wild' at the base – complements Speed's cartographic desire to impose spa-tial order on Ireland. According to Harley, this image disseminates

Fig. 3. 'The Kingdome of Ireland', John Speed, *Theatre of the Empire of Great Britaine*
(London 1611). Reproduced by permission of the Huntington Library,
San Marino, California.

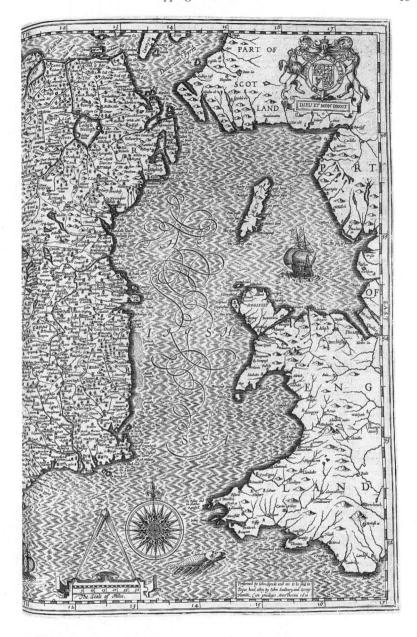

Fig. 4. 'The Kingdome of Scotland', John Speed, *Theatre of the Empire of Great Britaine* (London 1676). Reproduced by permission of the Newberry Library, Chicago, Illinois.

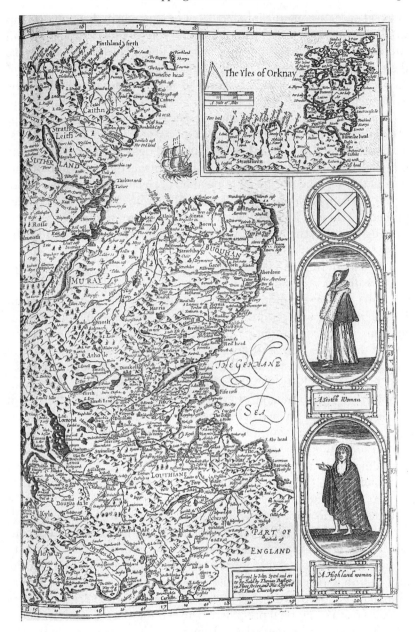

'a social order among the inhabitants of Ireland which through the map would become associated with the country as a whole' ('Meaning and Ambiguity in Tudor Cartography' 13). Although Harley does not make the connection, it is not difficult to see how the map's codification of hierarchical colonial relations works to inspire plantation, in part by assuaging potential British planters' anxieties. This becomes even more obvious once the map of Ireland is contrasted with the general maps of England and Scotland. On these maps representatives of Englishness and Scottishness appear in both the left and right borders. That is, the marginal figures encompass the geographic image; the land's inhabitants delimit the national territory. On the map of Ireland, on the other hand, the figures appear only on the left-hand margin. With the six figures pushed to one side, literally marginalized, the cartographic image opens a discursive space that serves to invite incoming British planters from the other side of the Irish Sea.

The bulk of Ireland's population, Colley points out, 'was never swept into a British identity to the degree that proved possible among the Welsh, the Scots, and the English' ('Britishness and Otherness' 314).[20] Jacobean Ulster, however, witnessed the emergence of a nascent British community, one that was introduced in an effort to render Ireland a pacified part of the multi-national British state. This is not to say that a cohesive British identity was instantly consolidated in Ulster – although, of course, a strong sense of Britishness eventually emerged there: 'the Protestant people of Northern Ireland', J. G. A. Pocock writes, constitute 'the last of the historic nations formed in the past of this archipelago' ('Contingency, Identity, Sovereignty' 301). Thus, Colley's work on the construction of British identity has been rightly criticized for 'excluding Ireland' and for failing 'to acknowledge the varieties of, and divisions within, British Protestantism'.[21] To draw attention to the early flowering of Britishness in Jacobean Ulster is to complicate further Colley's work, in terms of both its periodization and its inscription of a teleological narrative of forging a British identity.[22] The plantation reminds us that cultural contact in Ulster – triggered by economics, politics, religion, war – led not to a forging of identities, but rather to an uneven and ongoing, historically and culturally determined and determining, process of identity formation, reformation, and deformation. In fact, the arrival of British planters failed to disrupt national prejudices between the English and the Scots. The tenuousness of James's desired union as well as the 'peace' in Ireland was exposed on both islands during the Wars of the Three Kingdoms. The strains of these intra- and inter-island conflicts are not absent from later editions of the *Theatre*. In the 1652 reissue, the four royal portraits that formerly graced the map of Scotland have been replaced by less than flattering images of 'A Scotch Man' and 'A Scotch Woman' above portraits of 'A Highland Man' and 'A Highland woman' clad in plaid (fig. 4). In his description of Scotland in the first edition of the *Theatre*, Speed noted that 'The whole *Kingdome* is diuided in two parts ... the *South* whereof is the more populous and more beautified in manners, riches, and ciuilitie: the *North* more rude, retaining the customes of the *Wild Irish*, the ancient *Scot*' (131). In the first edition of the *Theatre*, Englishness and (Lowland) Scottishness are defined against Irishness. In the 1652 reissue, the demarcation of civil and wild Scot is harder to sustain. Under the pressure of Anglo-Scottish hostilities, the 'wild Scot' has become a part of the map's 'total image' of Scotland. As the Islands of the North Atlantic were mapped and remapped in the early modern period, as maps were decorated and redecorated, the bodies of Britain's and Ireland's heterogeneous inhabitants were fashioned and refashioned, reminding us that British identities were far from pure or stable. If a sense of Britishness was invented in Jacobean Ulster, it was tenuously reinvented throughout the seventeenth century, a century that laid the ideological groundwork for Britain's, Ireland's, and North America's real and imagined British communities.

NOTES

Many thanks to this volume's editors and to Elizabeth Harvey, Balachandra Rajan, and Paul Stevens for their valuable feedback.

1 Bacon *The Letters and the Life of Francis Bacon* III:227.

2 See Mignolo 'Misunderstanding and Colonization'. I am indebted to Mignolo's work on early modern / colonial maps, especially his idea of 'a performative (or enactive)' (210) production of space.

3 The English edition of Ortelius, *The Theatre of the World*, appeared in 1606. Speed's *Theatre* 'had done for Britain what Ortelius had done on a global scale': see Levy *Tudor Historical Thought* 196.

4 Richard Helgerson describes Speed as 'rabidly ... loyal to the crown': see his *Forms of Nationhood* 128.

5 Speed *Theatre* (London, 1611), dedication page.

6 Speed *Historie of Great Britaine* (London, 1611) 1241.

7 Speed's map of Scotland undercuts Helgerson's claim that what 'we see when we open *The Theater of the Empire of Great Britain* ... is not the king but the country' ('Forms of Nationhood' 145); however, the possibility that Speed is subversively putting James in his (national) place should not be ignored. That James appears on the map of Scotland and not on the map of Great Britain and Ireland is intriguing.

8 Marginal figures are also absent from the map of Wales. Does this absence suggest that Wales has been not only politically but also culturally absorbed by the English? In the text accompanying his map of England, Speed claims that 'the Welsh became one nation and kingdome with the English' (*Theatre* 5).

9 Much of the material printed on the reverse of Speed's maps is from Camden's *Britannia*, at times verbatim. Of course, the 'original *Britannia*, as we find it in early drafts . . . was an investigation of Roman Britain': see Levy *Tudor Historical Thought* 152.

10 Spelman *Of the Union*, in Galloway and Levack eds. *The Jacobean Union* 170.

11 *Conditions To Be Observed by the Brittish Vndertakers of the Escheated Lands in Vlster* (London, 1610), sig. A3.

12 *Calendar of the Carew Manuscripts* VI:124, 392–422, 245. 'The use of the term "Briton" in these early-seventeenth-century documents', Theodore Allen notes, 'anticipates by a century the Act of Union of 1707, uniting England and Scotland in one state, Great Britain': see Allen *The Invention of the White Race* I:273 n.16.

13 Colley 'Britishness and Otherness' 315, 316.

14 John Davies *The Works in Verse and Prose of Sir John Davies* III:204–5.

15 'From the time of the Ulster plantation', Roy Foster writes, 'Protestants constituted the political elite; segregation took the place of Anglicization': see his *Modern Ireland* 45. See also Michael J. Hill 'The Origins of the Scottish Plantations'. Hill notes that 'the Celtic Scots intermixed with the Irish, creating a cultural fusion in Ulster' (43). Challenging Colley's Anglocentric linking of Britishness and Protestantism, Hill also notes that 'a Celt converted to Protestantism would [not] become less culturally Celtic' (39).

16 See Andrews *Irish Maps*. 'Such outline "plantation" surveys', Andrews notes, 'belong to a colonial cartographic genre hardly known elsewhere in contemporary western Europe' (6).

17 Perhaps I should say 'Speed's' maps, for the geographic images of Ireland are gleaned from the work of other government surveyors, such as Robert Lythe, Francis Jobson, John Browne, and Richard Bartlett: see Andrews *Shapes of Ireland* 89–117.

18 'The colonizing policy of the new reign', Gottfried writes, 'probably motivates a long insertion describing the fertility of the country' ('The Early Development' 124). George Hill notes that 'Camden might have given us more light on the [Ulster Plantation] than he has deigned to afford, for he . . . had access to the Irish State Papers soon after their receipt in London': see his *An Historical Account of the Plantation in Ulster* i.

19 Camden *Britannia* (1607), trans. Edmund Gibson (1695) 1007.

20 Cf. Pocock: ' "Irish history" is not part of "British history", for the very good reason that it is largely the history of a largely successful resistance to being included in it; yet it is part of "British history", for exactly the same reason. In saying this, we move from the illusion, or verbal confusion, that "British history" is the history of a shared identity with a shared past, to

the more focused realisation that it is the history of the attempt, with its successes and failures, to create such an identity' (Pocock 'Contingency, Identity, Sovereignty' 295).

21 Crossman 'Introduction' in *Ireland in Proximity* 10.
22 ' "British history" is not simply the history of the coming together of the British: for much of the time, the theme of integration is matched by those of rejection and conflict' (Grant and Stringer 'Introduction: The Enigma of British History' in *Uniting the Kingdom?* 5).

V

Britain's brave new world

Bruited abroad: John White and Thomas Harriot's colonial representations of ancient Britain

Andrew Hadfield

Who really wanted there to be a British union? Certainly interest in the British problem was a force in British intellectual and political life from the 1580s onwards. How serious was anyone, though, about the prospect of a wider union? Raphael Holinshed's history of the British Isles, *Chronicles of England, Scotland, and Ireland* (1577, 1587), significantly makes no mention of Britain in its title. William Harrison's 'The History of Britain', which opens the work, distinguishes the island of Britain from its nearest neighbour, Ireland, and from 'little Britain', otherwise known as Armorica, or Brittany (Holinshed *Chronicles* I:3–6, 32, 52, 60). However, Harrison has no desire to relate the conception of Britain to the contemporary history of the island; in fact, quite the opposite, as he stresses the antiquity of the geopolitical entity he is describing. Harrison is retelling a Galfridian narrative of the decline of the Britons, eventually driven into Wales, Cornwall, and Armorica by the victorious Saxons, with whom many of the Britons intermarry (*Chronicles* I:13–14).[1] Equally, he is at pains to stress the number and variety of races living within the island owing to the wave of invasions. There are the Picts who travel from Scythia specifically to plunder the Britons; the Scots, who are driven to Ireland by the Picts but return later; the Roman invaders; and the Saxons, then the Danes, who force the Britons into Wales (*Chronicles* I:11–13, 48–50). Indeed, the Britons themselves prefigure the range of identities of the land by dividing up the island they possess, a precedent first established by their eponymous founder, Brutus (*Chronicles* I:195).

William Camden in his *Britannia*, published in Latin in 1586, translated into English in 1610, was sceptical of Geoffrey's abilities as a historian and he argued that Geoffrey had 'little authority among men of learning' (*Britannia* 2). Camden attempts to disprove the myth of Brutus (vii–viii), but his work has the same historical emphasis as Harrison's account and Holinshed's design, delving into the past to authenticate the truth with little concern to relate the histories and identities of the peoples who inhabited Britain at various times to a contemporary situation. Camden's aim is to separate out identities and establish their roots through tracing etymologies, basing his investigations on the principle that people who speak the same language must have the same origin (xviii). Camden, like Harrison, shows that Britain has been populated at various times by Britons (now Welsh), Scots, Picts, Romans, Saxons, and Danes (lxxxiv–clxiii).

Is it surprising that such works show so little interest in the conception of Britain? In effect, the British project involved a plan to unite the kingdoms of England and Scotland. Ireland was rarely considered to be part of Britain, unless the notion of the 'British Isles' was invoked (Hadfield 'Briton and Scythian'). Wales, as Camden's and Holinshed's works demonstrate, was considered to have been absorbed into England (Roberts 'Tudor Wales'). By the 1580s it was clear that Elizabeth would not have children and that the Tudor dynasty would end. It was most likely that her successor would be from the Scottish line of Stuarts, whether that meant James VI, who had become king of Scotland in 1567 with the forced abdication of his mother, Mary Queen of Scots, or his young cousin, Arbella Stuart (1575–1615) (Steen ed. *The Letters of Lady Arbella Stuart* 30). If Elizabeth were to die without further negotiation and planning for the succession, a Scottish claim to the English throne would unite Britain.

Furthermore, given the central role that Mary Queen of Scots played in English political life in the 1570s and 1580s before her execution in 1587, it is unthinkable that a history of Britain could have been written without taking into account her role and activities. England was technically at war with Spain, its queen having been declared a heretic by Pope Pius V, who asserted that she could legitimately be overthrown by her Catholic subjects. Many non-Catholic English men and women would not have welcomed the prospect of rule by a 'North Briton', especially in the light of the constitutional issues the question of Mary's imprisonment raised, the scandals she was involved in, and the plots to overthrow Elizabeth that she appeared happy to endorse.[2]

Mary's biography reads like an English nightmare. She had been brought up a strict Catholic at the French court. She was the daughter-in-law of Catherine de Medici, later the evil genius behind the Massacre of Saint Bartholomew's Day (1572), having married the sickly dauphin, Francis. Therefore, she had been used to unite England's two traditional foes, posing a threat alongside – at worst, in tandem with – Spain, whilst also being the heir to the throne of England. The spectre of her namesake, Mary I, who had allied herself with Spain through marriage to Philip II, signalled further undesirable associations. Mary's attempt to claim the English throne in 1558 when Mary I died, on the grounds that her half-sister, Elizabeth, was illegitimate, created further grounds for hostility. After she returned to Scotland, she was implicated in the murder of her second husband, Lord Darnley, in 1567, and married the Earl of Bothwell, also implicated in the murder, three months later, a union which led to civil war in Scotland, and Mary's enforced abdication and flight to England where she spent the last nineteen years of her life under arrest. Once she had been imprisoned Mary was the centre of a number of plots to overthrow Elizabeth and install her as monarch, action Mary endorsed on a number of occasions despite her protestations of innocence. The three major plots were the Ridolfi plot (1571), the Throckmorton plot (1583), and the Babington plot (1586), when she dictated a letter giving her consent to a rebellion which planned to overthrow Elizabeth.[3] Despite Elizabeth's reluctance to sign her death warrant, Mary was tried, condemned to death, and executed on 8 February 1587.[4]

In short, Mary was associated with aggressive Catholicism and the murder of Protestants, an alliance between England's traditional enemies, underhand dealing and connivance, and civil war, in both Scotland and France. She was thought to be lewd, inconsistent, capricious, arrogant, and deceitful. It is not surprising that so many clearly feared the Stuart claim (Phillips *Images of a Queen*). More to the point, however, as Anne McLaren has recently argued, the debates, especially those in Parliament, over the rights and wrongs of the execution of Mary, significantly changed the political climate in England. First, they contributed to an on-going battle between Elizabeth and her advisers and would-be advisers over the definition of the term 'counsel'. Elizabeth wished to limit this to advice that she sought and chose. As the queen informed her Parliament in 1589, 'Many come hither *ad consulendum, qui nesciunt quid sit consulendum*' (Many come hither to counsel, who are ignorant what counsel means). Predictably enough, many of her subjects felt they had a right to advise the monarch in Parliament as they saw fit, in line with their sense of what was best for the nation, i.e., that Mary should be executed (McLaren *Political Culture* ch. 4). Second, the debates transformed English perceptions of the Scots: 'From being, as they had been deemed by earlier apologists, brothers in Protestantism, the Scots became "strangers" (a term employed with equal venom to describe recusants within England) and "barbarians", an identification that underpins the

language of conquest which features so prominently in their debates'
(172).

When James succeeded to the English throne in 1603 there were plots
against him – albeit rather half-hearted – and the House of Commons
threw out his attempt to establish a formal union of Britain, which helped
to foster his distrust of democratic institutions (Levack *The Formation of the
British State*; McEachern *Poetics of English Nationhood* 138–61). Nevertheless
he did often style himself 'King of Britain' and, at last, works appeared
that seemed to be enthusiastic about the projected union of Britain.
The most notable example was John Speed's *Theatre of the Empire of Great
Britaine* (1611), which represented James as he appeared to see himself,
as the king who unified the four kingdoms of the British Isles. Perhaps
Speed's inclusion of Wales and Ireland as British kingdoms signals the
crucial change from the 1580s, and shows how the focus was no longer
on Scotland and England, emphasizing earlier English fears of a Scottish
Britain.

It is in terms of the anxieties induced by the political turmoil of the
1570s and 1580s that we have to read contemporary representations of
Britain. This is, I would suggest, the case with the illustrations of the
Britons and the Picts appended to Thomas Harriot's *Report*, when it was
reprinted in 1590 as the first part of Theodor De Bry's on-going project,
America (1590–1634).[5] Harriot's text has been interpreted in a variety of
ways, but has not really been related to debates over the question of
Britain and Britishness.[6]

Harriot's *Report* was first published in 1588 as a small quarto. Harriot,
a protégé of Sir Walter Raleigh's, who had worked with Raleigh since at
least 1582, had long been interested in voyages to the New World.[7] He
had used his scientific knowledge and navigational expertise to plan the
1584 voyage to the colony on Roanoke Island led by Philip Amadas and
Arthur Barlowe, and had then sailed on Richard Grenville's expedition
in 1585–6. One of Harriot's roles was to study the native Americans and
their environment in collaboration with the artist, John White, another
of Raleigh's protégés, who had already travelled on other voyages to the
Americas – probably on Martin Frobisher's expedition to Newfound-
land in 1577 – and who was later to become governor of the colony at
Roanoke.[8]

Harriot's *Report* was written partly as a defence of the colonial enterprise in Virginia, and partly as a scientific treatise, detailing the flora,
fauna, and people of the south-east coast explored by the English. Harriot
claimed that he had collected far more material on the 'straunge beasts,
fishe, trees, plants, and hearbes' of the region which he would publish in

due course, but the projected volume never materialized (20). The text we have has a clear polemical edge and promotional purpose. The preface, dedicated to the 'adventurers, favorers, and welwillers of the enterprise for the inhabitting and planting in Virginia' (5), admits in the second sentence that 'There have bin divers and variable reportes with some slaunderous and shamefull speeches bruited abroade by many that returned from thence', which need to be counteracted. The native Americans are shown as docile, helpful peoples who will present no physical challenge to any European settlers (if any are left alive after the importation of disease) (Greenblatt *Shakespearean Negotiations* 21–39). Indeed, Harriot admits that any fault has been on the side of the English: 'some of our companie towardes the end of the yeare, shewed themselves too fierce, in slaying some of the people, in some towns, upon causes that on our part, might easily enough have been borne withall' (30).

The divided nature of the text and the ideological forces at work within it, are, I would argue, even more in evidence when the *Report* was reprinted by De Bry with the added illustrations based on John White's original drawings, and one important plate derived from a painting by the French artist, Jacques Le Moyne De Morgues. As Paul Hulton has pointed out, De Bry tends to Europeanize the natives' faces and gestures (Harriot *Report* xi). The Algonquian Indians are seen to be civilized, reasonable people in the main, even if certain practices – praying with rattles around the fire (Plate XVII), performing ritual dances (Plate XVIII), worshipping idols (Plate XXI), tattooing themselves in bizarre ways (Plate XXIII) – and their basic appearance, mark them out as exotic curiosities, whose effects might grace a *Wünderkammer*. It is noticeable that the illustrations representing the Algonquians as un-European are all gathered at the end of the sequence. Before then, the reader has seen that they have a social structure which resembles that of European societies (Plates III, IV, VI, VII, VIII), a religious system (Plate V), recognizable styles and types of dress (IX), and an organized society based on marriage (Plates IV, VI, X). The Indians are shown in a variety of civilized and domestic situations: carrying their babies (albeit on their backs rather than 'in their armes before their brests'; p. 53) (Plate X); making boats out of trees (Plate XII); fishing (Plate XIII); broiling fish over a fire (Plate XIV); cooking meat in earthenware pots over a fire (Plate XV); and sitting down to eat (Plate XVI). A complete picture of an orderly, recognizable society, familiar to the reader, is carefully established – before the last plates complicate the impression.

Harriot wrote captions to the pictures in Latin, which Richard Hakluyt, who had probably put De Bry in touch with Harriot, translated into English. These further establish the sophisticated and relatively civilized state of the Algonquians, contrasting them favourably to their European counterparts. Next to Plate XIII, 'Their manner of fishynge in Virginia', Harriot writes:

Ther was never seene amonge us soe cunninge a way to take fish withall, whereof sondrie sortes as they fownde in their Rivers unlike unto ours. Which are also of a verye good taste. Dowbtless yt is a pleasant sighte to see the people, sometymes wadinge, and goinge somtymes failinge in those Riuers, which are shallowe and not deepe, free from all care of heapinge oppe Riches for their posteritie, content with their state, and liuinge frendlye together of those thinges which god of his bountye hath given unto them. (56)

There is something of a sting in the tail of this description as Harriot draws attention to the Algonquians' lack of true religion. However, there is a clear critique of European greed, an exultation of the life of the unaccommodated man, an appeal to the natural wealth and abundance of the New World, and a suggestion that no sensible person would stay in England if they could possibly travel to the Americas and live with these marvellous people. Similarly, the two plates which depict the Indians cooking and eating, XV and XVI, praise their habits at the expense of their European counterparts. Harriot emphasizes the social nature of meals, having described the careful methods of preparing and cooking food which are observed:

Then they putte it out into dishes, and sett before the companye, and then they make good cheere together. Yet they are moderate in their eatinge wher by they avoide sicknes. I would to god wee would followe their exemple. For wee should bee free from kynes of diseases which wee fall into by sumptwous and unreasonable banketts, continuallye deuisinge new sawces, and provocation of gluttonye to satisfie our unsatiable appetite. (60)

A common moral is drawn, one made often enough in works dealing with the New World, that Indian continence and restraint has much to teach the greedy Europeans.[9]

Harriot's captions encourage the reader to think of the native Americans in terms of European society.[10] In fact, the whole sequence appears to be designed to make the reader try to place the newly discovered peoples it represents within larger cultural, political, and religious schemes. The opening plate produced by De Bry (figure 5) shows Adam and Eve about to pluck the fatal apple from the tree of knowledge. In front of them, the lion lies down with the mouse and the rabbit as an

Fig. 5. 'Adam and Eve picking the apple', frontispiece to Theodor de Bry, 'The True Pictures and Fashions of the People in the Parte of America now Called Virginia, Discovered by Englishmen', appended to Thomas Harriot, *A Briefe and True Report of the New Found Land of Virginia* (1590). Reproduced by permission of the British Library.

emblem of peace within the Garden of Eden. Behind them a man labours
while a woman tends a baby in a shelter, clearly a sign of the division of
labour and the curse of work effected by the fall (Hadfield *Literature, Travel
and Colonial Writing* 115–17). The illustration provides a sense of drama
and wonder to the subsequent images, relating the European discovery
of the Americas to the fall of mankind.[11] What is the relationship between the Indians and Adam and Eve? Are the Indians on the verge of a
disaster, as the greedy and destructive Europeans enter their realm? Or,
should the sequence be read the other way round: is it the Europeans we
should concentrate on, and their discovery of a society that resembles
the Garden of Eden in the New World? Who, in a sense, has most to
gain from the encounter? Harriot's harrowing description of the diseases
which decimate the Indians and consolidate English superiority would
seem to suggest that both sets of questions are valid.

The three 'Pictures of the Pictes which in the Olde tyme dyd habite
one part of the great Bretainne', and the two illustrations of 'neighbour[s]
unto the Picte', which conclude the sequence, are equally problematic
(figures 6–9). However we choose to interpret these illustrations – and
their meaning is open to considerable dispute – it is significant that
De Bry's version of Harriot brings us back to the island that the explorers
and colonists left, encouraging the reader to contextualize the images in
terms of ancient and contemporary British politics. De Bry writes on the
frontispiece to the pictures that:

The Painter of whom I have had the first of the Inhabitants of Virginia, give
me these 5 Figures ... fownd as hy did assured my in a oold English chronicle,
the which I wold well sett to the end of these first Figures, *for to showe how that
the Inhabitants of the great Bretannie have bin in times past as sauvage as those of Virginia.*
(75, my emphasis)

However, despite De Bry's words, the illustrations deliberately refuse the
most obvious comparison (ancient Britons and American Indians). The
first point to note is that the emphasis is placed upon the Picts. Their
'neighbours', who appear to be considerably more civilized, are obviously the Britons. It is noticeable, however, that Harriot does not choose
to name them, remarking that 'Ther was in the said great Bretainne
yet another nation nigbour unto the Pictes', and proceeds to describe
their clothes without further comment ('which did apparell them selves
with a kind of cassake other cloath Jerkin ... The did also wear longe
heares, and their moustaches ... and did carye the picke or the lance
in their hande ... as you may see by this picture.'). It seems likely that

Fig. 6. De Bry, 'Som Pictures of the Pictes which in the Olde tyme dyd habite one part of the great Bretainne', Plate I, 'The truue picture of one Picte'. Reproduced by permission of the British Library.

Fig. 7. De Bry, 'Som Pictures of the Pictes', Plate II, 'The truue picture of a women Picte'. Reproduced by permission of the British Library.

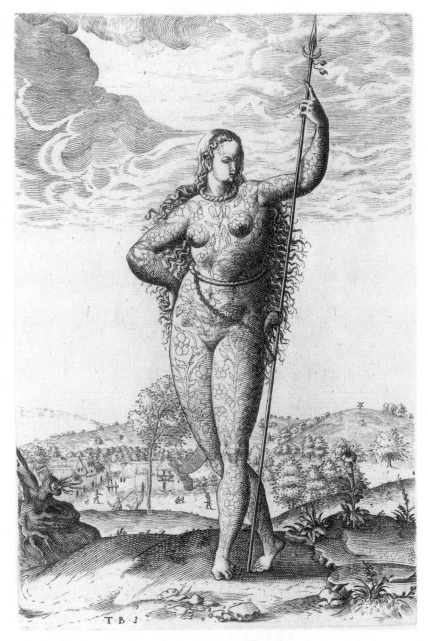

Fig. 8. De Bry, 'Som Pictures of the Pictes', Plate III, 'The truue picture of a yonge dowgter of the Pictes'. Reproduced by permission of the British Library.

Fig. 9. De Bry, 'Som Pictures of the Pictes', Plate IV, 'The truue picture of a man of nation neighbour unto the Picte'. Reproduced by permission of the British Library.

the startling avoidance of the expected comparison is designed to focus attention on the relationship between the Picts and the Indians.

The comparison is an inauspicious one, and serves to make a pointed contrast between the two peoples. The Picts were generally regarded as a savage, lawless race, whose main object was to plunder other, more established and successful races, as their supposed Scythian origins would suggest. They were notable for their lack of stability – they built no towns – and ferocious war paint, as the three illustrations here demonstrate.[12] Crucially, for my purposes here, they were associated solely with Scotland, where they fought and intermingled with the Scots, helping to form the Scottish people, and were invariably opposed to the Britons and Saxons (Kidd *British Identities* ch. 6).

In the first edition of the *Chronicles* (1577), Holinshed describes the Picts as 'a cruell kind of men and much given to warres . . . more desirous of spoyle than of rule or government'.[13] A woodcut included in the text shows the British king, Marius, defeating the Picts (figure 10). Marius eventually allowed the Picts to settle in Scotland.

The last illustration depicting the Virginian Indians shows a heavily tattooed figure and the caption explains how important such marks are to their chief men. Nevertheless, the inscriptions on the body are more regulated than those on the Picts and do not serve to define the Indians as a people (tattoos do not appear elsewhere in the sequence; Fleming 'Renaissance Tattoo' 44–8). The captions to the pictures of the Picts emphasize the importance of body paint. The woman Pict is shown to have griffin heads on her shoulders, lion faces on her 'low parts and thighs', half-moons on her breasts, and her belly has a sun (another contrast to the clothing of their neighbours, pointed out in the caption). The civilized behaviour of the Indians is in stark contrast to the savage aggression of the Picts, who are shown in hostile warlike poses, brandishing weapons and clutching the severed heads of their enemies. De Bry's opening remarks on the comparison between the Indians and the ancient Britons are, in fact, quite accurate. It is the neighbours of the Picts, however, who resemble the natives of Virginia, not the Picts themselves.

The sequence of illustrations would appear to offer coded but quite explicit advice to any English readers. A connection is made between the Britons – and, by implication, the English – and the docile, civilized peoples of the New World. In stark contrast are the Picts, who are truly threatening and savage. The reader is encouraged to look toward the New World for riches and success, both of which Harriot's text promises

Fig. 10. Raphael Holinshed, insert engraving of the Scots and Picts fighting the Britons, *Chronicles of England, Scotland, and Ireland* (1577). Reproduced by permission of the National Library of Wales.

anyone astute enough to get involved in the colonial project. The illustrated *Report* looks forward to texts produced two decades later, such as the report commissioned for the Virginia Company in 1609, *Nova Britannia*, which argued that the ancient Britons would have remained in savagery and ignorance if 'Julius Caesar with his Roman Legions (or some other) had not laid this ground to make us tame and civil', and William Strachey's *The Historie of Travell* (1612).[14] Britain's past can be repeated in the 'New World' and a new Britain established there.

The Picts, on the other hand, appear to warn the reader of a path that should not be taken. Given their association with Scotland it is not likely that they are simply included here to represent, metonymically, the people of ancient Britain, but to have a bearing on contemporary developments in Britain. Specifically the Picts represent the threat to England from a Scottish claim to the throne and, hence, a unification of Britain, which many saw as highly undesirable. It is extremely unlikely that any of those associated with the publication of De Bry's version of Harriot's *Report* would have been in favour of the Stuart claim to the throne.[15]

The 1580s were the time when English colonial projects were first planned and carried out, Harriot's *Report* being the definitive account of events in the very first of these. There were a huge number of works published in these years, designed to persuade Englishmen of the value and necessity of establishing colonies in the Americas (Hadfield *Literature, Travel and Colonial Writing* 97–8). The most important propagandist was Richard Hakluyt, who produced a collection of descriptions of voyages to the Americas in 1582, followed by his influential 'A Discourse of Western Planting' (1584), and the first edition of his major work, *The Principall Navigations, Voyages, Traffiques, and Discoveries of the English Nation* (1589). Hakluyt was driven by a fear that if Protestant England did not establish an empire in the Americas, then Catholic Spain would dominate the known world for the foreseeable future. In short, his goal was to continue the sectarian conflict within Europe in the Americas (Hadfield 'Rethinking the Black Legend'; Helgerson *Forms of Nationhood* ch. 4).

Hakluyt played a key role in De Bry's project and was instrumental in persuading De Bry 'to publish the Harriot–White material first as the first part of his projected *America*'.[16] It is unlikely that any of the subsequent material in De Bry's collection made the same impact as the engravings based on White's pictures (Hulton *America 1585* 19). The inclusion of the drawings of the Picts, with their implicit political message, would appear to be part of the larger overall religious design behind Hakluyt's colonial project, warning English and European Protestant readers that more dangerous savages lived within the realm than were to be found in the Americas.

De Bry (1528–98) also had little reason to be enthusiastic about a Catholic Stuart claim to the English throne. He was a Protestant who had been forced to flee his native Belgium during the long struggle of the Low Countries to free themselves from Spanish rule (Alexander *Discovering the New World* 8–9). De Bry's enterprise was a conspicuously Protestant collection which made a significant contribution to the 'Black Legend', the accounts of Spanish atrocities in the Americas and Europe as a means of promoting Protestant ventures (Maltby *The Black Legend in England*). A famous illustration to the account of Girolamo Benzoni's voyage to South America (1541–56), placed after a gruesome sequence of Spanish atrocities toward the Indians, shows gleeful natives pouring molten gold down the throat of a Spanish soldier with the words, 'Eat, eat gold, Christian', a richly evocative native response to colonial avarice. Closer to home, the Spanish Armada was defeated only two years before the start of De Bry's *America*.

It is also evident that Harriot and his patron, Sir Walter Raleigh, to whom the elaborate folio text was dedicated, were party to Hakluyt's thinking about English colonial expansion in the New World (Shirley 'Sir Walter Raleigh and Thomas Harriot' 18). Moreover, Raleigh was closely associated with Edmund Spenser at this point, through their Irish connections. In 1589, Spenser travelled back from his Munster estates to Elizabeth's court, probably in an attempt to secure patronage and publicity for *The Faerie Queene*. He recorded the visit some years later in *Colin Clouts come home againe* (1595), which he dedicated to Raleigh. A year later Spenser seriously offended James VI, through his portrait of the trial and execution of Duessa in *The Faerie Queene* (v. 9), a transparent allegory of the trial of James's mother, Mary Queen of Scots. James demanded that Elizabeth punish Spenser (McCabe 'The Masks of Duessa'). Later, in the 1590s, Raleigh appears to have hedged his bets as far as he could when he realized that the succession was likely to pass to the Stuart line (Philip Edwards *Sir Walter Raleigh* 25–6). It is more than likely that his association with Spenser was enough to damn him in James's eyes, a link compounded by Raleigh's association with forward Protestants such as Hakluyt. Indeed, most colonial propagandists were staunchly Protestant, indicating that Raleigh's involvement in projects such as De Bry's publication of the Harriot–White material signalled an opposition to the Stuart claim.

It is also worth noting a further link to Raleigh's later life and works. Raleigh's own account of his voyage to Guiana in search of the fabled city of El Dorado, *The Discoverie of the Large, Rich and Bewtiful Empire of Guiana* (1596), has to be read in terms of Raleigh's problems with Elizabeth and his anxieties as a courtier following his clandestine marriage to Elizabeth Throckmorton and their subsequent banishment from court (1592; Montrose 'The Work of Gender'). Raleigh demonstrates that his men show themselves to be continent and restrained in the face of the wealth and variety of opportunities presented to them in the Americas, a message to the queen that he has learned his lesson. He also includes a passage on the legendary Amazons of whom he has heard reports even though he has not seen them himself. He describes how the Amazons assemble with men once a year to choose partners and for one month 'they feast, daunce, & drinke of their wines in abundance'. If they conceive a son they leave it with the father, if a daughter, 'they nourish it, and reteine it, and as many as have daughters send unto the begetters a Present, all being desirous to increase their owne sex and kinde' (Raleigh *The Discoverie of the Large, Rich and Bewtiful Empire of Guiana* 146).

Raleigh's digression, which he signals himself ('And though I digresse from my purpose, yet will I set downe what hath been delivered me for truth of those women'; 146), appears to be an allegorical core to the whole text: that under female rule men are emasculated and their actions circumscribed. The Amazons' desire to separate the girls from the boys and live apart seems to be placed either as a warning to Elizabeth, or, more likely, as a coded comment for like-minded male readers.

Women's rule was one of the key political issues of Elizabeth's reign, with even her defenders, such as John Aylmer, sharing the basic assumption, with opponents like John Knox, that female government was an aberration that it would tax the finest minds to explain (McLaren *Political Culture* 59–69). In this context it cannot be an entirely innocent detail that two of the three Picts are female. Both women are recognizable as Amazons or warrior women, glaring back at the viewer.[17] De Bry, contrary to his usual practice of Europeanizing his subjects, has made the expression of the 'dowgter of the Picts' more aggressive and hence more alien than in Jacques Le Moyne De Morgues's original drawing. Should these fierce women be read as counterparts to Raleigh's Amazons? Women who, in essence, violate nature by daring to usurp male authority and rule? Mary Queen of Scots had been executed by the time De Bry's edition of the *Report* was published, but there was still the possibility that Arbella Stuart, now fifteen, could succeed Elizabeth as queen. It took a considerable time before the Stuarts and the Scots were not associated with all the perceived characteristics of female rule – civil war, the inversion of the proper order, factionalism, and contrived artifice (Neale *Elizabeth I and Her Parliaments* II:262). Moreover, given the hostility to female rule, especially in the second half of Elizabeth's reign, there were numerous commentators, some of them clearly associated with Raleigh and his circle, who felt that Elizabeth was in danger of turning into the Whore of Babylon she had supposedly destroyed in 1587.[18] The aggressive women Picts, both iconographically represented as virgins with long flowing locks, may be another sardonic comment on the decaying cult of Elizabeth's virginity (Fleming 'Renaissance Tattoo' 45).

John Shirley has suggested that '[t]he original purpose of Harriot's volume is difficult to determine' (Shirley 'Sir Walter Raleigh and Thomas Harriot' 19). He is right that there is no clear and straightforward link between the text and a context, and that much of what has been argued here can only be conjecture and surmise. Some of the details I have selected for scrutiny and attached importance to may well be anodyne or incidental. Within the context, however, of the Stuart succession, English expansion overseas, and the possible unification of Britain in the late 1580s and early 1590s, John White and Thomas Harriot's Picts suggest a covert colonial critique of an undesirable prospective political union by rehearsing historical national differences.

NOTES

I would like to thank Anne McLaren and the editors for commenting on earlier drafts of this chapter.

1 On the influence of Geoffrey of Monmouth's *Historia regum britanniae* in sixteenth-century England, see Kendrick, *British Antiquity*.

2 See Read *Lord Burghley and Queen Elizabeth* ch. 18; Fraser *Mary Queen of Scots*; Phillips *Images of a Queen*; Erskine-Hill *Poetry and the Realm of Politics* introduction, appendix 1.

3 For details see Read *Lord Burghley and Queen Elizabeth* chs. 3, 15, 18; Fraser *Mary Queen of Scots* 424–9, 469–70, 475–500.

4 Read *Burghley* ch. 18; Fraser *Mary Queen of Scots* chs. 25–6.

5 A convenient modern facsimile is edited by Paul Hulton. All subsequent references to this edition are in parentheses in the text, unless stated. Selections from De Bry's project can be found in Alexander *Discovering the New World*.

6 See Hulton and Quinn *American Drawings of John White*; Hulton 'Images of the New World'; Fleming 'The Renaissance Tattoo'; Hadfield *Literature, Travel and Colonial Writing* 115–26.

7 On the relationship between Raleigh and Harriot, see Shirley 'Sir Walter Raleigh and Thomas Harriot' 16–35.

8 On what is known of White's life, see Hulton and Quinn *American Drawings of John White* 1:12–24.

9 For other examples, see Hadfield *Literature, Travel and Colonial Writing* 71–91; Montaigne 'Of the Cannibals', in *The Essayes of Michael, Lord of Montaigne* (1603), trans. John Florio, 1:215–30.

10 For further examples, see Hadfield *Literature, Travel and Colonial Writing* ch. 2.

11 For this ubiquitous concept in New World writings, see Greenblatt, *Marvelous Possessions.*

12 Holinshed *Chronicles* (1587) I:11; V:3, 27, 47, and *passim.*

13 Holinshed *Chronicles* (1577) 67.

14 First text cited in Gibbons *Shakespeare and Multiplicity* 214; Strachey *The Historie of Travell into Virginia Britania* (1612).

15 On the close relationship between Harriot, Raleigh, Hakluyt, De Bry, and White, and the probable sequence of events that led to the publication of De Bry's version of the Harriot–White material, see Alexander *Discovering the New World* 64; Hulton *America 1585* 17–21; Quinn ed. *The Roanoke Voyages.*

16 Hulton, introduction to Harriot *Report* xiii.

17 See Shepherd *Amazons and Warrior Women.*

18 See McEachern *Poetics of English Nationhood* ch. 2; Hackett *Virgin Mother, Maiden Queen* ch. 6. On Elizabeth's second reign, see McLaren *Political Culture* introduction; Guy 'The 1590s: The Second Reign of Elizabeth I?' 1–19.

CHAPTER 11

The commonwealth of the word: New England, Old England, and the praying Indians

Linda Gregerson

Six months after the trial and execution of Charles I and two months after the formal declaration of an English commonwealth, amidst deliberative and legislative action on such urgent matters as the settling of army accounts, reforming of the admiralty, assessment and collection of taxes, impressment of sailors, billeting of soldiers, fen drainage, coinage, abolition of the Deans and the House of Lords, pursuit of the war in Ireland, and the sale of forfeited royal and bishopric lands, the Parliament of England turned its attention to a project we may at first imagine to be more remote. On the strength of reports from certain godly ministers in the field and with the intent of furthering their fledgeling mission, Parliament established a corporation, the Society for the Propagation of the Gospel in New England, and appointed sixteen members to its governing board.[1] The New England Company, as it came to be called, was endowed with certain legal powers and obligations within the commonwealth: it could sue or plead, be sued or impleaded in courts of law; it could purchase land and tenements in England and Wales, gather rents, and receive and invest the proceeds of charitable donation. Its mandate, the purpose of these accumulations and investments, was the maintenance of ministers for the conversion of the Indians in New England, the provision of clothing, tools, and other materials conducive to the settlement that was thought to go hand in hand with conversion, and the foundation of 'Universities, Schools, and Nurseries of Literature' for educating the natives and their children.[2]

Parliament's Act of 27 July 1646, 'for the promoting and propagating the Gospel of Jesus Christ in New England', construes a profound continuity and reciprocal obligation between the radically reconstituted commonwealth of England and Wales and the 'many hopeful Towns and Colonies' of New England. The authors of the Act refer to the North American settlers not merely as co-religionists but as co-nationals, part of an extended first-person plural. Since the godly 'of this Nation' (197) have largely exhausted their own estates in the course and labour of New England settlement, it becomes the duty of those still living within the ancient boundaries of the nation to support the work of conversion with money and material supplies: the authors 'conceive our selves of this Nation bound' to help (198). Accordingly, the Act mandates a national collection 'through all the Counties, Cities, Towns and Parishes of England and Wales' (198). Ministers are instructed to read the Act in the presence of their congregations 'upon the next Lords-day after the same shall be delivered unto them, and to exhort the people to a chearful and liberal contribution' (199). Nor is this exhortation intended to die a quiet death beneath the cover of a general appeal. Following their solicitation from the pulpit, ministers and their delegates are instructed to go from house to house to every inhabitant of their parish and 'to take the subscription of every such person in a schedule to be presented by them for that purpose' (200).

Despite some scepticism (monies collected earlier on behalf of the New England missionary enterprise had been poorly accounted for) and some confusion (the most prominent of the New England ministers continued to encourage private donations that bypassed the Society), this charitable fund-raising gradually assumed significant proportions. Between the establishment of the New England Company in 1649 and the Stuart Restoration of 1660, charitable donation to the Society exceeded £15,900 (Kellaway *The New England Company* 30–6). This was supplemented, as the Society exercised its rights to invest in urban and county real estate, by an additional £4,000 in rents. On the American side of the Atlantic, authority to disburse the money raised in England and Wales was vested in the Commissioners of the United Colonies, a confederate body that had been established in 1643 (some six years before the founding of the New England Company) to protect the common interests of the Plymouth, Connecticut, New Haven, and Massachusetts colonies.[3] In addition to bills of exchange and goods intended for direct distribution among the Indians (chiefly clothing, tools, and books), the Commissioners received from London a wide variety of merchandise intended for resale, having persuaded the Society in England that mercantilist activity of at least this limited scope would be the most effective means of transferring dispersable income across the ocean. The Society refused, however, to transfer its principal for reinvestment in New England, as the Commissioners urged it to do; primary investment was to remain firmly situated in England and Wales.

   The business of North American conversion thus involved a reciprocal cultivation and survey of Old and New England: on the one
side, counties and parishes systematically canvassed for benevolent donation, according to 'schedules' and subscription lists, and properties
purchased, administered, and leased; on the other side, ground brought
under cultivation, meeting houses and dwellings built, fourteen 'Praying
Towns' established for the furthering of Christian community among
the Algonquian tribes of eastern Massachusetts. These networks of exchange and affiliation may seem to have been modest in scale, tenuously
inscribed upon the political and economic landscapes that sustained
them. They were, however, far from modest in philosophy or intent, and
they were born of trauma and upheaval on both sides of the Atlantic.
Even modest parcels of land, for instance, bore an immoderate weight of
history: the Society's holdings in England and Wales included a significant proportion of Royalist estates sequestered in the course of civil war;[4]
the 'Praying Towns' in Massachusetts were conceived in part as a last
and fragile bastion against European encroachment. For the Algonquian,
ravaged by English disease and English appropriation, had no effective
means of securing (English) title to traditional tribal grounds in the context of traditional land use; the colonists recognized no proprietary right
to lands that remained uncultivated. 'Take care', John Eliot exhorted
the Commissioners, 'that due Accommodation of Lands and Waters
may be allowed them [the Algonquian tribes], whereon Townships and
Churches may be (in after-Ages) able to subsist; and suffer not the English
to strip them of all their Lands' (Kellaway *The New England Company* 87).
   The deepest reciprocities between the faithful of England and Wales
and their counterparts in New England, however, were manifested not
in acreage but in written words. John Eliot spent fifteen years learning
Algonquian, devising an orthography that could render it on the page,
and translating into that language both Old and New Testaments of the
Bible. That Bible, printed in 1663, was the first complete Bible of any kind
published in North America. It was also, as an instrument for Christian
conversion, 'without precedent in modern times, for there [had been]
no tradition of such Bible translation for missionary purposes' since the
patristic era of the Christian church.[5] Tellingly, Eliot's Algonquian Bible
predated the first Irish Bible by twenty-seven years and the first Scots
Gaelic Bible by over a century. In addition to the complete Algonquian
Bible, Eliot published preliminary translations of the books of Genesis,
Matthew, and the 'Psalms in meter' (1655–6), Richard Baxter's *Call to the
Unconverted* (1663), Lewis Bayly's *Practice of Piety* (1665), an *Indian Grammar*

(1666), an *Indian Primer* (1669), *Indian Dialogues* (1671), an *Indian ABC* (1671), a *Logic Primer* (based on the *Dialecticae* of Petrus Ramus, 1672), and Thomas Shepard's *Sincere Convert* (1689). All but the *Indian Dialogues* were published in Algonquian; a second edition of the Algonquian Bible was completed in 1685 (Kellaway *The New England Company* 122–46). Eliot's petitions for assistance from his English supporters and their New England agents routinely listed paper, type, and journeyman printers among his most urgent requests.

The New England mission also produced a remarkable series of publications printed in London, addressed to the people and Parliament of England, and affording an account of settlement and conversion among the Indians. Four such tracts or promotional pamphlets had been published prior to the founding of the New England Company, and a fifth appeared before the Society assumed responsibility for their production. Eleven tracts were published in all, each conveying its substance in colourful figures of futurity, as in *The Day-breaking, if not the Sun-Rising of the Gospell With the Indians in New-England,* and *The Light Appearing More and More Towards the Perfect Day.* These pamphlets are a conspicuous patchwork for the most part: letters written by Eliot and other ministers in the field; epistolary endorsements from the President of Harvard College, Commissioners of the United Colonies, and persons of note in Parliamentary England; partial transcriptions of the Indian converts in dialogue with their ministers and fellow congregants; sermons and exhortations delivered by the Indians in Christian assembly. Among the most distinctive features of these pamphlets are lists of questions propounded by the Indians in the course of their spiritual training. The following questions, for instance, were propounded by the Indians of Natick, near Roxbury, Massachusetts, in 1649, and were duly recorded by John Eliot, their pastor:

> *If but one parent beleeve, what state are our children in?*
> *How doth much sinne make grace abound? . . .*
> *If so old a man as I repent, may I be saved? . . .*
> *When we come to beleeve, how many of our children doth God take with us, whether all only young ones, or at what age?*
> *What meaneth that, Let the trees of the Wood rejoyce?*
> *What meaneth that, That the Master doth not thank his servant for waiting on him?*
> *What meaneth that, We cannot serve two masters?*
> *Can they in Heaven see us here on Earth?*
> *Do they see and know each other? Shall I know you in heaven?*
> *Do they know each other in Hell?*

When English-men choose Magistrates and Ministers, how do they know who be good men that they dare trust?

Seeing the body sinneth, why should the soule be punished, and what punishment shall the body have?

If all the world be burnt up, where shall hell be?

What is it to beleeve in Christ?

What meaneth, that Christ meriteth eternal life for us?

What meaneth that, Covet not thy neighbours house, etc.?

What meaneth that, The woman brought to Christ a box of Oyle, and washt his feet with tears, etc.?

What meaneth that of the two debtors, one oweth much, another but little?

If a wicked man prayeth, and teacheth, doth God accept, or what saies God?

At what age may maids marry?

If a man be wise, and his Sachem [native overlord] *weak must he yet obey him?*

We are commanded to honour the Sachem, *but is the* Sachem *commanded to love us?*

When all the world shall be burnt up, what shall be in the roome of it . . . ?

What meaneth God, when he sayes, yee shall be my Jewels? (Whitfield *The Light Appearing* 132–3)

The treatise in which these questions appear was published by Henry Whitfield, 'late pastor to the Church of Christ at Gilford in New England', with the explicit intention of countering false reports to the discredit of the New England mission. The questions, that is, are offered as a form of surety, interim report, and prospectus to an audience of interested investors, the Christian faithful of Parliamentary England. Whitfield acknowledges discouraging rumours that the New England mission is but 'a device or engine used . . . to cheat good people of their money' (Whitfield *The Light Appearing* 107). Witness to the contrary, says this testimony from the field, the good use to which your money has been put.

'*What meaneth that, We cannot serve two Masters?*' In the context of the Society for the Propagation of the Gospel in New England, the precept has two primary connotations. First, it asserts the claims of monotheism, that peculiar economy of faith which construes a 'jealous' God.[6] It is worth reminding ourselves that this postulate and its correlative hostility to doctrinal deviation are not the inevitable foundations of religious faith. William Strachey reports, in *The Historie of Travell* (1612), that the king of the Quiyoughcohanock Indians near Jamestown was wont to concede that 'he beleeved or [*sic*] god as much exceeded theires as our guns did their bow and arrowes, and many tymes . . . did send to the President at Iames Towne men with Presents entreating him to pray to his god for rayne, for his gods would not send him any' (Strachey *The Historie of Travell* 101). To Strachey's mind, the Quiyoughcohanock perversely resist a self-evident logic: we want your god to help us, we concede our gods are false, we give them up. But no; the Quiyoughcohanock gods, it appears, are still very much in the pantheon; they simply will not send rain. 'And in this lamentable Ignoraunce', the Englishman writes, 'doe these poore sowles live' (101). Thomas Mayhew, preacher of the gospel on Martha's Vineyard, reports the efforts of the 'praying Indian' Hiacoomes to convert one of his brethren. How many gods do the English have? asks the neophyte. Just one, says Hiacoomes. '[A]nd shall I (saith he) throw away these 37. gods for one?' (Whitfield *The Light Appearing* 111). To the unconverted, the bargain is patently a bad one. It is not simply that spiritual wealth is not assessed according to a single universal standard of weights and measures. The very numerability that signifies bounty in one system of faith is fatally discrediting in another.

'*What meaneth that, We cannot serve two Masters?*' The second assertion conveyed by the biblical precept is the opposition between God and Mammon,[7] the pursuit of this-worldly and other-worldly 'profit'. At the outposts of early modern empire – at the trading ports, in the meeting houses and village schools, in the 'factories' and on colonial plantations – we encounter the problematic overlay of two systems of circulating wealth: material and spiritual 'commodity'. The conversion of souls to Christianity confusedly motivates, overlays, competes with, and covers for the conversion of spices, fabrics, and metals into currency and back again. John Eliot, minister of the Gospel in Roxbury, Massachusetts, reports that the Sachems are hostile to the conversion of their dependents and subordinates. '*Cutshamoquin* . . . told me that the reason of this trouble was, because the Indians that pray to God . . . do not pay [the Sachem] tribute as formerly they have done' (Whitfield *The Light Appearing* 140). Eliot protests to his native informant that he has done his best to avoid direct conflict with the local authorities: '[O]nce before when I heard of his complaint that way, I preached on that text, *Give unto Caesar* . . . [H]e said its true, I taught them well, but they would not in that point do as I taught them' (140). When, however, the 'praying Indians', or 'meeting Indians', as they are called, itemize for Eliot all the labours they still perform, all the goods and money they routinely turn over to their Sachem, the inventory is so impressive that Eliot much 'wonders' at what he takes to be wildly divergent accounts. 'But the bottome of it lieth here', he concludes upon reflection, '[the Sachem] formerly had all or what he would; now he hath but what they will; and admonitions to rule better . . . ' (141). It is not simply that tribute and vassalage may be differently assessed and extracted in different social systems, but that identical measures of tribute and vassalage may be differently assessed and extracted within a *single* social system. Obeisance performed in one spirit may be superabundant; performed in another spirit, it is scant. The preacher's disingenuous stipulation ('Give unto Caesar all that is Caesar's') has venerable precedent, but Caesar and the Sachem have always known that their conflict with Christianity is real, and mortal. They too have heard the precept against two masters. When they hear themselves admonished from below, they know they rule on sufferance.

'*If a man be wise*', asks a convert in Massachusetts, '*and his* Sachem *weak must he yet obey him?*' The Parliament that sponsored the Society for the Propagation of the Gospel in New England during the early years of John Eliot's ministry had concluded in January of 1649 that conscience obliged them to kill a king. Far from resolving the divergent constructions of faith and allegiance, material interest and corporate identity that had pitted Kirk against Prayer Book, Ulster planter against Irish Catholic, Cavalier against Roundhead, Parliament against the king, and the Army against Parliament, the dismantling of monarchy and the Laudian church had unleashed yet further convulsions of centrifugal dissent. There were those who saw a providential, even an apocalyptic, link between turmoil in the Old World and that in the New. 'For the *Shaking of all Nations*', writes Ed[ward] Reynolds, 'maketh way for the coming of him, who is the desire of all Nations'.[8] J. D., 'Minister of the Gospell' in Old England, writes: '[T]hese godly persons who fled into *America* for shelter from *Prelaticall persecution*, doe now appeare to be carried there by a sacred and sweet providence of Christ'.[9] Sixteenth-century England had been a noted haven for religious refugees; by the middle of the seventeenth century, this trend had been dramatically reversed, more than 20,000 English emigrants having left the country to escape religious persecution (Morrill 'The Stuarts' 295; Smith *This Realm of England* 254–5). John Eliot was himself among the nonconforming churchmen who had fled the established Church and shores of England in order to practise his faith more freely; his mission to the Algonquian was a consequence, not the instantiating motive, of emigration (Kellaway *The New England Company* 82).[10] So the Lord 'counterplots the enemy in his designes', J. D. asserts, 'making the late Bishops persecuting of the Godly tend to the promoting of the Gospel'.[11] 'The Lord', writes Joseph Caryl, '*who is wonderful in Councel, and excellent in working*, hath so wrought, that the scorching of some of *his people* with the *Sun of persecution*, hath been the enlightning of those who were *not his people* with the *Sun of righteousnesse'* (Preface to Whitfield *The Light Appearing* 100).

One of the more convoluted debates among planters and preachers on both sides of the Atlantic had to do with the supposed origins of the American Indians. The debate was not merely speculative, despite its frequent abstruseness, nor was it disinterested: the genealogy of the Indians had direct bearing on the settlers' understanding of their own place in Providential design. In 1650, Thomas Thorowgood published the first edition of *Jewes in America, or, Probabilities that the Americans are of that Race*. Like the Rabbi Menasseh ben Israel of Amsterdam, and like Edward Winslow who drafted the Act that established the Society for the Propagation of the Gospel in New England and served on the Society's first board of governors, Thorowgood was convinced that the Amerindians had descended from the ten lost tribes of Israel. This theory, argues J. D. in his Appendix to *Glorious Progress*, has won 'the Generall consent of many judicious, and godly Divines', and 'doth induce *considering minds* to beleeve, that the conversion of the Jewes is at hand'.[12]

Despite a passage in the Massachusetts Charter declaring that conversion of the native populations was 'the principal end of this plantation', New England ministers had been slow to begin their evangelical work. Despite a general conviction, based on prophecies in the Books of Daniel and Revelation, that the millennium would be signalled by two mass conversions, that of the Jews and that of the Gentiles, the faithful disagreed on which conversion would precede the other, and what this boded for active proselytizing. John Eliot appears to have embraced the lost tribes theory for a period of seven years or so, but his mission to the Algonquian both preceded and outlived that period (Cogley 'John Eliot and the Origins of the American Indians'). The debate over tribal origins was dizzying in its complexity and confused in its practical import but clear, for all that, in its foundational assumptions: the fate of England's exiled population of believers, of the Gospel among the Amerindians, and of the English Reformation on its own native soil were indissolubly entwined. In letters addressed to fellow ministers in England and Wales in October of 1649, leading divines of Oxford and Cambridge endorsed the labours of the New England Company as 'not at all relating to, or ingaged in the unhappy differences of these sad and discomposed times', i.e., as a means of advancing the interests of the church while healing division within it (Kellaway *The New England Company* 26). For significant contingents in the Army (a large source of the Society's monetary support) and in Parliament, the New England church of the puritan diaspora afforded a template for work that had yet to be accomplished at home. To their minds, the New England church was bound to cast its beacon in two directions: its mission extended outward to the Indians, whatever their origins, and backward to the stalled Reformation in England.

The logic of eschatology was also entwined in New England with the fiduciary logic of mercantilism and plantation. Plantation requires that there shall be some palpable return on investment, some aggregate influx of wealth to the metropolitan centre that sponsors exploration and development. In its trade with the Orient, early modern Europe had had to reckon with an embarrassing imbalance in consumer demand: while the East afforded great quantities and varieties of merchandise much coveted in Europe, Europe appeared to have very little that the East coveted in return. Hence the pivotal usefulness of New World gold: it was not only desirable in itself; it could also promote the circulation of movable wealth in other parts of the world. Possessed of the one true faith, of course, Christian Europe could tell itself that it possessed a pearl worth all the wealth of the heathen nations combined, and indispensable to the well-being of those nations, if only they could be brought round to the proper understanding. Mr Eliot's letters, writes J. D. in his Appendix, 'are as a discovery of a far more precious *mine* in *America*, then those *Gold* and *Silver* ones of *India*: For they bring tidings of the *unsearchable riches of Christ* revealed unto poor soules in those parts.'[13] Moreover, writes Joseph Caryl, 'This gaine of soules is a *Merchandize* worth the glorying in upon all the *Exchanges*.'[14]

The problem with this impeccable rebalancing of the books is that it could not be made to work out very neatly in pragmatic terms. The New England mission to which John Eliot and Thomas Mayhew devoted their lives had to offer its underwriters the spiritual satisfaction of performing good works *in lieu of* material profit. The work of the gospel in Roxbury, in Natick, on Martha's Vineyard, in Pautucket, is 'difficult, not only in respect of the language, but also in respect of their barbarous course of life and poverty; there is not so much as meat, drink, or lodging for them that go unto them to preach among them, but we must carry all things with us, and somewhat to give unto them' (Eliot in Winslow *Glorious Progress* Civ). Eliot dwells, as well he might, upon the practical difficulties that attend conversion among a population afflicted with much material want. He appears to feel it as an advantage that he can offer the Algonquian a double advancement, both material and spiritual: 'they shall flock unto the Gospel, thereby to receive externall benificence and advancement, as well as spirituall grace and blessings' (Civ). From a less sanguine perspective, however, the practical difficulties Eliot describes are compounded by the further difficulties they engender, difficulties both heuristic and political. Christ preached among the Gentiles as a poor man, as Eliot himself points out, 'a poore underling, and his servants poore', yet his English servants come to the Indians armed with relative riches and power (CIV). Is it not possible that their example will be misleading? Might not the material incentive obscure or deform the spiritual? The Commissioners of the United Colonies cautioned Eliot that the Indians might 'onely follow Christ for loaves and outward advantage Remaining enimies to the yoak and goverment' (Kellaway *The New England Company* 92). Acknowledging the real and present danger of material bribes, one anonymous promoter of the New England mission tried to distinguish its methods from those of the Catholic competition on these very grounds: 'if wee would force them to baptisme (as the Spaniards do . . .) or if wee would hire them to it by giving them coates and shirts . . . wee could have gathered many hundreds, yea thousands it may bee by this time . . . ; but wee have not learnt as yet that art of coyning Christians'.[15]

According to Edward Reynolds, the Indians may measure the truth of (Reformed) Christianity and the disinterestedness of its promoters by the latter's opposition to worldly riches. Joseph Caryl thumpingly concurs: 'How much it doth become Christians to let Heathens see that they seek *them* more then *theirs*; That the gaining of them to Christ is more in their eye, then any worldly gain' (Preface to Whitfield *The Light Appearing* 100). The Indians, however, are not certain how to read this. '*What meaneth God*', they ask in Massachusetts, '*when he sayes, ye shall be my Jewels?*' To covet the souls of the Indians, rather than their furs and precious metals, is for Joseph Caryl to be absolved of mercenary motive, to be found pure. At some ideological distance, however, his words induce something of a chill. Add to the peculiar imperatives of monotheism the peculiar imperatives of a proselytizing church and you have a formidable institution hungry for expansion. The English faithful construed their mission as a merciful corrective to the murderous depredations they associated with the Spanish conquest – and thus with Roman Catholicism. The harms engendered in the name of faith, however, have never been exclusive to a single church. Hypocrisy and cynical self-interest on the part of the proselytizers afford tempting interpretive 'solutions' to the historical conjunction of material exploitation, violent demographic shifts, and Christian conversion. If sheer bad faith afforded a fully sufficient account, the interpretive conundrum would evaporate. To my mind, it does not.[16] '[I]n the old law', writes William Strachey, 'the elected Iew accompted every Iew his neighbour only, yet synce the time of Grace, we are taught to acknowledge every man . . . to be . . . our neighbour' (Strachey *The Historie of Travell* 19). Under the new law, the faithful are instructed to 'Goe, and baptise all Nations, . . . that all Nations might be . . . Partakers of . . . Redemption' (23, 28).

The planters in New England needed money for seed, for tools, for set- tled shelter, for books, for paper, for schools, and journeymen printers. 'I finde it absolutely necessary', writes John Eliot, 'to carry on civility with Religion' (Winslow *Glorious Progress* C4v). The civility he describes has two main branches: (1) that which Eliot calls 'cohabitation', the establishment of settled communities among the Indians so that they may function as congregations, and (2) literacy. Neither project is simple: land must be brought under cultivation, the habits and techniques of husbandry must be introduced, a language must be written down, the Bible trans- lated. The pragmatic difficulties of settlement and education, however, daunting as they may be, pale beside the epistemological difficulties of propagating a text-based religion among a people who have no tradition of literacy. The problem was especially keen for Protestant missionaries, who could not rely on the liturgical and sacramental mediations of the Roman Catholic church. This was what the Reformation had been *about*. Christ is represented in a book, as the Word that at once fulfils and super- sedes an earlier testament, the mere letter. What can this mean, though, to those for whom the letter itself is an innovation? The central textual strategy of the gospels, the parabolic logic that overturns while relying upon an earlier textual tradition, assumes mind-boggling complication in the New England plantation. John Eliot – he who transcribed the questions reprinted above – reports in 1658 on the exegetical progress of his converts. In a time of sickness and bad harvest, the Indians of Natick gather together for a day of fasting and prayer. The 'exhortations' they offer and which Eliot records are more elaborate than the questions of a decade earlier: the Indians have now been trained to perform their own ritualized *explication de texte*, and this at a time when they have 'none of the Scriptures printed in their own Language, save *Genesis*, and *Matthew*, and a few *Psalmes* in Meter' (Eliot 'Postscript' to *A further Accompt* D4r).

The Indian Waban takes his text from Matthew: 'I will have mercy and not sacrifice; for I came not to call the righteous, but sinners to Repentance' (Matthew 9:13). 'What!' says Waban, 'Doth not God love them that be righteous? Doth he not call them to him? . . . Is not God righteous?' Answer: 'These words are a Similitude . . . The righteous here are not meant those that are truly righteous, but those that are

Hypocrites; that seem righteous, and are not; that think themselves right-eous, but are not so indeed' (Eliot *A further Accompt* C2v, C2r–v). The Indian John Speene takes his text from Matthew as well (Matthew was the only gospel the Indians had so far): '*I . . . baptize you with water . . . but he that cometh after me . . . shall baptize you . . . with fire*'. This too is a similitude.

[Y]ou all know what fire will do; for when your Tobacco-pipes are filthy, foule, stinking, unfit for your use, you cast them into the fire, and that doth not burn them up, but burneth up all their filth, and maketh them clean and sweet, & fit for your use. So our hearts are filthy, and unfit for Gods use, but cast our hearts into the word, for there the Spirit is, and then the Spirit of God will burn out all our filth and sin, and make us sweet, and fit for the Lords use. (Eliot *A Further Accompt* D2r)

The God of the Englishmen speaks in figures, and nowhere so insistently as through the mouth of his Son.

Thomas Mayhew, out on Martha's Vineyard, records a homelier scene, less bookish, that he takes to be evidence of progress in spiritual un-derstanding among his converts. A five-day-old child of 'meeting Indians' has died. Mayhew beholds a remarkable change in the ceremonies of passage:

[H]ere were no black faces for it as the manner of the Indians is, nor goods buried with it, nor hellish howlings over the dead, but a patient resigning of it to him that gave it; . . . and as we were going away, one of the Indians told me he was much refreshed in being freed from their old customes, as also to hear of the Resurrection of good men and their children to be with God. (Whitfield *The Light Appearing* 116)

Conversion installs its own sort of double-entry system, one in which God's creatures are always and hopelessly in debt on account of their sins, but capable of being 'redeemed', bought back for salvation by Christ. The paradox of the Protestant ethic, whatever it may have done for capitalism, involves the profound discrediting of 'works'. In order that the macroeconomic vista be one of hope, the microeconomic vista must be one of despair: I can never make good on my debt to God; it is presumption (and a deadly sin) to think I can. According to what logic, then, should Reformed Christians invest in the propagation of the gospel?

'*Come forth ye Masters of money*', writes J. D. in his Appendix, 'part with your gold to promote the Gospel . . . If you give any thing *yearly*, . . . Christ will be your *Pensioner*. If you give anything into *banke*, Christ will keep *account* thereof, and reward it . . . [W]hat ever you give will be well and

wisely improved' (Winslow *Glorious Progress* E2r). That is, contributions
to the New England plantation for which he canvasses will be a *good
investment.* Wasn't it the founding purpose of the Reformation, however,
to remind the faithful that they cannot buy their way to heaven? Henry
Whitfield, though he publishes *The Light Appearing* in order to promote
plantations, paints a rather darker picture of what the investor may hope
to secure: 'Brethren, the Lord hath no need of us, but if it please him,
can carry his Gospel to the other side of the world . . . and leave us in
Indian darknesse' (Whitfield *The Light Appearing* 146–7). John Eliot finds
something of a middle ground: 'Your faithful and unwearied paines
about the Lords work for the good of his dear children here, and for the
furtherance of the kingdome of Christ among these poor Indians, shall
doubtlesse be had in remembrance before the Lord, not through merit,
but mercie' (Whitfield *The Light Appearing* 130). Not through merit: even
from *within* the project of missionary conversion, the point is not that the
Indians need the Englishmen (efficacious grace comes from God alone,
and God is not dependent upon the English instrument). The point is
rather that Englishmen, cast out of England by oppression and civil tur-
bulence, or remaining in England only to see their hopes of a purified
church give way to new forms of tyranny and fragmentation, require a
missionary project among tribes more dispersed than their own (when
he did not hold firmly to the lost-tribes-of-Israel theory, Eliot seems to
have held with the alternate theory that the Amerindians derive from
Tartarian or Scythian tribes; Cogley 'John Eliot and the Origins of the
American Indians' 213). They required this not in order to obtain grace
(grace cannot be earned), but to achieve an interim consolation, that of
community. With no guarantee that they would constitute the community of the saved, the agents of the Christian mission could perform the
work that marked them as the community of the hopeful.

The modern nation is a back-formation, part of the retroactive logic
of empire. Hence our common recourse to the colonial periphery when
we try to understand what the nation is and how it is perceived by
those who claim to constitute it. The community for which Eliot and
Mayhew proselytized was universalist and transcendent, a community
that rendered national boundaries and nationalist ideology obsolete, and
yet it was a community whose fate was indissolubly linked for many
seventeenth-century Englishmen with the fate of their own emergent
nation. The church was one, but its restoration to unity required a state-
based bastion of Reform. The Word was one, but the unifying instrument
of Reform was a multiplying vernacular. The constitutive paradox of

early modern Britain was at once an uncertain union of asymmetrically empowered ethnicities, cultures, languages, and administrative units and an uncertain union of secular and religious aspiration. This paradox was profoundly aggravated by the transatlantic colonial encounter. Historians and sociologists have begun to argue for the inseparability of state formation and empire-building in the early modern period (Armitage *Ideological Origins of the British Empire*; Adams *The Familial State*; Gorski *The Disciplinary Revolution*). While emphatically sharing that view, this chapter also suggests that the experience and experiments of colonialism are in many ways more complex than the language of empire would allow.

To a twenty-first-century reader, the catechistical exchanges reported by John Eliot as part of his effort to bring certain eastern Algonquian tribes into the one true faith contain a devastating cultural and political critique of his enterprise. The temptation is to imagine that only we are alive to the full weight of this critique and the full irony of these exchanges, but we would be better advised to underestimate neither the Algonquian nor the ministers who evangelized among them. Some of the 'questions' propounded by the Indian converts are not at all ambiguous in the force of their critique: '*Doe not Englishmen spoile their soules, to say a thing cost them more then it did? and is it not all one as to steale?*' Yet John Eliot duly records this question, along with others that cut to the contorted roots of Christian faith: '*I see why I must feare Hell, and do so every day. But why must I feare God?*' And, '*If God made hell in one of the six dayes, why did God make Hell before Adam had sinned?*' (Winslow *The Glorious Progress* C3r). It is far too crude to imagine that only the perspectives of postcolonial postmodernity can offer purchase on the full complexity of these questions, the circumstances in which they were propounded, and the (heavily mediated) circumstances in which they came to the attention of the faithful back in Parliamentarian and early Restoration England. '[L]et me give you a taste of their knowledge by their Questions', John Eliot writes (Winslow *Glorious Progress* C2r). They are, to his mind, very *good* questions; they accrue to the credit of both his converts and his mission. Why should we imagine he could only believe this if he believed his Algonquian interlocutors to be missing the point? At the outposts of early modern empire, in the prayer meetings as in the frankly mercantilist and military centres, we see the groundwork laid for the devastating exploitation that is still our heritage. At the same time, the improbable, even preposterous labours the New England congregations represent testify to a baffling component of *good* faith, and on both sides: a vision of commonwealth that considerably challenges our present analytical vocabularies.[17]

NOTES

I am greatly indebted to Steven Mullaney, Julia Adams, John Knott, and the editors for their suggestions and scrupulous critique, to Laura Stevens for sharing with me the fruits of her research, to John Schietinger and Erica Fenby for research assistance. Earlier versions of this chapter were delivered as papers at the annual meetings of the MLA in Washington DC (1996), at the conference on Archipelagic Identities 1485–1791 at Hertford College, Oxford (1999), to members of the English Department at the University of North Carolina, Greensboro, and to members of the Early Modern Colloquium at the University of Michigan. My thanks to the organizers of those events, and to members of the audience.

1 The New England mission was still quite new when the Society was established in 1649. On the Massachusetts mainland, John Eliot first preached to the Indians of Nonantum in the fall of 1646, his earlier attempts to interest them in Christian salvation having been met with flat rejection: 'they gave no heed unto it, but were weary, and rather despised what I said'. See Van Lonkhuyzen 'A Reappraisal' 401. On Martha's Vineyard, the Indian Hiacoomes converted to Christianity under the guidance of Thomas Mayhew, Jr, as early as 1642, but his example was chiefly scorned by other Wampanoags until the 'universal sicknes' of 1645–6 (Whitfield *The Light Appearing* 111).

2 Firth and Rait eds. *An Act for the promoting and propagating the Gospel of Jesus Christ in New England [27 July, 1649]*. In Firth and Rait *Acts and Ordinances* II:197–200. Further references are given by page number in the text.

3 Since the Commissioners, as William Kellaway observes, had originally been charged with protecting colonists *against* the Indians (as well as against the Dutch and French), there was at times some dissonance between their original and their newly augmented responsibilities (Kellaway *The New England Company* 62–3).

4 When the New England Company was reauthorized under the restored Stuart monarchy (its new charter was sealed on 7 February 1661), it was also allowed to regain control over the properties and rents it had obtained during the interregnum. In the case of its most valuable properties, however, estates purchased from the Royalist Thomas Bedingfield, this reassertion of title involved years of litigation and disrupted income. See Kellaway *The New England Company* 41–55.

5 I.e., since the versions produced by 'the almost legendary figures of the early Church – Ulfilas, Mesrop, and Cyril and Methodius'. See 'Bible Translations' in Hoxie *Encyclopedia of North American Indians* 67–9.

6 Stephen Greenblatt usefully estranges the notion in *Marvelous Possessions* 120.

7 This 'second' connotation is, of course, the explanation given by Christ himself in the biblical verse that prompts Eliot's Indian's question: 'No man can serve two masters: for either he will hate the one, and love the other; or else he will hold to the one, and despise the other. Ye cannot serve God and mammon' (Matthew 6:24; King James Version).

8 'How much', he continues, those winds and shakings which carried many good men out of *Old* into *New England* have made way to the publishing of the name of Christ in those barbarous places' (Ed[ward] Reynolds, Introductory epistle 'To the Christian Reader' in Eliot *A further Accompt* (1659) A2r).

9 J. D. Appendix to Winslow *Glorious Progress* E1r.

10 The authors of the *Dictionary of National Biography* (*DNB*) assert that Eliot was first ordained within the Anglican church; Kellaway (*The New England Company* 81–2) thinks this improbable.

11 J. D. Appendix to Winslow *Glorious Progress* E1r.

12 Ibid. D3v.

13 Ibid.

14 Caryl in Eliot *A Late and Further Manifestation of the Progress of the Gospel amongst the Indians in New-England* 267.

15 [Wilson, John?] *The Day-breaking* 15.

16 For some of the better-balanced attempts to assess the motives and impact of the New England missionaries, see Naeher 'Dialogue in the Wilderness'; Ronda 'Generations of Faith' and '"We Are Well As We Are"'; Salisbury 'Red Puritans'; Stevens 'The Poor Indians'; Van Lonkhuyzen 'A Reappraisal'.

17 For bibliographic listings of the eleven promotional pamphlets, see: Eliot 1–4, Eliot and Mayhew, Shepard, Whitfield, and *New Englands First Fruits*.

VI

Restoring Britain

CHAPTER 12

Orrery's Ireland and the British problem, 1641–1679

John Kerrigan

In 1669, the Earl of Orrery's *Guzman* was performed at Lincoln's Inn Fields. This charming, lightweight comedy – very different from the rhymed heroic dramas which made the Earl's reputation earlier in the decade – concerns a young gentleman of decayed fortune who pretends to be a magician in order to fleece the rich and advance the marriage prospects of his siblings. Francisco's skills are most apparent when the anti-hero, Guzman, who is obliged to fight a duel, visits the supposed sorcerer to purchase a charm against death. The scene is set with '*flashes of Fire*' and much dancing around by boys '*in hideous Dresses, making great Noises and Hums*'. Does Guzman require protection against sword-thrust or gun-shot?, Francisco asks. Shouldn't the charm be tested? Claiming that he has used the magic on himself, Francisco hands over a pistol which is charged with powder but not loaded. In the words of the stage direction: 'Guzm[an] *Shoots, and* Fran[cisco] *lets fall a Bullet at his own Feet, which he hastily takes up and shews to* Guzm[an] *who is amaz'd at the Shot.*'[1]

What suggested this trick to Orrery? His editor, William Smith Clark, scoured Spanish as well as English literature to find sources for the plot of *Guzman*, only to conclude that the author probably 'invented the whole flimsy structure'.[2] Clark overlooked, however, an episode in Ireton's Irish campaign which Orrery – then Lord Broghill – participated in, and promptly reported to the English public in *A Letter from the Lord Broghill to the Honourable William Lenthall Esq.* (1651). It seems that, after a bloody encounter with Catholic forces in North Cork, Broghill found, on the corpses of the defeated Irish, charms against death by sword-thrust and musket-shot, which had been distributed by the priests who sprinkled the troops with holy water as they went to fight. In his *Letter* Broghill transcribes one of these charms, and remarks: 'Certainly they are a people strangely given over to destruction, who though otherwise understanding enough, let themselves be still deluded by rediculous things, and by more rediculous persons; Had I been one of the charmed, I would have first tryed mine on the Priest which gave it.'[3]

Much could be said about Protestant attitudes to the Catholic Irishry's weakness for hocus pocus.[4] What interests me more immediately is the effect on the received picture of Orrery of this link between 'rediculous things' on a Munster battlefield and a gulling plot on the London stage, nearly two decades later, because literary scholars have underestimated the importance of his experiences of conflict and government in the peripheries of the archipelago. This is the more surprising given that the leading facts of his life – which was always centred on Ireland – were set out by Kathleen M. Lynch as long ago as 1965.[5] The best accounts of his prose romance, *Parthenissa*, by Paul Salzman and Nigel Smith, both see it as reflecting 'the pervasive political concerns of England in the Interregnum',[6] while the fullest, essay-length discussions of his plays, by Mita Choudhury and Nancy Klein Maguire,[7] are innocent of Irish data. As a result, scholars have failed to understand why his early plays in particular were so successful with audiences attuned to the politics of the Three Kingdoms and their relationship with the United Provinces, Spain, and France.

This, in turn, has led them to overlook how Orrery's interests were both compromised and advanced by the stresses, fractures, and volatile coalitions which emerged within the Stuart multiple monarchy in the mid-seventeenth century. I want to reinspect his career here in the light of those interactive perplexities, which involved religion and culture as well as high politics, and which constitute a large part of the multi-faceted question (which is grounded in state formation) that historians call the British problem. As will become apparent, Orrery's contributions to prose romance, drama, and polemic were not just historically symp-tomatic but were active responses to political difficulty designed both to realize literary possibilities and to intervene in politics in the (partly achieved) hope of extending Anglo-Protestant hegemony in Ireland and more largely around the archipelago.

It is true that Broghill's career was tied into specifically English politics in 1649 when, *en route* to join the exiled court on the continent, he was (the story goes)[8] intercepted in London by Cromwell and offered a choice between working for parliament and languishing in the Tower. He won Cromwell's trust, however, by campaigning with him in Munster, and governing for him in Scotland, and he renewed his influence at Whitehall by advising Charles II on advantageous ways of satisfying the Protestant interest in Ireland. So his moves from Royalism through cooperation with the Lord Protector into support for a Stuart Restoration only superficially resemble the gyrations of such English politician–writers as Edmund Waller. His shifts of allegiance were typical of those born into the New English families that had established themselves in Munster in the wake of the Tudor conquest, and who had stayed true to the Church of Ireland – those known by the mid-seventeenth century as Old Protestants – for whom the contest between king and Parliament was compounded by religious war and conflict over land ownership after the Irish Rebellion of 1641.

It would be a mistake, however, to view Broghill as merely representative, not just because he was unique in the mixture of piety, opportunism, physical courage, erudition, low avarice, and high imagination which made up his mental world, but because his Protestant community was heterogeneous even before the arrival of the dissenting Independents who followed Cromwell. It included such leaders as Inchiquin, whose switches of loyalty and faith (often conflicting with those of Broghill) were encouraged by his Gaelic background, and his Catholic relatives and clients.[9] By 1641, morever, the interests of the New English were patchily interwoven with those of the traditionally Catholic Old English and mere Irish. When Broghill's father, Richard Boyle, First Earl of Cork, was brought news of the rising, he was dining, in a neighbourly way, in the house of his Old English son-in-law the Earl of Barrymore,[10] with the Old Irish landowner, Viscount Muskerry, who was later a leading rebel. Such relationships did nothing to simplify the political choices which faced Old Protestants in the 1640s, and they adopted a variety of positions between the devoted Royalism of Broghill's brother, Viscount Shannon, who went into exile with Charles II and remained loyal even when cuckolded by the king, and the intellectual republicanism of his sister, Lady Ranelagh.

The range of literary culture caught up in these social intricacies can be quickly gauged by triangulating an Old English soldier, a Gaelic poet, and John Milton, around the deaths of two Boyle family members shortly after the outbreak of the Rebellion. In September 1642, Broghill and other Protestant Royalists recaptured a castle at Liscarrol from a group of Catholic rebels commanded by Garret Barry – a professional soldier in the Spanish service, who had published, in Brussels, in 1634 (with the strikingly ethnic assertion '*Composed by Captaine* GERAT BARRY *Irish*' on the title-page) one of the most sophisticated military treatises to appear in English before Orrery's own *Treatise of the Art of War* (1677). It must have added to the bitterness of the fray that, in dedicating his *Discourse of Military Discipline* to the head of his family, Barry had honoured one of the men who now opposed him: the same Earl of Barrymore that had married Broghill's sister, Alice, and who was killed by Barry's men, along with Broghill's brother, Kinelmeaky. Writing about this battle years later, the poet Dáibhí Ó Bruadair ignored the Protestant convert Barrymore and praised the Catholic *seanghaill* who took Kinelmeaky's life.[11] Earlier, though, he had lamented the death of Alice Boyle's second husband – surprisingly enough, a Catholic, Sir John Barry – and wished success to Barrymore's eldest son,[12] who went with his mother to England in 1645 and became, at Lady Ranelagh's prompting, a pupil of Milton.[13] So the literary contexts of Liscarrol link Garrett Barry and Ó Bruadair with the greatest puritan poet of the day, a poet whose life may have been saved at the Restoration by the mediation of Orrery at the instigation of Lady Ranelagh.[14]

Broghill's own literary connections were in one respect more circumscribed than those I have just sketched. Though he possibly learned some Gaelic in childhood,[15] he seems, as an adult, neither to have read the language nor to have understood the culture which the Cromwellians assaulted. It is unlikely that he knew the lines in which the poet Piarais Feiritéir, a tenant of the Boyles, praised his father as 'Iarla calma Corcaighe' ('the brave Earl of Cork'), and there is no sign of his responding to the innovative body of work in which Feiritéir registers the breakdown in relations between neighbours, and the fierceness of the Cromwellian 'gang from Dover'.[16] Feiritéir was caught up in the troubles which he lamented: initially on good terms with the planters, he was given arms to oppose the rebels, but he joined the rising, and, after several years holding Tralee Castle, he was treacherously executed. That Broghill knew something about him is clear from his complaints to Parliament about Inchiquin's dealings with Catholics, but he there mentions favours done to Feiritéir as a rebel with no reference to his being a poet.[17]

Despite his indifference to the fact that some of the finest verse of the age was being composed on the Boyle estates – an undervaluation of Irish that he shared with most of his Protestant contemporaries – Broghill's acquaintance with poets was extensive, and archipelagic. Did his appreciation of drama begin when he was five and six years old and visiting players (probably English) performed at his father's Lismore Castle?[18] As a young man at the Caroline court, he befriended Suckling and possibly D'Avenant. The former wrote him a marriage poem,[19] while the latter subsequently praised him as 'A great new World', lauded his cruelties in Munster – when he made the Lee run red with blood, and hanged a Catholic bishop[20] – and helped him, after the Restoration, get his plays staged in London. During the interregnum, Broghill exchanged poems with Cowley.[21] Irish politics linked him with Roscommon, and encouraged his correspondence with Denham. After the Restoration, he was admired by such younger writers as Dryden for pioneering rhymed heroic drama.[22] The origins of this mode have been disputed but, however the laurels are divided between Orrery and Katherine Philips, its emergence had an Irish dimension.

Philips was, of course, more a Welsh than an Irish writer. She moved from London to Pembrokeshire at fourteen and married a Presbyterian gentleman who represented West Wales constituencies in various interregnum Parliaments. She wrote elegies for her Welsh neighbours and a poem in praise of the 'Brittish language' (i.e. Welsh) used by Merlin, King Arthur, Caractacus, and Boadicea,[23] while she was flatteringly dubbed 'the wise and learned Druyde of Cardigan'.[24] Yet because her marriage portion was partly paid in Irish land that had been confiscated after the 1641 Rebellion,[25] she had to go to Dublin in 1662–3, when appeals against expropriation were being heard, to secure her husband's claim. It was then that Orrery was shown her translation of the third act of Corneille's *La Mort de Pompée*, and, no doubt attracted by the local topicality of a work which deals with the rights and wrongs of clemency after a civil war[26] in the context of conspiracies that threaten a victorious Caesar at the Egyptian edge of empire – cf. the plots against the Lord Lieutenant which stirred among Independents in Ireland – he encouraged her to complete her translation, and advanced £100 to buy costumes for its production at the Smock Alley theatre, shortly before the public première of his *Altemera*, the heroic play which took London by storm as *The Generall*.[27] Much remains obscure about Orrery's support for Philips, but the Cromwellian sympathies which persist in this Royalist poet's translation will not have made him less interested in seeing her work performed.

Philips's ideological ambiguity in 1662–3 is just one reminder of how Orrery's sizeable output – which includes not just romances, plays, and the *Art of War*, but religious poetry, state letters, and controversial pamphlets – was sustained by social networks that discouraged fixed positions, even after the concentrating shock of the 1641 rebellion and the consolidation of Protestant fortunes which followed Charles II's sponsorship of the Act of Explanation (written by Orrery to justify the Restoration land settlement in Ireland). In the 1660s the newly promoted Broghill had to get along with Irish Catholics who had rebelled in the 1640s and gone into exile with the king, and who now returned to court and to their lands in Munster – much as his father had found it necessary to deal with Old Irish and English landowners.[28] His contacts within Ireland may never have been as eclectic as those of, say, Ormond, the Old English leader of Protestant Royalism, but his tentacles reached further. Unlike Ormond, he inherited an estate in England, which he used for periods of retirement when politics became too hot, and which was well placed, in Somerset, for keeping an eye on supply lines between the West Country and Cork. More unusually, he construed his position archipelagically because of his dealings in Scotland.

Like many Royalist gentlemen, Broghill initially encountered the Scots in the débâcle of the First Bishops' War. He returned north, however, in 1655–6, as President of the Council in Edinburgh, when his task was to strengthen union by adapting the Scottish legal system to English practice, to extend the Protectorate's support-base by manipulating disagreements between the Remonstrant and Resolutioner factions within Presbyterianism (a strategy which, it was hoped, would control Ulster too), and to root out Royalist conspiracy.[29] The task was made easier for him by blood and marriage ties that linked Munster to Scotland,[30] but it still required political tact. Broghill's relationship with George Monck was probably cemented in 1647, during Monck's third visit to Ireland, when both sided with parliament's Lord Lieutenant, Viscount Lisle, against the volatile Inchiquin. It was in Scotland, however, as servants of Cromwell, that the two future agents of Charles II really worked together. In Edinburgh, Broghill developed his skills as a spymaster, and he was alerted to the seditious traffic between the West of Scotland and Ireland which preoccupied him beyond the change of regime.[31] It was all excellent preparation for the greatest crisis of his life – the Restoration – when he exploited his Presbyterian contacts, and his knowledge of underground Royalism, to plot with Monck and conspire to snatch Dublin Castle from the Army's commissioners. These, it seems to me, are the circumstances which precipitated his first popular success, *The Generall*, a play which loses much when thought about Anglocentrically.

Before turning to that drama, however, I want to show how Orrery's Ireland illuminates an earlier work: the huge, narratively convoluted but continuously readable *Parthenissa*, which began to be published in Waterford, in the year of the *Letter* to Lenthall, 1651, and which broke off with a London instalment in 1669, the year of *Guzman*.[32] This text is less *à clef* than some other romances of the period, such as Sir William Sales's *Theophania* (1655), Richard Brathwaite's *Panthalia* (1659), and Sir George Mackenzie's thinly veiled account, in Book III of *Aretina* (1660), of Anglo-Scottish politics from 1603 to the Restoration. *Parthenissa* starts from a rebellion in Armenia, at the edge of an expansionist Roman empire, against the background of the Social War (91–87 BC) between Rome and its dependent neighbours on the Italic peninsula. J. G. A. Pocock has argued that the War of the Three Kingdoms is difficult to analyse because it combined three different kinds of conflict: civil war in several spheres; imperialistic expansion by the English; and a *bellum sociale* resembling that fought between Rome and its neighbours, over citizenship rights and the like.[33] On the showing of *Parthenissa*, Broghill would agree with Pocock: in his partly topical romance, these modes of conflict are all present, compounded, and concatenated in ways that allow the reader to investigate the processes which generate crisis.

That *Parthenissa* has an Irish aspect is suggested by a letter to Broghill from his brother, the scientist Robert Boyle, in December 1649: 'I am not a little satisfied, to find', he writes,

that since you were reduced to leave your *Parthenissa*, your successes have so happily emulated or continued the story of *Artabbanes*; and that you have now given romances as well credit as reputation. Nor am I moderately pleased, to see you as good in reducing towns in *Munster*, as *Assyria*; and to find your eloquence as prevalent with masters of garrisons, as mistresses of hearts.[34]

This compliment turns on a comparison between the campaigns of a hero in the romance and those of Broghill, with Cromwell, in Ireland. Although *Parthenissa* draws from its sources – which include Polybius and Raleigh's *History of the World*[35] – a number of un-Irish set-piece battles fought with enormous armies, it also describes the long sieges, savage reprisals, piracy or privateering by sea, switches of allegiance, and confusing pacts which characterized war in the Irish theatre.

The rebellion in Armenia, for instance, quickly mounts to a siege which the hero of this part of the narrative, Artavasdes, resists. In describing his success, Broghill is far more attentive to logistics and tactics than is usual in romance – as one might expect from the defender of Lismore against the Irish in 1642 and Youghal against Castlehaven's Confederate troops in 1645. Like those rebels, Artavasdes' opponents have influence at court. More immediately (to isolate a source for this episode), like the Protestants of Cork, who learned from experience in 1644 to secure their garrison by expelling Papists, the Royalists in Artaxata are betrayed from within the siege.[36] 'That which brought us so often into hazard', Artavasdes says, 'was, that Artaxata was twice sett on fire, by the treachery of those within, which requiring many hands to quench it, robb'd us of so many hands for our defence' (I.i.160). Once the traitors have been identified, Broghill relishes their execution, then reveals how, like the Papists, their leader abuses his contacts: 'there was also one of the prisoners that being upon the point of Death, and repenting his Rebellion sent to me, and to discharge his conscience asur'd me that Celindus had a friend in the Kings Councell, who gave him constant Intelligence of our proceedings' (ibid.). This 'friend', Crassolis, resembles such courtiers as the Earl of Glamorgan: a counsellor trusted by Charles who (in Old Protestant eyes) put the interests of the Irish Catholics before those of the crown.

It was an uncomfortable fact for Broghill that, whatever the disloyalty of the Confederate Catholics, it was the besieged Old Protestants who broke the truce called by the king in 1643 so that he could boost his strength in England with Irish troops. At the time they made their case in declarations that Broghill recorded in his letter book – telling the Ulster Scots, for example, that they had been forced to accept the treaty by 'unsupportable sufferings', and explaining that they now end it because 'the Irish are like to obtaine an advantagious Peace, from his Ma[jes]tie by their insinuatinge, and by the wicked Counsell about him'.[37] In the romance, a similar matter is handled more obliquely:

Celindus who perceiv'd that force was unsuccessfull, & that two assaults had cost him neere 7000 men, lost all hopes of takeing Artaxata by storme, and therefore began to make his Approaches, and endeavour to possesse himselfe of that by industry & Tyme which valour had deny'd him; but not wholly to rely upon the blinde Events of Warre, he design'd to attempt somthing by Treaty . . . (I.i.161)

Working with Crassolis at court, Celindus puts terms to the king that are calculated to secure an advantageous peace, and to render his opponents 'surprizable' by making them drop their guard. As a gloss on Confederate motives[38] this could hardly be more jaundiced, but Broghill's account of the debates that went on around Charles I regarding the legitimacy of treating with rebels is absorbingly cogent.

Never less than refracted, Irish history in *Parthenissa* becomes virtual. In Book I of the Second Part, the king of Armenia, Artabazus, escapes the rebellion in his own realm by fleeing to a neighbouring province, where the loyal governor, Phanasder, provides enough men from his overstretched forces to rescue the princess Altazeera from Artaxata. The troops sent to England by Inchiquin during the cessation did Charles, in

practice, little good, and when the truce was broken the Munster Protestants followed him in looking to Parliament. It is perhaps not surprising
that this betrayal should be justified in the narrative by accusation. In the
romance, King Artabazus so ungratefully seizes power from Phanasder
in his province that Artavasdes turns against the monarch he had previously protected from rebels. Such changes of allegiance are common
in *Parthenissa*, and they are never more Irish than when associated with
Broghill's excuse that he was defending Charles's interests by joining his
opponents. As Surena puts it in Part II Book VI: 'If I have bin so unfortu-
nate, as seemingly to take up Arms against my King; yet I am so happie
as to be satisfy'd they are really for him' (II.vi.567). Inconveniently for
Broghill, this was also the justification which Confederates used for the
1641 rising.

What raises *Parthenissa* from apologia to literature, however, is precisely its willingness to seek out and develop such points of difficulty.
Artavasdes may be right to oppose Artabazus for being ungrateful, but
the rebel Surena's motives prove more ambiguous: justified in protecting
Parthenissa against the oppressive suit of his king, he allows noble resistance to rationalize personal ambition and misuses his growing power to
harass the heroine himself. As events unfold it becomes harder to catego-
rize causes as good or bad. The combination of local crisis-management
and expedient royal policy which made it impossible for Old Protestants
to be consistent created a writing-climate for Broghill in which scepticism and suppleness could flourish. Even when his virtuous characters
do not change sides, they find their natural equals – courageous, cour-
teous, and ardent in love – in those ranged against them, sparing them as
strangers because of their acts of valour, or pulling off a helmet to reveal a
friend in the ranks of the enemy. This mode of romance proved lastingly
attractive,[39] but it was peculiarly consoling to Broghill's contemporaries
in Ireland who knew what it was to fight against those who had been
allies, and who wanted to believe, once the civil wars were over, that the
amity of such characters as Artabbanes and Artavasdes, who met when
fighting one another, could be strong and true.

In the four books of *Parthenissa* published in 1669, Orrery is less
interested in the reduction of towns in Assyria and Munster than in
such Protectorate and Restoration topics as the spectacle of war at sea.
The romance continues to be troubled, however, by the fear of neighbourly betrayal which no doubt did afflict Old Protestants traumatized
by the 1641 Rebellion but which they also played up whenever the Dublin
government seemed likely to deal tolerantly with Catholics. Even after

206 *John Kerrigan*

the Restoration, when Ireland had been at peace for a decade, there is a pressurizing vigilance in Orrery's letters to Ormond about conspiracies, and the same anxiety dictates the tone of the treatise which he addressed to the Lord Lieutenant in 1662, *The Irish Colours Displayed*. There Orrery resists the royal counsels of reconciliation, describing the Irish as inveterate enemies of the English, and giving climactic emphasis to 'the late unparalell'd Massacres'.[40] The best way to avoid a repetition of the rising, he insists in his letters, is to have a Protestant militia ready for instant use.

Near the end of *Parthenissa* these views come through in the account of unrest in Nicomedia. As its name suggests, this city falls within the historical territory of Nicomedes of Bithynia, but it is held by an élite governing on behalf of Mithridates of Persia. Like Dublin or the Munster garrison towns, the place is divided. Numbers of the inhabitants are loyal to the wrong monarch, much as the 'Vulgar *Irish*', according to *The Irish Colours Displayed*, believe 'that the Kingdome of *Ireland* lawfully belongs to the Crown of *Spain*' (5). In the romance, 'a rich *Nicomedian*' (for which read an Old English Catholic), who is entertaining the Princess of Persia at his house, abducts her on behalf of a 'Conspirator's party' while 'the antient Inhabitants of the place' (the Gaelic Irish) take up arms against the government. Fortunately 'the then chief Magistrate of *Nicomedia*', being a wiser lieutenant than Ormond, has anticipated the unrest, and the hero of this section, Callimachus (who might here be Orrery), is able to 'the more hastily put the *Pontick* Militia of *Nicomedia* in Arms' (III.vi.15–17).

Those equations are speculative and circumstantial because the topicality of *Parthenissa* is not determinate. Its procedures owe much to the seventeenth-century belief – summarized by John M. Wallace – that

to moralize about contemporary affairs and yet to write a piece of literature [an author should] see in the local incidents the general rules that they typified. Then he had to find his fable, usually in history books, although no source was barred and a pure invention was quite permissible; and finally . . . work up his fable with all the expertise at his command. The reader . . . would reverse the process, going from particulars to generals to particulars again.[41]

This catches well the work of analysis, extrapolation, and analogy construction that has gone into *Parthenissa*. Broghill makes it impossible to read the romance as ancient history by mixing figures from different periods – Hannibal, Sulla, Pompey – and introducing pieces of 'pure invention' inspired by French romance (oracles, arduous quests, recovery from apparent death, erotic intrigues). Relevance to war in the

Three Kingdoms is local and fleeting, or elusively paradigmatic, or it lies
in the strands of resemblance which make a hero such as Artabbanes
suggest now one contemporary figure and now another.

Artabbanes is certainly prismatic. While Robert Boyle was right to
see Broghill in his make-up, he also smacks of Cromwell.[42] In Book III
of Part I, he turns into the historical figure of Spartacus, leading a slave
revolt and showing great military acumen. Because we are accustomed
to the Spartacus of Hollywood and Soviet ballet, it is easy to overlook how
unusual Broghill's positive account of him is. Elsewhere in early modern
Anglophone literature and political theory he seems to be ignored or
glancingly vilified. In his Preface, Broghill recommends Spartacus as
more admirable even than Masaniello, the Neapolitan fisherman who
led a 'Revolt . . . from the King of Spayne in the Present' (I, A2v). The
Europe-wide cult of Masaniello which followed the rising of 1647 awaits
its historian,[43] but medals pairing him with Cromwell were definitely
struck.[44] In the case of Artabbanes it looks as though war in Ireland
led Broghill to compound his Royalist liking for princely heroes with a
devotion to Protestant liberty under a low-born leader.

To read *The Generall* after *Parthenissa* is to be made to think harder about
the king of Spain. Although, as events would show, Spain posed less of a
threat to the stability of post-Restoration Ireland than did Louis XIV's
France, Old Protestants remembered how Catholic soldiers recruited by
Garret Barry and others for service in Spain's own *bellum sociale*, between
Castile, Catalonia, and Portugal, had stayed in Ireland in 1640–1 and
been deployed in the Rebellion.[45] Once the Cromwellian invasion took
hold, and Catholic landowners began to be dispossessed and sent into
Connaught or the West Indies, Spain was the country to which defeated
rebels went:

> *Transport, transplant,* mo mheabhair ar Bhéarla.
> *Shoot him, kill him, strip him, tear him.*
> *A Tory, hack him, hang him, rebel,*
> *a rogue, a thief, a priest, a papist.*
> Bíd na mílte dínn i n-aonacht,
> iad 'na mbanna dá dtarra[i]ng 'na gcéadaibh
> chum gach cuain ar fuaid na hÉireann,
> dá gcur don Spáinn ar áis nó ar éigin.[46]

These horrific lines, probably composed *c.* 1658 in County Cork,[47]
are not unique in seventeenth-century Irish poetry in their macaronic

representation of conflict.[48] They are peculiarly interesting, however, because they show a word which would have a long future in British politics ('*Tory*') returning to the Gaelic, from which it emerged in the 1640s, with heightened, sectarian overtones – overtones that would pejoratively attach it to the Duke of York's faction during the Exclusion Crisis of 1679–81, where it was polarized against the Scottish-derived label 'Whig'.[49] If the penetration but also appropriation of Gaelic by English at this point illustrates in miniature how the British and Irish problems became inextricable, the passage also shows that the problems of Ireland were bound up with Catholic hopes and Protestant fears about 'Spáinn'. The belief, reported by Orrery, that the king of Spain was properly the ruler of Ireland (above, p. 206) was widely current among the 'Vulgar *Irish*' throughout the period.

Nor was the Spanish threat perceived solely as coming from the Catholics. Shortly after the première of *The Generall*, in 1663, Orrery informed the king that republicans were working for an invasion of Ireland by Spain.[50] Clark (Orrery's editor) may be right to say that the setting of *The Generall* in Sicily is not significant, but when he backs this up by pointing out that Mora, the base of those rebelling in the play, is actually in Spain, not Sicily, one is inclined to wonder. For Masaniello's revolt in Naples was linked to a rising in the Spanish dominion of Sicily,[51] a place of strategic importance which interested Orrery enough for a 'map of Scicily' to be prominent in his library.[52] By choosing the locale he did, Orrery was able to correlate unrest in one island that was breaking its links with Spain (i.e. Sicily) with the troubles in another (i.e. Ireland) that accompanied the Restoration – an event that Orrery wanted to construct as freeing Munster from the threat of Catholic hegemony long associated with Spanish power.

Like a number of heroic dramas written in the 1660s – for which it provided the pattern – *The Generall* is about the overthrow of a usurper. Having seized power in Sicily, put the legitimate heir (Melizer) in prison, and sent his general, and rival for the heroine Altemera, into banishment, the play's unnamed usurper-king finds himself confronted by rebels and uncertainly backed by an army that wants its general back. This general, Clorimun, is another of Orrery's prismatic characters: primarily a version of Monck, he has touches of Broghill himself (who was General of the Horse in Ireland for Parliament and Major-General of the Army in 1662), and like both men he is drawn into events reluctantly, expressing a preference for retirement. Once involved, his contribution is decisive. The jealousy of the usurper and the pleas of Altemera ignite his loyalty to Melizer, and he helps effect a Restoration in the course of which he is reconciled to Lucidor, the leading rebel and Altemera's lover.

As a dramatist Orrery has been seen by Choudhury as a propagandist for Charles II, and by Maguire as a troubled ex-Cromwellian who is driven by guilty repetition-compulsion to return to the same clutch of issues. My own view is very different. In his plays, as in *Parthenissa*, Orrery strikes me as calculating: both critical of Carolean policy and cannily defensive. The latter was particularly necessary when he wrote *The Generall* because his role in the run-up to the Restoration had been more duplicitous than he retrospectively claimed.[53] Apart from anything else, he had compromised the position of the Church of Ireland by networking with the 'Presbyterian knot'.[54] When he plotted in this way from Munster, Broghill was only partly smoothing the way for Monck in Scotland and England. He was also preparing, as some recognized at the time, to set hard conditions for the king – resisting the Restoration which did occur for the sake of another (more advantageous to Old Protestants) which did not. Despite his part in the conspiracy to seize Dublin Castle and other garrisons in 1659, he was not an unconditional Royalist, and he expressed surprise at the swift liberality of the invitation issued to Charles by the London Parliament.[55] He was slow to make the advances which his Royalist relatives expected, and careful to write critically to Thurloe about 'odd plots here concerning the King'.[56]

In *The Generall* these awkward facts are finessed, while open resistance to the Cromwells is subtly discredited. Thrasolin, an officer working for the usurper, as Broghill did for the Protectorate, proves more useful to Melizer (i.e. Charles II) than those who are frankly rebellious because he can orchestrate unrest in the army, and persuade the usurper to recall the general. Since the seeds of conflict are already sown between Clorimun and the usurper, it is then only a matter of time before Melizer's Restoration is secured. Who, though, are the rebels, in their Irish-sounding stronghold, Mora? Since they are not fighting in support of Melizer[57] – though their leader is reconciled with Clorimun, who, by that stage, is – they can hardly put us in mind of, say, the English Royalists of Booth's rebellion. A 1660s audience would have pricked up its ears at 'Rebels' and 'Confederacy' when Thrasolin describes the usurper's mistrust of his own men: 'Sometimes hee thinkes, the Rebells being nigh, / That wee and they are in Confederacy' (I.[i.]86–7). *The Generall* is hardly more *à clef* than *Parthenissa*, but these rebels sound very like Catholic Confederates: justly opposed by the usurper and his general – until he treats with them – they can as properly be turned to Royalist ends by the right sort of well-intentioned collaborator.

If *The Generall* were simply an apology for Monck, this section of the plot might be taken as rendering more palatable the truce which he made with the Spanish-trained mere Irish leader, Owen Roe O'Neill, in 1649[58] – that year of shifting alliances which provoked Milton in his *Observations on the Articles of Peace* to denounce the Belfast presbytery for its similarly dangerous accommodation with Catholic rebels. Yet the dénouement of the play, in which the darkly named Lucidor is given the hand of Altemera by Melizer, would more immediately have put contemporaries in mind of the post-1660 situation of Catholic moderates. From the grudging point of view of Orrery, the Ormondist-fringe Confederates were the great winners in the Restoration game – the chief beneficiaries of the restored king's mercy – because many had rebelled in 1641, yet, due to their later seeming fidelity,[59] they were granted lands and favour. Certainly, the passive Royalism of the rebels in Act v –

> To their true sovereigne gladly they submitt.
> Against the usurpers pow'r they made defence,
> But they to you are all obedience.   (v.[i.]402–4)

– most naturally evokes the dutifulness of loyal Catholics, while not excluding the thought that hard-line followers of O'Neill were being indulged by Melizer/Charles II, who responds to the submission by saying:

> My mercies still shall be to those more great,
> Which to it trust, and for it doe not treat.
> Past faults I'le never to Remembrance bring.
> (409–11)

Any suggestion of laxity is qualified, however, by Melizer's wisdom in giving Clorimun, the character who most resembles Monck and Broghill, the authority and military means to protect Sicily/Ireland against invasion from Catholic Europe (Puglia was at this date under Spanish control, of course): 'Now *Clorimun*', he declares, 'The *Apulian* king on *Scicily* does fall, / And of this Warr I make you Generall' (417–18).

It is worth recalling the circumstances in which *The Generall* was performed. Before its public première, the play (or a version of it) was privately staged in Dublin in front of the Lord Lieutenant, Ormond, under the title *Altemera*. In London, in 1664, it opened to an audience which included Charles II. Both occasions gave Orrery the chance to set up for admiration the royal policy of oblivion, while avoiding (through the impersonality of drama) full endorsement of the king's tolerance, and pressing for power in Dublin to be exercised by his own faction. Once that is noticed, the play's willingness superficially to harmonize with official policy itself seems calculated, and the tenor of the work can be squared with Orrery's more aggressive *Irish Colours Displayed* and its elaborately documented partner, *An Answer of a Person of Quality to a Scandalous Letter* – both published in 1662, the year of *The Generall*'s Irish performances, in reply to Peter Walsh's *Letter Desiring a Just and Mercifull Regard of the Roman Catholicks of Ireland* (1662?). Brought out anonymously not least to conceal Orrery's involvement with those he now called 'the late horrid Usurpers',[60] these pamphlets whitewash the erratic record of Old Protestant Royalism and condemn the conduct of Irish Catholics into the period covered by *The Generall*. Whatever Walsh may claim, Orrery scoffs, 'not the Birds nor the Flies contributed lesse to [the Restoration] then the *Roman* Catholique *Irish*'.[61]

The Old English Franciscan Walsh is an interesting target for Orrery to have selected because he was execrated by such firm Romanists as Ó Bruadair for his willingness to obey the king rather than the Pope in spiritual matters.[62] As so often in Irish politics, the compromiser was perceived by all sides as especially threatening. In his *Letter* to Ormond, Walsh admits that wrongs had been done by Catholics, but says that they have been punished by the scourge of war, and that Protestants have behaved badly too. The Lord Lieutenant should even-handedly 'preserve the ... people of so many different Nations of the Brittish Monarchy'.[63] Orrery responded to this by warning against the adoption of measures which might strengthen Catholic rebels. A powerfully built passage in *The Irish Colours Displayed* predicts endless contention in Ireland given the long history of animosity, the differences of habit and language, and the 'enmity' which naturally holds between a 'subjected people' and 'their Conquerors'. Orrery must have written this with a copy of Spenser's *View of the State of Ireland* in hand, because he ends up refuting the Latin tag with which Sir James Ware, in his 1633 preface, had rebuked the poet's pessimism: 'When all these thoughts ... run thorough my head, I cannot hope to live so long as to hear *Iam cuncti gens una sumus* [now we are one people] plaid by the *Irish* Harp, though I know it was sung by some *English* in their discourses about the beginning of the late Kings

Reign' (4–7). Orrery prefers to cite Spenser on the savagery of Irish funerals (5), and to recommend his policy toward Papists. As he puts it in the *Answer*: 'The BEAST if *pamper'd*, will *Kick*, if kept *low*, OBEY' (82).

Walsh lacks Orrery's forensic skill, but he qualifies his divisive pessimism, in *The Irish Colours Folded* (1662), by invoking other multiple monarchies and cultural genealogies. Comparing the 1641 Rebellion with the rising in Catalonia, he points out that the Spanish now sit amicably with 'the *Catalonians*, who . . . transferred the Dominion over them to a Foreign Prince, [and] murdered . . . all the *Spaniards* that came in their way' (4). Pursuing a line that reflects the relatively integrationist experience of the Old English, he says that the Irish are as capable of getting on with their conquerors as their conquerers were with theirs: 'The *Brittains*, the *Danes*, the *Saxons*, and the *Normans* are now so incorporated in *England*, as the memory of all distinction is lost amongst them' (3). Orrery had categorized Ormond as culturally English (*Irish Colours Displayed* 9–10); Walsh is more interested in his Anglo-Norman ancestors, and how they kept their lands. If Ormond adopts the mercy and justice of his forebears, he predicts, peace will break out and 'the posteri[t]y of those that proclaim lowdly the English interest, must within an age, admit themselves to be called Irish as well as the Descendants from the first Colony of English planted in *Ireland*' (11).

Three and half centuries later it is still too early to say whether Walsh was right. It took the Old Protestants decades to feel secure enough in their Irishness and hostile enough to England to generate what has been called colonial nationalism, and to this day, in Ulster, the Presbyterian pieces of the jigsaw do not fit. Yet Ulster also complicated Orrery's perception of the British problem – as can be seen from the way he and other Irish Protestants used the word 'British'.[64] Early in *The Irish Colours Displayed* he sweepingly describes his theme as 'The contention lying . . . between His Majesties *British* Protestant Subjects, and His *Irish* Romane Catholique in the Kingdome of *Ireland*' (2). Later, though, he applies 'British' exclusively to the Ulster Scots and writes instead about the 'English' – itself an ambiguous term, which sometimes includes the Anglo-Normans who remained Catholic, and sometimes more restrictively the Old Protestants and Cromwellians. His less than frank assertion that Charles II could rely on 'His Protestant Subjects in *Ireland*, whom I look upon all as one body' (*Irish Colours Displayed* 15) would crumble in 1666 when the covenanters revolted in Scotland. 'I consider Ireland as consisting of three sorts of people', he then told Ormond: 'the protestants, the Scotch presbyters and other sectaries, and the papists'.[65]

Orrery's self-presentation as not Irish, not fully British, and not yet Anglo-Irish, but as – in a peculiar sense – one of 'the English in Ireland', was shaped by his London life as a young man, and by periods in Somerset. It was, however, focused by the conflicts of the 1640s and 1650s, when the Old Protestants were caught between Scottish complications in Ulster and rebellious Gaelic Irish, and by their vulnerability after the Restoration – a vulnerability which hindsight tends to underestimate, compounded as it was by archipelagic interconnections and a changing international scene that brought war with France and the United Provinces close to the shores of Munster. Those are the springs of Orrery's fear, in 1666, that unrest in Scotland would spread to Presbyterian Ulster and incite Catholics to plot a rising with help from the continent. In his letter to Ormond about the 'three sorts of people' in Ireland, Orrery predicts that Louis XIV will send arms, encouraged by the presence in France of 'the desperatest sort of Irish'. What made the dangers worse, as he pointed out, was that the London Parliament (which had already refused to countenance an Act of Union on commercial grounds)[66] was damaging the revenue on which the defence of Ireland depended by legislating against the import of Irish cattle.[67]

All this explains why Orrery, whose *Parthenissa* and *The Generall* are so rooted in Irish conditions, and who was so staunch in defending the interests of Munster Protestants against England,[68] should have gone on to write plays that are unique on the early Restoration stage in dealing with English history (and should have added, in 1676, a romance about Henry VIII called *English Adventures*). *Henry the Fifth* and *The Black Prince* do not represent the full spread of his drama, even in the 1660s: *Mustapha*, for instance, a tragedy about false counsellors, is set in Hungary among the Turks, and his most searching usurper play *Tryphon* revisits the cruces of *The Generall* in a setting vaguely drawn from Josephus' history of the Maccabees. They are the clearest symptoms, however, of an Englishness which was the more assertive and anxious for being Irish, and threatened by the power of France – a preoccupation not just in the history plays but in the long poem called 'A Vision' that Orrery wrote in 1675, and in his *Art of War*.

The constructed Englishness of *Henry the Fifth* is most immediately displayed in the homogeneity of its *dramatis personae*. In giving Owen Tudor a large (and unhistorical) role as Henry's confidant, Orrery erased his Welsh descent: nothing in the play recalls the fractious exchanges between MacMorris, Fluellen, Pistol, and Jamy in Shakespeare. Orrery's

English characters are, inevitably, virtuous, courageous, and faithful, though their sharing a code of love and honour with the French élite does smooth Henry's path to achieving his territorial rights and the hand of the Princess Katherine. This code is richly capable of generating dramatic tension. Owen Tudor, for instance, feels obliged to woo the princess on the king's behalf when requested, even though he loves her himself. It is significant that his predicament should be counterpointed with an intrigue in which the Duke of Burgundy breaks a treaty with the English king, because although it is only in a limited sense political it transposes the dilemmas which Broghill and others faced when choosing between obedience to the crown and self-interest in the 1650s.

No doubt the huge success enjoyed by *Henry the Fifth* when it opened in 1664 partly stems from this ability to tent the wounds of both loyalty and betrayal. The French accept Henry as their monarch, for example, not just because of his victories but because they are persuaded that 'since *Charles the Fair* / Our Kings insensibly Usurpers were'.[69] This translates into the thought that, since the demise of Charles I, the Three Kingdoms had almost inadvertently been governed by usurpers – from Oliver Cromwell through his sons Richard and (in Ireland) Henry. Now, as King Henry puts it, 'English and French . . . but one people are, / And both shall have my equal love and care' (v.[vii.]551–2). What makes this different from other Restoration appeals for reconciliation between former enemies is its multinational setting. The king asserts a unity which (as at the end of *The Generall*) would join Irish Catholics to the English – a reconciliation somewhat speciously conjured up by a language of 'one people' not used by the English in Ireland about the mere Irish but about the English of England,[70] especially when hoping for an Act of Union or relaxation of customs dues.

Does that mean that Orrery's *Henry the Fifth* can, like Shakespeare's,[71] be read as shadowing a suppression of rebellion in Ireland – as putting on stage the reconquest which Orrery joined Cromwell to achieve but which he now wished to think of as always a royal cause? Here is what the Archbishop of Canterbury says to the French about the conflict among the barons and the Peasants Revolt that marred the reign of Richard II:

> Civil Wars our Isle destroy'd:
> Our Swords against our selves were long imploy'd.
> Whilst sick with Civil War, Prides worst disease,
> We bled in *France*, and lost three Provinces.
> But, now when those Intestine Wars are done,
> We come here to receive, or take our own.
>
> (IV.[i.]53–8)

This so transparently and plausibly blames the loss of most of Ireland on the first English Civil War that alert spectators would have interpreted *Henry the Fifth* as saying *inter alia* that the crown should now receive or take its own in Ireland and not succumb to a show of peace from the Catholics. As Orrery put it in his *Answer* to Walsh, 'The Crown hath often lost by Credulity what it hath got by Valour; it hath lost by pretence of Peace what it had gain'd in open War: The Kings interest in *France* was thus lost, the GOD of peace prevent the like in *Ireland*' (*Irish Colours Displayed* 83).

These intimations are not surprising in a play which was completed in Dublin, in 1662, when Orrery was preoccupied with the Walsh controversy, and which opened in 1664 when he was in London working on the Act of Settlement.[72] Yet the work's potency as political fantasy depends on the France it presents suggesting not just contemporary Ireland but the France of Louis XIV that threatened it. It revels in the idea that Charles II could maintain by force the medieval title 'King of France' that the Stuart monarchs clung to and that Louis XIV was challenging at the time, and indulges the equally unlikely notion that the policy of 'closer union' that both crowns entertained could be clinched on terms advantageous to England by an ill-equipped Royal Navy and under-funded army.[73] A truer measure of the relative power of the two states emerged in the very month that *Henry the Fifth* was licensed (November 1663), when the king's last toehold in France, Dunkirk, taken from Spain by Cromwell, was not exactly lost by credulity in pretence of peace but sold to Louis to help Charles pay his bills.

Orrery was not alone in feeling, by 1662, that the greatest threat to the Three Kingdoms was no longer posed by the Protectorate enemies, Spain and the United Provinces. Anti-French sentiment ran so high in 1661 that there was rioting in London. He was more alert to the danger than many at court, however, because of his Munster perspective. When Charles II was drawn into war with the United Provinces, in March 1665, Orrery could believe that the Dutch were plotting an insurrection with Ludlow and other recidivists;[74] but his fear of Irish Catholicism made him more nervous of France – rightly, as it proved, not just because Louis XIV did go to war against the Three Kingdoms in January 1666 but because he later sent troops to Ireland in support of James II. If Orrery, however, was ahead of much highly placed thinking in 1662, by the time *Henry the Fifth* was performed it was so acceptable that the king allowed his court to be projected into its fantasy. In his role as Owen Tudor, Betterton wore Charles II's coronation robe; Harris, as Henry, that of the Duke of York; and Smith, as the Duke of Burgundy, the robe of the Earl of Oxford. When Orrery began his second dramatic celebration of English arms in France, later in 1664, it was at the king's command.

Even more than *Henry the Fifth*, *The Black Prince* rewrites history as romance. Bluntly warlike in its prologue (which predicts a coronation of Charles II in Paris), it revels in the paradoxes of duty and devotion that are thrown up by rivalry between Edward III, his son the Black Prince, Lord Delaware, and the captive king of France, as they seek the favours of bright Plantagenet. This drama of English nobility and French defeat was just one of Orrery's contributions to the war effort during a year (1666) in which he raised a militia in Munster, made plans to rebuild the fort at Kinsale, and kept Ormond informed about the landing of priests, public masses, and a visit by French ships to Kerry. He even gave him a résumé of a play put on by a Jesuit schoolmaster about a pastor who, with the help of his scholars, destroyed the wolves (i.e. the Protestants) that had ravaged his flock – evidence that Irish Catholics could be as topical as Orrery in their drama.[75] Anxiety was widespread in the Three Kingdoms, but the apprehensiveness in County Cork was such that Orrery was unable to write a letter recommending *The Black Prince* without discussing the likelihood of French arms reaching the Irish.[76] In some ways appropriately, because the play is set in the aftermath of war, *The Black Prince* was not staged until October 1667, by which time a treaty had been ratified with France and her allies. It is a sign of the problematic position of Munster within the British entity, however, that Orrery had to seek guidance from Ormond as to whether the waters around the province were excluded from the peace declared in 'the British seas'.[77]

No doubt this continuing sense of exposure contributed to the treatment of a merchant called Lynch, who had the misfortune to raise Orrery's suspicions in October 1667 – as *The Black Prince* was being premièred – with a letter that he was carrying in French about procuring items from Ireland. Explaining to Ormond that he '*looked upon the cerf, mouton, and poules des Indes as being false names . . . for ammunition, horse, foot, &c.*', Orrery said that he had only menaced, not injured, Lynch by tying lighted gunpowder matches to his fingers.[78] What would have happened to Lynch had he not managed to placate his tormenter can be deduced from the fate of Guillaume Preudhomme who was similarly treated in 1669 (the year of *Guzman*) and, according to a doctor, 'burned to the very sinews, which was a naughty thing'.[79] For a man of Orrery's make-up – refined, but inured to atrocities – the risk of another 1641 licensed ruthlessness. It would have confirmed rather than challenged his belief that little had changed to have known that, while he was torturing

Preudhomme, Charles II and his inner circle – including Sir Richard Bellings, son of a leading Confederate Catholic – were negotiating with Louis XIV the secret Treaty of Dover. The deceiving counsellor Crassolis, who misled King Artabanus in *Parthenissa*, was active again at court.

Orrery discovered as much when his enemies, and some former allies, weakened his influence in 1672 and deprived him of his powers in the Lord President's court of Munster.[80] The sense that history was regressing to the condition of 1641 can only have been enhanced for him by the recruitment, in Ireland, of troops for Louis XIV's armies. Under pressure from the House of Commons in 1675, Charles recalled a brigade of soldiers – many of them Irish – from the French service, but he then committed the blunder of leaving them together in Ireland under Catholic officers.[81] A similar build-up of Irish forces had been unacceptable to Parliament forty years earlier under Strafford, and it was not pleasing now. When the House voted against granting the king any supply, Orrery responded by writing his 'Vision', in which the headless ghost of Charles I appears to his sleeping son and urges him to respect law and property while the Genius of France, laden with guns and money bags, tempts him with Popery, absolutism, and French gold. This poem about 'poore Englands Fate' nowhere mentions Ireland, but, as surely as *Henry the Fifth*, it was generated by Irish circumstances.[82]

For wealthy Protestants, Restoration Munster was a place of increasing affluence; its big houses filled up with fine carpets, silver dishes, expensive looking-glasses, and oriental porcelain.[83] Yet fears of another 1641 grew during the 1670s, fed by reprints from London – publication was banned in Dublin – of Sir John Temple's *History of the Irish Rebellion* (1646), with its inflated massacre statistics. Orrery had always regarded the rebellion as an archipelagic phenomenon because he saw how the Irish Catholics had been emboldened by the Scottish covenant into pressing Charles I for concessions; so the covenanter rising of 1666 left him with anxieties which the king's toleration toward the Catholics (which might have pulled Old Protestants and Ulster Presbyterians together) did nothing to allay. Repeatedly after 1674, signs of unrest in Scotland prompted the Dublin government to send troops to Ulster, and there was continuous vigilance regarding contacts between Presbyterians across the North Channel. From the composition of 'A Vision' in 1675 to the letters which he wrote shortly before his death, in 1679, harassing Ormond about the Popish plot, Orrery was busy with security: rousing the militia, and, despite his gout, supervising from a sedan chair the reconstruction of the fort at Kinsale.

The regressive political psychology of this decade helps explain why, when reading Orrery's last major work, the *Art of War* (1677), one is so often reminded of *Parthenissa* and *The Generall*. Though the urge to warn Charles II about the French threat encourages him to illustrate his text with examples from Louis XIV's campaigns against the Spanish, he keeps adverting to the Irish rebellion, and, when discussing foreign policy, to the ongoing revolts in Sicily which the French now fed with supplies. When he writes about treachery within garrisons, and about how to deal with fires during sieges, it is the Protestant towns of Munster in the 1640s that he has in mind, just as he had when writing about the siege of Artaxata in *Parthenissa*.[84] When he urges the usefulness of pikes, or the prudence of having passwords, he invokes encounters like the one described in his 1651 *Letter to Lenthall* – triumphs he was revisiting as he prepared his unfinished and now lost history of the Confederate Wars.

So the opening boast of the *Art of War*, that 'no one Nation in the World, hath acquir'd more Glory by Arms, than the *English*', and the disquisition which follows on why English soldiers are as courageous as the Greeks and Romans, follows *Henry the Fifth* in celebrating an Englishness constructed by Ireland – a position which verges on paradox when Orrery, who is elsewhere happy to call Ireland 'my Countrey' (*Irish Colours Displayed* 3), and who now lived permanently in Munster, calls the English 'my Countreymen'.[85] What the comparison with classical soldiery also brings into focus, however, is Orrery's relative reluctance to institute any categorization that would support a contrast between English civility and Irish barbarousness. When discussing Caesar's wars, for instance, he praises the Celtic leader Vercingetorix as 'a Person worthy to command a National Army', and he is sarcastic about the Greek and Roman habit of referring to their opponents as 'barbarous Nations (as they were pleas'd to term them)' (168, 130). Even in *Parthenissa*, where Hannibal's 'barbarous Affricans' and the Parthians who carry their enemies' heads on spears, 'according to their barbarous custome', resemble the savage Irish of Spenser (I.iv.351; II.viii.755), Orrery had made it clear that the leaders of these forces, though sometimes (like Hannibal himself) gripped by primitive passions, were capable of noble behaviour. While he was happy in his controversy with Peter Walsh to echo the charge of barbarism levelled against the Irish by earlier propagandists and still heard after the Restoration,[86] his slights were primarily tactical.

The implications of this are various, but one point worth bringing out, given the way post-colonial theory and New Historicism (with its New World interests) have encouraged literary scholars to assimilate early modern Ireland to the history of colonialism, is that, by highlighting the dynamics of the British problem, an archipelagic approach encourages us to qualify accounts of Anglo-Irish relations that concentrate on the westward enterprise, in which Ireland figures as a mid-Atlantic stepping-stone to the Americas.[87] That Protestants of English stock compared the Irish with wild Native Americans is not in dispute;[88] but the works of Orrery show that such a construction was far from automatic. Because he could not afford to underestimate his opponents by taking their inferiority for granted, he was more pragmatic than programmatic in contrasting English with Irish mores (the more salient contrast, for him, was between élite and poorer social groups).

It would thus be misleading to elide his attitudes with those developed in the more systematically colonialist Elizabethan and early seventeenth-century treatises, even though he was a hard-line advocate of expropriation, who bent his energies to redistributing Catholic-owned estates and to entrenching the big-house, landed society that would develop, after the victories of William III, into the Anglo-Irish Ascendancy. His intellect was mobilized by unpredictable conflict and messy accommodation with competing groups across the Atlantic islands, including a sizeable Catholic élite within Munster. *Parthenissa* is evidently a product of those contingencies, but the polished eloquence of the heroic plays – which can be misread as complacent – is just as fraught with the strain of maintaining, or manufacturing, a display of loyalty. In Orrery we see history and place fostering an early modern sensibility more archipelagic than purely Irish or English, and a remarkable body of writings not readily assimilable to so-called 'English literature'.

NOTES

This chapter was researched and written during my tenure of a British Academy Research Readership (1998–2000). I am grateful to Alison McCann of the West Sussex Record Office for help with the Petworth House Archives and to Lord Egremont for permission to quote from them.

1 *The Dramatic Works of Roger Boyle Earl of Orrery* ed. William Smith Clark II 2 vols. (Cambridge, MA: Harvard University Press, 1937) I; II.[iv.]202–364.

2 *Dramatic Works of Roger Boyle*, I, 437.

3 *A Letter from the Lord Broghill to the Honourable William Lenthall Esq.* (London, 1651), 5.

4 For examples see Barnabe Riche, *A New Description of Ireland* (London, 1610) A3r, A4v–B2v, D2r–v, H1r–v, H4r–Ir, I2r–K1r; *The Irish Sections of Fynes Moryson's Unpublished 'Itinerary'* ed. Graham Kew (Dublin: Irish Manuscripts Commission, 1998), 104–5. That the assumption of superiority did not

protect its possessors from superstition is suggested by the medical advice sent by John [?Nunnsig] to the Countess of Orrery in 1668 (Edward MacLysaght ed. *Calendar of the Orrery Papers* (Dublin: Stationery Office, 1941) 61–2).

5 Kathleen M. Lynch *Roger Boyle First Earl of Orrery* (Knoxville: University of Tennessee Press, 1965); cf. now Patrick Little 'The Political Career of Roger Boyle, Lord Broghill, 1636–1660' Ph.D. thesis (Birkbeck College, University of London, 2000), which does not, however, discuss literary material.

6 Paul Salzman *English Prose Fiction 1558–1700: A Critical History* (Oxford: Clarendon Press, 1985) 190; Nigel Smith *Literature and Revolution in England, 1640–1660* (New Haven: Yale University Press, 1994) 244, discusses *Parthenissa* as 'native heroic romance . . . for English people'.

7 Mita Choudhury 'Orrery and the London Stage: A Loyalist's Contribution to Restoration Allegorical Drama' *Studia Neophilologica* 62 (1990) 43–59; Nancy Klein Maguire 'Regicide and Reparation: The Autobiographical Drama of Roger Boyle, Earl of Orrery' *English Literary Renaissance* 21:2 (Spring 1991) 257–82, rpt in her *Regicide and Restoration: English Tragicomedy, 1660–1671* (Cambridge: Cambridge University Press, 1992).

8 It was given currency by Thomas Morrice's life of Orrery, included in the anonymously edited *Collection of the State Letters of the Right Honourable Roger Boyle* (London, 1742) 10–11.

9 See, for example, John A. Murphy 'Inchiquin's Changes of Religion' *Journal of the Cork Historical and Archaeological Society* 72 (January–February 1967) 58–68, and 'The Politics of the Munster Protestants' *Journal of the Cork Historical and Archaeological Society* 76 (January–June 1971) 1–20; see also Little 'Political Career of Roger Boyle' ch. 3.

10 On the match, see Nicholas Canny *The Upstart Earl: A Study of the Social and Mental World of Richard Boyle First Earl of Cork, 1566–1643* (Cambridge: Cambridge University Press, 1982) 47–8.

11 'Cuirfead cluain ar crobaing'/'I shall put a cluain' in *Duanaire Dáibid Uí Bruadair: The Poems of David Ó Bruadair* 3 vols. ed. Revd John C. Mac Erlean, Irish Texts Society (London: David Nutt, 1910–17), II:48–97, 53. It is a measure of Ó Bruadair's hostility to English Protestantism that he was willing to see Oliver Stephenson as Old English when his family arrived in Ireland in the same New English wave of Tudor immigration as that of Kinelmeaky himself.

12 'Is boct mo beata'/'My life is now so poor' *Duanaire Dáibid Uí Bruadair* I: 50–67; 'Is olc an ceart'/ ''Twould be an act of shabbiness' *Duanaire Dáibid Uí Bruadair* I: 78–89, 83.

13 James G. Taafe 'John Milton's Student, Richard Barry: A Biographical Note' *Huntington Library Quarterly* 25 (1962) 325–36.

14 William Riley Parker *Milton: A Biography* 2 vols. 2nd edn rev. Gordon Campbell (Oxford: Clarendon Press, 1996) I:572.

15 As did at least three of his brothers: see Canny *Upstart Earl* 127.

16 Ibid. 128; *Dánta Piarais Feiritéir* [ed. Patrick Dineen] with translations by Pat Muldowney (Aubane, Co. Cork: Aubane Historical Society, 1999) 60–1, 32–3.

17 *Articles Exhibited to the Honourable House of Commons Assembled in Parliament, Against the Lord Inchiquine Lord President of Munster, Subscribed by the Lord Broghill and Sir Arthur Loftus Knight* (London, 1647) 2.

18 For these visits in the context of Boyle-family and Munster great-house entertainments more largely, see Alan J. Fletcher *Drama, Performance, and Polity in Pre-Cromwellian Ireland* (Cork: Cork University Press, 2000) 230.

19 'Upon my Lord Brohalls Wedding' in *The Works of Sir John Suckling, The Non-Dramatic Works* ed. Thomas Clayton (Oxford: Clarendon Press, 1971).

20 'Poem to the Earl of Orrery' (comp. 1650–7) lines 3, 553–96, in *Sir William Davenant: The Shorter Poems, and Songs from the Plays and Masques* ed. A. M. Gibbs (Oxford: Clarendon Press, 1972).

21 Ted-Larry Pebworth 'The Earl of Orrery and Cowley's *Davideis*: Recovered Works and New Connections' *Modern Philology* 76:2 (1978) 136–48.

22 See, for example, the Dedication to Dryden's *The Rival Ladies* (1664).

23 *The Collected Works of Katherine Philips: The Matchless Orinda* 3 vols. ed. Patrick Thomas, Germaine Greer, and Ruth Little (Stump Cross: Stump Cross Books, 1990–3) I:202–3.

24 Sir Edward Dering *Letter-Book* (University of Cincinnati Library, Phillipps MS 14932) Letter 3 (29 September 1662). Cf. 'Roger Boyle, Earl of Orrery To Orinda' in *Poems by Several Persons* (Dublin, 1663), which concludes: 'If there be *Helicon*, in *Wales* it is. / Oh happy Country! which to our Prince gives / His title, and in which *Orinda* lives' (*Collected Works of Katherine Philips* III:188).

25 *Collected Works of Katherine Philips* II:57.

26 Cf. Andrew Shifflett ' "How Many Virtues Must I Hate?"': Katherine Philips and the Politics of Clemency' *Studies in Philology* 94 (1997) 103–35.

27 Evidence of the plans to seize Dublin Castle and murder the Lord Lieutenant (of which Orrery appears to have had some intelligence) surfaced in March, May, and June 1663. *Pompey* and *Altemera* were staged in February. Cf. Philips 'To my Lord Duke of Ormond, Lord Lieutenant of Ireland, on the discovery of the late Plot' in *Collected Works of Katherine Philips* I:222–3, and *Orinda to Poliarchus* Letter 33 in II:95–6, 96.

28 Cf. S. J. Connolly *Religion, Law, and Power: The Making of Protestant Ireland 1660–1760* (Oxford: Clarendon Press, 1992) 19.

29 F. D. Dow *Cromwellian Scotland, 1651–1660* (Edinburgh: Donald, 1979) chs. 8–9; T. C. Barnard 'Planters and Policies in Cromwellian Ireland' *Past and Present* 61 (1973) 31–69, 53–60; Julia Buckroyd 'Lord Broghill and the Scottish Church, 1655–1656' *Journal of Ecclesiastical History* 27 (1976) 359–68; David M. Walker *A Legal History of Scotland* Vol. IV: *The Seventeenth Century* (Edinburgh: T. and T. Clark, 1996) 69–70; Little 'Political Career of Roger Boyle' ch. 5.

30 Little 'Political Career of Roger Boyle' 153–4.

31 Dow *Cromwellian Scotland* 187–94.

32 On the complex publishing history see C. William Miller 'A Bibliographical Study of *Parthenissa* by Roger Boyle Earl of Orrery' *Studies in Bibliography* 2 (1949–50) 115–37.

33 'The Atlantic Archipelago and the War of the Three Kingdoms' in Brendan Bradshaw and John Morrill eds. *The British Problem*, c. *1534–1707: State Formation in the Atlantic Archipelago* (London: Macmillan, 1996) 172–91.

34 *The Works of the Honourable Robert Boyle* 5 vols. ed. Thomas Birch (London, 1744), V:239.

35 *Parthenissa* 3 parts in 6 tomes (London, 1655–69) Preface; I, A2r.

36 See the confession of a plotting friar before execution and the attempted betrayal of Cork to Muskerry by its Mayor and aldermen described in *A Manifestation Directed to the Honourable Houses of Parliament in England, Sent from the Lord Inchequin, the Lord Broghill [and others]* (London, 1644) 9–10, and, for a more balanced analysis, John A. Murphy 'The Expulsion of the Irish from Cork in 1644' *Journal of the Cork Historical and Archaeological Society* 69 (1964) 123–30.

37 BL Add MS 25287 pp. 6–12.

38 For a nuanced account of these see Micheál Ó Siochrú *Confederate Ireland 1642–1649* (Dublin: Four Courts, 1999) ch. 2.

39 See, for example, Colley Cibber's praise for the 'irresistably Inviting' *Parthenissa*, when introducing his adaptation from it, *Perolla and Izadora. A Tragedy* (London, 1706) A2r.

40 *The Irish Colours Displayed, In A Reply of an English Protestant to a Late Letter of an Irish Roman Catholique* (London, 1662) 6.

41 John M. Wallace ' "Examples Are Best Precepts": Readers and Meanings in Seventeenth-Century Poetry' *Critical Inquiry* 1 (1974) 273–90, 286.

42 In dialogue with the Roman Ventidius, Artabbanes presses the advantages of monarchical over republican government, but even there his emphasis is as much on the value of rule by one man (who might be Lord Protector) as it is on the merits of inheritance (II.iii.237–72).

43 In addition to such negative depictions as T. B.'s play, *The Rebellion of Naples* (1649), Broghill would have access to James Howell's translations – as *An Exact Historie of the Late Revolutions in Naples* (London, 1650) and *The Second Part of Massaniello* (London, 1652) – of Alessandro Giraffi's more balanced *Le rivolutioni di Napoli Descritte dal Signor A. G.* (Venice, 1647).

44 Rosario Villari 'Masaniello: Contemporary and Recent Interpretations' *Past and Present* 108 (August 1985) 117–32, 125–6.

45 R. A. Stradling *The Spanish Monarchy and Irish Mercenaries: The Wild Geese in Spain 1618–68* (Blackrock: Irish Academic Press, 1994) 38; J. H. Elliott 'Revolts in the Spanish Monarchy' in Robert Forster and Jack P. Greene *Preconditions of Revolution in Early Modern Europe* (Baltimore: Johns Hopkins University Press, 1970) 109–30.

46 Éamonn mac Donnchadh an Dúna 'Mo lá leóin go deó go n-éagad' lines 129–36 in Cecile O'Rahilly ed. *Five Seventeenth-Century Political Poems* (Dublin: Dublin Institute for Advanced Studies, 1952). Meidhbín Ní Úrdail translates: '*Transport, transplant*, is my recollection of English. *Shoot him, kill him, strip him, tear him. A Tory, hack him, hang him, rebel, a rogue, a thief, a priest, a papist.* Thousands of us are together, they as a bond [bail] transporting themselves

in their hundreds to every harbour throughout Ireland, being sent to Spain willingly or unwillingly.'

47 O'Rahilly ed. *Five Political Poems* 85; Michelle O Riordan ' "Political" Poems in the Mid-Seventeenth-Century Crisis' in Jane Ohlmeyer ed. *Ireland from Independence to Occupation, 1641–1660* (Cambridge: Cambridge University Press, 1995) 112–27, 121.

48 Other examples are quoted and discussed in Joep Leerssen *Mere Irish and Fíor-Ghael: Studies in the Idea of Irish Nationality, its Development and Literary Expression prior to the Nineteenth Century* (1986; Cork: Cork University Press/Field Day, 1996) 202–28.

49 *Oxford English Dictionary*, 'Tory', 'Whig'.

50 *Calendar of the State Papers Relating to Ireland* [hereafter *CSPI*], *1663–1665* ed. Robert Pertland Matiaffy (London: His Majesty's Stationery Office, 1908), 151.

51 H. G. Koenigsberger 'The Revolt of Palermo in 1647' *Cambridge Historical Journal* 8 (1944–6) 129–44.

52 A booklist in the Petworth House Archives (Orrery Papers MS 13190) – which records many theological and ecclesiastical works, Catholic as well as Protestant, the usual classical texts (e.g., 'Homers Iliads', Cicero, Sallust, Lucan), legal and political treatises (including 'Matchevills Works' in Folio), books about travel (Hakluyt), and modern literature (not least 'All Dryden's plays') – gives 'Maps' as a general heading but only specifies the map of Sicily under it.

53 Aidan Clarke *Prelude to Restoration in Ireland: The End of the Commonwealth 1659–1660* (Cambridge: Cambridge University Press, 1999) 260–1, 263, 287.

54 Ibid. 263, on Broghill's 'approach to Robert Douglas and a number of other prominent members of the Edinburgh presbytery associated with the loyalist "Resolutioner" group with whom he had negotiated during his time as president of the Scottish council'.

55 Ibid. 292–3.

56 Ibid. 276.

57 As the king puts it: 'And, *Lucidor*, since you to armes did fly / But to preserve your mistresse' Chastitie' (v.i.389–90).

58 Hard-pressed by the Confederates, and told by Cromwell to protect English interests as best he could until an invasion was launched, the always Royalist-inclined Monck exploited O'Neill's disaffection with more moderate or compromising factions in the Confederation to persuade him into a pact that allowed O'Neill to buy Parliamentary gunpowder. Monck was required to explain this extraordinary deal to the Council of State, and reprimanded. The scandal was not forgotten: when Thomas Gumble wrote his *Life* in 1671, he felt obliged to justify the pact at length, and then excused it by saying: 'This Action, little can be said for it, but the usual Arguments of Necessity and Self-preservation' (*The Life of General Monck, Duke of Albemarle* (London, 1671) 27). As for Catholic historians, the pro-O'Neill author of the *Aphorismical Discovery* was so embarrassed that he ignored the truce, merely saying that, when

Ormond and Inchiquin signed an instrument for O'Neill to buy ammunition, 'he made his waies with Colonell Monke', while Richard Bellings,
the Old English Ormondist, stressed the treachery to the Confederate
cause which O'Neill's willingness to treat with Monck demonstrated, though
he was careful to say nothing to the detriment of Monck, who had become,
thanks to the Restoration, a Royalist hero (*Aphorismical Discovery of Treasonable
Faction* in John T. Gilbert ed. *A Contemporary History of Affairs in Ireland* 3 vols. in
6 (Dublin: Irish Archaeological and Celtic Society, 1879–80) II:1, 37; Richard
Bellings *History of the Irish Confederation and the War in Ireland, 1641–1643*
ed. John T. Gilbert, 7 vols. (Dublin: John T. Gilbert, 1882–91), VII:117ff.).

59 See, for example, *Irish Colours Displayed* 5.

60 *An Answer of a Person of Quality to a Scandalous Letter* (Dublin, 1662) 18.

61 *Irish Colours Displayed* 12.

62 'Ionnsa d'féinn éirionni' ('Tis sad for Erin's Fenian bands') *Duanaire Dáibid
Uí Bruadair* II:8–11.

63 *A Letter Desiring a Just and Mercifull Regard of the Roman Catholicks of Ireland, Given
about the End of October 1660* (Dublin?, 1662?).

64 See, for example, Connolly *Religion, Law, and Power* 114–24.

65 *State Letters* 198.

66 Barnard 'Planters and Policies' 60–6.

67 An Irish Cattle Bill was narrowly passed, after heated debate, on 23 November
1666.

68 See, for example, his speech to the General Convention, held in Dublin in
1660, saying 'that rather then Ireland should bee the least Mote in the Ey
of England hee would loose his right hand, but rather then England should
be a beame in the ey of Ireland he would loose his head' (quoted by Clarke
Prelude to Restoration 271).

69 v.[iii.]291–2; in *Dramatic Works of Roger Boyle* I.

70 Cf. James Kelly 'The Origins of the Act of Union: An Examination of
Unionist Opinion in Britain and Ireland, 1650–1800' *Irish Historical Studies*
25 (1986–7) 236–63, 237–46; T. C. Barnard 'Crises of Identity Among Irish
Protestants 1641–1685' *Past and Present* 127 (1990) 39–83, 42–3; Jim Smyth
' "Like Amphibious Animals": Irish Protestants, Ancient Britons, 1691–1707'
Historical Journal 36 (1993) 785–97, and ' "No Remedy More Proper": Anglo-
Irish Unionism Before 1707' in Brendan Bradshaw and Peter Roberts eds.
British Consciousness and Identity: The Making of Britain, 1533–1707 (Cambridge:
Cambridge University Press, 1998) 301–20.

71 See, for example, David J. Baker *Between Nations: Shakespeare, Spenser, Marvell,
and the Question of Britain* (Stanford: Stanford University Press, 1997) ch. 1;
Christopher Highley *Shakespeare, Spenser, and the Crisis in Ireland* (Cambridge:
Cambridge University Press, 1997) ch. 6.

72 Contrast the exclusively English reading by John Butler 'The Mirror of
a King: The Earl of Orrery and Shakespeare on King Henry V' *Cahiers
Élisabéthains* 45 (April 1994) 65–75.

73 See, for example, Keith Feiling, *British Foreign Policy 1660–1672* (London:
Macmillan, 1930) 63, 69, 73, 149, 218.

74 *State Letters* 124–5.

75 *State Letters* 140–1, 187, 205; cf. Liam Irwin 'The Earl of Orrery and the Military Problems of Restoration Munster' *Irish Sword* 13 (1977–9) 10–19.

76 To Viscount Conway and Killulta, 17 July 1666; *CSPI 1666–1669* 156–8.

77 *State Letters* 297.

78 *CSPI 1666–1669* 476–8; for anti-French sentiment more largely at this date see Steven C. A. Pincus *Protestantism and Patriotism: Ideologies and the Making of English Foreign Policy, 1650–1668* (Cambridge: Cambridge University Press, 1996) ch. 25.

79 *CSPI 1666–1669* 725–6.

80 Lynch *Roger Boyle* 140–4, 163–4; Ronald Hutton *Charles II: King of England, Scotland, and Ireland* (Oxford: Clarendon Press, 1989) 298–9.

81 C. T. Atkinson 'Charles II's Regiments in France, 1672–1678' *Journal of the Society for Army Historical Research* 23 (1945) 53–65, 129–36, 161–72; Hutton *Charles II* 328–9, 363.

82 Petworth House Archives, Orrery Papers MS 13187.

83 T. C. Barnard 'The Political, Material and Mental Culture of the Cork Settlers, *c*. 1650–1700' in Patrick O'Flanagan and Cornelius G. Buttimer eds. *Cork: History and Society: Interdisciplinary Essays on the History of an Irish County* (Dublin: Geography Publications, 1993) 309–65, 322–33.

84 Compare, for example, n. 36 above with *A Treatise of the Art of War* (London, 1677) 43.

85 *Art of War* 1, 12. There is a symptomatic split in the make-up of his last book, *Poems on Most of the Festivals of the Church* (1681); it greets the reader with preliminaries produced in London ('Printed for *Henry Herringman* at the Anchor in the Lower Walk of the *New-Exchange*') but the body of the work was apparently printed by William Smith in Cork.

86 On the persistence of such accounts see Nicholas Canny 'Identity Formation in Ireland: The Emergence of the Anglo-Irish' in Nicholas Canny and Anthony Pagden eds. *Colonial Identity in the Atlantic World* (Princeton: Princeton University Press, 1987) 159–212, 198–201, but note Barnard 'Crises of Identity' esp. 78–80.

87 The classic account remains Nicholas Canny *Kingdom and Colony: Ireland in the Atlantic World 1560–1800* (Baltimore: Johns Hopkins University Press, 1988).

88 See, for example, James Muldoon 'The Indian as Irishman' *Essex Institute Historical Collections* 3 (1975) 267–89, but also Patricia Coughlan's thoughtfully complicating 'Counter-Currents in Colonial Discourse: The Political Thought of Vincent and Daniel Gookin' in Jane H. Ohlmeyer ed. *Political Thought in Seventeenth-Century Ireland: Kingdom or Colony* (Cambridge: Cambridge University Press, 2000) 56–82.

CHAPTER 13

Jacobite literature and national identities
Murray Pittock

Jacobitism and its literature and culture have long had the status of an irritant to conventional British historiography, partly because the political inadequacy and military defeat of the Stuart cause are insufficient explanation for its reach and significance, which are thus deemed sentimental and ahistorical. In fact, there are good underlying reasons to accept the importance of Jacobitism, both as a phenomenon in its own day, and through the subsequent influence of its rhetoric. As I have argued elsewhere, nothing could better show this importance than the wrath with which many critics and historians greet the notion that (for example) Samuel Johnson was a Jacobite, or that Jacobitism was an important political and cultural option. Sometimes commentators seem to think that the evaluation of such possibilities is a personal insult to the long-dead writers involved. Hostility and indignation are signs of the importance of the interpretation of the topic at issue, for our understanding of Jacobitism has a deep bearing on our understanding of the eighteenth century in general, and, indeed, of the development of Britain itself.

Jacobite discourses do not simply represent the interests of one side in a dynastic struggle long overtaken by events; rather, they are a set of minority concerns which were suppressed, political options which were not implemented, and religious and national dimensions long ignored. Of these, arguably the most important are the status of Ireland and of Catholicism itself: and in Ireland, Jacobite rhetoric, and the linkage of the Stuarts to the Fianna, survived and renewed itself in the memorializing language of nineteenth- and twentieth-century nationalism. The envisioning of the nation and national identity as feminine, present in both Scotia and Eire, was alike the target of Government propaganda in 1745 and 1798 aimed at feminine 'unnaturalness': 'Delicacy of sentiment, mercy, tenderness, and compassion, the peculiar ornaments of the fair sex, were by them [the Jacobite women] exchanged for wild transports of lawless ambition, the lust of power, cruelty, revenge, and all the wild horrors of destructive war.'[1] As I shall show, the eroticization of violent deliverance played a key role in Jacobite discourse, just as it was to do in the intonations of Cathleen Ni Houlihan 150 years later. When Padraig Pearse recommended a return to Irish eighteenth-century poetic traditions, Roger Casement suggested the Jacobite marching song 'Tearlais Og' for the Irish Volunteers, and Sean O'Casey addressed his 'Songs of the Wren', 'in deference to an old Gaelic song' dealing with a metaphorical returning Stuart,[2] they knew what they were doing, just as Daniel Corkery did in his idealization of the pure Irishness of the makers of the Jacobite *aisling*, and as Yeats understood in his praise of the Jacobite *aisling* or in his modelling Red Hanrahan on Eoghan Ruadh Ó Suilleabhain (1748–84), one of its chief practitioners.[3] Similarly, Francis Ledwidge's poem, 'The Blackbirds', written on those who took part in the Irish rising of 1916 and critiqued by Eavan Boland in *Object Lessons* (1996), may have its ancestry in the 'Blackbird' cycle of eighteenth-century Jacobite songs, and beyond them the 'Blackbird's Son' which is Fionn's sword, and the 'Blackbird speech' (swordplay) loved by the Fianna, itself a name meaning 'warband' or 'warriors' (Boland *Object Lessons* 141–2). So after 1687, Tyrconnell, James's Lord Lieutenant, was a 'swordsman' in Irish verse, while his supporters, such as Sarsfield, who defended James II and VII's Patriot Parliament of 1689 with its declaration of Irish sovereignty, became as much heroes of subsequent nationalist rhetoric as did Grattan's Parliament of 1782 (Leerssen *Mere Irish and Fior-Ghael* 257).

Jacobite literature, then, is a critically important discourse for understanding the language of Irish nationality, just as it is, in a different way, for understanding Scottish literature. Whereas in Ireland the *aisling* and related Jacobite material transmuted itself to express a new generation of politics, notably those of Daniel O'Connell, in Scotland it fulfilled the classic lineaments of decadence: a rigid insistence on form and theme at the expense of any renewing dimension of content (Leerssen *Mere Irish and Fier-Ghael* 284, 286; O'Callaghan *History of the Irish Brigades* 193, 634; Pittock *Jacobitism* 58). Hence Lady Nairne's (1766–1845) famous 'Will Ye No Come Back Again?' reworks material from the 1740s to express longing for the return of a Stuart king as the male mate of a female Scotland at a time when the song's subject had been dead for thirty years. With decadence comes elegy, and with elegy nostalgia, which breeds sentiment: and such was the fate of Scottish Jacobite literature, one early and knowingly mocked in *Waverley* Chapter 22, where Flora McIvor seduces Waverley into sympathy for active rebellion by paradoxically dwelling on the inevitability of defeat and the fading quality of the civilization she wishes to defend.[4] No one ever became a revolutionary by reading *Fingal* (1762), no matter how strong its stress on the Fianna and their swordplay. The use of both swords and oaks as symbols in his Ossian poetry is part of Macpherson's reinterpretation of Jacobite topoi in an age of Sentiment (Pittock 'James Macpherson and Jacobite Code'). By contrast, Yeats's transformation of the 'Fianna' into the 'Fenians', a term of the 1848 and 1867 Risings, in his *Wanderings of Oisin* (1889), illustrates the literary gulf between the afterlife of Scottish and Irish Jacobite literature as expressions of national identity even more surely than his possible reference to Macpherson's *Temora* in the phrase 'A terrible beauty is born' from 'Easter 1916', one first identified by Derick Thomson (Thomson *Macpherson's Ossian* 264).

On the other hand, it is arguable that Jacobite literature in Scotland is responsible in no small part for the survival of Scottish literature itself. The preservation of a self-consciously 'national' literature through the Vernacular Revival (most of the leading figures of which were clear Jacobites or had Jacobite associations), the importance of Jacobite politics, imagery, and ideas to most of the main Scottish writers before 1850, and to a degree since, and the preservation of the female nation typology with its historic Jacobite associations, are all indicators within Scotland's national literature of the influence of Jacobitism, which are frequently ignored. Scott's *Highland Widow* (1826), Stevenson's *Kidnapped* and *Catriona*, J. M. Barrie's *Farewell, Miss Julie Logan* (1932), John Buchan's *Witch Wood* (1927), Naomi Mitchison's *The Bull Calves* (1947), Violet Jacob's *Flemington* (1911), and Compton Mackenzie's and Hugh MacDiarmid's cultivation of the Jacobite white rose as a symbol for Scottish identity (in which guise it is currently worn by Nationalist members of the Scottish Parliament) are but a small sample of the legacy of the literature of the Jacobite struggle. In its earlier manifestation, Archibald Pitcairne (1652–1713), Allan Ramsay (1684–1758), James Macpherson (1736–96), James Boswell (1740–95), Robert Fergusson (1750–1774), and Robert Burns (1759–96) all displayed the importance of Jacobite themes and images in the construction of nationality, as arguably did Lord Byron (1788–1824), whose adoption of *Raubberomantik* poses follows on from that of 'Corsica' Boswell in stressing the national, freedom-loving qualities of highland *banditti*.[5]

I have begun my discussion in this fashion to stress the important influence of Jacobite discourse on literary history, particularly in Scotland and Ireland (though English Tory ruralism and the locative politics of 'Country' identity indicate that England too has its part to play: the

Johnsonian fear of ruined churches, and the toppled oaks and dismissed chaplains of Jane Austen's Sotherton are both, perhaps at one remove, evidence of this – both Johnson and Austen had Jacobite sympathizers in their families). In what follows, the particular rhetorical qualities and themes of Jacobite literature will be discussed, as will the part they play in providing a critique of the post-1688 British state. For there is no doubt that Jacobite literature's significance, both in eighteenth-century terms and in those of its subsequent legacy, can best be discerned through its status as an oppositional language. In this dimension as in others, it lies athwart many of the ideas of 'four nations' British history, which has, like its Whig ancestors, often attempted to construct ideas of Britishness within an evolutionary paradigm which projects a concern for a collective 'British' identity and praxis far back beyond its nineteenth-century heyday. To take only one example, Linda Colley, an outstanding scholar in dealing with the eighteenth century on its own terms, is enabled by the events of 1916–22 to avoid Irish Britishness (which would not fit her Protestant=British thesis) in her discussion of the making of British identity in *Britons* (1992), while also eliding (as modern secularism and ecumenism enable her to do) the huge gulfs of distrust and dislike between 'Protestants' which existed in that century. 'Back to the future' is the motto of history like this, just as surely as it was of William Stubbs's Ancient Constitution, Lord Acton's anti-Papal English particularism, and E. A. Freeman's Teutonism (Kenyon *The History Men*; Pittock *Jacobitism* 3–4). By contrast, in the Presbytery of Caithness it is reported in 1755 that the Episcopalian minister 'would rather his hearers were proud Papists than Presbyterians', while at Fordyce 40 per cent of the population are estimated to have turned Catholic following the suppression of the Episcopalian meeting-house in 1745.[6] The 1717–21 conversations between the Nonjuring British Catholics (i.e. Anglicans and Episcopalians) and the Orthodox still form a major theological document in the latter tradition (Ware *The Orthodox Church*), while, lest any think these the activities of the fringe of a fringe, the preservation of Catholic estates by Protestant neighbours in northern England after the 'Fifteen, argued for by Leo Gooch, is arguably one indicator of class solidarity's ability to outweigh the claims of religion (Gooch *The Desperate Faction?*). In 1788 (the year after Pitt had argued against the repeal of the Test and Corporation Acts on the grounds of the danger posed by Nonconformists), the dissenter Gilbert Wakefield 'found the marks of Antichrist in the Church of England'. In 1831, Coleridge remarked that 'hatred to the Church of England' was the main 'active principle' of dissenters, while the lowbrow 'Dissidence of Dissent' was Arnold's target in the 1860s (Cannon *Samuel Johnson* 25–33ff.). Protestant identity only very slowly replaced Anglican hegemony, if indeed it ever did so fully: in 1853, Anglican reviewers reacted in distaste to the virulent anti-Catholicism of Charlotte Brontë's *Villette*, the author of which bore the marks of heavy exposure to Methodism, with its overtones of unpleasant and un-Anglican enthusiasm.[7] The preservation of Anglican hegemony was one of the key aims of the Revolution of 1688–9; but its effects were far more wide-reaching, and their endurance and significant place in the British state of our own day are reasons why hostility to Jacobite rhetoric and a desire to minimize or ridicule Jacobite support or sympathy continue in the present day. The twenty years after 1688 were, quite simply, critical in the establishment of the lineaments of a Britishness which endured till the 1960s, and of which Jacobite discourse formed the major initial critique. Externally, the Revolution opened the gates to the struggle with France for world domination and to the development of a large-scale British empire financed by sophisticated credit arrangements sourced in an ever more dominant London; internally, the state was centralized to an unprecedented degree, both economically and politically. The Council of Wales was abolished; the Irish Parliament curtailed and its abolition considered; the Scottish Estates brought into an incorporating Union with the English Parliament and the Scottish Privy Council dissolved, while the Stannaries of Cornwall, suspected of Jacobitism, did not meet under William II and III and George I, and thereafter dwindled into desuetude. The Convocation of Canterbury and York, 'a major representative institution', was suppressed from 1717 (Szechi and Hayton 'John Bull's Other Kingdoms'). Every occasion of major conflict with France betwen 1689 and 1801 led to ever-greater concentration of government in London. Power was centralized, and an economic and commercial powerhouse built on the metropolis provided the credit for the massive military spending which secured an empire.

This was Great Britain. By contrast, those who wished to restore the Catholic Stuarts to the throne aimed at a diversity of ends which to a greater or lesser extent would have undermined this state. There was no question, for virtually all British Jacobites, that the Stuarts would be restored to all their three kingdoms of England, Scotland, and Ireland (though French foreign policy on occasion leant toward a restoration in Scotland and/or Ireland alone), but the Britain of James III and VIII would, it was generally hoped, be a very different place. Irish Jacobites frequently desired Catholic hegemony, and the end of 'Saxon' rule in

Ireland; Scottish Jacobites wanted to restore the Edinburgh Parliament, (mostly) the Episcopal Church, and the pre-1688 status quo; English and Welsh Jacobites abhorred the financial revolution, higher taxes, pro-Hanoverian foreign policy, and the threat to the Anglican High Church posed by the Lutheran Georges. Many Jacobites also wanted religious toleration, and an end to the oppressive enclosures of land and emphasis on property rights under the new regime, widely regarded as corrupt: these and other radical measures gained at least the intermittent support of many of the poor. The inherent marginality of the Jacobite rainbow coalition was nonetheless a threat, countered via politics, literature, main force, and, eventually, through the teleology of civility emplaced by Enlightenment, with its emphasis on progress away from the limited and barbaric toward the commonality of British acculturation.[8] In this, the discourse of Scottish Jacobite literature, with its emphasis on the tradition of a patriotism surviving through centuries of heroic resistance against overwhelming odds, had its very success turned back on it in a portrayal of Scotland as bloody, brutish, warlike, and given to a misdirected ferocity better expended on French regulars at Quebec, Ticonderoga, and Waterloo than on the ancient enemy it had once gloried in overcoming. In its traditional form, the rhetoric of patriot valour spoke of the battle of a small nation for its independence, won only by the unparalleled quality of Scottish heroism, and now betrayed for gold by an indolent nobility corrupted by luxury (a similar myth surrounds the nobles' attitude to Wallace, and received its latest airing in *Braveheart* (1995)), as once the Roman empire had been bought and sold by the corrupt descendants of L. Mucius Scaevola, Scipio Africanus, and Cato the Elder. On 4 November 1706, the Duke of Hamilton asked the Estates in a rhetorical passion his actions belied: 'shall we in half an hour yield what our forefathers maintained with their lives and fortunes for many ages? Are none of the descendants here of those worthy patriots who defended the liberty of their country against all invaders'. Two weeks later, protesters from an entirely different social background who burned 'the Articles of Union at Dumfries' spoke in similar terms of Scotland's 'sacred and civil liberties . . . purchased and maintained by our ancestors with their blood'. It was this discourse to which Burns was bidding adieu when he wrote 'The English steel we could disdain, / Secure in valor's station' (Szechi *'Scotland's Ruine'* 160, 177–8, 179; Burns *Poems and Songs* 512). Frequently it was linked to a classicizing mode which, as Barbour himself had done, made of the heroes of historic Scotland the stuff of secondary epic.

In this guise, Viscount Dundee was described in Tacitean terms as 'last and best of Scots' in the Latin elegy of Archibald Pitcairne, translated by Dryden, whose own *Aeneid* of 1697 was strongly laced with Jacobitical imagery. The use of Vergil's epic as a coded referent for the Stuarts was to become central to eighteenth-century Jacobite rhetoric in both England and Scotland (Pittock *The Invention of Scotland* 35, '*The Aeneid* in the Age of Burlington' 231–49).

For the roots of Jacobite literature, however, we must reach much further back than the events of 1688–9. The main themes which were associated to some degree or another with Jacobite sympathies were (i) sacred poetry extolling high Anglican and Episcopal positions under threat, and tending to endorse a sacramental monarchy; (ii) the status of the land as woman, and the king as her husband, traditional in Irish and Scottish culture, and frequently realized through the representation of eroticized violence; (iii) the identification of poverty with purity and 'honesty', as opposed to the corruption and double-dealing of the Whig state; (iv) Vergilian exemplars, particularly *Eclogue* IV and the *Aeneid*; (v) retreat poetry, often linked to Horace and the topographical poem, beginning with the fate of Strafford as the stag in Sir John Denham's *Cowper's Hill*; (vi) the identification of the Stuart cause with the mythological tradition of Ireland and Scotland, in particular the Fianna; (vii) their association as patriot monarchs with English (or more usually Scottish) language, habit, or custom: Juvenal was sometimes used here as an avatar of the critique of a great empire ruined by cosmopolitanism – 'iam pridem Syrus in Tiberim defluxit Orontes' ('Syrian Orontes has long been discharging into the Tiber'). Naturally, these themes were most characteristic of Jacobite literature at differing levels: (i) is found mostly in the commonplace-books, sermons, histories, and propaganda of the Jacobite-leaning clerisy; (ii) and (iii) are wide-spread in more popular Jacobite verse and its descendants; (iv) is found at every level, from Pope's *Dunciad* and Dryden's *Astraea Redux* to the correspondence of Jacobite gentlemen and the popular propaganda of the era; (v) is more common in high culture; (vi) in Gaelic writing; and (vii) in Scots, although it is also found in England. All have their roots before 1688 (Pittock *Poetry and Jacobite Politics*).

In the castle and university patronage which preserved a version of Scottish court culture after the departure of the monarchy in 1603, there was frequently a close association between Latin and the strongest expressions of Scottish patriotism. In 1626, for example, Arthur Johnston (whose Laudian work Dr Johnson was still looking for in Aberdeen in the 1770s) attacked what he saw as the end of (or at the very least a threat to) the Auld Alliance in his poem 'On the Rupture of the Peace Between France and Scotland', while in his verse on William Alexander, Earl of Stirling, he bemoans the corrupting influence which the Thames has on Scottish talent, and in 'De Pluvius Anglicanis et Scotia Sereni- tate', humorously remarks that it has been raining in England for two months while in Scotland the sun shines.[9]

This Scoto-Latin tradition provided one of the earliest uses of the *Aeneid* as a commentary on the Stuarts, when in 1660 James Kennedy welcomed Charles II home as 'Aeneas Britannicus'. After the Revolution, Richard Maitland, Earl of Lauderdale, dedicated his part-translation of the *Aeneid* to James VII's wife, Mary of Modena. Within this context of the use of the *Aeneid*, Gavin Douglas's sixteenth-century translation into Scots, with its promise to 'kepand na sudroun bot our awin langage', became part of the alliance of the vernacular and the classical seen in Scotland since the era of resistance to Reformation English,[10] and crys- tallized in the Jacobite anti-Unionism of educated patriots after 1707. Thomas Ruddiman, who came to Edinburgh as a result of a meeting with Pitcairne, edited Douglas's *Aeneid*, a quotation from which headed Ramsay's elegy on Pitcairne's memory (which has strong Aenean over- tones) read to the Easy Club at the time when Ramsay changed his Club pseudonym to 'Gavin Douglas' (Pittock *Poetry and Jacobite Politics* 154).

In James Philp of Almerieclose's *Graemeid*, the last Latin epic attempted in Britain, the Jacobite hero Viscount Dundee (also celebrated in clas- sical terms by Pitcairne, of course) comes from Angus, termed 'locus Aeneadum' in Philp's Latin: 'Aeneas' and 'Angus' were interchangeable Scots Christian names. Nor is this only a turn-of-the-century phe- nomenon. The coded identification of James with Aeneas and Charles with Ascanius can be found in the Oliphant of Gask correspondence from 1743, in the tract *Aeneas and His Two Sons* (1746) and in *Ascanius, or the Young Adventurer* (1746–7). Similarly Donald MacLeod of Gualtergill is described by Bishop Robert Forbes as 'The Faithful Palinurus' (Pittock *The Myth of the Jacobite Clans* 237; Forbes *The Lyon in Mourning* 1:183; Oliphant *The Jacobite Lairds of Gask* 100).

Jacobite poets frequently pursued this theme. William Hamilton of Bangour's 'earliest known achievement' in verse was a translation of the final third of *Aeneid* X, dealing with the bad kingship of Mezentius, just as Alexander Robertson of Struan lighted on *Aeneid* V. William King (1689– 1761) described Flora MacDonald as 'the Cyprian goddess' guiding her protégé safely to Carthage; a motto from Vergil's fourth (Augustan)

Eclogue headed a 1720 Ode on Charles's birth (Pittock *Poetry and Jacobite Politics* 173; Forbes *Lyon in Mourning* II:263, III:67), and the 1721 *Health to the Lost Shepherd* shows Ascanius as a shepherd–king.[11] Irish Gaelic verse, incidentally, likewise portrayed the Stuart as a herdsman. '*Fuimus Troes*' became a consistent tag of both Jacobite hope and lament from at least the beginning of the eighteenth century (it is found in Arbuthnot and John Daniel's account of Charles Edward, for example; Pittock '*The Aeneid* in the Age of Burlington' 241–2). Indeed, it was such a commonplace that Scott put it in the mouth of the Baron of Bradwardine as the typifying signature of Jacobite antiquarianism. One cannot perhaps claim that Vergil's epic was uniquely seen as Jacobite property, but the rise of Gothicism from the Patriot Whigs to the Scottish Enlightenment is suggestive of a cultural defence mechanism against the Trojans on the one hand (for Aeneas' great-grandson, Brutus, was the founder of Britain in Galfridian lore) and the Fianna on the other. 'Rule Britannia' and *Alfred* belong together in more ways than one.[12]

The praise-of-retreat ('What sweet delight a quiet life affords, / And what it is to be of bondage free') poetry of William Drummond of Hawthornden (1600–49), as well as being a theme most suited to a Horace with an absent Maecenas, foreshadows the same topos in Jacobite poetry such as that of Alexander Robertson of Struan (1670–1749) and the Countess of Winchilsea (1661–1720) (Kastner *The Poetical Works of William Drummond* xvi, xl; Pittock 'From Edinburgh to London' 22). It has its origins in the Horatian Augustanism of James VI's Castalian Band at the Scottish court before 1603, and the king's failure to live up to the hopes of his Scoto-Britane Castalians became thereafter a source for the use of Horatian rhetoric as an implicit reproach. In 1617, when James returned to Scotland, Drummond's 'Forth Feasting' presents Scotland in traditional guise as a neglected woman:

> Ah! why should Isis only on thee shine?
> Is not thy Forth as well as Isis thine?
> Though Isis vaunt she hath more wealth in store,
> Let it suffice thy Forth doth love thee more . . .
>> (Eyre-Todd ed. *Scottish Poetry* 205–6; Edwin Morgan
>> 'How Good a Poet is Drummond?')

Drummond's introduction of 'the vocabulary of a lady lamenting her fickle, departed love' then emerges into clearer view: 'When in her arms she doth thee fold . . . Loath not to think on thy much loving

Forth'. Scotia's intimacy with her icon has turned to the beginnings of reproach.

The presence of this identification of the land with an abandoned and neglected woman is one which readily conflates with the Jacobite songs of a later era, just as the Horatian/Apollonian identification of James as the sun whose beams are withdrawn ('Triste solum sine sole' ('alone and sad without the sun')) finds a ready echo in the identification of Fionn as returning messianic king with the sun: 'We raised Image of Sun / The banner of great Fionn of the Fian' (Pittock 'From Edinburgh to London' 24; Meek 'The Gaelic Ballads of Scotland' 42). James Macpherson drew on this traditional Gaelic characterization of Fionn ('the sun-beam of battle; the standard of our king'), and allied it (as Fiona Stafford points out in *The Sublime Savage* 63–4, 70–1, 138ff., 147) with 'Virgil's Troy rather than Homer's', collocating Aenean imagery with that of the Fianna just as the classical legends of Jacobite medals (e.g. 'Sola Luce Fugat' ('he dispels them by his light alone')) had their counterpart in Gaelic verse describing the returning Charles as the 'sun', or in the sunflowers of enduring Stuart loyalty which feature in Joseph Enzer's Jacobite plasterwork for the House of Dun in Montrose Basin in the 1740s (Noel Woolf *The Medallic Record* 46–7, 53). In similar vein, the returning Augustus of a restored Aenean Stuart could be articulated in terms of Horace's *Odes* IV:v, 'lucem redde tuae, dux bone, patriae'. The status of Augustus as 'dux bone' ('good leader') was a slippery one throughout the so-called Augustan period, and part of this slipperiness was of a piece with the nature of the dynastic contest itself (Erskine-Hill *The Augustan Idea*). As Pope remarked, 'The *Aeneid* was evidently a party piece', and he should have known, for the 1743 *Dunciad* is pronounced in its dependence on the darker books of Vergil's epic, particularly Book VI. The 'universal Darkness' of Pope's climax is that of an underworld from which there is no Aenean return to cast light on a Britain where 'Dunce the second reigns like Dunce the first'. Pope is explicit in his comparison of his poem with Vergil's because the mock-heroic was one of the subgenres through which the reversals of politico-cultural disappointment were expressed. Darkness, Dulness's element, can accompany the mock-heroic moment of climax elsewhere: for example in Canto III of *The Rape of the Lock*. As in the 'naked Temples' (i.e. bereft of the Sacrament) of *Windsor Forest* (1713) over whose ruins stalked the 'stately Hind' (cf Dryden's *The Hind and the Panther* (1687)), a hint of Catholic apologetics was a comfortable companion for Jacobite Augustanism (*The Poems of Alexander Pope* ed. Butt 196, 350; Pittock *Poetry and Jacobite Politics* 107). 'Pius Aeneas' foreshadowed Augustus, whose

piety was endorsed by his adoption of the title 'Pontifex Maximus' in
12 BC. This priestly title of the Roman emperors in its turn passed to
the Papacy; combined with the myth that Brutus, great-grandson of
Aeneas, was the founder and begetter of Anglo-Irish monarchy, it had
a powerful attraction as an image to legitimist Jacobitism, often being
accompanied by a nostalgic, sacral, and intensely traditionalist vision of
the crown (Pittock *Poetry and Jacobite Politics* 11ff.).

In Ireland, where the legitimacy of the Stuarts derived rather from
the fact that the roots of the Scottish monarchy's foundation myth lay
in Irish rulers, the *aisling* poetry of figures such as Aoghan Ó Rathaille
(c. 1675–1729) and Eoghan Ruadh Ó Suilleabhain (1748–84) presents
a male speaker who encounters a woman, Ireland, in a dream vision.
The woman awaits the return of her (Stuart) deliverer from over the sea,
the expulsion of those who imprison and rape her, and a fertile renewal
based on union with her true lover. As Ó Rathaille puts it in 'Gile na
Gile' ('Brightness Most Bright'):

> All in derision they tittered – a gang of goblins
> and a bevy of slender maidens with twining tresses.
> They bound me in bonds, denying the slightest comfort,
> and a lumbering brute took hold of my girl by the
>   breasts.
>
> I said to her then, in words that were full of truth,
> how improper it was to join with that drawn gaunt
>   creature
> when a man the most fine, thrice over, of Scottish blood
> was waiting to take her for his tender bride.
>
> (Ó Tuama *An Duanaire* 150ff.)

While in Ireland the woman-nation is usually passive, envisioned in the
suffering bonds of oppression by the poet who reports her plight, in
Scotland, by contrast, the woman is often the speaker, calling for a deliverance in which she sometimes participates. For example, in 'Tho
Georthie Reigns in Jamie's Stead', a song of the 1740s which later formed
a model for Burns's radical anthem 'For a' that and a' that', the woman
(Scotland) appeals thus:

> He's far beyond Culbin [Sands – near Elgin] the night
> That has my heart for a that
> He wears the Pistol by his Side
> That'll gar me laugh for a that
> The highland coat the filobeg [philabeg]

> The tartan hoas and a that
> He wears that's o'er the hill the night
> And will be here for a that.
> He wears the broad Sword by his side
> Well knows he how to draw it
> The Target & the tartan plaid
> The Shoulder belt & a that.

The woman-nation, whose 'heart' belongs to the Stuart prince, is aroused to liberating war in sexual terms: 'the Pistol by his Side / That'll gar me laugh for a that'.[13] In other songs, 'His Quiver hang down by his thigh' (Donaldson *The Jacobite Song* 56–8), or alternatively the sheer excitement of imminent victory achieves the same effect. The king at the central point of the capital is the symbol of that armed and renewed sovereignty which brings fertility, just as the movement deeper into the heart of the House of Dun is one toward the sunflowers of a bright, glorious, and fecund Restoration. Prince Charles himself is often presented with the colouring of corn and fertile land: he can be 'The Yellow-hair'd Laddie' in Scots, *Tearlach Ruadh* ('ruddy Charles') in Scots Gaelic, or *ban* ('the fair one') in Irish Gaelic. Similarly of course, the original 'Golden Boy' of *Eclogue* IV promises an era where 'waving corn will slowly flood the plains with gold' (Pittock *Poetry and Jacobite Politics* 148–9; National Library of Scotland MS 2910 30r; Gillies 'Gaelic Songs of the "Forty-Five"' 44; Virgil *The Pastoral Poems* 54–5). Seduction songs were often used as the model for Scottish Jacobite song-cycles which equated the land with a woman. In particular the gipsy abductor of 'Three Gipsies Came to our Ha Door' or 'The Gipsy Laddies' became instead an erotic deliverer, a Highland or Stuart hero, who came to take his bride Caledonia, 'o'er the hills and far awa', a phrase repeated in Jacobite song manuscripts from Banff to Oxford in a manner which provides evidence for the distribution of such songs.[14] Intriguingly, when three different 'over the hills' songs appear in the Rawlinson MSS in the Bodleian Library, the odd orthography of 'awa', with a final 'w', suggests that these are Scots songs taken down by an English speaker – indeed they are explicitly described as such. Another 'Scotch Song' in Rawlinson pushes back the 'Bonnie Laddie' motif (a common theme in Scottish Jacobite song-cycles, emphasizing the youth and appeal of the returning king) to 1715–16, with 'The Princely Laddy' as a descriptor for 'James the VIII'. The orthography here looks Englished also. Most famously, 'The Bonnie Bonnie Banks o Loch Lomond' ceased to be a simple love song and became an asseveration of the return to its native place of the soul of a Jacobite betrayed by

King's Evidence to his doom at Carlisle, whose return by the 'low road' is nonetheless that of an insubstantial spirit who can no longer enjoy the physicality of fighting or love – these he 'will never meet again' (Bodleian MS Rawl Poet 155/113, 142, 145, 176; Pittock, 'The Culture of Jacobitism' 139).

The distribution of these songs and their themes is a major question, which cannot be fully explored here, but it appears clear that songs under categories (ii) and (iii) in particular, and (i) (sacred verse) to a lesser extent, expressed a Jacobite literary discourse which appears not only in a wide variety of sources, but also in different languages. For example, there is the case of the Scottish ballad 'Molly Stewart', reworked into Burns's version of 'It was a for our rightfu king' (Burns *Poems and Songs* 694). Here the antecedents are in Scots and Irish Gaelic: Sìleas Na Ceapaich's 'Do Righ Seamus', with its refrain where the Scottish nation is addressed as 'My Little Mollie O' and the Irish air 'Mo Mhali Beag O'. Perhaps similarly, 'Macpherson's Rant', known best in Burns's version ultimately based on a contemporary Banff broadside of 1700, may bear relation to 'Macpherson's Tune', played by a Leinster highwayman on the bagpipe (not the fiddle as in Banff) while he was led to the gallows.[15] Both versions exhibit the folk topos of the social bandit (cf. Hobsbawm's 1969 study, *Bandits*, and the *Raubberomantik* cult which links Byron, 'Corsica' Boswell, and Jacobite themes – 'Corsica' was a synonym for Britain in Jacobite code) (Hobsbawm *Bandits* 12, 35, 112). Just as MacPhersen breaks his fiddle beneath the gallows in defiance of the society which has condemned him, so similar instrument-breaking defiances by the resistant folk hero can be found in 'The Minstrel Boy' and a story of Culloden where William Farquharson, who had played 'The Braes of Mar' en route to the battlefield, on reaching it broke it over his knees and 'never played again' (Tayler and Tayler *Jacobites of Aberdeenshire* 418ff.). Fiddles (like harps) were political, and clear signatures of the transmission of subversive ideas. In 1793, the MP Arthur Cole-Hamilton 'threw his glass at' a 'blind fiddler's head' in Belfast for playing 'The White Cockade' at a time of mounting Jacobin tension (Whelan 'The United Irishmen' 283). Maire Bhui Ni Laoghaire's contemporary *aisling* likewise calls for help for Ireland from monarchic Spain not Republican France, in a continuation of the Jacobite tradition, although Irish literature was shortly to adapt the young and ageing woman of the Jacobite *aisling* for its own purposes. In Scotland in 1797, following the founding of the United Scotsmen, George III became described in radical circles as 'Geordie Whelps', after the title of a Jacobite song (Leerssen *Mere Irish and Fior-Ghael* 284; Wells *Insurrection* 73), while another such song, 'The Sow's Tail to Geordie', became one of the most popular radical songs. In similar vein, 'whelp' was a coded term for George in an eighteenth-century Munster song and in the late Scottish Jacobite version of 'Welcome, Royal Charlie', musically one of the best of the Jacobite songs (Meikle *Scotland and the French Revolution* 67, 86, 120, 147).

Harp or pipes were the instruments used to play 'The Blackbird', 'The Flowers of Edinburgh', and 'The White Cockade' among those in western Ireland supportive of the Irish Brigades (O'Callaghan *History of the Irish Brigades* 269, 605), while 'The White Cockade' itself exists in both Scottish and Irish versions in English and Gaelic (Leerssen *Mere Irish and Fíor-Ghael* 283). Dance music was also used: 'The Auld Stewarts Back Again' was recorded as the air to a 'new dance' in 1749 at a gathering where 'Over the Water to Charlie' was also played (Forbes *The Lyon in Mourning* ii:254). Airs returned in different forms: 'King James's March to Ireland' (1692) reappearing, for example, as 'Lochaber No More'.[16] Communal activities such as drinking (among men) or 'waulking' / trampling the cloth (among women) were opportunities for Jacobite singing: there are a number of fine Gaelic waulking-songs. In Ireland, hurling was adopted as a means of gathering together by Jacobites (Public Record Office SP 63/388/41–2), as it was by nationalists during the Celtic Revival. Drinking has clear (if rather negative) connotations with regard to Jacobitism, and some songs (such as 'Here's to the King Sir') appear to be 'toast' songs, where 'Up your sword and down your gun' implies the raising and draining of the glass (Pittock 'The Culture of Jacobitism' 139). Explicit appeals to drink are, of course, also found: 'The Loyal Health', 'Here's a Health to the King the Crown does belong to', and 'A Scotch Song on the 10th of June' are all examples of this (Bodley Rawl MS Poet 155/3, 142; MS Firth e6f62).

The link between poverty, purity, and the theme of honesty was also very important in Jacobite writing. The sense that 1688, by so drastically altering the law of primogeniture, marked a watershed in the nature of property rights was a strong one, reinforced by the financial revolution and the perceived emergence of a new moneyed order with no roots in land or location. This is the tapsalteerie world portrayed in John Gay's *Beggar's Opera* (1728), which uses a number of Jacobite or Jacobite-leaning airs, including 'Over the hills and far away'. 'Gentlemen of the road' could indeed be 'fine gentlemen' as 'Captain' Macheath may be: for a third of James's army did not serve again after 1688, and some at least turned to highway robbery. When Jemmy Twitcher says 'What we win, gentlemen, is our own by the law of arms and the right of conquest', it can be taken as an indicator that Macheath's gang takes its example from a regime whose founder, William, had already been allied with his namesake the Conqueror by Gay's friend Pope in *Windsor Forest* (1713) (Gay *Dramatic Works* 21, 22, 48, 85; *The Beggar's Opera* 22, 31, 63, 77, 82; Childs *The Army, James II and the Glorious Revolution*). Jacobites could take such ironies as a badge of pride: the Duke of Wharton 'thought of himself as Macheath', for example (Blackett-Ord *Hell-Fire Duke* 221). Within a broader context, the decade after George I came to the throne seemed, in manifestations such as the South Sea Bubble and the scandal of Jonathan Wild (afterwards identified with Peachum/Walpole) – to say nothing of the conduct of the 'Great Men' of the state in general – to reveal the realities of a world 'turned upside down'. This sense of institutionalized inversion of inherited value is present in a vast range of texts, from Henry Fielding's *Jonathan Wild* (1743) and Swift's *Gulliver's Travels* (1726) to the bawdy and savage satire of Jacobite verse and the cynical note seen in the street literature of chaos and disappointment which greeted the pricking of the South Sea Bubble in 1720:

> So if ye gang near the South Sea Hoose
> The willywhas [rogues] will grip yer gear.
> Syne a the lave [fellow-Scots] maun fare the waur,
> For oor lang biding here [London].

Just as the crown ('But the very dogs o England's court / Can bark and howl in German') and its 'great man' were mocked, so too was London as the centre of the financial revolution.[17] The sense of the overturning of an old order and the unpredictability and doubtful legitimacy of the new was strong for many people, and intensified in groups such as smugglers, who resented the encroachment of taxation on traditional practices. Strong smuggling areas such as Montrose were frequently also intensely Jacobite. Rural discontent, from the Windsor Blacks to the Irish Whiteboys, drew on aspects of Jacobitical symbolism and associations to render their own threat more disturbing to the powers that be. Financial change, the enclosure of land, and the lack of religious toleration in many areas (Catholics, Scots Episcopalians, even dissenters) were other elements which sustained a different vision of eighteenth-century Britain from that powerfully purveyed in an increasingly centralized state with aggressive foreign-policy aims and a growing commodity industry, which through the medium of newspaper advertisement, the mushrooming of provincial titles and improved dissemination, was creating the first homogeneous middle-class audience Britain had known. In this context, 'honest' is frequently used as a coded term for Jacobite: it is, for example, used thus concerning the Jacobites at Lichfield Races in 1743, in a letter describing a dinner-party at which Dr King was present in 1749, and of a similar gathering at the Jacobite Lord Barrymore's a few years earlier. Both Mrs Caesar and the Duchess of Ormond thought of Swift as 'honest', and it is this rhetoric on which Burns draws in his depiction of 'The honest man, though e'er sae poor' as a radical exemplar, or which Hogg uses in his neo-Jacobite poem 'Donald MacGillavry' (where Donald is characterized as the epitome of incorruptible fairness), which obliquely hints at the early nineteenth-century radicalism of the Lowland trades (Higgins *Swift* 146; Burns *Poems and Songs* 602; MacQuoid *Jacobite Songs* 83). There are links here too with the gendered nation and conception of the land as female: Jacobite writers criticize 'O Beautiful Britannia' for 'playing the jade', while the Whig Defoe famously reinterprets the links between sexual and financial 'honesty' in praise of the fertility of trade in *Moll Flanders* and *Roxana*: 'an Estate is a Pond, but Trade is a Spring', as he elsewhere remarked, underscoring its link to fertility (Hogg *The Jacobite Relics*; Dijkstra *Defoe and Economics*).

Jacobite literature then lies at the heart of many of the literary references of its own century, and their expressions of cultural, political, and national identity, while having an afterlife, not only in the radical period of the 1790s, but in a large part of the ensuing rhetoric of Irish nationalism, where it survived in transmuted form. In 'Glory O! Glory O! to the Bold Fenian Men', 'Three Flowers', 'Four Green Fields', and many other rebel songs, the encounter between patriot and woman in Ireland's Anglophone literature echoes the structure of the *aisling*, as surely as James Clarence Mangan (1800–49) Englished 'Roisin Dubh' for Young Ireland. In a less grisly revenant mode than these 'Bog Queens' (ironized by Paul Muldoon's encounter with the maiden 'Anorexia' in a mock *aisling* dealing with the hunger strikes), Scottish literature in the twentieth century, from Dark Mairi in *Butcher's Broom* (1934) to Chris (Caledonia) in *A Scots Quair* (1932), frequently echoes the traditional representations of the woman-nation that find their apogee in the Jacobite era (Pittock *Celtic Identity and the British Image*).

National identity and literary history are linked to this rhetoric, whose destabilizing allegiances to Scotland, Ireland, Catholicism, and high Anglican ruralism force us to consider a more complex set of British identities than those which cast back the shadow of the Victorian noonday to a century when Britain's very existence was contested, both by a defeated dynasty who stood for a multi-kingdom monarchy and through the French foreign policy which on repeated occasions explicitly endorsed attempts to split its superpower enemy into its component nations (McLynn 'An Eighteenth-Century Scots Republic?'). When the politics of this was forgotten, the language and themes of its expression remained, though contributing to and subsisting in a different form.

NOTES

1 *The Female Rebels*, in Mackenzie *Scottish Pageant* 247.
2 Ruth D. Edwards *Patrick Pearse* 203; Austin Morgan *James Connolly* 116; Cullen 'The Political War Ballads of Sean O'Casey' 171.
3 Corkery *The Hidden Ireland*. For Yeats's stress on the importance of the *aisling*, see Zimmerman 'Yeats, the Popular Ballad and the Ballad Singers' 188; for Red Hanrahan, see Thuente *W. B. Yeats and Irish Folklore*.
4 The invitation to 'die like your sires' in Flora's song, itself a tradition derived from an Ossianic last bard, is a joke of Scott's with his audience which prevents us reading what follows save in the frame of mind of a teleological Whig.
5 For the use of 'Corsica' in Jacobite-leaning code, see Greenwood *William King* 77, 170–1.
6 National Archives of Scotland GD 95/11/11/(2); CH 2/47/5; RH 15/105/3, 23/2. I am indebted to Dr Clotilde Prunier for these and other references to Episcopalian and Catholic confluence, evidence for which can also be found in texts such as Macmillan *The Aberdeen Doctors*; Henderson *Chevalier Ramsay*; Henderson ed. *Mystics of the North East*.
7 See Mozley *The Christian Remembrancer*.
8 Colin Kidd has done valuable work on this, in *Subverting Scotland's Past* and in a series of succeeding articles, in a debate opened by Ash in *The Strange Death of Scottish History*.
9 Geddes and Leade *Musa Latina Aberdonensis* I:xix, xxiii, 180–1, 219; II:xv, xviii, 241; Baldwin *The Latin and Greek Poems of Samuel Johnson* 3.
10 Geddes and Leade *Musa Latina* III:167ff., 173; National Library of Scotland Dep. 221/62, MS 2/5.
11 Chapman 'Jacobite Political Argument' 285–9.
12 Cf. Gerrard *The Patriot Opposition* for an examination of Whig Gothic.
13 Aberdeen University Library MS 2222.
14 George Farquhar's *The Recruiting Officer* (1705) provides one of the earliest examples of this song in print. See Pittock ed. *James Hogg*.
15 Sileas Na Ceapaich (1660–1729) is edited in Ó Baoill *Bardachd Shilis na Ceapaich*.
16 Ramsay's repertoire is particularly full of such songs; Pittock ed. *James Hogg*.
17 'So if ye gang' recorded in Kirkpatrick *Traditional Songs of Scotland*; MacQuoid ed. *Jacobite Songs* 64.

VII
Historians respond

CHAPTER 14

Literature and the new British and Irish histories

Jane Ohlmeyer

This volume invites literary critics of the English Renaissance 'to take up, work with, and work upon the paradigm of the British history' with a view to generating 'disciplinary cross-pollination'. Collectively these chapters mark an important first step toward stimulating conversations between historians and their literary counterparts around issues of identity, ideology, perception, and representation in the early modern period. Writing from the perspective of a historian of seventeenth-century Ireland and Britain, these overtures are not only welcome but also essential in helping to ensure that current debate centred on the 'new British and Irish histories' remains provocative and controversial, yet dynamic and constructive.

This debate started among historians, especially political and military ones, but has been taken up by other scholars of the early modern period. Yet historians are far from clear about what is meant by the 'new British history'. For some it constitutes a distorting and irritating intrusion and for others it offers a useful vehicle for enriching national history and the interactions between the Three Kingdoms. The awkward terminology associated with the debate – the 'British problem', 'the British history', the 'new British history', the 'new British and Irish histories', and 'Atlantic archipelagic history' – reflects the diversity of opinion.[1] Moreover, there is even disagreement over when the term might usefully be applied. Some have suggested that prior to the personal Union of the Crowns in 1603 – never mind the political union between England and Scotland in 1707 or between Britain and Ireland in 1800–1 – the concept of 'British history' is misleading. Others argue that the formation of a distinctive 'British' identity is a product of the eighteenth and early nineteenth centuries (Broun, Finlay, and Lynch eds. *Image and Identity* 93–4; Colley *Britons*). Certainly when viewed from the perspective of Ireland (and Scotland and Wales), it could be argued that the phrase 'British history' remains a synonym for English history and excludes

Ireland.[2] Much more helpful is the 'composite monarchies' or 'multiple kingdoms' model first articulated by Professor H. G. Koenigsberger and the increased use of more neutral terms – 'Three Kingdoms' or, if Wales is to be included, 'Four Nations' – to describe the interactions within and between the Stuart kingdoms (Koenigsberger 'Dominium Regale'). Conrad Russell developed this model for England, Jenny Wormald for Scotland, and Michael Perceval-Maxwell for Ireland (Russell *The Fall of the British Monarchies*; Wormald 'The Creation of Britain'; Perceval-Maxwell 'Ireland and the Monarchy'). Yet even these tend to downplay the economic, social, cultural, linguistic, and religious commonalities that often criss-crossed the Stuart monarchies and transcended the geographical boundaries and political mind-sets associated with the White Cliffs of Dover, Hadrian's Wall, or the Boyne Valley. While it is critical to acknowledge and appreciate the real regional and national differences and diversities within the Three Kingdoms, to ignore these linkages and the wider contacts that the Stuart monarchies enjoyed, particularly with the continent and the Atlantic world, would be foolhardy.

How then does this volume contribute to this important yet, at times, irascible debate? Literary sources are invaluable in enriching our understanding of the processes that underpinned one of the principal themes of this book: identity formation. Clearly identity formation defies any easy explanation, particularly in the multi-lingual, religiously diverse, and culturally complex contexts of early modern Britain and Ireland where 'Englishness', 'Irishness', 'Scottishness', and 'Welshness' meant a variety of things to different people. Moreover, it proved an iterative process that was defined and re-defined by prevailing political, religious, cultural, and socio-economic developments in and between three kingdoms (never mind interactions with Europe and the New World), by the slippery nature of Stuart kingship, and by personal, local, and regional loyalties.[3] Many of the chapters in this volume shed light on an often overlooked topic: the emergence and development of 'Englishness', particularly during the late sixteenth and early seventeenth centuries (though occasionally some of the contributors appear to conflate 'Englishness' with 'Britishness'). While it is critical to acknowledge the continuities between the medieval and early modern periods, it might also be helpful to chart how the nature of 'Englishness' changed over time: how, for example, did the Wars of the Three Kingdoms and the political and constitutional upheavals of the 1650s modify the conclusions reached here?

Of course 'Englishness' extended well beyond the geographic and national boundaries of England. Linda Gregerson and Andrew Hadfield introduce an Atlantic dimension in their chapters, while in his discussion of English Catholicism Christopher Highley provides a refreshing alternative to the Protestant-centred interpretation of 'Englishness'. Despite the trans-nationalism of Catholicism, religious allegiance did little, Highley convincingly argues, to forge a common bond among the English, Scottish, and Irish exiles who preferred to attend their own colleges, to fight alongside their compatriots in Irish and Scottish regiments, and, where numbers permitted, to live in segregated communities. Certainly in the case of English and Irish recusants, experiences of diaspora merely served to heighten concepts of 'Englishness' and 'Irishness' (Cunningham 'The Culture and Ideology of Irish Franciscan Historians'; Hiram Morgan 'Faith and Fatherland'). However, in the case of Irish Catholics (but, interestingly, not English ones), a sense of fealty to the Stuarts as the legitimate monarchs of the Three Kingdoms played an increasingly important role in defining identity. The Irish generally welcomed the arrival of James VI of Scotland as king of England and Ireland, seeing him as Ireland's 'spouse' and rightful sovereign (Ó Buachalla 'James Our True King'). Even the exiled Archbishop of Armagh, Peter Lombard, dedicated his *Episcopion Doron* to James and in the preface congratulated him on his accession as Ireland's rightful ruler. He went on to beg the king to end the persecution of Irish Catholics and to grant liberty of conscience since the Irish were, Lombard maintained, his faithful and devoted subjects (Silke 'Primate Lombard' 131). This sense of loyalty to the House of Stuart also featured in the attitudes of many Scottish Protestant exiles and only dissipated with the outbreak of civil war after 1638.[4] Yet, whether abroad or at home, this volume lacks a detailed discussion of 'Scottishness' and Scotland's contribution to the emergence of a sense of 'Britishness', despite the wealth of material – maps, masques, prose, poetry, and political tracts – generated by the Union of the Crowns in 1603 and the fact that James VI and I sought, with some success, to foster a common sense of nationhood for his English and Scottish subjects.[5]

Scotland and the Scots may have been given short shrift in this volume but many of the chapters successfully tease out and explore the geographical parameters of major English canonical texts, particularly Shakespearean drama.[6] Yet one wonders if Shakespeare merits the attention that his plays have been accorded here? Surely one aspiration of this volume should have been to promote alternative texts and to interrogate prose, plays, and poetry – written in the various languages associated with the Four Nations together with more 'obscure' English-language

texts – that have never formed part of the accepted canon of 'English
Literature', which is itself inherently Anglocentric.[7] Equally, more attention might have been devoted to sources not traditionally regarded
as 'literary'. Christopher Ivic's analysis of John Speed's *Theatre of Empire*
does mark a welcome departure in this respect and underscores the
importance of interrogating visual sources in conjunction with written
ones. Other images and tracts – especially cultural, political, and religious ones – invite similar treatment from literary scholars. For instance,
in a stimulating discussion of the very real problems involved in interrogating English sermons from an interdisciplinary perspective, Mary
Morrissey has urged us to analyse sermons 'in a way that utilizes both
their rhetorical artfulness and their political engagement' (Morrissey
'Interdisciplinarity and the Study of Early Modern Sermons' 1111).

Contemporary histories might also be scrutinized, to paraphrase Dr Morrissey, 'as both texts and events'. In their chapters
Richard McCabe and Mary Floyd-Wilson highlight the significance
of Holinshed's *Chronicles* and the particular way in which it shaped English
attitudes and informed Shakespeare's *Cymbeline*. It is a shame that other
histories, by Irish and Scottish writers, did not receive similar analysis in
this volume. For instance, equally significant, albeit in an Irish and continental context, was *Foras Feasa ar Éirinn*, a synthesis of Irish history
from earliest times to the Anglo-Norman invasion, by Geoffrey Keating
(Séathrún Céitinn), an Old English priest from County Tipperary,
who defended the native and Old Irish against their many critics
(Cunningham *The World of Geoffrey Keating*; 'Representations of King,
Parliament and the Irish People'; 'Seventeenth-century Interpretations
of the Past'; Bradshaw 'Geoffrey Keating'). The fact that Keating's
history became a 'best-seller' in manuscript form, rather than in
print, also demonstrates the need to include unpublished works in
these discussions.[8] Unlike Keating's history, George Buchanan's *Rerum
Scoticarum Historia* (Edinburgh 1582) circulated widely in print throughout early modern Europe, appearing in nineteen editions before
1762, but it also helped to determine how contemporaries perceived
Scotland. Similarly Buchanan's political writings, especially *De Juri
Regni* (Edinburgh 1579), profoundly shaped the thinking of radical
Presbyterians, particularly one of his pupils, Andrew Melville; it irri-
tated and threatened James VI and I, another tutee and the future king
of the Three Kingdoms; and it won the admiration of contemporary
scholars (including Tycho Brahe) and later writers, most notably John
Milton (Williamson 'George Buchanan, Civic Virtue and Commerce';

McGinnis and Williamson 'Britain, Race, and The Iberian World Empire').

The apparent reluctance of many scholars of English literature to engage with the likes of Buchanan or Keating in the way that they have with Holinshed perhaps stems from Keating's decision to write in Irish and Buchanan's preference to pen his most important works in Latin. However, to allow English-language texts to dominate any discussions surrounding 'the paradigm of the British history' only serves to accentuate further the Anglocentric nature of the discourse.[9] While English became the language of government, of the courts, and of commerce, a significant proportion of the population, especially ordinary people, continued to speak Welsh, Cornish, Manx, Scots, and Scottish and Irish Gaelic for much of the early modern period. The importance of using Gaelic-language sources in unravelling the mentality, attitudes, and political ideology particularly – though by no means exclusively – of Irish Catholics and Scottish Gaels has captured the imagination of both historians and literary scholars.[10] In his chapter Murray Pittock draws on some of the Gaelic literary sources relating to Scottish Jacobitism; but what of Irish Jacobitism, which, thanks to the recent studies by Breandán Ó Buachalla and Eamonn Ó Ciardha, is now well documented?[11] Much more controversial amongst scholars of early modern Ireland is the debate over the purpose and nature of bardic poetry in the sixteenth and seventeenth centuries.[12] This has generated further general – and at times heated – discourse about the response of the Gaelic world to the processes inherent in conquest and colonization, together with re-evaluations of the significance of poetry and prose written in the vernacular.[13] Less contentious is the Latin-language material, which remains largely inaccessible to the modern reader because so much languishes untranslated.[14] This is ironic since these Latin tracts, composed in the intellectual lingua franca of early modern Europe, were specifically written for an international, scholarly audience, often with the explicit intention of defending reputations and shaping continental attitudes about the prevailing political cultures in the Stuart monarchies.[15] Surely serious study of these non-English-language works and the contexts in which they were generated and disseminated will serve to provide more nuanced accounts of the politics of language and highlight how literature was used as a political tool throughout the Stuart dominions. Collectively they demonstrate the varied nature of responses to events and highlight the different ways in which writers from the Three Kingdoms perceived themselves and others.

These criticisms are, perhaps, unfair, since no single article or volume can construct 'a new critical cartography' that is chronologically complete, geographically and linguistically inclusive, and stimulates cross-disciplinary discourses. How, then, might this be achieved? Some research topics lend themselves more readily to a 'Three Kingdoms', or – to borrow Derek Hirst's phrase – a multi-centred, approach than others. Events, such as the Union of the Crowns in 1603, the Wars of the Three Kingdoms of the 1640s, or the political unions of 1707 (with Scotland) and of 1800–1 (with Ireland), are obvious instances where the histories of the Stuart monarchies intersect and interact. Individuals who enjoyed political, military, landed, commercial, literary, or intellectual interests in one or more of the Stuart kingdoms also invite 'holistic' analysis. Thus John Kerrigan, in his splendid chapter on Roger Boyle, Baron Broghill and later Earl of Orrery, deftly situates the poet–politician's writings in their British and Irish contexts and highlights wider continental perspectives and this might serve as a useful model for future case studies.[16] Consider also the example of the infamous puritan prophetess Lady Eleanor Davies. Born in England to an English father of French extraction (George Touchet, Lord Audley, who also held an Irish title, Earl of Castlehaven), she spent much of her youth in County Fermanagh and married the legal imperialist, Sir John Davies, and shortly after he died wed Sir Archibald Douglas, one of the king's Scottish favourites. To what extent did her Irish experiences, her Scottish connections, and the overt Catholicism of her Irish relatives influence her writings and sharpen her awareness of 'Great Brittaines foure crownes or kingdoms' (Cope *Handmaid of the Holy Spirit* 4; Cope ed. *Prophetic Writings of Lady Eleanor Davies*)?

In addition to paying greater attention to writers who were particularly sensitive to or products of the Three Kingdoms, the patronage networks that enmeshed and sustained these figures need to be unravelled. From the early seventeenth century, vibrant intellectual, literary, and cultural groups emerged, especially in London, which represented a critical point of contact for the peoples of the Stuart monarchies. For example, the publication in 1646 of *The Irish Rebellion* by Sir John Temple, a New English planter who was clearly influenced by Edmund Spenser's *View of the State of Ireland* (first published in Dublin in 1633), emanated from the embittered Protestant refugees who gathered at the Pall-Mall home of Katherine, Lady Ranelagh, herself a sister of Orrery and an intimate of John Milton (he tutored her children and nephew).[17] Temple's hyperbole immediately impacted on government propagandists and later writers, including Milton, who imbibed his prejudices and maintained that the barbarism and incivility of the Irish denied them individual rights and liberties. The Ranelagh–Orrery network also included another Irish Protestant exile: the Stuart statesman and antiquarian, Arthur Annesley, Earl of Anglesey, whose excellent library attracted many scholars and writers including Samuel Pepys and Lucy Hutchinson.[18] Detailed analysis of writers, their patrons, and their intellectual networks – which often included a Three Kingdoms, continental, and/or Atlantic dimension – might paint more textured pictures than the ones that currently exist.

Moreover, how did writers portray and represent their patrons? A number of leading English and Irish poets and playwrights – most notably John Dryden but also John Dancer, Thomas Flatman, and John Wilson – enjoyed the largesse of the first Duke of Ormond, together with his sons, the earls of Ossory and Arran, and his grandson, the second duke.[19] Did these writers render the Butlers of Ormond as 'English' (as they appear to have seen themselves), as 'Irish' (by virtue of their birth and ancestry), or as 'British' (as we might dub them)? Or were they more concerned with depicting the family's sense of honour and dignity or, in the case of the Butler women, their virtue? While passing references to Butler links with Ireland and Britain do appear, the poets writing in English concerned themselves more with the first duke's position as a loyal servant to the Stuarts, as a premier courtier, and as an extraordinary statesman, and with Ossory's role as a faithful commander and military hero (comparable to Caesar or 'a Carthaginian prince').[20] Fairly typical was the tribute paid to father and son by Elkanah Settle, a mediocre poet of Irish Protestant birth, who lived in London:

two such worthies in one age, and in one family, I cannot but think their noble and heroick mindes could not have a less original than the transmigrated spirits of a Philip and an Alexander: That restless and daring courage shone in the son, and that solid prudence and judgement in the father; that one had a soul fit to conquer a world and the other to govern it.[21]

Juxtaposed to this image of Ormond as the 'most illustrious cavalier' is that of him as the 'unkinde desertor'. Catholic writers – most notably Nicholas French, Bishop of Ferns, and the anonymous author of the 'Aphorismical Discovery of Treasonable Faction' – lambasted the duke for his 'betrayal' of his Irish supporters; while the Gaelic poets vented their scorn against him for denying them his patronage.[22] For example, in 'How Queer this Mode' the late seventeenth-century poet, Dáibhí Ó Bruadair ridiculed Ormond for his anglicized ways:

> With haughty, upstart ostentation lately swollen,
> Though codes of foreign clerks they fondly strive to master,
> They utter nothing but a ghost of strident English.
>
> (Mac Erlean *The Poems* 1:19)

Fortunately for Ormond's historical legacy, his portrayal as an honourable aristocrat and loyal, royal servant has prevailed in part because this was the image that he strove to promote. The duke's very public dispute with Anglesey during the early 1680s – over Ormond's behaviour during the 1640s and particularly his relationship with the Confederate Catholics – highlights this.[23] He claimed that Anglesey's tract, which had circulated widely especially in the coffee-houses, 'deduces consequences, raises inferences, and scatters glances injurious to the memory of the dead, and the honours of some living; among those . . . yet living, I find myself worst treated' (Ormond *A letter from His Grace James Duke of Ormond* preface). This direct slight on the duke, and the perceived attack on Charles I, led Ormond to undermine Anglesey's position at court and to secure his dismissal from office.[24] Ironically it was the publication of the memoirs of James Touchet, third Earl of Castlehaven, who aimed to justify his own position as a Catholic Confederate during the 1640s, that sparked this bitter pamphlet war between these Stuart statesmen.[25] As it was, Castlehaven's family honour had been severely tarnished as a result of his father's trial and execution in 1631 (for being party to the rape of his own wife and for sodomizing his servants). The stigma of the scandal dogged his relations throughout the seventeenth century despite the best efforts of the dead earl's sister, Lady Eleanor Davies. Throughout the 1640s she complained about the treatment received by her brother – 'A peere of two kingdomes a noble man here, a prince or earle in Ireland, whose estate sometime inferior to none'; proclaimed his innocence; and lamented the damage done to 'The house of Audley no obscure one, though one much envied, and such a one then come of no Sodome seed, but like Isaack rather sacrificed.'[26]

Issues such as honour and virtue feature in the recent writings of English social and gender historians; yet much work remains to be done on the Irish and Scottish side especially for the cultural, social, gender, and economic history of the early modern period. Admittedly the sources are less rich than for England but until serious research is undertaken in these areas, and the various branches of the historical profession engage more fully with each other, meaningful comparative, integrative, and multi-centred scholarship remains problematic. This, combined with the different training and approaches adopted by the literary and historical professions, further frustrates interdisciplinary scholarship. However, as a number of chapters in this volume demonstrate, these obstacles can be surmounted. While it is critical to respect the very different disciplinary agendas, every effort should be made to identify common problems and research interests, which facilitate and foster cross-disciplinary, collaborative scholarship that transcends the mellifluous boundaries that divided and encompassed the Stuart world.[27]

NOTES

I am grateful to the editors, Derek Hirst, Eamonn Ó Ciardha, and my colleagues – David Ditchburn, Andrew MacKillop, Allan Macinnes, Mary Morrissey, Steve Murdoch, Micheál Ó Siochrú, and David Worthington – for discussing and debating many aspects of this chapter with me.

1 For my own position see Ohlmeyer 'Seventeenth-century Ireland' 449.

2 For a recent example of this see Peter Clarke ed. *The Cambridge Urban History of Britain II 1540–1840*. Yet one wonders how an urban history of 'Britain' (especially post 1800–1) can be written without some discussion of Dublin, the second largest city of empire from the late seventeenth, and throughout the eighteenth, century. For an interesting discussion of Wales, see Philip Schwyzer's chapter above.

3 For an important recent study see Kidd *British Identities*.

4 See Murdoch *Britain, Denmark-Norway and the House of Stuart*, particularly the introduction which offers a fresh analysis of the 'Scottishness' and 'Britishness' of James VI and I and Charles I. I am grateful to Dr Murdoch for allowing me to read this in advance of publication.

5 See Ferguson *The Identity of the Scottish Nation*; Williamson *Scottish National Consciousness*; Broun, Finlay, and Lynch eds. *Image and Identity*; Mason ed. *Scots and Britons* and *Kingship and Commonweal*, especially ch. 6; Keith Brown 'The Origins of a British Aristocracy', 'Scottish Identity in the Seventeenth Century'; Robertson ed. *A Union for Empire*, especially Part II.

6 For a fascinating discussion of the political significance and popularity of Shakespeare's plays, especially Joseph Ashbury's production of *Othello*, in late seventeenth-century Ireland, see Patrick Tuite 'Theatrical Representation'. I am grateful to Dr Tuite for allowing me to read his thesis in advance of publication.

7 In this respect Davidson ed. *Poetry and Revolution* marks an important new departure, albeit English writers predominate.

8 Dermod O'Connor published an English version of it in 1723 but it was not until the early twentieth century that the Irish Texts Society published the

full text in Irish and English – Geoffrey Keating, *Foras Feasa ar Éirinn*. For further details see Cunningham *The World of Geoffrey Keating* 10–13, 187–90, and Cunningham and Gillespie 'Patrick Logan and *Foras Feasa*'.

9 The linguistic barrier remains a very real one; however, given the wealth of material that has been translated into English by bodies like the Irish Texts Society and the Scottish Texts Society this should not be insurmountable.

10 For excellent, albeit dated, overviews of the Irish-language material see Ó Cuív 'The Irish Language', 'Irish Language and Literature'; also see Cunningham 'Irish Language Sources'. For Scotland see Ó Baoill *The Harps' Cry*.

11 Ó Buachalla 'James Our True King' and the magisterial (and untranslated) *Aisling Ghéar. Na Stíobhartaigh Agus An tAos léinn* 1603–1788; together with Ó Ciardha 'Gaelic Poetry'; 'The Stuarts and Deliverance'; 'The Unkinde Deserter'.

12 For the development of the debate – sparked in large part by the publication of Dunne 'The Gaelic Response' – see Caball 'Bardic Poetry', 'Faith, Culture and Sovereignty', and *Poets and Politics*, especially his introduction; Ó Riordan '"Political" Poems' and *The Gaelic Mind* – for Breandán Ó Buachalla's response to *The Gaelic Mind* see 'Poetry and Politics', and for Brendan Bradshaw's see 'The Bardic Response'.

13 For Ireland see Cunningham 'Native Culture'; Ó Buachalla 'James our True King'; Mac Craith 'The Gaelic Reaction'. For Scotland see Dawson 'Calvinism and the Gaidhealtachd'; Macinnes 'Scottish Gaeldom', 'Crown, Clan and Fine', 'Gaelic Culture', and *Clanship, Commerce and the House of Stuart*.

14 For an excellent introduction see Benignus Millet 'Irish Literature in Latin'. Richard Stanihurst, who features in this volume as a contributor to Holinshed's *Chronicles*, subsequently published in Latin on Ireland's past in *De rebus in Hibernia gestis* (Antwerp 1584), translated in Lennon *Richard Stanihurst* 131–60. Similarly Sir William Herbert, a contemporary of Spenser and fellow undertaker on the Munster Plantation, whose *c.* 1591 treatise on the government of Sir James Croft in Ireland, written in Latin, is now available in translation in *Sir William Herbert* ed. Keaveney and Madden.

15 For Irish examples see the chapters by Cunningham and Ó hAnnracháin in Ohlmeyer ed. *Political Thought* and Carroll 'Irish and Spanish Cultural and Political Relations'.

16 Of course, these individuals tended to be members of the élite: Scottish peers like Hamilton and Argyll, the English Duke of Buckingham, or Irish lords, such as Ormond, Antrim, or the Earl of Clanricard, might be regarded as men of the Three Kingdoms. Increasingly historians examine them in this context, see Scally 'Counsel in Crisis'; Keith Brown *Noble Society in Scotland*; Treadwell *Buckingham and Ireland*; Barnard and Fenlon eds. *The Dukes of Ormond*; Ohlmeyer *Civil War and Restoration*.

17 Though the careers of her father, Richard Boyle, first Earl of Cork, and her brothers have been well documented, Lady Ranelagh has received

surprisingly little attention from historians despite the fact that her archive is extensive, albeit dispersed. For her circle see Webster 'New Light on the Invisible College'; Barnard 'The Hartlib Circle'.

18 For the sales catalogue of Anglesey's library, see *Bibliotheca Angleseiana, sive Catalogus Variorum Librorum* .... For his contact with Mrs Hutchinson and Pepys, see British Library, Additional MSS 18,730, Annesley's Diary 1675–84, entries for 2 September 1676 and 8 October 1682: 'The morning was much delighted in reading pious Mrs Hutcheson's diary and put thereby in mind of close walking with god as she did.' On 21 August 1682 he recorded that 'Lady Ranelagh, Mr Pepys and many friends' came to dinner. Mrs Hutchinson dedicated her translation of Lucretius' verse to Anglesey (Norbrook 'Lucy Hutchinson's "Elegies" ' 484–5).

19 Steve Zwicker and I are currently working on an article on 'John Dryden and the Patronage of the Dukes of Ormond'.

20 Anonymous *A brief compendium . . . Thomas Earl of Ossory* 3.

21 *An heroick poem on the Right Honourable Thomas Earl of Ossory* .

22 See particularly French *The Unkinde Desertor*, and J. T. Gilbert ed. *A Contemporary History* where the 'Aphorismical Discovery' is reprinted. Also see Kelly ' "Most Illustrious Cavalier" ' and Ó Ciardha 'The Unkinde Deserter'.

23 [Arthur Annesley, earl of Anglesey,] *A letter from a person of honour in the countrey written to the Earl of Castlehaven*. Ormond responded with *A letter from His Grace James Duke of Ormond*. This in turn provoked a hard-hitting response from Annesley, *A letter from the Right Honourable Arthur Earl of Anglesey Lord Privy Seal*.

24 Ormond *A true account of the whole proceedings betwixt His Grace James Duke of Ormond, and the Right Honor [sic] Arthur, Earl of Anglesey*; [Peter Pet?,] *The Happy Future State of England*.

25 Touchet *The memoirs of James, Lord Audley*.

26 Eleanor Davies *The word of God, to the citie of London, from the Lady Eleanor* 9, 6–7; *The crying charge* .

27 For instance, collaboration between individual historians and literary scholars can prove very fruitful as the publications of Derek Hirst, Kevin Sharpe, and Steven Zwicker demonstrate. Equally, bodies such as the Folger, Huntington, and Newberry Libraries that actively encourage cross-disciplinary dialogue have an important role to play, particularly if they are willing to adopt less of an Anglocentric agenda.

CHAPTER 15

Text, time, and the pursuit of 'British identities'

Derek Hirst

The editors of this volume lament, and with some justice, the reluctance of historians to engage with 'literary' texts and with literary scholars. Historians usually look to processes – the rise of this, the crisis of that. They are wary of the pressures of what they conceive as 'the literary' on texts that they often take to be transparent evidence of the past, since authorial self-consciousness and artifice, they reason, devalue texts as evidence for the narratives they seek to construct. Few historians have adjusted to demonstrations that the archive, as much as the epic, is a rhetorical and narrative construct. Fewer still recognize as a corollary that just as literary scholars are challenging the concept of canon, so historians ought to be open to the permeability of generic and disciplinary distinctions among texts. Yet the generic self-consciousness that has been the hallmark of 'the literary' might seem a particular asset for historians and others concerned with issues of mentality in general, and with identity in particular. We now know enough of practices of censorship and self-censorship to recognize the constraints on those who sought to question received wisdom, let alone to challenge official positions. A prime value of the 'literary' text to the historian is, or ought to be, precisely its self-consciousness and its artifice. After all, multiplicity of voice is inherent in the dialogue form, while ambivalence, ambiguity, and irony are the very idiom of literary expressiveness. Sensitivity to such devices allows cultural historians, indeed cultural scholars in general, a better sense of the boundaries of what could be articulated, even of what might be thought.[1] A sense of boundaries is surely crucial for an understanding of issues of identity.[2]

Establishing whatever it was that was 'British' in the early modern period is a singularly tricky business. Since Jane Ohlmeyer has in this volume eloquently expounded some of those difficulties from viewpoints north of Tweed and west of the Irish Sea, this chapter will turn in the other direction. Historians of early modern England are familiar with a series of set-pieces in which issues that seem recognizably 'British' impinged directly on English political consciousnesses. The debates on a projected union with Scotland, of 1604–7, in the 1650s, and again at the end of the seventeenth century, unleashed repeated displays of chauvinism and intolerance; so, even more fiercely, and from a different angle, did the Irish Revolt of 1641.[3] Such displays have been set alongside the paeans to Englishness of lawyers who felt England's common law was under threat, as well as the predictable Shakespearean soliloquies, to construct a historian's version of national consciousness: an intransigent insularity that seems complicated only by England's troubling peninsularity.[4]

The chapters in this volume tell a very different story. They alert us to the intensely polemical nature of effusions of Englishness by showing how various were early modern approaches to the nation and its people.[5] We learn that some of those who sought to represent the nation reached far beyond the merely English for their subject matter and their illustrations. We learn too that under that most 'British' king, James, court masques explored novel images of national origin and identity, while Shakespeare's *Cymbeline* admitted the bellicose ancient Briton as well as the indomitable Anglo-Saxon into the pantheon. Perhaps most importantly (because they have been so central to the writing of England and its destiny), we learn that Shakespeare's history plays contain sharply discordant national voices that are never entirely stilled. Instantiating the editors' promise that this volume would enrich our understanding of English identity in particular, Matthew Greenfield finds fissures in the English polity imagined in *1 Henry IV*, and thus questions easy assumptions that an English nation, with its implied unity, confronted subject others; and Pat Parker pushes a related argument to the heart of *Henry V*, to suggest the intensity of the Welsh challenge to the king's English doings. The Jacobean court masquers were of course singing for their suppers, but there is no denying the evidence assembled in these chapters that 'Britain' was a proposition that had a life. That life was not simply the creation of the publicists of state, or of dramatists looking for something new. Even the most alienated – indeed, especially the most alienated – from Catholic exiles in Rome to Jacobites of various hues, found new ideologies cut across by inherited tensions and loyalties. Exile and exclusion always challenge identity; yet we might wonder whether the extravagant assertions of Englishness with which the late sixteenth and seventeenth centuries abound are not the Ur-texts of national pride they have sometimes seemed, but instead acts of contest, excited by the presence of an alternative pole whose power of attraction we have too little recognized.[6] Such speculation, it goes without saying, is a tribute to the discoveries of the literary scholars who have contributed to this volume.

Ambivalence about English identity and English claims on others is clearly reflected in a variety of sources, which have been the preserve of the literary scholar. Cultural scholars, however, may want to go beyond reflections to try to situate the ironies: for when we talk about the meaning of identity surely what we have in mind is a matter of experience, a template of feeling, loyalties, and constraints. Here, it is the historian who is best placed to savour, if not perhaps to detect, irony, for the central irony is a historical one. Richard Helgerson outlined the ways in which Shakespeare's generation fleshed out the meaning of nationhood in terms of land, law, history, the Spanish foe, and so on (Helgerson *Forms of Nationhood*). As that generation reached maturity, it was inexorably confronted with the subversion of the 'England' it had conjured. Elizabeth might stand proudly and self-containedly on a map of England in the famous Ditchley portrait, yet her land was scarcely self-contained. England's subordination of Ireland was becoming painfully obvious – even as the increasing likelihood of the Stuart succession raised its own questions about name and nation. It would have been surprising if the observant and the sensitive had avoided a certain sense of conflictedness. Indeed, Shakespeare and his contemporaries laboured under a further dilemma. At precisely the moment England was beginning to acquire empire, in Ireland, in Virginia, with all the coercion of others that that brought, at home a sense of English liberties, even of 'the liberty of the subject', was emerging (Sacks 'Parliament, Liberty and the Commonweal'). Shakespeare showed repeatedly – and not just in Lear's tirade on the heath – his interest in matters of social and individual justice. He was by no means alone in finding it hard to reconcile English liberties at home with English claims and conduct beyond England's ancient borders.[7] The historian might be forgiven for being surprised that literary scholars should express wonderment at the ironies they uncover in representations of England.

The 'new British' scholarly agenda engages with geographical, cultural, and historical challenges; and these are difficult enough. The editors of this volume defend themselves against the charge of 'Anglocentrism' Nicholas Canny has directed against so much of that agenda by urging that English identities too have to be delineated; but that defence may not convince the sceptic, particularly in view of what must seem the token presence here of the Gael and the American Indian (Canny 'Irish, Scottish and Welsh' 147–8). Although the chapters in this volume throw valuable light on some less familiar texts (Orrery's plays, Harriot's drawings, various masques, exilic works, Holinshed's Irish *Chronicles*), there remains some justice to Matthew Greenfield's intimation that the 'new British' agenda has in practice tended merely to bring a new set of questions to bear on familiar components of the English canon. Methodological problems, however, must also be confronted. The introversion of many historians may be lamented, but the editors' ability to refer to 'Shakespeare' as an 'iconic text' exposes a crucial, and troubling, area of disciplinary difference. Chapters in this volume amply demonstrate how multifaceted was that icon. Yet we still need to ask what the demonstration of textual complexity tells us even of English 'identity', let alone of the 'British identities' this volume promises. Without substantially more data, we may be left with little more than a recognition of new textual perturbations.

Let us take as an example Richard McCabe's fascinating exploration of Holinshed's collection of Irish narratives (Giraldus's, Campion's, John Hooker's). McCabe charts the overlay of new Protestant supremacy on a work of old English hegemony, as Campion gives place to Hooker. His endeavour tells us much about Holinshed's text and of the fervour of Hooker's Protestantism, but it provides only a limited perspective on English 'identity'. A different understanding of one writer's sense of the English/Irish world and its dilemmas emerges when we relate the case for the royal prerogative in the Irish Parliament advanced by Holinshed's Hooker with John Hooker's concern elsewhere to circumscribe the royal prerogative in the English Parliament.[8] Like so many who followed him in the pursuit of empire, he urged practices outside England that he deemed anathema at home. Hooker's two faces, one turned toward Elizabeth's England and the other toward Holinshed's Ireland, remind us that fractures were replicated, in both metropole and periphery. The literary scholars in this collection are to be commended for moving beyond the anecdotal approach of new historicism, whose promises of enlightenment through the ostensibly artless selection of 'historical' detail too often misled; but it is not always apparent that we have been provided with a more powerful key to open the barriers separating the text from its writer and his/her world. In the British field, more than most, the settings of authors and texts alike were not only multifaceted, but also multiply fractured. Only by trying to catch the refractions, and the pressures and tensions, are we likely to approach British, or even English, 'identities'.

John Kerrigan's study of the Earl of Orrery's plays and romances provides a model. It is not simply an exploration of a particularly exposed and imaginative individual; in its attention to alignments in various arenas, and in its demonstration of the way those alignments inflected Orrery's writings, it suggests what an interdisciplinary approach to works of British imagination might look like. Instead of merely invoking the authority of J. G. A. Pocock to demonstrate the existence of a historical and conceptual problem that then forms a passive context for an exercise in textual unfolding, Kerrigan insists on the mutual interplay of texts and contexts, and demonstrates how each pressed on the other. For him, identities are a matter of process and situation, as well as representation; and only an interdisciplinary approach as sophisticated as his is likely to uncover them. Orrery as Anglo-Irish politician followed, of course, a more complicated path than most; nevertheless, Orrery as playwright clearly expected audiences, in London as well as Dublin, to share at least some of his concerns, and of his alertness too. Although Orrery's published writings were emphatically Anglocentric, Kerrigan's study looks beyond merely English attitudes and relationships. Nevertheless, his is an interdisciplinary road with little traffic on it. This is the more regrettable since not only are interrogations of identity always likely to gain most from interdisciplinary approaches; as important, truly British studies – lacking as these do an established canon or narrative, lacking at many points the archives from which to construct such a narrative – have most to offer such approaches.

How might we sustain that claim? We might look at Linda Gregerson's and Christopher Highley's readings of the efforts of exiles to achieve a sustainable English Christian identity, but since their approaches are so close to that of the historian we probably need to go further. Indeed, the matter is sufficiently important that I would like to breach the normal etiquette for writers of afterwords by urging the gains to be had from Kerrigan's multi-centred approach. My contention is that there are texts that we can, with care, bring into colloquy with other texts, and with multiple histories, to throw light far beyond text and writer. Indeed, it seems possible to arrive, if not yet at past identities, at least at a grid of beliefs and attitudes that is more than the sum of the parts. I want to look again at that familiar text, Shakespeare's *The Tempest*, not because it is in any way representative, but because it is the great text of the expanding English imagination. In the figure of the most vividly conjured 'other' in early modern English literature, set within an implied Irish frame,[9] we might – I will suggest – engage with the elusive topic of this volume.

Whatever the resonances of the mantled, shapeless, and hairy 'wild Irishman' in Speed's 1611 British atlas, Caliban's obvious anagram – 'can[n]ibal' – seems to push this savage to a distant frontier. On that frontier, the charge of cannibalism was strategic, and provided an essential legitimation for aggression. European accounts of the Indian tended to shift to outright hostility as active colonization became the order of the day, since the drive to exploit a region to which the newcomers had scant claim brought to the fore the charge of cannibalism (Sheehan *Savagism and Civility* 37; Hulme *Colonial Encounters* 164 n.73). If a people was to be subjugated, expropriated, extirpated, then it helped if they could be put beyond the bounds not simply of civility but even of humanity; and cannibalism was the ultimate savagery. Accordingly, the charge of cannibalism resonates through the early literature of American conquest, as voyagers strategically misinterpreted the rituals they observed, or simply invented.[10]

Cannibalism was not a new-found practice, and nor was the denigration of those deemed cannibals. Herodotus wrote the founding text of the cannibal legend: the Scythians on the Black Sea not only followed distressingly unsettled transhumant practices, they also practised cannibalism; and with them the Greeks had endless war.[11] The resurrection of that analysis, and that potent charge, in the sixteenth century surely cannot be attributed only to the general resurgence of classical learning; nor was it as unpolemical as we might imagine from Montaigne's ability, as he reflected on the cannibal, to roam freely between the New World and the Scythians.[12] It was for out-savaging the Scythian that King Lear disinherited Cordelia – and the Scythian of Lear's imagination is very much the cannibal (*King Lear* 1.i.116–18).[13] Scythian barbarism was a by-word. Marlowe's Tamburlaine was a Scythian, while Joannes Boemus, whose influential conspectus of the world was published in translation in London in the busy year of 1611, and whose Latin text was used by Spenser, deemed the unsettled and bloody Scythians the most barbarous of all the peoples of the earth; Samuel Purchas, borrowing from the same sources, agreed with him two years later. To Robert Sibthorpe, preaching of *Apostolike Obedience* in 1627, the Scythian and the ordinary barbarian were antonyms, as distinct as 'bond or free, Iew or Grecian'.[14] The figure of the Scythian even shaped the seminal claim to the Caribbean, and Columbus delighted in the word 'cannibal' as a near-cognate of 'the Great Khan'.[15]

The political significance lies in the line connecting the Gaelic Irish and their Scottish kin to the Scythians. My aim here is not to reiterate Spenser's estimate of the Scythian connection,[16] but to stress how wide-spread was the assumption that the connection existed. Spenser's great editor W. L. Renwick noted that 'The Scythian and Spanish origin of the Irish is in nearly all the chronicles', and he goes on to quote from Camden's *Britannia* of 1610 in support. In the following year – *The Tempest*'s year – 1611, Speed's *Theatre of the Empire of Great Britaine* repeatedly stressed the Scythian home of the Irish. Those medieval Gaels who followed European fashion by asserting a common and potent, and in their case non-Greco-Roman, ancestor could not have known how embarrassing their choice would prove to their descendants when expanding horizons and appetites raised the stakes in the contest between the savage and the civil.[17] The Spanish theorist of empire, Las Casas, was convinced that the early Irish had been cannibals, and his contemporary John Mair probably had in mind the predictive implications of such a claim when he denied the relevance of Las Casas's source (St Jerome) to Scotland; for Mair questioned whether the flesh-eating sins of ancestors could be visited on their successors through the generations (Elliott *The Old World and the New* 34; Mair *History of Greater Britain* 44–45).

Others were eager to attribute Scythian extremes, even cannibalism, to the modern Gael. Both Canny and Arthur Williamson have observed, though they do not quite explain, the charges vented by Spenser's contemporaries. It may have been ideology but it was also ethnology that allowed James VI to dismiss his Highlanders and Islanders as cannibals. In similar fashion, Sir Henry Sidney slighted Shane O'Neill as 'that canyball', while fifty years later Sir John Davies denounced those living under Gaelic rule as 'little better than Cannibals who do hunt one another'.[18] John Speed's interest in Irish cannibalism, their delight in blood as a dietary supplement, and reports of their 'filthie abominable acts... against Nature, committed with Beasts', is similarly programmatic – and, displayed as it is in his *Theatre of . . . Great Britaine*, perhaps more emblematic (Speed *Theatre of the Empire of Great Britaine* 138, 143, 145). The term 'cannibal' came easily to these minds, thanks to the continuities between the north-eastern marches of the Hellenic world, medieval Gaeldom, and the bloody present.[19]

Yet Shakespeare did not quite add to the fashionable blood-libel chorus against the Gael, although he surely admitted it into his play. Caliban's name and appearance could not but conjure the cannibal; but Shakespeare balanced the horror of that figure with the famous cry for autonomy – 'This island's mine by Sycorax my mother, / Which thou tak'st from me... I am all the subjects that you have, / Which first was mine own king' (I.ii.331–2, 341–2). The cry is striking not simply for its pathos, but also for its powerful echoes of the protest by the great Gaelic chieftain Shane O'Neill a generation earlier – a protest Holinshed carefully set before Shakespeare and his other readers. Shane O'Neill's declaration, 'Mine ancestors were kings of Ulster . . . so now Ulster is mine and shall be mine',[20] underscores the tangled ideologies Shakespeare articulated through the triangulated geographies of his play. His decisions to write Ireland across the brave new world, and to indulge that dispossessory 'cannibal' slur against the Gael are clear enough. He did not, however, dismiss out of hand the Gaels' own possessory arguments, for in the end Caliban's cry went unrefuted; and nor was Shakespeare alone in his receptivity to those arguments. In a little-noticed passage in Spenser's *View*, Eudoxus – the altogether English protagonist in the dialogue – complains about the extent of support in England for O'Neill claims of possessory right to Ulster.[21] Although there was no English equivalent of Las Casas, Acosta, Oviedo, no English Montaigne, Gaelic or 'savage' claims to rights do not seem to have gone unnoticed.

The triangulated geographies of *The Tempest* provide a pattern for us as we puzzle at the problem of identity. Critics and theorists may succeed in teasing out of the text answers to questions of an identity understood as the subjectivity of the author and the agency of the words on the page. Identity understood in cultural or national terms poses other difficulties for critics, who may discern key features but are unlikely to succeed in setting those features in perspective. For that, we must surely look for points of triangulation beyond the text. Triangulation can be horizontal – thus, by reading across Gaelic sources Murray Pittock is able to show the appeal of the Stuart legend to the imaginations of the excluded. Triangulation can go more deeply, as Kerrigan's work shows. Some such effort is needed if identity is to be – as it most surely was – more than a trope. Without an appreciation of the reach of the cannibal legend, we could debate endlessly what Shakespeare's antihero has to say of 'the savage', and its application to England; but we would not hear him speak of the heirs of the Scyths. It was the latter who, in the years up to 1611, more sharply confronted English, lowland Scottish – indeed, British – identities.

As Shakespeare's generation well knew, identity is a matter of nature and nurture, or of genes and experience as we might have it. Time – which changes contexts as well as understandings – is involved, as well as text; and few contexts were as multiple, various, changing, as those having to do with matters British. The British identities that preoccupy this volume's contributors are more than most a matter of dynamics and not statics; they are also, in all cases, complicated and multivalent. Historians and literary scholars must therefore look to each others' labours if they are to uncover, in the archive as well as in the text, the whorls and creases that are the marks of selfhood or identity, whether collective or individual.

NOTES

1 A salutary object lesson here is John Kerrigan's study of Orrery's works, in this volume.
2 I should make clear that, like the other contributors to this volume, I do not intend subjectivity when I speak of identity.
3 See, conveniently, Levack *The Formation of the British State*, and Russell *The Fall of the British Monarchies*.
4 The word-play is Donald R. Kelley's in 'Debate: History, English Law and the Renaissance' 143. Historians' recapitulations of early modern English chauvinism are too numerous to chronicle.
5 I use the phrase 'early modern' in preference to the 'Renaissance' of the title to this volume since it does not seem that Jacobite literature, for example, can comfortably be included under the usual definitions of the Renaissance.
6 This suggestion would certainly hold for John Lilburne, the 'freeborn Englishman' of the later 1640s, who flourished his identity both against Parliament's allies, the Scots, with their quasi-federal vision, and also against the second British king, Charles Stuart.
7 Eltis *The Rise of African Slavery in the Americas* provides a brilliant and sobering analysis of what I am tempted to call the dangerous inheritance of English liberty.
8 Snow ed. *Parliament in Elizabethan England* esp. p. 28. Hooker's scorn, to which McCabe draws notice, for 'busie headed lawiers and malecontented gentlemen [who] dispute the princes prerogative with their Littletons tenures', would probably have struck Elizabeth as deeply ironic.
9 See Baker 'Where is Ireland in *The Tempest?*' Baker's case could, however, be reinforced. Throughout the play we are alerted to a morbid wetness. That wetness, and the diseases it brought, provide the burden of Caliban's repeated curses on Prospero, and Prospero retaliates in kind by confining Caliban and his co-conspirators 'i' th' filthy-mantled pool . . . the foul lake [that] O'erstunk their feet' with 'horse-piss'. Sebastian and Antonio similarly comment on the rottenness of the island's air. Three times we are told of the island's 'fens', and also of its 'bogs' and damp 'flats'; furthermore, Prospero's cell has a wind-break around it (I.ii.322–3; II.i.47–9; IV.i.182–4, 199; V.i.10). This land seems less enchanted than cursed, its topography owing more to painful reports of exposure and dysentery in Irish quagmires during the Elizabethan conquest than to travellers' tales of distant lands.

10 See Hulme *Colonial Encounters* 13–87, for a provocative study of the importance of the cannibal legend to early modern Europe.
11 Herodotus *The Persian Wars* iv. For Herodotus' preoccupation with the antitype, see Hartog *The Mirror of Herodotus.*
12 Montaigne *The Essayes of Michael, Lord of Montaigne* 105–19. Anthony Grafton
   observes that 'Cannibals...had always according to legend inhabited
   Scythia.' Nevertheless, it was surely the contemporary bearing of the
   Herodotean charge that drove Sebastian Munster to select Scythian cannibals for graphic inclusion in his 1546 edition of Ptolemy's *Geography*, to
   which Grafton draws notice (Grafton *New Worlds, Ancient Texts* 104).
13 I am grateful to Joe Loewenstein for the latter reference, and for observing
   to me that the homeland of Medea, whose magic Prospero invokes when he
   draws the circle on the ground, was Colchis, on the Black Sea, in what was
   to become known as the land of the Scyths.
14 Boemus *Manners, Lawes, and Customes of all Nations* 105–16; Purchas *Pilgrimage*
   333; Sibthorpe *Apostolike Obedience* 8. Canny has noted the impact of the 1611
   Boemus: 'Ideology of English Colonization' 587; for traces of the Latin text
   in Spenser's *View*, see Renwick edition 64, 79, 81.
15 *Oxford English Dictionary* s.v. 'cannibal'.
16 See especially Hadfield 'Briton and Scythian' 390–408.
17 Renwick *View* 265; Speed *Theatre of the Empire of Great Britaine* 131, 137–
   8, 143, 145. For the subject in general, see Matthews 'The Egyptians in
   Scotland'; Hoffman 'Outsiders by Birth and Blood' 8–10. One version of
   the Declaration of Arbroath has the Scots hailing 'de Maiori Schithia',
   ('from Greater Scythia'): Fergusson ed. *The Declaration of Arbroath* 50. For the
   general subject of origin legends, see Susan Reynolds 'Medieval Origines
   Gentium'. Although neither Mair nor Buchanan was eager to accept the
   case, both did accept Bede's testimony that the Picts were Scythians; and
   everybody conceded that the Picts had inhabited Ireland as well as Scotland,
   and intermarried with the Scoti: Major [alias Mair] *A History of Greater Britain*
   54–5; Buchanan *History of Scotland* I:88, 91, 120. Bede's claim is to be found
   in the first chapter of the first book of the *Ecclesiastical History of the English
   People.*
18 Williamson 'Scots, Indians and Empire' 64; Canny 'Ideology of English
   Colonization' 587. To King James, it is true, cannibals seem to have been
   not just the anthropophagi who by then constituted the term's main referent
   but also those who lived 'vpon raw flesh' – a practice that contemporaries
   thought wide-spread in the Gaelic world (Sommerville ed. *King James* 201);
   Speed also registered the Irish propensity for raw flesh, but bracketed it firmly
   with cannibalism: Speed *Theatre of the Empire of Great Britaine* 138. Spenser's
   interest in the bloody ways of the Gael is notorious. For the most accessible
   version, see *A View of the State of Ireland* ed. Hadfield and Maley 66, 101–2.
19 The Scythian connection seems to have been a very British concern, for
   the Spanish, having to do with settled empires in the New World, proved
   far more interested in Herodotus' Egyptians. Thus, for the Spanish theorist

of empire José de Acosta, the Scythians were primarily of interest for their mobility, which provided an analogue for the Amerindians' migrations over the land-bridge from Asia (Pagden *The Fall of Natural Man* 175, 193–5).

20 Holinshed *The Second Volume of Chronicles, with a continuation by John Hooker alias Vowell* 113–14.

21 Eudoxus declares feelingly, on hearing Irenius dismantle Hugh O'Neill's possessory claims, that he will now be able 'the better [to] satisfye them whom I have often harde to obiecte these doubts' (Renwick *View* 149–50).

Bibliography

Adams, Julia. *The Familial State: Ruling Families and Merchant Capitalism in Early Modern Europe.* Ithaca: Cornell University Press, forthcoming.

Alexander, Michael, ed. *Discovering the New World, Based on the Works of Theodor de Bry.* London: London Editions, 1976.

Allen, Theodore. *The Invention of the White Race.* 2 vols. London: Verso, 1994.

Allen, William. *The Letters and Memorials of William Cardinal Allen (1532–1594).* Introd. Thomas Francis Knox. London: David Nutt, 1882.

Anderson, Benedict. *Imagined Communities: Reflections on the Origin and Spread of Nationalism.* Revised edn. New York: Verso, 1991.

Andrews, J. H. *Irish Maps.* Dublin: Eason and Son, 1978.

Shapes of Ireland: Maps and Their Makers, 1564–1839. Dublin: Geography Publications, 1997.

Andrews, K. R., N. P. Canny, and P. E. H. Hair, eds. *The Westward Enterprise.* Liverpool: Liverpool University Press, 1978.

[Annesley, Arthur]. *A letter from a person of honour in the countrey written to the Earl of Castlehaven: being observations and reflections upon His Lordships memoires concerning the wars of Ireland.* London, 1681.

Annesley, Arthur. *A letter from the Right Honourable Arthur Earl of Anglesey Lord Privy Seal, in answer to his grace the Duke of Ormond's letter of November the 12th, 1681...* London, 1682.

Anon. *A brief compendium of the birth, education, heroick exploits and victories of the truly valorous and renowned gentleman, Thomas Earl of Ossory...* London?, 1680.

The supplication of certaine masse-priests falsely called Catholikes. London, 1604.

Archer, Jayne. 'Women and Alchemy in Early Modern England'. Unpublished Ph.D. dissertation. University of Cambridge, 2000.

Armitage, David. 'Greater Britain: A Useful Category of Historical Analysis?' *American Historical Review* 104 (1999): 427–45.

The Ideological Origins of the British Empire. Cambridge: Cambridge University Press, 2000.

Ash, Marinell. *The Strange Death of Scottish History.* Edinburgh: Ramsay Head Press, 1980.

Axton, Marie. *The Queen's Two Bodies: Drama and the Elizabethan Succession.* London: Royal Historical Society, 1977.

Ayscu, Edward. *A Historie Contayning the Warres, Treaties, Marriages, and Other Occurrents betweene England and Scotland* (1607).

Bacon, Francis. *Of the Advancement and Proficiencie of Learning* (1st, Latin, edn 1605). Trans. Gilbert Wats. London, 1674.

The Letters and the Life of Francis Bacon. 7 vols. Ed. James Spedding. London, 1861–74.

New Atlantis (1627). In *Francis Bacon: A Critical Edition of the Major Works*. Ed. Brian Vickers. Oxford: Oxford University Press, 1996.

Baker, David J. *Between Nations: Shakespeare, Spenser, Marvell, and the Question of Britain*. Stanford: Stanford University Press, 1997.

'Where is Ireland in *The Tempest*?' In *Shakespeare and Ireland*. Ed. Mark Thornton Burnett and Ramona Wray. Basingstoke: Macmillan, 1997.

'"Wildehirissheman": Colonialist Representation in Shakespeare's *Henry V*'. *English Literary Renaissance* 22 (1993): 37–61.

Baldwin, Barry. *The Latin and Greek Poems of Samuel Johnson*. London: Duckworth, 1995.

Barber, C. L. *Shakespeare's Festive Comedy: A Study of Dramatic Form and its Relation to Social Custom*. Princeton: Princeton University Press, 1959.

Barber, Peter. 'England II: Monarchs, Ministers, and Maps, 1550–1625'. In *Monarchs, Ministers, and Maps: The Emergence of Cartography as a Tool of Government in Early Modern Europe*. Ed. David Buisseret. Chicago: University of Chicago Press, 1992.

Barnard, T. C. 'The Hartlib Circle and the Cult and Culture of Improvement in Ireland'. In *Samuel Hartlib and the Universal Reformation*. Ed. Mark Greengrass, Michael Leslie, and Timothy Raylor. Cambridge: Cambridge University Press, 1994.

Barnard, T. C., and Jane Fenlon, eds. *The Dukes of Ormond, 1610–1745*. Woodbridge, Suffolk: Boydell Press, 2000.

Barroll, J. Leeds. *Shakespearean Tragedy: Genre, Tradition, and Change in Antony and Cleopatra*. London: Associated University Presses, 1984.

Bartlett, Robert. *Gerald of Wales 1146–1223*. Oxford: Clarendon Press, 1982.

Bartley, J. O. *Teague, Shenkin and Sawney: Being an Historical Study of the Earliest Irish, Welsh and Scottish Characters in English Plays*. Cork: Cork University Press, 1954.

Beare, Philip O'Sullivan. *Selections from the Zoilomastix of Philip O'Sullivan Beare*. Ed. Thomas J. O'Donnell. Dublin: Irish Manuscripts Commission, 1960.

Berry, Philippa. *Of Chastity and Power: Elizabethan Literature and the Unmarried Queen*. London: Routledge, 1989.

Bibliotheca Angleseiana, sive Catalogus Variorum Librorum . . . London, 1686.

Blackett-Ord, Mark. *Hell-Fire Duke: The Life of the Duke of Wharton*. Windsor Forest, Berks.: The Kensal Press, 1982.

Boemus, Joannes. *Manners, Lawes, and Customes of all Nations*. 1611.

Boland, Eavan. *Object Lessons: The Life of the Woman and the Poet in our Time*. London: Vintage, 1996.

Boling, Ronald J. 'Anglo-Welsh Relations in *Cymbeline*'. *Shakespeare Quarterly* 51 (2000): 33–66.

Bolton, Edmund. *Hypercritica*. 1618.

Bossy, John. 'Catholicity and Nationality in the Northern Counter-Reformation'. In *Religion and National Identity*. Ed. Stuart Mews. Oxford: Blackwell, 1982.

Bottigheimer, Karl. 'Kingdom and Colony: Ireland in the Westward Enterprise 1536–1660'. In K. R. Andrews, N. P. Canny, and P. E. H. Hair eds. *The Westward Enterprise*.

Bradshaw, Brendan. 'The Bardic Response to Conquest and Colonisation'. *Bullán* 1 (1994): 119–22.

'The Beginnings of Modern Ireland'. In *The Irish Parliamentary Tradition*. Ed. Brian Farrell. Dublin: Gill and Macmillan, 1973.

'The Elizabethans and the Irish'. *Studies* 66 (1977): 38–50.

'The Elizabethans and the Irish: A Muddled Model'. *Studies* 70 (1981): 233–44.

'The English Reformation and Identity Formation in Ireland and Wales'. In Bradshaw and Roberts eds. *British Consciousness and Identity*.

'Geoffrey Keating: Apologist of Irish Ireland'. In *Representing Ireland: Literature and the Origins of Conflict, 1534–1660*. Ed. Brendan Bradshaw, Andrew Hadfield, and Willy Maley. Cambridge: Cambridge University Press, 1993.

The Irish Constitutional Revolution in the Sixteenth Century. Cambridge: Cambridge University Press, 1979.

'Nationalism and Historical Scholarship in Modern Ireland'. *Irish Historical Studies* 26 (1989): 329–51.

'Native Reaction to the Westward Enterprise: A Case-Study in Gaelic Ideology'. In K. R. Andrews, N. P. Canny, and P. E. H. Hair eds. *The Westward Enterprise*.

'Sword, Word and Strategy in the Reformation in Ireland'. *Historical Journal* 21 (1978): 475–502.

'The Tudor Reformation and Revolution in Wales and Ireland'. In Bradshaw and Morrill eds. *The British Problem*.

Bradshaw, Brendan, and John Morrill, eds. *The British Problem, c. 1534–1707: State Formation in the Atlantic Archipelago*. London: Macmillan, 1996.

Bradshaw, Brendan, and Peter Roberts, eds. *British Consciousness and Identity: The Making of Britain, 1533–1707*. Cambridge: Cambridge University Press, 1998.

Brady, Ciarán. *The Chief Governors: The Rise and Fall of Reform Government in Tudor Ireland*. Cambridge: Cambridge University Press, 1994.

'Comparable Histories?: Tudor Reform in Wales and Ireland'. In Ellis and Barber eds. *Conquest and Union*.

'The Decline of the Irish Kingdom'. In *Conquest and Coalescence: The Shaping of the State in Early Modern Europe*. Ed. Mark Greengrass. London: Edward Arnold, 1991.

'The Road to the View: On the Decline of Reform Thought in Tudor Ireland'. In *Spenser and Ireland: An Interdisciplinary Perspective*. Ed. Patricia Coughlan. Cork: Cork University Press, 1989.

Broun, D., R. J. Finlay, and M. Lynch, eds. *Image and Identity: The Making and Remaking of Scotland through the Ages.* Edinburgh: John Donald, 1998.

Brown, Keith. *Noble Society in Scotland from the Reformation to the Revolution.* Edinburgh: Edinburgh University Press, 2000.

'The Origins of a British Aristocracy: Integration and its Limitations before the Treaty of Union'. In Ellis and Barber eds. *Conquest and Union.*

'Scottish Identity in the Seventeenth Century'. In Bradshaw and Roberts eds. *British Consciousness and Identity.*

Brown, Paul. ' "This thing of darkness I acknowledge mine": *The Tempest* and the discourse of colonialism'. In *Political Shakespeare: Essays in Cultural Materialism.* Ed. Jonathan Dollimore and Alan Sinfield. Manchester: Manchester University Press, 1985.

Buchanan. George. *History of Scotland.* London, 1735.

Burgess, Glenn. 'Introduction: The New British History'. In *The New British History: Founding a Modern State 1603–1715.* Ed. Glenn Burgess. London: I. B. Tauris, 1999.

Burns, Robert. *Poems and Songs.* Ed. James Kinsley. Oxford: Oxford University Press, 1992.

Caball, Marc. 'Bardic Poetry and the Analysis of Gaelic Mentalities'. *History Ireland* 2 (1994): 46–50.

'Faith, Culture and Sovereignty: Irish Nationality and its Development, 1558–1625'. In Bradshaw and Roberts eds. *British Consciousness and Identity.*

Poets and Politics: Continuity and Reaction in Irish Poetry, 1558–1625. Cork: Cork University Press, 1998.

Caesar, Julius. *The Gallic War.* Trans. H. J. Edwards. Cambridge, MA: Harvard University Press, 1986.

Calderwood, James. *Metadrama in Shakespeare's* Henriad. Berkeley: University of California Press, 1979.

Calendar of the Carew Manuscripts, preserved in the Archiepiscopal Library at Lambeth. 6 vols. London: 1873.

Camden, William. *Britain, Or a Chorographicall Description of the Most flourishing Kingdomes, England, Scotland, and Ireland, and the ilands adjoyning, out of the depth of Antiquitie.* Trans. Philemon Holland. London, 1610.

Britannia. London, 1586.

Britannia (1607). Trans. Edmund Gibson. London, 1695.

Remains Concerning Britain. Ed. R. D. Dunn. Toronto: University of Toronto Press, 1984.

Campion, Edmund. *Two Bokes of the Histories of Ireland.* Ed. A. F. Vossen. Assen: Van Gorcum, 1963.

Cannon, John. *Samuel Johnson and the Politics of Hanoverian England.* Oxford: Clarendon Press, 1994.

Canny, Nicholas. 'Edmund Spenser and the Development of an Anglo-Irish Identity'. *Yearbook of English Studies* 13 (1983): 1–19.

The Elizabethan Conquest of Ireland: A Pattern Established, 1565–76. Hassocks, Sussex: The Harvester Press, 1976.

The Formation of the Old English Elite in Ireland. Dublin: National University of Ireland, 1975.

From Reformation to Restoration: Ireland, 1534–1660. Dublin: Helicon, 1987.

'The Ideology of English Colonialization: From Ireland to America'. *William and Mary Quarterly* 30 (1973): 575–98.

'Irish, Scottish and Welsh Responses to Centralisation, *c.* 1530–*c.* 1640: A Comparative Perspective'. In *Uniting the Kingdom?: The Making of British History*. Ed. Alexander Grant and Keith J. Stringer. London: Routledge, 1995.

Kingdom and Colony: Ireland in the Atlantic World, 1560–1800. Baltimore, MD: Johns Hopkins University Press, 1988.

Carey, John. *The Irish National Origin-Legend: Synthetic Pseudohistory*. Cambridge: Department of Anglo-Saxon, Norse, and Celtic, University of Cambridge, 1994.

Carley, James. 'Polydore Vergil and John Leland on King Arthur: The Battle of the Books'. *Interpretations* 15 (1984): 86–100.

Carrafiello, Michael E. *Robert Parsons and English Catholicism, 1580–1610*. London: Associated University Presses, 1998.

Carroll, Clare. 'Irish and Spanish Cultural and Political Relations in the Work of O'Sullivan Beare'. In *Political Ideology in Ireland, 1541–1641*. Ed. Hiram Morgan. Dublin: Four Courts, 1999.

Cartari, Vincenzo. *The Fountaine of Ancient Fiction*. Trans. Richard Linche. London, 1599.

Chapman, Paul. 'Jacobite Political Argument in England 1714–66'. Unpublished Ph.D. dissertation. University of Cambridge, 1983.

Childs, John. *The Army, James II and the Glorious Revolution*. Manchester: Manchester University Press, 1980.

Clarke, Aidan. *The Old English in Ireland, 1625–42*. London: MacGibbon & Kee, 1966.

Clarke, Peter, ed. *The Cambridge Urban History of Britain II 1540–1840*. Cambridge: Cambridge University Press, 2000.

Clegg, Cyndia. *Press Censorship in Elizabethan England*. Cambridge: Cambridge University Press, 1997.

Cogley, Richard W. 'John Eliot and the Origins of the American Indians'. *Early American Literature* 21 (1986–7): 210–25.

Colley, Linda. 'Britishness and Otherness: An Argument'. *Journal of British Studies* 31 (1992): 309–29.

Britons: Forging the Nation, 1707–1837. New Haven: Yale University Press, 1992.

Comyn, David, ed. and trans. *The History of Ireland*. 4 vols. London: Irish Texts Society, 1902–14.

Conditions To Be Observed by the Brittish Vndertakers of the Escheated Lands in Vlster. London, 1610.

Cope, Esther S. *Handmaid of the Holy Spirit: Dame Eleanor Davies, Never Soe Mad a Ladie*. Michigan: Ann Arbor, 1992.

ed. *Prophetic Writings of Lady Eleanor Davies*. Women Writers in English 1350–1850. Oxford: Oxford University Press, 1995.

Corkery, Daniel. *The Hidden Ireland*. 2nd edn. Dublin: M. H. Gill and Son, 1925.

Corthell, Ronald. 'Robert Persons and the Writer's Mission'. In *Catholicism and Anti-Catholicism in Early Modern English Texts*. Ed. Arthur F. Marotti. New York: St Martin's, 1999.

Craig, Thomas. *De unione regnorum Britanniae tractatus* (1606). Ed. and trans. C. Sanford Terry. Edinburgh: Scottish Historical Society, 1909.

Cronin, Michael. *Translating Ireland: Translation, Languages, Cultures*. Cork: Cork University Press, 1996.

Crossman, Virginia. 'Introduction'. In *Ireland in Proximity: History, Gender, Space*. Ed. Scott Brewster *et al*. London: Routledge, 1999.

Cullen, Patrick. 'The Political War Ballads of Sean O'Casey, 1916–18'. *Irish University Review* (1983): 168–79.

Cunningham, Bernadette. 'The Culture and Ideology of Irish Franciscan Historians at Louvain 1607–1650'. In *Ideology and the Historians*. Ed. Ciarán Brady. Dublin: Lilliput Press, 1991.

'Irish Language Sources for Early Modern Ireland'. *History Ireland* 4 (1996): 44–8.

'Native Culture and Political Change in Ireland, 1580–1640'. In *Natives and Newcomers: Essays on the Making of Irish Colonial Society, 1534–1641*. Ed. Ciaran Brady and Raymond Gillespie. Dublin: Irish Academic Press, 1986.

'Representations of King, Parliament and the Irish People in Geoffrey Keating's *Foras Feasa ar Éirinn* and John Lynch's *Cambrensis Eversus* (1662)'. In Ohlmeyer ed. *Political Thought*.

'Seventeenth-century Interpretations of the Past: The Case of Geoffrey Keating'. *Irish Historical Studies* 25 (1986): 116–28.

The World of Geoffrey Keating: History, Myth and Religion in the Seventeenth Century. Dublin: Four Courts, 2000.

Cunningham, Bernadette, and Raymond Gillespie. 'Patrick Logan and *Foras Feasa ar Éirinn*, 1696'. *Éigse* 32 (2000): 146–52.

Curran, John E. Jr. 'Royalty Unlearned, Honor Untaught: British Savages and Historiographical Change in *Cymbeline*'. *Comparative Drama* 31 (1997): 277–303.

Davidson, Peter, ed. *Poetry and Revolution: An Anthology of British and Irish Verse, 1625–1660*. Oxford: Oxford University Press, 1998.

Davies, Ceri. *Latin Writers of the Renaissance*. Cardiff: University of Wales Press, 1981.

Davies, Eleanor. *The crying charge*. N.p., 1649.

Prophetic Writings of Lady Eleanor Davies. Ed. Esther S. Cope. Oxford: Oxford University Press, 1995.

The word of God, to the citie of London, from the Lady Eleanor . . . N.p., 1644.

Davies, John. *A Discovery of the True Causes Why Ireland Was Never Entirely Subdued [and] Brought Under Obedience of the Crown of England Until the Beginning of His*

Majesty's Happy Reign (1612). Ed. James P. Myers, Jr. Washington, DC: The Catholic University of America Press, 1988.

The Works in Verse and Prose of Sir John Davies. 3 vols. Ed. Alexander B. Grosart. Blackburn, Lancashire: printed for private circulation, 1869–76.

Davies, Norman. *The Isles: A History.* London: Macmillan, 1999.

Davies, R. R. *Domination and Conquest: The Experience of Ireland, Scotland, and Wales, 1130–1300.* Cambridge: Cambridge University Press, 1990.

'The Peoples of Britain and Ireland, 1100–1400: IV Language and Historical Mythology'. *Transactions of the Royal Historical Society,* 6th ser., 7 (1997): 1–24.

Dawson, Jane. 'Anglo-Scottish Protestant Culture and Integration in Sixteenth-Century Britain'. In Ellis and Barber eds. *Conquest and Union.*

'Calvinism and the Gaidhealtachd in Scotland'. In *Calvinism in Europe, 1540–1620.* Ed. Andrew Pettegree, Alasdair Duke, and Gillian Lewis. Cambridge: Cambridge University Press, 1994.

Dean, C. *Arthur of England: English Attitudes to King Arthur and the Knights of the Round Table in the Middle Ages and Renaissance.* Toronto: Toronto University Press, 1987.

Deane, Seamus. 'Introduction'. In *Nationalism, Colonialism, and Culture.* Minneapolis: University of Minnesota Press, 1990.

De Quincey, Thomas. *Autobiography from 1785 to 1803.* In *Collected Writings.* 14 vols. Ed. David Masson. Edinburgh: Adam and Charles Black, 1889–90.

Dijkstra, Bram. *Defoe and Economics.* Basingstoke: Macmillan, 1989.

Dobin, Howard. *Merlin's Disciples: Prophecy, Poetry, and Power in Renaissance England.* Stanford: Stanford University Press, 1990.

Dollimore, Jonathan, and Alan Sinfield, eds. *Political Shakespeare: Essays in Cultural Materialism.* Manchester: Manchester University Press, 1985.

Dollimore, Jonathan, and Alan Sinfield. 'History and Ideology: The Instance of Henry V'. In John Drakakis ed. *Alternative Shakespeares.* London: Methuen, 1986.

Donald, M. B. *Elizabethan Copper: The History of the Company of Mines Royal, 1568–1605.* London: Pergamon Press, 1955.

Donaldson, William. *The Jacobite Song.* Aberdeen: Aberdeen University Press, 1988.

Donno, Elizabeth Story. 'Some Aspects of Shakespeare's Holinshed'. *Huntington Library Quarterly* 50 (1987): 229–48.

Drummond, William. *The Poetical Works of William Drummond of Hawthornden.* 2 vols. Ed. L. E. Kastner. Edinburgh: Scottish Text Society, 1913.

Dunne, Tom. 'The Gaelic Response to Conquest and Colonisation: The Evidence of the Poetry'. *Studia Hibernica* 20 (1980): 7–30.

Edwards, Francis. *Robert Persons: The Biography of an Elizabethan Jesuit, 1546–1610.* St Louis, Missouri: Institute of Jesuit Sources, 1995.

Edwards, Philip. *Sir Walter Raleigh.* London: Longman, 1953.

Threshold of a Nation. Cambridge: Cambridge University Press, 1979.

Edwards, Ruth Dudley. *Patrick Pearse*. London: Gollancz, 1977.

Eliot, John. *A brief narrative of the progress of the Gospel amongst the Indians in New-England, in the year 1670*. London, 1671.

A further Accompt of the Progresse of the Gospel amongst the Indians in New-England and Of the means used effectually to advance the same. With Abraham Peirson, *Some Helps for the Indians*. London, 1659.

A further Account of the progress of the Gospel Amongst the Indians in New-England. Being a Relation of the Confessions made by several Indians. London, 1660.

A Late and Further Manifestation of the Progress of the Gospel amongst the Indians in New-England. Declaring their constant Love and Zeal to the Truth: With a readinesse to give Accompt of their Faith and Hope; as of their desires in Church Communion to be Partakers of the Ordinances of Christ . . . London, 1655. Rpt in *Tracts Relating to the Attempts to Convert to Christianity the Indians of New England. Collections of the Massachusetts Historical Society* 3rd ser., 4 (1834): 261–87.

Eliot, John, and Thomas Mayhew, Jr. *Tears of Repentance: Or, a further Narrative of the Progress of the Gospel amongst the Indians in New-England: Setting forth, not only their present state and condition but sundry confessions of sin by divers of the said Indians, wrought upon by the saving Power of the gospel; together with the manifestation of their faith and hope in Jesus Christ, and the work of grace upon their hearts*. London, 1653. Rpt. *Tracts Relating to the Attempts to Convert to Christianity the Indians of New England. Collections of the Massachusetts Historical Society* 3rd ser., 4 (1834): 197–260.

Elliott, J. H. *The Old World and the New*. Cambridge: Cambridge University Press, 1970.

Ellis, Steven. 'Historiographical Debate: Representations of the Past in Ireland: Whose Past and Whose Present?' *Irish Historical Studies* 27 (1991): 289–308.

'Tudor State Formation and the Shaping of the British Isles'. In Ellis and Barber eds. *Conquest and Union*.

'Writing Irish History: Revisionism, Colonialism, and the British Isles'. *Irish Review* 19 (1996): 1–21.

Ellis, Steven G., and Sarah Barber eds. *Conquest and Union: Fashioning a British State, 1485–1725*. London: Longman, 1995.

Eltis, David. *The Rise of African Slavery in the Americas*. Cambridge: Cambridge University Press, 2000.

Empson, William. *Some Versions of Pastoral*. New York: New Directions, 1974.

Erskine-Hill, Howard. *The Augustan Idea in English Literature*. London: Edward Arnold, 1983.

Poetry and the Realm of Politics: Shakespeare to Dryden. Oxford: Clarendon Press, 1996.

Eyre-Todd, George, ed. *Scottish Poetry of the Seventeenth Century*. Glasgow: William Hodge & Co., n.d.

Fanning, Ronan. 'The Meaning of Revisionism'. *Irish Review* 4 (1988): 15–19.

Ferguson, William. *The Identity of the Scottish Nation: An Historic Quest*. Edinburgh: Edinburgh University Press, 1998.

Fergusson, J., ed. *The Declaration of Arbroath*. Edinburgh: Edinburgh University Press, n.d.

Firth, C. H., and R. S. Rait, eds. *An Act for the promoting and propagating the Gospel of Jesus Christ in New England [27 July, 1649]*. In *Acts and Ordinances of the Interregnum, 1642–1660*. 3 vols. London: Wyman and Sons, 1911.

Fisher, Jasper. *Fuimus Troes, or The True Trojanes* (1633).

Fleming, Juliet. 'The Renaissance Tattoo'. *Review of Ethnographic Studies* 31 (1997): 35–52.

Floyd-Wilson, Mary. 'Temperature, Temperance, and Racial Difference in Ben Jonson's *The Masque of Blackness*'. *English Literary Renaissance* 28 (1998): 183–209.

Forbes, Robert. *The Lyon in Mourning*. 3 vols. Ed. Henry Paton. Edinburgh: Edinburgh University Press, 1895.

Foster, Roy. *Modern Ireland, 1600–1972*. London: Allen Lane, 1988.

Fraser, Antonia. *Mary Queen of Scots*. London: Weidenfeld and Nicolson, 1969.

French, Nicholas. *The Unkinde Desertor of Loyall Men and True Friends*. Paris, 1676.

Galloway, Bruce R. *The Union of England and Scotland, 1603–1608*. Edinburgh: John Donald, 1986.

Galloway, Bruce R., and Brian P. Levack, eds. *The Jacobean Union: Six Tracts of 1604*. Edinburgh: Scottish History Society, 1985.

Gay, John. *Dramatic Works*. Ed. John Fuller. Oxford: Clarendon Press, 1983.
  The Beggar's Opera. Ed. Edgar V. Roberts. London, 1969.

Geddes, William Duguid, and William Watt Leade, eds. *Musa Latina Aberdonensis*. 3 vols. Aberdeen: New Spalding Club, 1892–1916.

Gerrard, Christine. *The Patriot Opposition to Walpole: Politics, Poetry, and Myth, 1725–1742*. Oxford: Clarendon Press, 1994.

Gibbons, Brian. *Shakespeare and Multiplicity*. Cambridge: Cambridge University Press, 1993.

Gilbert, J. T., ed. *A Contemporary History of Affairs in Ireland*. 3 vols. Dublin: Irish Archaeological Society, 1879.

Gilbert, William. *De Magnete*. London, 1600.

Gillespie, Raymond. 'Explorers, Exploiters and Entrepreneurs: Early Modern Ireland and Its Context, 1500–1700'. In *An Economic Geography of Ireland*. Ed. B. J. Graham and L. J. Proudfoot. London: Academic Press, 1993.

Gillies, William. 'Gaelic Songs of the "Forty-Five"'. *Scottish Studies* 30 (1991): 19–58.

Gooch, Leo. *The Desperate Faction?: The Jacobites of North-East England 1688–1745*. Hull: University of Hull Press, 1995.

Gorski, Philip. *The Disciplinary Revolution: Calvinism, Confessionalism, and State Power in Early Modern Europe*. Chicago: University of Chicago Press, forthcoming.

Gottfried, Rudolph B. 'The Early Development of the Section on Ireland in Camden's *Britannia*'. *English Literary History* 10 (1943): 17–30.

Grafton, Anthony, with April Shelford and Nancy Siraisi. *New Worlds, Ancient Texts: The Power of Tradition and the Shock of Discovery*. Cambridge, MA: Harvard University Press, 1992.

Grant, Alexander, and Keith J. Stringer. 'Introduction: The Enigma of British History'. In *Uniting the Kingdom?: The Making of British History*. Ed. Alexander Grant and Keith J. Stringer. London: Routledge, 1995.

Greenblatt, Stephen. *Marvelous Possessions: The Wonder of the New World*. Oxford: Clarendon Press, 1991.

Renaissance Self-Fashioning: from More to Shakespeare. Chicago: University of Chicago Press, 1980.

Shakespearean Negotiations: The Circulation of Social Energy in Renaissance England. Berkeley: University of California Press, 1988.

Sir Walter Raleigh: The Renaissance Man and his Roles. New Haven: Yale University Press, 1973.

Greenfeld, Liah. *Nationalism: Five Roads to Modernity*. Cambridge, MA: Harvard University Press, 1992.

Greenwood, David. *William King: Tory and Jacobite*. Oxford: Clarendon Press, 1969.

Grueber, Herbert A. *Handbook of the Coins of Great Britain and Ireland in the British Museum*. London: British Museum, 1899.

Gruffydd, R. Geraint. 'The Renaissance and Welsh Literature'. In *The Celts and the Renaissance: Tradition and Innovation*. Ed. Glanmor Williams and Robert Owen Jones. Cardiff: University of Wales Press, 1990.

Gurr, Andrew. 'Introduction'. *Henry V*. Cambridge: Cambridge University Press, 1992.

Guy, John. 'The 1590s: The Second Reign of Elizabeth I?' In *The Reign of Elizabeth I: Court and Culture in the Last Decade*. Ed. John Guy. Cambridge: Cambridge University Press, 1995.

Hackett, Helen. *Virgin Mother, Maiden Queen: Elizabeth I and the Cult of the Virgin Mary*. Basingstoke: Macmillan, 1995.

Hadfield, Andrew. 'Briton and Scythian: Tudor Representations of Irish Origins'. *Irish Historical Studies* 28 (1993): 390–408.

Literature, Travel and Colonial Writing in the English Renaissance, 1545–1625. Oxford: Clarendon Press, 1998.

'Rethinking the Black Legend: Sixteenth-Century English Identity and the Spanish Colonial Antichrist'. *Reformation* 3 (1998): 303–22.

Hall, Edward. *Hall's Chronicle; containing the History of England during the reign of Henry the Fourth, and the succeeding Monarchs, to the End of the Reign of Henry the Eighth . . . Carefully collated with the Editions of 1548 and 1550*. Ed. Henry Ellis. London, 1809.

Hamilton, Henry. *The English Brass and Copper Industries to 1800*. 2nd edn. London: Frank Cass and Co. Ltd, 1967.

Harley, J. B. 'Meaning and Ambiguity in Tudor Cartography'. In *English Map-Making, 1500–1650*. Ed. Sarah Tyacke. London: British Library, 1983.

Harley, J. B., and Kees Zandvliet. 'Art, Science, and Power in Sixteenth-Century Dutch Cartography'. *Cartographica* 29 (1992): 10–19.

Harriot, Thomas. *A Briefe and True Report of the New Found Land of Virginia* (1590).

Hartog, François. *The Mirror of Herodotus: The Representation of the Other in the Writing of History*. Trans. Janet Lloyd. Berkeley: University of California Press, 1988.

Hartwig, Joan. 'Cloten, Autolycus, and Caliban: Bearers of Parodic Burdens'. In *Shakespeare's Romances Reconsidered*. Ed. Carol McGinnis Kay and Henry E. Jacobs. Lincoln: University of Nebraska Press, 1978.

Heaney, Seamus. 'An Open Letter'. In *Ireland's Field Day*. Notre Dame: University of Notre Dame Press, 1986.

Helgerson, Richard. *Forms of Nationhood: The Elizabethan Writing of England*. Chicago: University of Chicago Press, 1992.

Henderson, G. D. *Chevalier Ramsay*. Aberdeen: Nelson, 1952.

 ed. *Mystics of the North East*. Aberdeen: Third Spalding Club, 1934.

Henry, Bruce Ward. 'John Dee, Humphrey Llwyd, and the Name "British Empire"'. *Huntington Library Quarterly* 35 (1971–2): 189–90.

Herbert, William. *Sir William Herbert: Croftus, sive de Hibernia Liber*. Ed. Arthur Keaveney and John Madden. Dublin: Irish Manuscripts Commission, 1992.

Herford, C. H., and Percy Simpson eds. *Ben Jonson*. 11 vols. Oxford: Clarendon Press, 1925–52.

Herodotus. *The Persian Wars: A Companion to the Penguin Translation of Books 5–9 from Herodotus, The Histories, Translated by Aubrey de Selincourt, Published in the Penguin Classics*. Ed. Stephen Usher. Bristol: Bristol Classical Press, 1988.

Hicks, L., ed. *Letters and Memorials of Father Robert Persons, S.J.: Volume 1 (to 1588)*. Catholic Record Society 39. London: Catholic Record Society 1942.

Higgins, Ian. *Swift: A Study in Disaffection*. Cambridge: Cambridge University Press, 1995.

Highley, Christopher. *Shakespeare, Spenser, and the Crisis in Ireland*. Cambridge: Cambridge University Press, 1997.

Hill, George. *An Historical Account of the Plantation in Ulster at the Commencement of the Seventeenth Century, 1608–1620*. Belfast, 1877.

Hill, J. Michael. 'The Origins of the Scottish Plantations in Ulster to 1625: A Reinterpretation'. *Journal of British Studies* 32 (1993): 24–43.

Hobsbawm, Eric. *Bandits*. London: Weidenfeld and Nicolson, 1969.

Hodgen, Margaret T. *Early Anthropology in the Sixteenth and Seventeenth Centuries*. Philadelphia: University of Pennsylvania Press, 1964.

Hoffman, Richard C. 'Outsiders by Birth and Blood: Racist Ideologies and Realities around the Periphery of Medieval European Culture'. *Studies in Medieval and Renaissance History* n.s. 4 (1983): 1–14.

Hogg, James. *The Jacobite Relics* (Series I). Paisley: Alex. Gardner, 1874.

Holderness, Graham. '"What ish my nation?": Shakespeare and National Identities'. *Textual Practice* 5 (1991): 74–93.

Holinshed, Raphael. *Chronicles of England, Scotland, and Ireland*. 6 vols. London, 1807–8; repr. with an introduction by Vernon Snow. Ed. Henry Ellis. New York, 1965, 1976.

 The First and Second Volumes of Chronicles, comprising The description and historie of England, The description and historie of Ireland, and The description and historie of Scotland. London, 1587.

 The Second Volume of Chronicles, with a continuation by John Hooker alias Vowell. London, 1586.

Homer. *The Iliad*. 2 vols. Trans. A. T. Murray. London: Heinemann, 1947.

Hooker, Richard. *Ecclesiastic Polity*. 1597.

Howard, Jean, and Phyllis Rackin. *Engendering a Nation: A Feminist Account of Shakespeare's English Histories*. London: Routledge, 1997.

Hoxie, Frederick E., ed. *Encyclopedia of North American Indians*. Boston: Houghton Mifflin, 1996.

Hughes, Paul L., and James F. Larkin, eds. *Stuart Royal Proclamations*. 2 vols. Oxford: Clarendon Press, 1973.

Hulme, Peter. *Colonial Encounters: Europe and the Native Caribbean, 1492–1797*. London: Methuen, 1986.

Hulton, Paul. *America 1585: The Complete Drawings of John White*. London: British Museum, 1984.

   America (1590–1634). New York: Dover, 1972.

   'Images of the New World: Jacques Le Moyne De Morgues and John White'. In K. R. Andrews, N. P. Canny, and P. E. H. Hair eds. *The Westward Enterprise*.

Hulton, Paul, and David Beers Quinn, eds., *The American Drawings of John White, 1577–1590*. 2 vols. London: British Museum, 1964.

Ivic, Christopher. 'Incorporating Ireland: Cultural Conflict in Holinshed's Irish *Chronicles*'. *Journal of Medieval and Early Modern Studies* 29 (1999): 473–98.

Johnston, Dafydd, ed. *Gwaith Lewys Glyn Cothi*. Cardiff: University of Wales Press, 1995.

Jones, Emrys. 'Stuart *Cymbeline*'. *Essays in Criticism* 11 (1961): 84–99.

Jordan, Constance. *Shakespeare's Monarchies: Ruler and Subject in the Romances*. Ithaca: Cornell University Press, 1997.

Kastan, David Scott. *Shakespeare After Theory*. London: Routledge, 1999.

   Shakespeare and the Shapes of Time. Hanover, NH: University Press of New England, 1982.

Kastner, L. E., ed. *The Poetical Works of William Drummond of Hawthornden with 'A Cyprus Grove'*, 2 vols. Edinburgh: Scottish Text Society/William Blackwood, 1913.

Kearney, Hugh. *The British Isles: A History of Four Nations*. Cambridge: Cambridge University Press, 1989.

Keating, Geoffrey. *Foras Feasa ar Éirinn: The History of Ireland*. 4 vols. Ed. David Comyn and P. S. Dinneen. London, 1902–14.

Keeler, Laura. *Geoffrey of Monmouth and the Late Latin Chroniclers, 1300–1500*. Berkeley: University of California Press, 1946.

Kellaway, William. *The New England Company 1649–1776: Missionary Society to the American Indians*. London: Longmans, Green and Co., 1961.

Kelley, Donald R. 'Debate: History, English Law and the Renaissance'. *Past and Present* 65 (1974): 24–51.

Kelly, Billy. '"Most Illustrious Cavalier" or "Unkinde Desertor"? James Butler, first duke of Ormond, 1610–1688'. *History Ireland* 1 (1993): 18–22.

Kendrick, T. D. *British Antiquity*. London: Methuen, 1950.

Kenyon, John. *The History Men: The Historical Profession in England since the Renaissance*. London: Weidenfeld and Nicolson, 1983.

Kidd, Colin. *British Identities Before Nationalism: Ethnicity and Nationhood in the Atlantic World, 1600–1800.* Cambridge: Cambridge University Press, 1999.

Subverting Scotland's Past. Cambridge: Cambridge University Press, 1993.

Knight, Wilson G. *The Crown of Life: Essays in Interpretation of Shakespeare's Final Plays.* London: Methuen, 1958.

Knox, Thomas Francis, ed. *The First and Second Diaries of the English College, Douay.* London: David Nutt, 1878.

Koebner, Richard. '"The Imperial Crown of this Realm": Henry VIII, Constantine the Great, and Polydore Vergil'. *Bulletin of the Institute of Historical Research* 26 (1953): 29–52.

Koenigsberger, H. G. 'Dominium Regale or Dominium Politicum et Regale'. Rpt in Koenigsberger *Politicians and Virtuosis: Essays on Early Modern History.* London: Hambledon, 1986.

Kurland, Stuart M. '*Hamlet* and the Scottish Succession?' *Studies in English Literature* 34 (1994): 279–300.

Leerssen, Joseph T. *Mere Irish and Fior-Ghael: Studies in the Idea of Irish Nationality, its Development and Literary Expression prior to the Nineteenth Century.* Amsterdam: John Benjamins, 1986.

Lennon, Colm. *Richard Stanihurst: The Dubliner, 1547–1618.* Dublin: Irish Academic Press, 1981.

Sixteenth-Century Ireland: The Incomplete Conquest. Dublin: Gill and Macmillan, 1994.

Levack, Brian P. *The Formation of the British State: England, Scotland and the Union, 1603–1707.* Oxford: Clarendon, 1987.

Levin, Richard. *The Multiple Plot in English Renaissance Drama.* Chicago: University of Chicago Press, 1971.

Levy, F. J. *Tudor Historical Thought.* San Marino: Huntington Library, 1967.

Lim, Walter. *The Arts of Empire: The Poetics of Colonialism from Ralegh to Milton.* Newark: University of Delaware Press, 1998.

Lindley, David. *Thomas Campion.* Leiden: E. J. Brill, 1986.

Lloyd-Morgan, Ceridwen. 'The Celtic Tradition'. In *The Arthur of the English: The Arthurian Legend in Medieval English Life and Literature.* Ed. W. R. J. Barron. Cardiff: University of Wales Press, 1999.

Llwyd, Humphrey. *The Breviary of Britayne.* Trans. Thomas Twyne. London, 1573.

Loomie, Albert J. *Guy Fawkes in Spain: The 'Spanish Treason' in Spanish Documents.* London: University of London, 1971. (*Bulletin of the Institute of Historical Research*, special supplement 9.)

The Spanish Elizabethans: The English Exiles at the Court of Philip II. New York: Fordham University Press, 1963.

Lucan. *Pharsalia.* Trans. J. D. Duff. London: Heinemann, 1969.

Mac Craith, Mícheál. 'The Gaelic Reaction to the Reformation'. In Ellis and Barber eds. *Conquest and Union.*

MacDougall, Hugh A. *Racial Myth in English History: Trojans, Teutons, and Anglo-Saxons.* Montreal: Harvest House, Ltd, 1982.

Mac Erlean, J. C., ed. *The Poems of Dáithí Obruadair*. 2 vols. London: Irish Texts Society, 1910.

Macinnes, Allan I. *Clanship, Commerce and the House of Stuart, 1603–1788*. East Linton, East Lothian: Tuckwell Press, 1996.

'Crown, Clan and Fine: The "Civilising" of Scottish Gaeldom, 1587–1638'. *Northern Scotland* 13 (1993): 31–59.

'Gaelic Culture in the Seventeenth Century: Polarization and Assimilation'. In Ellis and Barber eds. *Conquest and Union*.

'Scottish Gaeldom, 1638–51: The Vernacular Response to the Covenanting Dynamic'. In *New Perspectives on the Politics and Culture of Early Modern Scotland*. Ed. John Dwyer, Roger A. Mason, and Alexander Murdoch. Edinburgh: John Donald, 1982.

Mackenzie, Agnes Mure. *Scottish Pageant 1707–1802*. Edinburgh: Oliver and Boyd, 1950.

Maclean, John, ed. *The Life and Times of Sir Peter Carew*. London: Bell and Dalby, 1857.

Macmillan, D. *The Aberdeen Doctors*. London: Hodder and Stoughton, 1909.

MacQuoid, G. S., ed. *Jacobite Songs and Ballads*. London: Walter Scott, n.d.

McCabe, Richard A. 'The Masks of Duessa: Spenser, Mary Queen of Scots, and James VI'. *English Literary Renaissance* 17 (1987): 224–42.

McCoog, Thomas M. 'Establishment of the English Province of the Society of Jesus'. *Recusant History* 17 (1984): 121–39.

The Society of Jesus in Ireland, Scotland, and England 1541–1588. New York: E. J. Brill, 1996.

McEachern, Claire. *The Poetics of English Nationhood, 1590–1612*. Cambridge: Cambridge University Press, 1996.

McFarland, R. 'Jonson's *Magnetic Lady* and the Reception of Gilbert's *De Magnete*'. *Studies in English Literature* 11 (1971): 283–93.

McLaren, A. N. *Political Culture in the Reign of Elizabeth I: Queen and Commonwealth, 1558–1585*. Cambridge: Cambridge University Press, 1999.

McLeod, Bruce. *The Geography of Empire in English Literature, 1580–1745*. Cambridge: Cambridge University Press, 1999.

McLynn, Frank. 'An Eighteenth-Century Scots Republic? – An Unlikely Project from Absolutist France'. *Scottish Historical Review* 59 (1980): 177–81.

Major, John. *A History of Greater Britain* (1521). Ed. and trans. Archibald Constable. Edinburgh: The University Press for the Scottish History Society, 1892.

Maley, Willy. 'Shakespeare, Holinshed and Ireland: Resources and Contexts'. In *Shakespeare and Ireland: History, Politics, Culture*. Ed. Mark Thornton Burnett and Ramona Wray. London: Macmillan, 1997.

Maltby, William S. *The Black Legend in England: The Development of Anti-Spanish Sentiment, 1558–1660*. Durham, NC: Duke University Press, 1971.

Mapstone, Sally. 'Shakespeare and Scottish Kingship: A Case History'. In *The Rose and the Thistle: Essays on the Culture of Late Medieval and Renaissance Scotland*. Ed. Sally Mapstone and Juliette Wood. East Linton, East Lothian: Tuckwell Press, 1998.

Marcus, Leah. *Puzzling Shakespeare: Local Reading and Its Discontents.* Berkeley: University of California Press, 1988.

Mason, Roger A. 'Scotching the Brut: Politics, History and National Myth in Sixteenth-Century Britain'. In *Scotland and England 1286–1815*. Ed. Roger A. Mason. Edinburgh: John Donald, 1987.

'The Scottish Reformation and the Origins of Anglo-British Imperialism'. In Mason ed. *Scots and Britons.*

ed. *Kingship and Commonweal: Political Thought in Renaissance and Reformation Scotland.* East Linton, East Lothian: Tuckwell Press, 1998.

ed. *Scots and Britons: Scottish Political Thought and the Union of 1603.* Cambridge: Cambridge University Press, 1994.

Matthews, William. 'The Egyptians in Scotland: The Political History of a Myth'. *Viator* 1 (1970): 289–306.

Meagher, John C. 'The First Progress of Henry VII'. *Renaissance Drama*, new series 1 (1968): 45–73.

Meek, Donald. 'The Gaelic Ballads of Scotland: Creativity and Adaptation'. In *Ossian Revisited*. Ed. Howard Gaskill. Edinburgh: Edinburgh University Press, 1991.

Meikle, Henry W. *Scotland and the French Revolution.* Glasgow: James Maclehose, 1912.

Mignolo, Walter. 'Misunderstanding and Colonization: The Reconfiguration of Memory and Space'. *South Atlantic Quarterly* 92 (1993): 209–60.

Mikalachki, Jodi. 'The Masculine Romance of Roman Britain: *Cymbeline* and Early Modern Nationalism'. *Shakespeare Quarterly* 46 (1995): 301–22.

Miller, Liam, and Eileen Power, eds. *Holinshed's Irish Chronicle.* Dublin: Dolmen Press, 1979.

Millet, Benignus. 'Irish Literature in Latin, 1550–1700'. In *New History of Ireland*, III. Ed. T. W. Moody *et al.* Oxford: Clarendon Press, 1976.

Miscellanea XII, Catholic Record Society 26. London, 1926.

Monmouth, Geoffrey of. *Histories of the Kings of Britain.* London: J. M. Dent, 1911.

Histories of the Kings of Britain. Trans. Lewis Thorpe. Harmondsworth: Penguin, 1966.

Montaigne, Michel de. *The Essayes of Michael, Lord of Montaigne* (1603). 3 vols. Trans. John Florio. London: Everyman, 1910.

Montrose, Louis. 'The Work of Gender in the Discourse of Discovery'. *Representations* 33 (1991): 1–41.

Moran, Patrick Francis. *Spicilegium Ossoriense.* Dublin, 1874.

Morgan, Austin. *James Connolly.* Manchester: Manchester University Press, 1988.

Morgan, Edwin. 'How Good a Poet is Drummond?' *Scottish Literary Journal* 15 (1988): 14–24.

Morgan, Hiram. 'Faith and Fatherland in Sixteenth-century Ireland'. *History Ireland* 3 (1995): 13–20.

'Mid-Atlantic Blues'. *Irish Review* 11 (1991 /2): 50–5.

Morrill, John. 'The Fashioning of Britain'. In Ellis and Barber eds. *Conquest and Union.*

'The Stuarts'. In *The Oxford Illustrated History of Britain*. Ed. Kenneth O. Morgan. Oxford: Oxford University Press, 1984.

Morrissey, Mary. 'Interdisciplinarity and the Study of Early Modern Sermons'. *Historical Journal* 42 (1999): 1111–23.

Moryson, Fynes. *An Itinerary*. 3 vols. London, 1617.

Mozley, Anne. *The Christian Remembrancer* (April 1853).

Mullaney, Steven. 'After the New Historicism'. In *Alternative Shakespeares*, II. Ed. Terence Hawkes. London: Routledge, 1996.

Munday, Anthony. *The English Roman Life*. Ed. Philip J. Ayres. Oxford: Clarendon Press, 1980.

Murdoch, Steve. *Britain, Denmark-Norway and the House of Stuart 1603–1660: A Diplomatic and Military Analysis*. East Linton, East Lothian: Tuckwell Press, 2000.

'NACBS Report on the State and Future of British Studies in North America'. *British Studies Intelligencer* 7th ser. 10 (2000): 11–27.

Naeher, Robert James. 'Dialogue in the Wilderness: John Eliot and the Indian Exploration of Puritanism as a Source of Meaning, Comfort, and Ethnic Survival'. *New England Quarterly* 62 (1989): 346–68.

Neale, J. E. *Elizabeth I and Her Parliaments*. 2 vols. London: Cape, 1957.

Nearing, Homer, Jr. 'The Legend of Julius Caesar's British Conquest'. *PMLA* 64 (1949): 889–929.

Neill, Michael. 'Broken English and Broken Irish: Nation, Language, and the Optic of Power in Shakespeare's Histories'. *Shakespeare Quarterly* 45 (1994): 1–32.

New Englands First Fruits; in respect. First of the Conversion of some, Conviction of divers, Preparation of sundry of the Indians. 2. Of the progresse of Learning, in the Colledge at Cambridge in Massachusetts Bay. With divers other speciall Matters concerning that Countrey . . . London, 1643.

Norbrook, David. 'Lucy Hutchinson's "Elegies" and the Situation of the Republican Woman Writer (with text)'. *English Literary Renaissance* 27 (1997): 468–521.

O Baoill, Colm, ed. *Bardachd Shilis na Ceapaich*; by Sileas Macdonald. Edinburgh: Scottish Gaelic Texts Society, 1972.

ed. *The Harps' Cry: An Anthology of Seventeenth-century Gaelic Poetry*. Edinburgh: Birlinn, 1994.

Ó Buachalla, Breandán. 'James Our True King: The Ideology of Irish Royalism in the Seventeenth Century'. In *Political Thought in Ireland since the Seventeenth Century*. Ed. David G. Boyce, Robert Eccleshall, and Vincent Geoghegan. London: Routledge, 1993.

'Poetry and Politics in Early Modern Ireland'. *Eighteenth-Century Ireland* 7 (1992): 149–75.

O'Callaghan, John Cornelius. *History of the Irish Brigades in the Service of France*. Glasgow, 1870.

Ó Ciardha, Eamonn. 'Gaelic Poetry and the Jacobite Tradition 1688–1719'. *Celtic History Review* 2 (1996): 17–22.

'The Stuarts and Deliverance in Irish and Scots-Gaelic Literature'. In *Kingdoms United? Great Britain and Ireland since 1500: Integration and Diversity*. Ed. S. J. Connolly. Dublin: Four Courts, 1999.

'The Unkinde Deserter and the Bright Duke: The Dukes of Ormond in the Irish Royalist Tradition'. In *The Dukes of Ormond, 1610–1745*. Ed. T. C. Barnard and Jane Fenlon. Woodbridge: Boydell Press, 2000.

O Corráin, Donnchadh. 'Irish Origin Legends and Genealogy'. In *History and Heroic Tale*. Ed. Tore Nyberg. Odense: Odense University Press, 1983.

O Cuív, Brian. 'Irish Language and Literature 1691–1845'. In *New History of Ireland*, IV. Eds. T. W. Moody *et al.* Oxford: Clarendon Press, 1976.

'The Irish Language in the Early Modern Period'. In *New History of Ireland*, III. Ed. T. W. Moody *et al.* Oxford: Clarendon Press, 1976.

Ohlmeyer, Jane. ' "Civilizinge of those rude partes": Colonization within Britain and Ireland, 1580s–1640s'. In *The Origins of Empire: British Overseas Enterprise to the Close of the Seventeenth Century*. Ed. N. P. Canny. Oxford: Oxford University Press, 1998.

Civil War and Restoration in the Three Stuart Kingdoms: The Career of Randal MacDonnell, Marquis of Antrim, 1609–1683. Cambridge: Cambridge University Press, 1993.

'Seventeenth-century Ireland and the New British and Atlantic Histories'. *American Historical Review* 104 (1999): 446–62.

ed. *Political Thought in Seventeenth-century Ireland: Kingdom or Colony?*. Cambridge: Cambridge University Press, 2000.

Oliphant, T. L. Kingston. *The Jacobite Lairds of Gask*. London: Charles Griffin & Co., 1870.

Olsen, Thomas G. ' "Drug-Damn'd Italy" and the Problem of British National Character in *Cymbeline*'. *Shakespeare Yearbook* 10 (1999): 269–96.

O Riordan, Michelle. *The Gaelic Mind and the Collapse of the Gaelic World*. Cork: Cork University Press, 1990.

' "Political" Poems in the Mid-seventeenth Century'. In *Ireland from Independence to Occupation, 1641–1660*. Ed. Jane Ohlmeyer. Cambridge: Cambridge University Press, 1995.

Ormond, James, Duke of. *A letter from His Grace James Duke of Ormond, Lord Lieutenant of Ireland, in answer to the Right Honourable Arthur Earl of Anglesey Lord Privy-Seal . . .* London, 1682.

A true account of the whole proceedings betwixt His Grace James Duke of Ormond, and the Right Honor [sic] Arthur, Earl of Anglesey, late Lord Privy-Seal, before the King and Council . . . London, 1682.

Ortelius, Abraham. *The Theatre of the whole World*. London, 1606.

Osborn, James M. *Young Philip Sidney*. New Haven: Yale University Press, 1972.

O Tuama, Sean, *An Duanaire, 1600–1900: Poems of the Dispossessed*. Trans. Thomas Kinsella. Portlaoise: Dolmen Press, 1994.

Padel, O. J. 'Some South-Western Sites with Arthurian Associations'. In *The Arthur of the Welsh: The Arthurian Legend in Medieval Welsh Literature*. Ed. Rachel

Bromwich, A. O. H. Jarman, and Brynley F. Roberts. Cardiff: University of Wales Press, 1991.

Pagden, Anthony. *The Fall of Natural Man: The American Indian and the Origins of Comparative Ethnology*. Cambridge: Cambridge University Press, 1982.

Palmer, William. 'Gender, Violence, and Rebellion in Tudor and Early Stuart Ireland'. *Sixteenth-Century Journal* 23 (1992): 699–712.

Parker, Patricia. *Shakespeare from the Margins: Language, Culture, Context*. Chicago: University of Chicago Press.

Patterson, Annabel. 'Back by Popular Demand: The Two Versions of *Henry V*'. In *Shakespeare and the Popular Voice*. Oxford: Basil Blackwell, 1989.

Reading Holinshed's Chronicles. Chicago: University of Chicago Press, 1994.

Perceval-Maxwell, Michael. 'Ireland and the Monarchy in the Early Stuart Multiple Kingdom'. *Historical Journal* 34 (1991): 279–95.

Persons, Robert. *A Brief Apologie or Defense of the Catholic Ecclesiastical Hierarchie*. Antwerp, 1602.

A Conference about the next Succession to the Crown of England, divided into Two Parts (n.p., 1 S94). New York: Da Capo Press, 1972.

'Father Persons' Memoirs (concluded) . . . Punti per la Missione d'Inghilterra'. Ed. and trans. J. H. Pollen as 'Notes Concerning the English Mission'. In *Miscellanea* IV, Catholic Record Society 4. London: Catholic Record Society, 1907.

The Jesuit's Memorials for the intended Reformation of England, under the first Popish Prince. Introd. Edward Gee. London: Printed for Richard Chiswel, 1690.

Letters and Memorials of Father Robert Persons, S.J., Volume I (to 1588). Ed. L. Hicks. Catholic Record Society 39. London: Catholic Record Society, 1942.

'The Memoirs of Father Robert Persons'. Ed. J. H. Pollen. *Miscellanea* II, Catholic Record Society 2. London: Catholic Record Society, 1906.

'An Observation of Certain Apparent Judgements of Almighty God Against such as have been Seditious in the English Catholic Cause' (1598). In *'Father Persons' Memoirs (concluded) . . . Punti per la Missione d'Inghilterra'*. Ed. and trans. J. H. Pollen as 'Notes Concerning the English Mission'. In *Miscellanea* IV, Catholic Record Society 4. London: Catholic Record Society, 1907.

A Treatise of Three Conversions of England from Paganism to Christian Religion. English Recusant Literature, 1558–1640 304. Ilkley: Scolar Press, 1976.

Pet, Peter (?). *The Happy Future State of England: Or, A Discourse by Way of Letter to the late Earl of Anglesey, Vindicating him from the Reflections of an Affidavit published by the House of Commons Ao 1680 by occasion whereof observations are made concerning infamous witnesses*. London, 1688.

Phillips, J. E. *Images of a Queen: Mary Stuart in Sixteenth-Century Literature*. Berkeley: University of California Press, 1964.

Pittock, Murray G. H. '*The Aeneid* in the Age of Burlington: a Jacobite Text?' In *Lord Burlington: Architecture, Art and Life*. Ed. Toby Barnard and Jane Clark. London: Hambledon Press, 1995.

Celtic Identity and the British Image. Manchester: Manchester University Press, 1999.

'The Culture of Jacobitism'. In *Culture and Society in Britain 1660–1800.* Ed. Jeremy Black. Manchester: Manchester University Press, 1997.

'From Edinburgh to London: Scottish Court Writing and 1603'. In *The Stuart Courts.* Ed. Eveline Cruickshanks. Stroud: Sutton, 2000.

The Invention of Scotland. London: Routledge, 1991.

Jacobitism. Basingstoke: Macmillan, 1998.

'James Macpherson and Jacobite Code'. In *From Gaelic to Romantic.* Ed. Fiona Stafford and Howard Gaskill. Amsterdam: Rodopi, 1998.

The Myth of the Jacobite Clans. Edinburgh: Edinburgh University Press, 1995.

Poetry and Jacobite Politics in Eighteenth-Century Britain and Ireland. Cambridge: Cambridge University Press, 1994.

ed. *James Hogg: The Jacobite Relics of Scotland.* 2 vols. Edinburgh: Edinburgh University Press, 2002–3.

Pocock, J. G. A. 'The Atlantic Archipelago and the War of the Three Kingdoms'. In *The British Problem, c. 1534–1707.* Ed. Brendan Bradshaw and John Morrill. London: Macmillan, 1996.

'British History: A Plea for a New Subject'. *Journal of Modern History* 47 (1975): 601–28.

'Contingency, Identity, Sovereignty'. In *Uniting the Kingdom? The Making of British History.* Ed. Alexander Grant and Keith J. Stringer. London: Routledge, 1995.

'Two Kingdoms and Three Histories? Political Thought in British Contexts'. In Mason ed. *Scots and Britons.*

'Limits and Divisions of British History: In Search of the Unknown Subject'. *American Historical Review* 87 (1982): 311–36.

Pope, Alexander. *The Poems of Alexander Pope.* Ed. John Bult. London: John Methuen, 1965.

Porter, Jerome. *The Flowers of the Lives of the Most Renowned SAINCTS of the Three Kingdoms ENGLAND SCOTLAND, AND IRELAND Written and collected out of the best authors and manuscripts of our nation, and distibuted according to their feasts in the Calender.* 1632.

Powel, David. *The Historie of Cambria.* London, 1584.

Principe, Lawrence M. *The Aspiring Adept: Robert Boyle and His Alchemical Quest.* Princeton: Princeton University Press, 1998.

Purchas, Samuel. *Pilgrimage.* 1613.

Quinn, David B. ' "A Discourse of Ireland" (circa 1599): A Sidelight on English Colonial Policy'. *Publications of the Royal Irish Academy* 47 section C, no. 3 (1942): 151–66.

The Elizabethans and the Irish. Ithaca, NY: Cornell University Press, 1966.

Raleigh and the British Empire. London: Hodder & Stoughton, 1947.

'Reflections'. In *The European Outthrust and Encounter: The First Phase c. 1400–c. 1700: Essays in Tribute to David Beers Quinn on his 85th Birthday.* Ed. Cecil H. Clough and P. E. H. Hair. Liverpool: Liverpool University Press, 1994.

The Roanoke Voyages, 1584–1590. 2 vols. London: Hakluyt Society, 1955.

Quint, David. 'Alexander the Pig: Shakespeare on History and Poetry'. *Boundary 2* 10 (1982): 49–68.

R. A. [Amershan] *The Valiant Welshman, or the true chronicle history of the life and valiant deedes of Caradoc the Great, King of Cambria, now called Wales* (London: R. Lownes, 1615). Rpt in *Tudor Facsimile Texts*. Issued for subscribers by John S. Farmer, 1913.

Rabelais, François. *The Complete Works of François Rabelais*. Trans. Donald M. Frame. Berkeley: University of California Press, 1991.

Raleigh, Walter. *The Discoverie of the Large, Rich and Bewtiful Empire of Guiana*. Ed. Neil L. Whitehead. Manchester: Manchester University Press, 1997.

Read, Conyers. *Lord Burghley and Queen Elizabeth*. London: Cape, 1960.

Reynolds, Ed[ward]. Introductory epistle, 'To the Christian Reader'. In John Eliot, *A Further Accompt*. 1659.

Reynolds, Susan. 'Medieval Origines Gentium and the Community of the Realm'. *History* 68 (1983): 375–90.

Rhodes, J. T. 'English Books of Martyrs and Saints of the Late Sixteenth and Early Seventeenth Centuries'. *Recusant History* 22 (1994): 7–25.

Richards, W. Leslie, ed. *Gwaith Dafydd Llwyd o Fathafarn*. Cardiff: University of Wales Press, 1964.

Roberts, Peter. 'Tudor Wales, National Identity and the British Inheritance'. In Bradshaw and Roberts eds. *British Consciousness and Identity*.

Robertson, John, ed. *A Union for Empire: Political Thought and the British Union of 1707*. Cambridge: Cambridge University Press, 1995.

Ronan, Myles V. *The Reformation in Ireland Under Elizabeth, 1558–1580 (From Original Sources)*. London: Longmans, Green and Co., 1930.

Ronda, James P. 'Generations of Faith: The Christian Indians of Martha's Vineyard'. *William and Mary Quarterly* 3rd ser., 38 (1981): 369–94.

'"We Are Well As We Are": An Indian Critique of Seventeenth-Century Christian Missions'. *William and Mary Quarterly* 3rd ser., 34 (1977): 66–82.

Rossi, Joan Warchol. '*Cymbeline*'s Debt to Holinshed: The Richness of III.i'. In *Shakespeare's Romances Reconsidered*. Ed. Carol McGinnis Kay and Henry E. Jacobs. Lincoln: University of Nebraska Press, 1978.

Rubinstein, Frankie. *A Dictionary of Shakespeare's Sexual Puns and Their Significance*. London: Macmillan, 1984.

Russell, Conrad. 'The British Problem and the English Civil War'. *History* 72 (1987): 395–415.

The Fall of the British Monarchies 1637–1642. Oxford: Clarendon Press, 1991.

Sacks, David H. 'Parliament, Liberty and the Commonweal'. In *Parliament and Liberty from the Reign of Elizabeth to the English Civil War*. Ed. J. H. Hexter. Stanford: Stanford University Press, 1992.

Salisbury, Neal. 'Red Puritans: The "Praying Indians" of Massachusetts Bay and John Eliot'. *William and Mary Quarterly* 3rd ser., 31 (1974): 27–54.

Sawday, Jonathan. *The Body Emblazoned: Dissection and the Human Body in Renaissance Culture*. London: Routledge, 1995.

Scally, John. 'Counsel in Crisis: James, Third Marquis of Hamilton and the Bishops' Wars, 1638–1640'. In *Celtic Dimensions of the British Civil Wars*. Ed. John R. Young. Edinburgh: John Donald, 1997.

Scott, A. B., and F. X. Martin, eds. and trans. *Expugnatio Hibernica: The Conquest of Ireland*. Dublin: Royal Irish Academy, 1978.

Settle, Elkanah. *An heroick poem on the Right Honourable Thomas Earl of Ossory*. London, 1681.

Shakespeare, William. *Cymbeline*. Ed. J. M. Nosworthy. London: Routledge, 1988.

    Hamlet. In *The Norton Shakespeare*. Ed. Stephen Greenblatt. New York: W. W. Norton, 1997.

    Henry V. In *The Norton Shakespeare*. Ed. Stephen Greenblatt. New York: W. W. Norton, 1997.

    King Richard II. Ed. Peter Ure. London: Methuen. 1964.

    The Poems. Ed. F. T. Prince. London: Methuen, 1960.

    Richard II. Ed. Anthony Hammond. London: Methuen, 1981.

    The Riverside Shakespeare. 2nd edn. Ed. G. Blakemore Evans *et al*. Boston and New York: Houghton Mifflin, 1997.

    Venus and Adonis. Ed. C. Knox Pooler. London: Methuen, 1927.

Sheehan, Bernard W. *Savagism and Civility: Indians and Englishmen in Colonial Virginia*. Cambridge: Cambridge University Press, 1980.

Shepard, Thomas. *The Clear Sun-shine of the gospel breaking forth upon the Indians in New-England*. London, 1648. Rpt. *Tracts Relating to the Attempts to Convert to Christianity the Indians of New England. Collections of the Massachusetts Historical Society* 3rd ser., 4 (1834): 26–66.

Shepherd, Simon. *Amazons and Warrior Women: Varieties of Feminism in Seventeenth-Century Drama*. Brighton: Harvester, 1981.

Sherman, William. *John Dee: The Politics of Reading and Writing in The English Renaissance*. Amherst: University of Massachusetts Press, 1995.

Shirley, John W. 'Sir Walter Raleigh and Thomas Harriot'. In *Thomas Harriot: Renaissance Scientist*. Ed. John W. Shirley. Oxford: Clarendon Press, 1974.

Sibthorpe, Robert. *Apostolike Obedience*. 1627.

Siculus, Diodorus. *Bibliotheke historike English and Greek*. 12 vols. Trans. C. H. Oldfather. London: Heinemann, 1961.

Sidney, Henry. 'Sir Henry Sidney's Memoir of his Government of Ireland, 1583'. Ed. Henry F. Hore. *Ulster Journal of Archaeology* 3 (1856): 33–52, 85–109, 336–57; 5 (1857): 299–323; 8 (1860): 179–95.

Sidney, Philip. *Complete Works*. 4 vols. Ed. A. Feuillerat. Cambridge: Cambridge University Press, 1912–26.

Silke, John J. 'The Irish Abroad, 1534–1691'. In *A New History of Ireland*. III Ed. T. W. Moody *et al*. Oxford: Clarendon, 1976.

    'Primate Lombard and James I'. *Irish Theological Quarterly* 22 (1955): 124–50.

Sinfield, Alan. 'Masculinity and Miscegenation'. In *Faultlines: Cultural Materialism and the Politics of Dissident Reading*. Berkeley: University of California Press, 1992.

Skelton, R. A. *County Atlases of the British Isles, 1579–1850*. London: Carta, 1970.

Smith, Lacey Baldwin. *This Realm of England: 1399 to 1688*. 6th edn. Lexington, MA: D. C. Heath and Co., 1992.

Snow, Vernon F., ed. *Parliament in Elizabethan England: John Hooker's Order and Usage.* New Haven: Yale University Press, 1977.

Sommerville, Johann P., ed. *King James VI and I: Political Writings.* Cambridge: Cambridge University Press, 1994.

Speed, John. *The Historie of Great Britaine Vnder the Conquests of the Romans, Saxons, Danes and Normans.* London, 1632.

The Theatre of the Empire of Great Britaine. London, 1611.

Spelman, Henry. 'Of the Union'. In *The Jacobean Union: Six Tracts of 1604.* Ed. Bruce R. Galloway and Brian P. Levack. Edinburgh: Scottish Historical Society, 1985.

Spencer, Janet M. 'Princes, Pirates, and Pigs: Criminalizing Wars of Conquest in *Henry V*'. *Shakespeare Quarterly* 47 (1996): 160–77.

Spenser, Edmund. *The Faerie Queene.* In *The Poetical Works of Edmund Spenser.* Ed. J. C. Smith and E. de Selincourt. London: Oxford University Press, 1912.

'The Shepheardes Calender'. In *The Yale Edition of the Shorter Poems of Edmund Spenser.* Ed. William A. Oran *et al.* New Haven: Yale University Press, 1987.

A View of the Present State of Ireland, by Edmund Spenser. Ed. W. L. Renwick. London: Scholartis Press, 1934.

A View of the State of Ireland (1633): From the First Printed Edition. Ed. Andrew Hadfield and Willy Maley. Oxford: Blackwell, 1997.

The Works of Edmund Spenser. Ed. Edwin Greenlaw *et al.* 11 vols. Variorum Edition. Baltimore: Johns Hopkins University Press, 1932–58.

Stafford, Fiona. *The Sublime Savage: A Study of James MacPherson and the Poems of Ossian.* Edinburgh: Edinburgh University Press, 1988.

Stallybrass, Peter. 'Patriarchal Territories: The Body Enclosed'. In *Rewriting the Renaissance: The Discourses of Sexual Difference in Early Modern Europe.* Ed. Margaret W. Ferguson, Maureen Quilligan, and Nancy D. Vickers. Chicago: University of Chicago Press, 1986, 123–42.

Stanihurst, Richard. *De rebus in Hibernia gestis* (Antwerp, 1584). In Lennon, *Richard Stanihurst.*

Steen, Sara Jayne, ed. *The Letters of Lady Arbella Stuart.* Oxford: Oxford University Press, 1994.

Stevens, Laura Marie. '"The Poor Indians": Native Americans in Eighteenth-Century Missionary Writings'. Unpublished Ph.D. dissertation. University of Michigan, 1998.

Stevenson, David. *The Scottish Revolution, 1637–1644: The Triumph of the Covenanters.* Newton Abbot: David and Charles, 1973.

Strachey, William. *The Historie of Travell into Virginia Britania* (1612). Ed. Louis B. Wright and Virginia Freund. London: Hakluyt Society, 1953.

Strong, Roy. *The Renaissance Garden in England.* London: Thames and Hudson, 1979.

Szechi, Daniel, ed. *'Scotland's Ruine': Lockhart of Carnwath's Memoirs of the Union.* Aberdeen: Association for Scottish Literary Studies, 1995.

Szechi, Daniel, and David Hayton. 'John Bull's Other Kingdoms'. In *Britain in the First Age of Party, 1680–1750.* Ed. Clyve Jones. London: Hambleton, 1987.

Tayler, Alistair, and Henrietta Tayler. *Jacobites of Aberdeenshire and Banffshire in the Forty-Five*. Aberdeen: Milne & Hutchison, 1928.

Temple, John. *The Irish Rebellion . . . Together with the Barbarous Cruelties and Bloody Massacres which ensued thereupon*. London, 1646.

Thomson, Derick S. 'Macpherson's *Ossian*: Ballads to Epics'. In *The Heroic Process*. Ed. Bo Almqvist, Seamus O Cathan, and Padraig O Healai. Dun Laoghaire: Glendale Press, 1987.

Thornborough, John. *A Discourse Plainely proving the evident utilitie and urgent necessitie of the union of England and Scotland*. London, 1604.

Thuente, Mary Helen. *W. B. Yeats and Irish Folklore*. Dublin: Gill and Macmillan, 1980.

Touchet, James. *The memoirs of James, Lord Audley, Earl of Castlehaven, his engagement and carriage in the wars of Ireland from the year 1642 to the year 1651 written by himself*. London, 1680.

Treadwell, Victor. *Buckingham and Ireland 1616–1628: A Study in Anglo-Irish Politics*. Dublin: Four Courts Press, 1998.

Tuite, Patrick. 'Theatrical Representation, Public Performance, and the Cultural Garrisoning of Colonial Ireland'. Unpublished Ph.D. dissertation. University of Wisconsin-Madison, 2000.

Van Lonkhuyzen, Harold W. 'A Reappraisal of the Praying Indians: Acculturation, Conversion, and Identity at Natick Massachusetts, 1646–1730'. *New England Quarterly* 63 (1990): 396–428.

Veech, Thomas McNevin. *Dr Nicholas Sanders and the English Reformation 1530–1581*. Louvain: University of Louvain, 1935.

Verstegan, Richard. *A Restitution of Decayed Intelligence* (1605). Ed. D. M. Rogers. London: Scolar Press, 1976.

Virgil. *The Pastoral Poems*. Trans. E. V. Rieu. Harmondsworth: Penguin, 1954.

Wainewright, J. B. 'Some Letters and Papers of Nicholas Sanders'. In *Miscellanea* XII, Catholic Record Society 26. London: Catholic Record Society, 1926.

Wallace-Hadrill, J. M. *Bede's Ecclesiastical History of the English People: A Historical Commentary*. Oxford: Clarendon Press, 1988.

Ware, Timothy. *The Orthodox Church*. Harmondsworth: Penguin, 1982.

Weimann, Robert. *Shakespeare and the Popular Tradition in the Theater: Studies in the Social Dimension of Dramatic Form and Function*. Ed. Robert Schwarz. Baltimore: Johns Hopkins University Press, 1978.

Wells, Roger. *Insurrection: The British Experience 1795–1803*. Gloucester: Alan Sutton, 1986.

Whelan, Kevin. 'The United Irishmen, the Enlightenment and Popular Culture'. In *The United Irishmen*. Ed. David Dickson, Daire Keogh, and Kevin Whelan. Dublin: Lilliput Press, 1993.

Whitfield, Henry. *The Light Appearing More and More Towards the Perfect Day. Or, a Farther Discovery of the Present State of the Indians in New-England, Concerning the Progresse of the Gospel Amongst them. Manifested by Letters from such as Preacht to them there* (London, 1651). Rpt in *Tracts Relating to the Attempts to Convert to Christianity the Indians of New England. Collections of the Massachusetts Historical Society* 3rd ser. 4 (1834): 100–47.

Strength out of Weaknesse; or a Glorious Manifestation of the Further Progresse of the Gospel among the Indians in New-England. Held forth in Sundry Letters from divers Ministers and others to the Corporation established by Parliament for promoting the Gospel among the Heathen in New-England; and to particular members thereof . . . London, 1652. Rpt. *Tracts Relating to the Attempts to Convert to Christianity the Indians of New England. Collections of the Massachusetts Historical Society* 3rd ser., 4 (1834): 149–96.

Wickham, Glynne. 'Riddle and Emblem: A Study in the Dramatic Structure of *Cymbeline*'. In *English Renaissance Studies: Presented to Dame Helen Gardner in honour of her Seventieth Birthday*. Ed. John Carey. Oxford : Clarendon Press, 1980.

Wiles, David. *Shakespeare's Clown: Actor and Text in the Elizabethan Playhouse*. Cambridge: Cambridge University Press, 1987.

Williams, Glanmor. *Religion, Language, and Nationality in Wales: Historical Essays*. Cardiff: University of Wales Press, 1979.

Williams, Gwyn A. *Madoc: The Making of a Myth*. Oxford: Oxford University Press, 1987.

Welsh Wizard and British Empire: Dr John Dee and a Welsh Identity. Cardiff: University College Cardiff Press, 1980.

Williams, Michael E. *The Venerable English College Rome: History 1579–1979*. London: Associated Catholic Publishers, 1979.

Williams, Raymond. *Politics and Letters*. New York: Schocken Books, 1979.

Williamson, Arthur H. 'From the Invention of Great Britain to the Creation of British History: A New Historiography'. *Journal Of British Studies* 29 (1990): 267–76.

'George Buchanan, Civic Virtue and Commerce'. *Scottish Historical Review* 75 (1996): 20–37.

'Patterns of British Identity: "Britain" and its Rivals in the Sixteenth and Seventeenth Centuries'. In *The New British History: Founding a Modern State, 1603–1715*. Ed. Glenn Burgess. London: I. B. Tauris, 1999.

'Scotland, Antichrist and the Invention of Great Britain'. In *New Perspectives on the Politics and Culture of Early Modern Scotland*. Ed. John Dwyer, Roger A. Mason, and Alexander Murdoch. Edinburgh: John Donald, 1982.

'Scots, Indians and Empire: The Scottish Politics of Civilization'. *Past and Present* 150 (1966): 46–83.

Scottish National Consciousness in the Age of James VI: The Apocalypse, the Union and Shaping of Scotland's Public Culture. Edinburgh: John Donald, 1979.

Williamson, Arthur, and Paul McGinnis. 'Britain, Race, and the Iberian World Empire'. In *The Three Kingdoms in the Seventeenth Century*. Ed. Allan Macinnes and Jane Ohlmeyer. Dublin: Four Courts, 2000.

[Wilson, John?]. *The Day-breaking, if not the Sun-Rising of the Gospell With the Indians in New-England* (London, 1647). Rpt *Tracts Relating to the Attempts to Convert to Christianity the Indians of New England. Collections of the Massachusetts Historical Society* 3rd ser., 4 (1834): 1–23.

The English Martyrologe conteyning a summary of the lives of the glorious and renowned Saintes of the three Kingdomes, England, Scotland, and Ireland. St Omers College, 1608.

Winslow, Edward. *The Glorious Progress of the Gospel, amongst the Indians in New England. Manifested by three Letters, under the Hand of that famous Instrument of the Lord Mr. John Eliot, And another from Mr. Thomas Mayhew jun: both Preachers of the Word, as well to the English as Indians in New England* . . . London, 1649. Rpt in *Tracts Relating to the Attempts to Convert to Christianity the Indians of New England. Collections of the Massachusetts Historial Society* 3rd ser. 4 (1834): 69–98.

Woolf, D. R. *The Idea of History in Early Stuart England.* Toronto: University of Toronto Press, 1990.

Woolf, Noel. *The Medallic Record of the Jacobite Movement.* London: Spink, 1988.

Wormald, Jenny. 'The Creation of Britain: Multiple Kingdoms or Core and Colonies?' *Transactions of the Royal Historical Society* 6th ser., 2 (1992): 175–94.

'Gunpowder, Treason, and Scots'. *Journal of British Studies* 24 (1985): 155–6.

Zimmerman, G. D. 'Yeats, the Popular Ballad and the Ballad Singers'. *English Studies* (1969): 185–97.

Index